Elmer C. Yazzie
ACTIVE BODY
1996
watercolor and gouache

Acts 2:42 speaks of such Body-of-Christ activities as teaching, unity, breaking of the bread, and prayer.

These four activities take place effectively when the triune God's time frame is used, represented in the design by three center circles.

As Christians actively participate in the Christian life, they face trials, but fruitfulness prevails. The four red steps symbolize the trials, which come at unpredictable times. The three corn plants with seven ears and twelve tassel buds symbolize the complete fruitfulness of the Christian.

Fruitful plants yield new seeds. The two rings of the design, one yellowish and the other green, hold the seeds for the next crop. There are forty-nine (7 x 7) in one and fifty-six (7 x 8) in the other.

The activities of the Body should never cease. The background of the early dawn sky, midday sky, evening sky, and night sky represent this fact.

The source of the activities of the Body-of-Christ is the one true God, Jehovah. The design's opening faces east, the direction of life. The prophet Ezekiel said, "I saw the glory of God coming from the east." The main entrance to the Temple in Jerusalem faced east. Many cultures throughout the world consider east to be the most important direction.

This painting was inspired by the Holy Spirit as Pastor Don Byker was preaching on Acts 2:42 in Rehoboth, New Mexico.

Flourishing in the Land

A Hundred-Year History of Christian Reformed Missions in North America

Flourishing in the Land

A Hundred-Year History of Christian Reformed Missions in North America

Scott Hoezee

Christopher H. Meehan

Christian Reformed Home Missions
Grand Rapids, Michigan/Burlington, Ontario

William B. Eerdmans Publishing Company
Grand Rapids, Michigan/Cambridge, U.K.

Copyright © 1996

William B. Eerdmans Publishing Company
255 Jefferson Ave. SE, Grand Rapids, MI 49503
also
P.O. Box 163, Cambridge CB3 9PU U.K.

Printed in the United States of America

Christian Reformed Home Missions
2850 Kalamazoo Ave. SE
Grand Rapids, MI 49560

Library of Congress Cataloging-in-Publication Data
Hoezee, Scott, 1964–
    Flourishing in the Land : A 100-Year History of Christian
Reformed Missions in North America / Scott Hoezee and
Christopher H. Meehan.
        p.   cm.
    ISBN 0-8028-3795-6 (alk. paper)
    1. Christian Reformed Church — Missions —United
States. 2. Reformed Church — United States — Missions —
United States. 3. Christian Reformed Church. Board of Home
Missions — anniversaries, etc.   I. Meehan, Christopher H.,
1949– II. Title.
BV2766.C553H64   1996
266'.5731'08997 — dc20   96–11541
                                                                    CIP

Contents

Acknowledgments

Approximately three months after signing on to write this book I realized it was going to be much more work than I had originally thought. What kept it from becoming an impossible project, however, were the marvelous contributions of so many people.

Specifically, I wish to acknowledge Sandra De Groot, project developer for William B. Eerdmans Publishing Company. During the nearly two years in which I worked on this project, Sandy was a steady source of encouraging words and warm smiles. When delays frustrated the writing process, when relevant photos could not be found, when an ice storm grounded our flight to New Mexico — whatever the circumstances, Sandy maintained enthusiasm for this project and for my part in it, and for that I give her my heartiest thanks.

I also acknowledge John Rozeboom, his assistant — Gert Rotman, and the entire Home Missions staff for their constant cooperation, helpful feedback, and steady encouragement. The staff at Calvin College's Heritage Hall in the Hekman Library, including director Herbert Brinks and assistant James De Jonge, were also invaluable research assistants at many stages of this project.

I thank my three student researchers, who spent many hours bent over Xerox machines to get me copies of the many articles and essays which went into the research. Claudette Grinnell, Coleman Moore, and Tim Steen all spent time tracking down and copying articles, which in turn freed me up to read and then write about those articles.

I thank my co-writer, Chris Meehan, whom I have greatly enjoyed getting to know and whose sidebar vignettes throughout this book add a real sparkle and liveliness to the finished product. Chris's feedback on the individual chapters as we went along was also very, very helpful.

I thank my editor, Jan Walhout, for her timely reading of the material and for her excellence in editing. Her suggested changes always made my writing grammatically correct, but, equally important, her work also made each chapter easier to read and understand.

For each individual chapter I am indebted to people who

provided materials, consented to interviews, proofread drafts, and made suggestions.

Chapter One

Thanks go to Edward T. Begay, Keith Kuipers, Elmer and Sharon Yazzie, Agnes Natewa, and Mike Meekhof, all of whom were gracious hosts on a trip to New Mexico and all of whom consented to be interviewed. Thanks also to the Yazzies for proofreading the final chapter draft and for giving us access to the Rehoboth archives, recently organized by Henry Ippel in a way which made it a joy to delve into the Rehoboth files and records. Thanks in general also to Al Mulder, whose long experience in and abiding love for New Mexico and its people enabled him to provide us with much rich material and also a keen proofreader's eye.

Chapter Two

Thanks to Gerrit Koedoot for an interview, John Rozeboom for an excellent and invaluably rich thesis on Jewish missions, and Mitch Glazer of Jews for Jesus for helpful background material.

Chapter Three

Thanks to Joel Nederhood, David Feddes, and the Back to God Hour staff for their help. Thanks also to Harold Dekker for proofreading the draft and for offering helpful insights.

Chapter Four

Thanks to Leonard Verduin for a helpful correspondence, Don Postema for an interview and for proofing the final draft, Bill Van Groningen for being such a wonderful campus pastor and for providing great material from Queen's University, and Edson "Bill" Lewis, who kept me regularly informed on all new developments in the emerging Christian Reformed Campus Ministry Association.

Chapter Five

Thanks to Duane VanderBrug for several readings of various

stages of the draft and for offering not only important corrections but also sharp insights into this area of denominational history. Thanks to Robert Price for an interview and for providing me with a copy of his incisive thesis.

Chapter Six

Enormous thanks to Harold Bode for tireless work photocopying relevant articles, collecting important books, and taking a great deal of time to write up his own chronology of chaplaincy — a document essential to the writing of this chapter. Thanks also to Jacob Heerema and Harold Dekker for reading and commenting on the draft.

Chapter Seven

Special thanks to Gary Teja and Gary Schipper for providing materials and proofreading the draft. My thanks to John Wagenveld and Arlene Nyenhuis, who also sent materials in the area of ministry to Hispanics and the history of various CRC efforts in this field.

Chapter Eight

Hearty thanks to John Rozeboom, whose thirty-page summary of the *Gathering* program became a primary resource. Thanks also to John, Al Mulder, Duane VanderBrug, and Peter De Boer, all of whom took the time to read several drafts of the final chapter and who then offered needed corrections, critique, and balancing.

My sincere thanks to the staff at Eerdmans and to William B. Eerdmans, Jr., both for bringing me in on this project and for assistance all along the way. Thanks to Aaron Phipps, whose computer wizardry boggles the mind and whose layouts and designs catch and please the eye. Thanks to my congregation of Calvin Christian Reformed Church and to council president Ronald Rozema for supporting this project. Their giving me time off when it was needed and their general willingness to encourage my reading and writing are vastly appreciated.

Lastly, thanks to my wife, Rosemary, and my daughter, Julianna, who put up with many months of my bringing home musty archive folders, of my spending long hours at the word processor, and of my leaving to attend many a production meeting. Their patience and understanding undergird this book in invisible but vital ways. My thanks goes to them but also, more importantly, my abiding love.

— Scott Hoezee

I brought to this book a knowledge of the Christian Reformed Church that I gained as religion editor for the *Grand Rapids Press*. I held that job from 1983 to 1987.

So I had some knowledge and sense of this church that is so powerfully entrenched in the West Michigan area. But I gained a much richer, fuller, and far more personal understanding of this church in the process of helping Reverend Scott Hoezee chronicle the fascinating hundred-year history of Christian Reformed home missions.

Scott is on the top of the list of persons I want to highlight. He is the one who set the literary direction for this book. He is the pilot who guided me into places where I could find interesting, compelling stories.

My wife, Mary, also offered important support. It's hard enough having a husband who writes at all hours of the day for a newspaper. Then to have him batting away on the computer in his spare time is another intrusion. Besides putting up with the hours required for this history, Mary came along when I spent a week interviewing folks in New Mexico.

There are many others to whom I want to give a pat on the back. There are all of those wonderful Home Missions workers and church members in the Southwest. I'll miss several if I name only a few. But I remember the enjoyable afternoon spent talking in Keith Kuipers's living room; the enjoyable lunch we had at a colorful cafe in downtown Gallup, New Mexico, with Marla Jasperse and her husband, Joel; the pain as Zuni Indian Loren Tuscon Christian talked about his battle with demon rum; and the deep kindness of Reverend Michael Meekhof and his wife, Ardith.

I especially recall the sunny winter weekend I spent in Los Angeles, where it seemed to me Jesus Christ was definitely alive and well in the First Community Church. Reverend Stan Ver Heul and Reverend Tom Doorn are doing powerful work in that place.

So many others touched me in the course of helping to write this book: a Cambodian pastor near Holland, Michigan; the East Coast son of a Jew killed in a concentration camp; a hospice chaplain helping widows and widowers get through the holidays in Grand Rapids, Michigan; a young radio preacher and wise old TV minister in Chicago, Illinois; a corporate chaplain fighting memories of convenience-store killings in Orlando, Florida; a burly, bearded holy-man minister at the University of Michigan.

A special tribute has to go to Reverend Tymen E. Hofman, a Canadian who did more than his fair share of work in helping me gather the details of the Home Missions story in the country of his birth. A good friend, Charlie Ryman, graciously spent time trying to give me a deeper understanding of Native American spirituality. Through Charlie, I was able to ask better questions and especially to listen more intently when talking to Navajo and Zuni Indians on the New Mexico mission field.

There were John Rozeboom's huge heart and soothing smile, Gert Rotman's timely calls about plane tickets and other details, and the steady editing of Jeanne Ambrose.

Overall, I'm grateful for the chance to help tell a story that reveals the efforts of hardy spirits doing important work in a tumultuous hundred-year period that only God could hold together.

— Christopher H. Meehan

Foreword

Flourishing in the Land produced stacks of photographs, both prints and slides — hundreds, maybe thousands, of pictures illustrating the hundred-year story of Christian Reformed work in God's North American harvest field. Some of them were recent and colorful, most of them old black and whites.

The photographs usually focus on people. How appropriate! The *Flourishing* story is a story about persons. Church buildings, governing boards, and landscapes are all part of the story, but it's the people who hold my interest and entice me to read. They are leaders of the mission, converts to Christ, a spouse of a mission worker, babies held in adult arms, little kids standing by. I hear them say, "Look! I'm here too."

I'm grateful to Sandra De Groot for her caring inventory of all the *Flourishing* photos, only a small percentage of which ended up in the book. Sandy's care in sorting and choosing shows respectful treatment of the people in the pictures, skillful attention to honoring their dreams, and due notice of their high calling and sacrifice for the gospel's sake.

Who were the persons whose eyes look out of the prints and lock on mine? In the old days, most of them were not smilers, at least for the camera. I'm invited to look more deeply into their eyes to size up these strangers.

By themselves the photos disclose little. But coupled with text, the photos confirm something of great importance. The heroes of *Flourishing in the Land* are ordinary Christian people. The great story of the mission of the triune God to reach and redeem a lost world is acted out through the dreams and common sense, the gifts and foibles, the noble and frivolous actions of people who look like people I know, who look like me.

The photos in this book bring the hero stories down to earth. I'm encouraged seeing that the people God used before and employs today are distinguished by one main thing: Knowing God's love themselves, when opportunity, challenge, or plain need arises, they go out and give to others who do not know. I pray for courage to live up to their example. This book is for them, for workers in God's harvest yesterday, today, and tomorrow.

— *John Rozeboom*
Executive Director
Christian Reformed Home Missions

Introduction

As he went about his work in the Executive Mansion in late 1896 (it would not regularly be called the White House until Theodore Roosevelt's presidency), President Grover Cleveland presided over a union which, with that year's inclusion of Utah, encompassed forty-five states stretching from Delaware to California. Although the country was enduring a severe economic depression, it was growing fast: In just the past ten years alone, between 1886 and 1896, seven territories had been granted statehood.

With the massacre of the Indians at Wounded Knee in 1890, armed conflict with the Native Americans appeared to be over, leaving the white majority free to continue their westward expansion unopposed. By 1893 the Great Northern Railroad reached all the way to Seattle, and with this greater ease of travel came increased desire for more settlements in the West. Hence Congress initiated policies like the 1887 General Allotment (or Dawes) Act, which furthered the breakup of Indian reservations by giving white settlers the right to stake agricultural claims even on Indian land. The result was that between 1887 and 1934 the Indians lost sixty percent of the land formerly granted to them by the government.

Meanwhile, in the East the Industrial Revolution sparked an explosion in urban growth. The promise of the city proved, however, to be an empty one for many. As an economic depression took hold in 1893, unemployment became widespread, especially among the masses of immigrants who earlier had looked to America as the land of opportunity.

In the South residual tensions of the Civil War and of Emancipation continued to rise as whites sought ways to keep blacks under their collective thumb. Poll taxes and grandfather clauses requiring literacy tests were instituted as ways to circumvent laws allowing blacks to vote. At the same time the Supreme Court, under the rubric of "separate but equal" legislation, continued to affirm the segregation of blacks from whites in places like passenger trains.

But by 1896, despite its problems, the 120-year-old American republic was definitely in its ascendancy. And as the nation expanded, so also did its churches. Indeed, the nine-teenth century was known as the Protestant century as wave after wave of immigrants expanded the base of the larger main-line churches and also of the smaller, more sectarian ones. As such churches became more inwardly secure, they began to look outward. Through a kind of religious Manifest Destiny, many American Christian leaders began calling for greater zeal to evangelize "the heathen" both at home and abroad. [1]

Sparked by religious revivals earlier in the century and led by charismatic evangelists like Dwight L. Moody, Robert E. Speer, and John R. Mott, the great mission century was at a high point by 1896. Numerous agencies were springing up around the country to train young people as missionaries. One of the largest mission movements was the Student Volunteer Movement. Founded in 1886, this organization aimed to bring the gospel to the corners of the earth. Toward that end upwards of three thousand to four thousand young people were recruited, trained, and sent out by the end of the

FIGURE 1 The Great Northern Railroad fueled white settlement of the West.

1880s. By 1900, Student Volunteer Movement mission leader John R. Mott grandly declared that the movement's goal was "the evangelization of the world in this generation." [2]

Of course, as has often been true in American history, the goals of politics and religion tended to coincide and mix, with the result that mission expansion sometimes looked suspiciously like territorial expansion in disguise. With the inauguration of William Mc Kinley in 1897, American Christians found a friend in Washington to support their mission aims. Mc Kinley meanwhile capitalized on mission zeal to foster American territorial expansion. When commenting on why he began a war with the Philippines in 1898, Mc Kinley stated that he felt it was his duty "to uplift and civilize and Christianize" the Filipinos. [3] Not surprisingly, President Mc Kinley was the keynote speaker at the 1900 meeting of the Ecumenical Missionary Conference.

As this flurry of mission activity was taking place, the nearly forty-year-old Christian Reformed Church was struggling to find its mission voice. A product of two ecclesiastical schisms — one in 1834 in the national Netherlands Reformed Church and a second schism in 1857 in the Reformed Church in America — the devout Dutch members of the Christian Reformed Church were often criticized for their slow move toward missions and evangelism. Even one of the denomination's most ardent cheerleaders, Reverend Henry Beets, would write in 1946, "Our CRC was *slow* in meeting the challenge of the Great Commission." [4]

For most of its first half-century, the Christian Reformed Church concentrated on consolidating its resources and refining its doctrines. Though the denomination experienced rapid growth, it came almost exclusively through a sharp spike in Dutch immigration. Hence, in the last years of the nineteenth century the number of Christian Reformed congregations would more than triple, from 39 in 1880 to 144 by the turn of the century, with a concurrent rise in membership from 12,000 to nearly 54,000.

Still, during this same period, active mission outreach was rare in the CRC, and officially organized work was virtually nonexistent. In later years some would blame this lack of mission zeal on a theological problem related to the Calvinist theology of election, reprobation, and limited atonement. Others would claim that the desire to form "Dutch only" ghettos inhibited a drive to bring in people from other traditions (indeed, most Christian Reformed congregations would worship exclusively in the Dutch language until well into the twentieth century). Still others would claim that a concern for missions actually was present right from the beginning but that practical considerations, lack of resources, and the denomination's relative youth forced it to postpone organized mission work. [5]

Whatever the reasons, the fact remains that little if any officially organized and funded mission work was done prior to 1896. The first effort of any kind came in 1879, when on July 13 Reverend Tamme Vanden Bosch (1843–1913) was installed as the denomination's first home missionary. The 1880 Synod subsequently officially recognized his labor and established committees on home and foreign missions.

The focus of Vanden Bosch's work was church planting in

FIGURE 2 Dutch immigrants like these poured into the United States in the late nineteenth century.

areas with concentrations of Dutch Reformed immigrants. Vanden Bosch was essentially an itinerant preacher who collected and then organized Dutch Christians into churches to be affiliated with the Christian Reformed denomination. His travels took him to northern Michigan, Wisconsin, Iowa, and as far away as North Dakota, Nebraska, and Kansas. Though his work focused on the Dutch immigrants who were already in the New World, Vanden Bosch did succeed in expanding the denomination's outreach by convincing the 1881 Synod to give him a $100 grant to "distribute Bibles among the heathen."

But this pioneering work in missions was short-lived because Vanden Bosch was released from service already in 1882. Judged by some to be erratic and unstable in his methods, Vanden Bosch later left the CRC and eventually became an agent for the Chicago Tract Society. But meanwhile the ongoing lack of enthusiasm for mission work was evidenced by the fact that no one stepped forward to take up Vanden Bosch's task until 1886, when Reverend Marcus J. Marcusse was installed as the denomination's second home missionary. In his four years of work Marcusse also focused on church planting among the Dutch — a work which resulted in eleven new churches.

FIGURE 3 Reverend Tamme Vanden Bosch (1843–1913) was installed as the denomination's first home missionary.

Other home missionaries followed, but the overall zest for mission work remained mild. While many of the churches in America were busy recruiting missionaries, the CRC seemed largely content to do self-maintenance. Even as late as 1905 the denomination was giving an average of only two cents per family per week to the cause of missions.

In much of the country, 1910 was a banner year for missions as college students in the Student Volunteer Movement increased their mission zeal. In that same year SVM leader John R. Mott convened an international missions conference in Edinburgh to promote "the evangelization of the world in this generation."

But during the 1910-1911 school year the students at Calvin College and Seminary, the official educational institutions of the CRC, evidenced little of the mission zeal animating their peers on other campuses. Of twelve Calvin campus societies, only one was dedicated to missions — and it was by no means the most popular society. Indeed, articles in the Calvin College newspaper, The Chimes, were sharply critical of the Student Volunteer Movement and its rallying slogan. Karl Wm. Fortuin, a seminary student, reflected the thinking of many when he alleged in a 1910 article that the methods and slogans of the then-popular mission movements were un-Reformed, insufficiently tied to Christ's command, too emotional, and more interested in human methodology than in reliance on God's Spirit. True mission zeal, according to Fortuin, springs only from obedience to God's command, not from a desire to convert souls. [6]

Fortuin's comments sparked a good deal of theological debate, which climaxed in a 1911 on-campus speech by Reverend John Hiemenga. In the speech, also printed in The Chimes, Hiemenga urged greater mission zeal among Calvin's students and in the denomination generally, but he was careful to point out that such zeal and mission work must not compromise the Reformed heritage. After all, Hiemenga claimed, our Lord's command is to bring the gospel to the whole world, and, since, as providence would have it, we Calvinists already have received the purest understanding of that gospel, who could do mission work better than we? [7]

If the CRC had been obviously dedicated to mission work, then all of this theological posturing might have been the necessary theoretical backing to inform and motivate the practical work. But in the absence of widespread mission zeal or work, such discussions have an arid feel to them — as though, while a house was burning down, bystanders on the sidewalk merely stood around dithering about the most proper method for rescuing the children on the second floor.

The simple fact is that many in the early days of the CRC appeared more interested in maintaining their Dutch ethnicity and staunch doctrines than in reaching out to those beyond their kin. Indeed, Harvey Smit has perceptively observed that in the mission debate chronicled in the Calvin College Chimes, it may be no coincidence that those who wrote articles favoring increased missions did so in English, whereas those who opposed such moves wrote in Dutch. [8]

Yet, throughout the history of the Christian Reformed Church, there have always been those who called for more mission work among the Native Americans of North America, among the Jews, in the cities, and on the western frontier. Despite the overall lack of mission zeal among many of the Dutch Calvinists, there were always some who agitated passionately for greater concern and deeper com-

FIGURE 4 Christian Reformed Church office building on Kalamazoo Avenue in Grand Rapids, Michigan, which houses the Christian Reformed Board of Home Missions.

passion for the lost — especially the lost among their own North American neighbors.

This book tells the story of these dedicated mission visionaries and workers. Although theirs were often lonely voices, although they often did not receive a great deal of attention or acclaim, and although they often labored for decades with few measurable results, the people whose efforts are chronicled on the pages ahead have one salient characteristic in common: an enormous dedication to the gospel and its advance among all people.

The story begins in 1896. As indicated earlier, there were sporadic mission efforts prior to this time, but 1896 stands out as a new beginning in Christian Reformed home missions. It was in that year that the denomination commissioned and sent out its first missionaries whose sole interest would go far beyond church planting among the Dutch. The efforts begun among the Navajo and Zuni of the American Southwest in the fall of 1896 were the first of a new era; for the next one hundred years, similar CRC mission programs would spring up all over the United States and Canada.

The stories of these dedicated kingdom workers deserve to be told and savored, not merely as interesting pieces of history but as goads to continue the spirit in which they carried out their work. Even when many of their brothers and sisters were reluctant to engage in missions, these men and women, on hearing Jesus' plea for more workers in his ripe harvest fields, did not merely ask that others be sent but responded, "Here we are, send us!"

Chapter One

Going West

Navajo and Zuni Missions

He named it Rehoboth, saying, "Now the Lord has given us room,
and we will flourish in the land."

Genesis 26:22

Westbound travelers on Interstate 40 cannot help being struck by his red weather-worn face and especially by his dark eyes, which stare directly into every car passing the giant billboard just outside Gallup, New Mexico. The man's visage, along with the feather headdress which frames it, is the classic Indian stereotype — the man looks like he could have walked directly off the set of a 1930s cowboy-and-Indian movie. Next to his hard-bitten face, in bold black letters, are the words "Welcome to Indian Country."

This billboard is one of many which greet present-day visitors to Gallup. A host of other billboards advertise scores of souvenir shops or "trading posts" which hawk all manner of Native American wares — from authentic silver and turquoise jewelry and woven wool blankets to made-for-tourists Kachina dolls, feather headdresses, and "Indian Country" plastic key chains.

Gallup lives up to its billboard hype. The famous Route 66, which winds through the heart of Gallup, is a highly commercialized, Las Vegas-like strip of shops, restaurants, hotels, and even gas stations, all designed to catch the eye of

tourists who are hungry for an "authentic" slice of the Old West and of the Indians who have for centuries called the West home. Even at the highway exit which takes travelers to Rehoboth, visitors are now greeted by a ring of outsized, garishly painted (and, to Native Americans, quite offensive) wooden teepees which surround a "Trading Post" souvenir shop, gas station, and Denny's restaurant.

Seeing Gallup today makes it exceedingly difficult to imagine how very different it looked only one century ago. On October 10, 1896, when Christian Reformed missionaries Andrew Vander Wagen and Herman Fryling emerged from their train into the Gallup depot, they saw no billboards announcing that they were in "Indian Country" — but neither did they need any, for in 1896 New Mexico was still a largely undeveloped United States territory bristling with what has now passed into the lore of the Old West. (Along with Arizona, New Mexico did not gain admission to the union as a full state until 1912, when President William Taft signed the proclamations making New Mexico and Arizona the forty-seventh and forty-eighth states respectively.)

1

FIGURE 1–2 Sign at entry to Gallup, New Mexico, 1996; Gallup in 1896.

By 1896 Gallup boasted a population of no more than eight hundred people, most of whom were employed in local coal mines or Indian trade. Although the town was deemed too small and unstable to have its own bank, it did boast two dozen saloons and a half-dozen casinos. Having left the very Dutch and comparatively staid Grand Rapids, Michigan, only five days earlier, the Christian Reformed Church's first missionaries to "the heathen" must have felt an enormous culture shock as they stretched their legs that day near the Gallup depot. Fryling later recalled,

The first thing we saw when we arrived in Gallup was a few Navaho men wearing a belt [sic] with cartridges and a sixshooter or pistol in a scabbard. Even the whites living out in the country were all armed with a gun and a big long hunting knife. We had heard people talk about the wild and woolly west, but in Gallup we saw the reality.[1]

So began the journey of the Vander Wagens, the Frylings, and, through them, the Christian Reformed Church into the Southwest and into the often complex world of Christian missions to Native Americans. What led up to this beginning? How had the Christian Reformed Church — notably slow in starting any kind of mission work — chosen this particular field to be its first concerted mission effort?

The Beginning

By the 1880s the Christian Reformed Church was beginning to take a few halting steps in the direction of missions. The denomination's first missionary, Tamme Vanden Bosch, had resigned his original missionary commission in 1882 after only two years of work. In 1889, however, the synod, through its newly established Board of Heathen Missions, approached Vanden Bosch again, this time with the offer of mission work among the Sioux Indians in the Dakotas. Vanden Bosch agreed, and so began his work in South Dakota.

But the times were not favorable. The Indians, who had suf-

FIGURE 3 Herman and Jennie Fryling, left, Andrew and Effa Vander Wagen, center, possibly Mr. and Mrs. James De Groot, right. Camp at Cienega, Arizona, July 1898.

fered so many humiliations in the past century, had been making spiritual and tribal comebacks through the Ghost Dance revival, which had been sweeping through Indian tribes since 1870. The Ghost Dance was a ritual which ostensibly put the Indians in contact with their ancestors, from whom they sought increased power for their struggle with the white man. It was widely believed by many Indians that a new era of Indian resurgence would begin in the spring of 1891. As tensions rose on all sides, a confrontation became nearly inevitable, and, indeed, in December of 1890, the Seventh Cavalry massacred a large number of Lakotan Ghost Dancers at Wounded Knee Creek in South Dakota.

FIGURE 4
Johannes Groen.

FIGURE 5 Spring Street CRC, Grand Rapids, Michigan.

In the midst of this tension, ferment, and conflict, Vanden Bosch's work among the Sioux went badly. Vanden Bosch became quickly discouraged and frustrated. Less than one year into his new assignment, he once again resigned his denominational mission post.

During the 1890s, however, other voices continued to call for greater work among the Indians, though not everyone agreed that this was the best field of endeavor to choose. Some wished instead to target the large populations of Jews living in urban centers like Paterson, New Jersey, or Chicago, Illinois. Others felt there was vital work to be done among the blacks living in the recently emancipated South. Still others asserted that work among the Indians was futile on several counts. Some believed, for instance, that, given their antipathy toward the white man, the Indians would surely never accept the white man's religion, so why even bother to proffer it? Some thought, as did many other Americans in the late nineteenth century, that the Indians were a dying breed. Finally, the more cynical of the denomination were of the opinion that the Indians were simply too stupid, hard-hearted, and lazy ever to be converted into solid Christians capable of being organized into formal congregations.[2] Some on the floor of synod went so far as to claim that any race which ate the entrails of animals was simply "beyond redemption."[3]

But many, notably mission secretary Johannes Groen, continued to herald the cause of the Indians. Groen pointed out that many white men went to the Southwest only to

make a profit off the Indians through cheap exploitation. Christians, he insisted, needed to go there not to pad their own pockets but actually to help the Indians in the name of Christ. The church needed to be a distinctly different presence as it labored in the midst of this vanishing race to bring them to Christ's light.

Groen succeeded in convincing the denomination to send him on a kind of fact-finding tour of Southwestern reservations. When he returned in early 1896, he reported that, while the Indians were indeed mired in many terrible sins, they were in fact an industrious people capable of making progress in civilization — that is, in becoming Christian. His encouraging report emboldened the denomination to search for and commission its first full-time missionaries to the American Southwest and to the Navajo who made their home there.

The search ended in Herman Fryling. Born in the Dutch province of Friesland in 1869, Fryling immigrated to the United States along with his parents in 1880. A graduate of Calvin Theological School, Fryling, with his wife, Katie, accepted the challenge of going into the Southwest as the denomination's first full-time missionaries to "the heathen." They would be joined on their journey by lay workers (and newlyweds) Andrew and Effa Vander Wagen. Like Fryling, Vander Wagen had also been born in Friesland, in 1868, and had immigrated to the United States in the same year as Fryling.

On September 29, 1896, in a stirring ceremony at Spring Street CRC in Grand Rapids (now First CRC), Fryling was ordained to the Christian Reformed ministry, and Vander Wagen was charged to engage in mission work as a lay missionary. Six days later the Frylings and the Vander Wagens boarded a westward-bound train, and so began their long journey.[4]

Fort Defiance

When the Vander Wagens and the Frylings arrived in Gallup on that October day in 1896, they had not yet reached their final stopping place — it was merely the end of the Santa Fe line. Reaching their destination of Fort Defiance, Arizona, would require a thirty-mile ride by horse and wagon over muddy, rutted roads which wound through the flat landscape and between the towering red mesas of western New Mexico and eastern Arizona.

Andrew Vander Wagen, "who was well-acquainted with horses," Fryling recalled, managed to secure a team of horses to be hitched to the Belknap spring wagon which the missionaries had brought with them from Michigan. Since they had arrived on a Saturday and did not wish to travel on the Lord's Day, the couples remained in Gallup until Monday.

The Vander Wagens decided to make the first trip to Fort Defiance while the Frylings waited behind, in part because of the frail health of Katie Fryling. The two-day journey was indeed a difficult one as thunderstorms turned the roads into fetid swamps of mud. On the first night the Vander Wagens managed to find lodging in an abandoned shack which had once served as a trading post. As the sun began to set that evening, however, Andrew and Effa realized that they had not thought to bring matches with them and so were forced to spend the night in the cold darkness. (After that experience Effa made certain that on future trips they always carried matches with them, stored in an old bottle to keep them dry.) The next day they arrived at Fort Defiance, and within a few days Andrew returned to Gallup for the Frylings. [5]

Fort Defiance was built by the U.S. government near the apex of white encroachment on Indian lands in the mid nineteenth century. As the name suggests, the fort was a "defiant" statement that the white man — through his military presence — was there to stay. When the government established a school there for Indian children, the Methodist Episcopal Church petitioned the government for permission to establish a missionary outpost there as well.

But the M.E. church found the work among the Navajo neither easy nor, in the end, desirable and so decided to abandon the mission. Upon their arrival, Vander Wagen and Fryling were told by an M.E. missionary that the work among the Navajo was fraught with discouragement and, for

FIGURE 6 Towering Red Mesas; Navajo hogan in bottom center of photo.

FIGURE 7 Fort Defiance circa 1898.

FIGURE 8–9 Navajo hogans are made of logs arranged in circular form, caulked with mud; a hole three or four feet in diameter is left in the top for smoke to escape. The door always faces east. The Zuni pueblo at right.

that reason, his denomination was prepared to sell the entire mission outpost to the Christian Reformed Church at a bargain price. Fryling felt this was a golden opportunity which God's providence had dropped right into their laps. So the missionary parsonage and the work among the Navajo tribe were turned over to the CRC. According to Fryling, the Christian Reformed Church became thereby the only Protestant denomination doing any kind of mission work among "the neglected people" of the Navajo at that time.

The Navajo

Although not as well-known to many Americans as some other tribes, the Navajo tribe is now the largest in the United States.[6] When the Frylings and Vander Wagens arrived, the tribe numbered approximately 25,000. Today that number has soared to more than 250,000, living on some 25,000 square miles of reservation land in New Mexico and Arizona.

By 1896 the Navajo tribe, like most Indian tribes at that time, had already waged and lost its battles with the white man. By the mid nineteenth century the Navajo had already been living in the Southwest for over four hundred years, having migrated there from the northern portion of what is now called North America. Some believe the Navajo originally may have come from as far away as the upper regions of present-day Canada. Referring to themselves as *Diné*, or "The People," the Navajo received their present name from the Spanish,

whom they encountered in the 1500s, after Columbus and his Spanish ships landed in the New World. It was also the Spanish who, by introducing the Navajo to sheep and goats, helped to create the now common Navajo trades of shepherding and the weaving of woolen blankets.

Significantly, the Spanish also brought with them the Christian faith of Roman Catholicism. But unlike other tribes (e.g., the Zuni) who lived together in pueblos, the Navajo were and are a largely nomadic people scattered over a wide area. Although members of the same clan tended to live in fairly close proximity to one another, the Navajo people generally were and are not village dwellers. Thus it was not hard for them to escape the influence of Spanish missionaries since there were no central Navajo villages in which the Catholics could establish missions.

Instead, the Navajo were free to make forays into Spanish

FIGURE 10 Navajo weaver and medicine man.

FIGURE 11 Navajo dress.   FIGURE 12 Medicine man.

culture, picking and choosing which of its elements they wished to assimilate and which they wished to disregard. In fact, as Peter Iverson notes in his history of the Navajo, it is precisely this adaptability of the Navajo people — their ability to assimilate new practices and cultures in their own unique way — which has been a key ingredient in helping the Navajo to survive where other tribes have faltered.

But by the mid nineteenth century even the scattered Navajo got caught up in a larger movement which did finally impinge on their freedom. On February 2, 1848, the Mexican War ended with the signing of the Treaty of Guadalupe Hidalgo. Under its terms, Mexico was to cede the entire Southwest territory to the United States, including the area now encompassing New Mexico, Arizona, Colorado, Nevada, Utah, and California. Whereas the Spanish and Mexicans had largely left the Indians to their own devices, the white man was intent on changing matters drastically. For with the arrival of the white man, a new concept also arrived: land ownership. To the Navajo, no one can "own" a piece of land; one can only be a steward of it. Yet the white man insisted that all tracts of land have strict boundaries and be divided along the lines of who held title to which areas.

By 1860 the Navajo were feeling so cramped and abused that they waged a retaliatory attack on the newly built Fort Defiance in Arizona. In this instance, however, the scattered nature of the Navajo tribe (which had been advantageous in previous encounters with outsiders) proved to be a disadvantage. The loosely organized Navajo were no match for

FIGURE 13 The view from Kit Carson's cave, located near Fort Wingate. The cave derives its name from a story that during the days of the Indian wars, Kit Carson held three hundred Navajo captive here. At the end of the cave is a small spring which for years had provided water for Navajo horses and sheep.

the tightly organized United States Army. Led by Navajo leaders Manuelito and Barboncito, the attack on Defiance was unsuccessful. Unfortunately, however, the conflict prompted the U.S. government to begin taking steps against the Navajo. The famed Indian killer Kit Carson was called upon in 1863 to help track down and round up the Navajo. Meanwhile, a new fort, Fort Sumner, was built in southeastern New Mexico as further evidence of the white man's abiding presence.

Under the leadership of Kit Carson and General James Carleton, the Navajo were systematically, though slowly, flushed out of their camps and hiding places and brought to Fort Defiance and to nearby Fort Wingate. As the number of captive Indians grew, however, these forts could no longer accommodate the Navajo prisoners. The result was one of the darkest episodes in Navajo history: The Long Walk. The Navajo were forced to march more than two hundred fifty

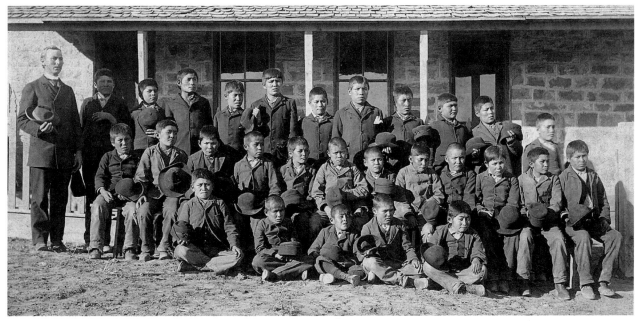

FIGURE 14 Herman Fryling with Indian children at Fort Defiance circa 1896.

FIGURE 15 Kit Carson.

miles to Fort Sumner near the end of 1864. Many of them died along the way from hunger, exposure, or mistreatment by the Army soldiers who oversaw this torturous march.

The Navajo interned at Fort Sumner would remain prisoners of the U.S. government for four years, until, on June 1, 1868, the Navajo leaders, including Barboncito, signed a treaty with the government. The Navajo would be permitted to leave the fort in order to live on a 3.5-million-acre reservation in northeastern Arizona and northwestern New Mexico (to which they would once more have to walk). In addition, the Navajo would be provided with sheep and cattle with which to begin a new life. Although there were several additions to this reservation in the next thirty years, this initial grant of land was still the bulk of Navajo territory when the Christian Reformed missionaries arrived in 1896.

When the Frylings and Vander Wagens arrived, the Navajo were once again a scattered people, living in the wide-open spaces of their sizeable reservation. Since they did not arrange themselves into pueblos or villages, the only way for missionaries to witness to the Navajo was either by traveling from camp to camp and hogan to hogan or through working in government schools in places like Fort Defiance. The disadvantage of the first option was that the distances to be covered were indeed considerable, making sustained contact with any

one family or clan very difficult. The disadvantage of the second method was that it put the missionary in touch only with the children and not directly with the adults of the tribe.

Another complicating factor for the fledgling missionaries was the Navajo language itself. Although the missionaries quite quickly began gathering a basic working vocabulary, they found communication difficult. Indeed, the Navajo language is considered to be one of the most difficult languages in the world. They also discovered for themselves the very obstacles which had so frustrated the Methodist Episcopal missionaries, one of which was the Navajo penchant for listening to new ideas, picking and choosing what they wanted to accept, and then disregarding the rest.

Despite the difficulties and hardships of their new environment, Fryling and Vander Wagen quickly applied themselves to their new task. Herman Fryling labored under great adversity and hardship on this new mission field. His wife, Katie, whose health had been declining steadily for some time, died on February 4, 1897, only five months after their departure from Grand Rapids.

These personal and vocational hardships not withstanding, Fryling and the Vander Wagens labored on, trying to create a positive Christian impression on any and all Navajo with whom they came into contact. Since the children in the school were the easiest group to target, the missionaries, taking a cue from their own Reformed heritage, decided to establish Bible and catechism classes to teach the children the Christian faith, which, it was hoped, would then be brought home by the children to the parents. Meanwhile, despite the language barrier, Vander Wagen and Fryling also sought to befriend adult Navajo who came to Fort Defiance to check

FIGURE 16 Effa Vander Wagen gave the sick people medicine, and the Zuni began to trust the missionaries.

FIGURE 17 Leonard P. Brink sitting in a chair that was used by a photo studio in Gallup for several photo sessions with many Rehoboth staff. See also figures 29 and 45.

on their children or buy supplies from the fort's trading post.

By the summer of 1897, the CRC's work among the Navajo saw its first expansion forty miles to the east in a place called Tohatchi, New Mexico. Tohatchi, meaning "water is scratched out," was the location of yet another government school for children from the surrounding area. Andrew Vander Wagen was the first to make the long trip on horseback from Fort Defiance to Tohatchi in the summer of 1897, and Fryling soon followed. The two of them made regular visits both to the children in the school and to the various camps and hogans in the valleys and hills around the outpost. A formal Christian Reformed mission outpost was established at Tohatchi in 1898.

By the fall of 1897, the Vander Wagens had already pulled up stakes to begin a new work in the Zuni pueblo forty miles south of Gallup (see below). Fryling, feeling very much alone now, requested some new missionary assistants, specifically to help the budding work at Tohatchi. He received this assistance from Mr. and Mrs. James E. De Groot, who would be "camp workers" in Tohatchi and Fort Defiance until 1900. During the De Groots' tenure, property was secured in Tohatchi, and a mission outpost was constructed early in 1899.

The De Groots were replaced in 1900 by one of the Christian Reformed Church's most remarkable missionaries to the Indians — Leonard P. Brink — who would minister in New Mexico until his death in 1936. He would work at Tohatchi until 1913, then at the Rehoboth school and several other sites including Farmington and Shiprock. Brink was a deeply committed and highly intelligent worker who would distinguish himself for his able study of the Navajo language. The fruit of this laborious study was many translations of Bible books, catechism material, and Christian hymns.[7]

But to do this work, Brink, hailed as the Christian Reformed "Cadmus to the Navajo," had to render into written form a language which had previously been only oral. Along the way his translation work forced him to grapple with other frustrations, including the fact that the Navajo language contains no fewer than twelve different verbs meaning "to give" and nine different expressions for "to eat." Because the Navajo tongue also produces sounds for which there are no English equivalents, Brink invented new alphabetical characters. Brink's goal was to produce a Navajo dictionary which would likely contain more than fifteen thousand words, a goal toward which he continued to labor throughout his nearly four decades of work in New Mexico. Somehow Brink also found time in his busy schedule to write regular articles about the mission work for the denominational periodical *The Banner*, thus keeping the larger denomination informed of what was happening in that remote corner of the Southwest.

Disagreeable Work and New Beginnings

According to Fryling, the Christian Reformed Church was the first denomination in the Southwest to evangelize by means of Bible instruction of children in the government schools. The method proved effective enough, however, that before long the Roman Catholic Church also established the St. Michael's mission outpost nine miles south of Fort Defiance, where, after demanding equal time with the Protestants, it received permission to hold Bible classes for the children in the boarding school. Apparently, however, conflict soon followed.

According to the testimony of Fryling, the Catholics attempted to undercut the Christian Reformed Church's mission outreach by poisoning the children against the Protestants and their version of Christianity. In what is undoubtedly a mild understatement, the missionaries eventually reported to synod that the work at Fort Defiance had become "disagreeable" because the Catholics' classes not only passively curtailed the amount of time Fryling could spend with the children but also actively undercut Fryling both theologically and personally.

Reportedly the Catholic workers would tell the Navajo not only that Protestant theology was false but also — and even worse — that the Protestants themselves were secretly out to steal the Indians' land and rob them of their freedom.[8] (Of course, at that time both Protestants and Catholics expressed suspicion toward each other. L.P. Brink himself once lamented the denomination's abandoning of Fort Defiance, in part, he said, because had we stayed in the Fort, "we could better keep an eye on [Roman Catholic] tactics"!) By 1904 the work was proving sufficiently troublesome that the Christian Reformed synod decided to end the Fort Defiance work and sell the mission property there to a group of Presbyterian mission workers.

Meanwhile, the methods of these fledgling missionaries came in for some in-house criticism as well. By 1906 a number of Christian Reformed congregations were expressing great dissatisfaction with what they were hearing from the Indian mission field. Some believed the method of targeting primarily children was un-Reformed. Some were also quite uncomfortable with using children as a kind of intermediary through whom to reach parents, claiming that this was

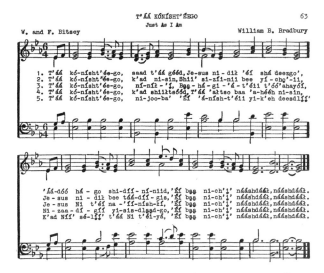

FIGURE 18 Hymn "Just As I Am" from *Jesus Dayoodláanii Biyiin*, Navajo gospel hymnal.

FIGURE 19 Translator Leonard P. Brink at his desk along with Jacob C. Morgan.

Churches in Classis Red Mesa

The following list shows the churches of Classis Red Mesa, the year each church began, its location, the year it organized, and its current pastor.

The "Indian Mission Field" was transferred from the Board of Foreign Missions to the Board of Home Missions in 1964, after the transfer of "off-reservation work" in 1960. Classis Red Mesa was organized with the approval of synod in 1982. Mr. Ernest P. Benally began serving in January 1996 as Red Mesa ministry director on behalf of Christian Reformed Home Missions and Classis Red Mesa.

Began	Location	Organized	Pastor
1897	Zuni, NM, CRC	1987	Michael Meekhof
1898	Tohatchi, NM, CRC	1983	Stanley Jim
1899	Rehoboth, NM, CRC	1906	Donald Byker
1912	Crownpoint, NM, CRC	1971	Robert L. Jipping
	Toyee and Whitehorse Lake, NM		
1915	Toadlena, NM, CRC	Emerging	Ray Slim †
	Newcomb, NM		
1925	Farmington, NM, Maranatha	1962	James Vande Lune
1926	Naschitti, NM, CRC	1982	Ray Slim †
1928	Gallup, NM, Bethany	1956	W. Keith Bulthuis
1930	Fort Wingate, NM, CRC	1982	Johnny Harvey ††
1930	Tohlakai, NM, Bethlehem	1982	Recruiting
1934	Red Valley, AZ, CRC	1992	Howard Begay ††
1934	Shiprock, NM, Bethel	1985	Recruiting
1934	Teec Nos Pos, AZ, Four Corners	1982	Paul H. Redhouse ††
1942	Sanostee, NM, CRC	Emerging	Ray Slim †
1950	Church Rock, NM, CRC	1983	Corwin Brummel
	Pinedale, NM		
1962	Albuquerque, NM, Fellowship	1978	John W. Dykhuis
1965	Window Rock, AZ, CRC	1980	Gary Klumpenhower
	Navajo, NM		
1993	Kayenta, AZ, Mission	Emerging	Jerome Sandoval

† Pastor Ray Slim serves as area pastor-trainer for all three churches
†† Those named as pastor are volunteer leaders of local ministry teams.

Other Ministries in Red Mesa

1903	Rehoboth Christian School	K-Grade 12
1908	Zuni Christian Mission School	K-Grade 8
1977	Crownpoint Christian School	K-Grade 6
1982	SW Campus Christian Fellowship	Campus ministry
	Albuquerque, NM	

Rehoboth Christian Hospital was founded in 1910. The Luke Society was formed in 1965 to accept sponsorship of the hospital and assure its continuance. In 1984 the hospital merged with the McKinley General Hospital in Gallup, NM, to become Rehoboth-McKinley Christian Health Care Services.

FIGURE 20 Church Rock Chapel in 1962.

"Off-Reservation" Churches and Ministries

Following World War II off-reservation ministries among Native American people were started in Brigham City, UT (Intermountain Indian School); Chicago, IL; Denver, CO; Phoenix, AZ (Cook Christian Training School and Phoenix Indian School); San Francisco, CA (Friendship House); and Salt Lake City, UT. Today small congregations continue in Denver and Salt Lake City.

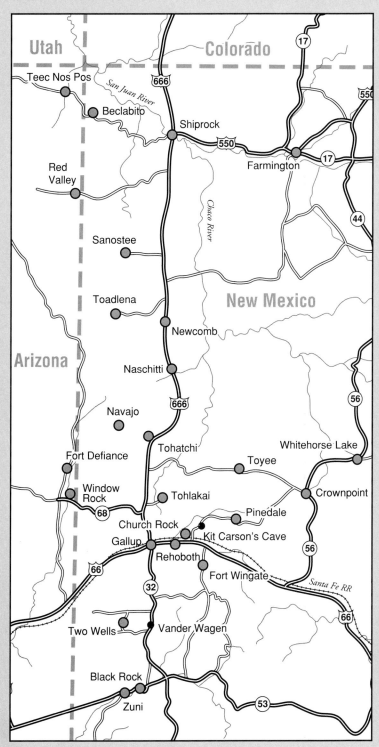

Red Mesa ministries now discontinued

1896 School work, Fort Defiance, AZ
1918 CRC mission in Kimbeto, NM
1928 CRC mission, San Antone, NM
1929 CRC mission, Two Wells, NM
1930 CRC mission, Star Lake, NM
1954 Bethany Christian School/Gallup NM
1979 CRC mission, Beclabito, NM
1990 CRC mission, Chinle, AZ

FIGURE 21 The Bethlehem Chapel at Tohlakai, NM.

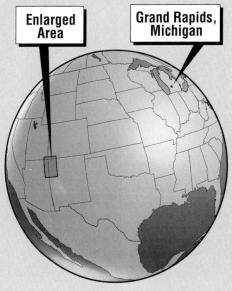

likely why the mission work had thus far proven to be so ineffective.

Indeed, by the missionaries' own admission, the work among the Navajo had a slow and "troublesome" start. By 1900 Fryling had worked for four years among the Navajo at Fort Defiance and, beginning in the summer of 1897, also in Tohatchi. Despite his best efforts, he could report few if any true conversions and no apparently significant inroads into the Navajo culture. But by 1901 matters began to improve. In a 1901 article in the denominational weekly *The Banner of Truth,* missionary L.P. Brink reported with joy the conversion of several Navajo children.

In January of 1901 a thirteen-year-old girl named Mattie

FIGURE 22 Nona Gardy, standing, and Mattie Green.

Green asked Fryling to baptize her into the Christian faith. Having determined that this request sprang from a sincere heart and a well-informed mind, Fryling joyfully accepted her profession of faith. Shortly thereafter he received a second request for baptism, from fourteen-year-old Nona Gardy. On January 14, 1901, at Fort Defiance — in the presence of a number of Navajo and some government workers — Fryling, "his voice and hands trembling with emotion," baptized the girls in the name of the triune God. The next week Fryling, Brink, and Vander Wagen held a special Communion service at which these new converts sacramentally celebrated the death of Jesus. Sadly, only sixteen days after her baptism, Mattie Green died of tuberculosis. From her deathbed she told her grieving mother, "Do not cry for me, for I am going to heaven to be happy forever." Later that year Nona Gardy also died of what was then commonly called consumption.[9]

By March of 1901 the sadness the missionaries felt over these deaths was ameliorated by a measure of joy as five other children asked to be baptized by Reverend Brink. Also encouraging was the fact that by July of 1901 the work in Tohatchi had advanced sufficiently that a Communion worship service could be held in the mission congregation there. Shortly after this, two Navajo were married in a Christian ceremony — probably the first Christian marriage ceremony ever to take place among the Navajo people.

Still, the work among the Navajo continued to be difficult. The Tohatchi congregation, for instance, was scattered over an area of two hundred square miles, making communal worship services difficult to arrange. Even *huisbezoek,* or home visitation, was a task which required long trips taking several days. Yet L.P. Brink knew that, aside from the fact that such home visits were an old Dutch custom, the Navajo people needed to be met and witnessed to on their home turf. Although he spent long hours at the Tohatchi mission station doing his translation work, Brink also routinely traveled by horse and buggy to seek out the Indians living amid the mesas of New Mexico.

FIGURE 23 Missionary's home, Tohatchi, NM.

Since the trips took several days to complete, Brink and his interpreters routinely accepted the hogan hospitality of the Navajo they visited. Occasionally they took shelter wherever they could when the distances between camps were considerable. Brink's *Banner* articles often detailed the kind of rugged ministry in which he was engaged.

We made quite a trip last week … [traveling] ten miles through one of the worst sandstorms that ever were. Not only did sand pass thru the air like clouds, but also sticks and pebbles innumerable. We were exceedingly glad to get inside of a trading store for a while. After talking to some Indians there for a while, we decided it was not the kind of place we wanted to stay in for the night, so we hied us off to a place about eighteen miles further, where there were mountains and timber, and we could be sheltered against the storm. When we reached the place in the evening, there was no one there and so we prepared to camp out for the night. Hastily, I sent my interpreter to the nearby trading store to get us some corned beef and crackers, and while he was gone I started two fires, one great big one to serve as a heating-stove and the other a little one to serve as a cooking stove. Soon the coffee was boiling and we feasted on coffee, crackers, and corned beef.[10]

On another occasion Brink recalled being invited to stay the night with a Navajo medicine man who listened quite attentively to Brink's Christian witness to Christ as the only true Savior: "To sleep on a hogan floor seemed a joy, after serving the Master thus. We became more and more convinced that in order to labor successfully among the Navaho's [sic], the Navaho must be visited in his hogan."[11]

By 1909 Brink's labors were yielding enough fruit that the need for a formal mission church building became apparent. In his *Banner* articles Brink began to plead with the members of the denomination to put aside some of their financial resources to pay for this needed mission outpost. As the Tohatchi congregation grew, there was no building large enough to hold the congregation on those occasions when they all gathered for worship. The small government school building in which they had been holding worship was insufficient as dozens of converts were being baptized, most of whom willingly made long journeys to attend the outpost's Sunday-afternoon worship services. Brink even reported that when two hundred Indians came for Christmas services in 1909, he had to conduct worship in shifts, speaking to thirty Indians, sending them out, and then replacing them with thirty more, until finally all had been inside for worship. Some of these attenders also needed overnight lodging since the length of their trip back home meant they would need to start out at first light on Monday morning.

By late 1910 Brink's passionate and persistent pleas resulted in the construction of the Tohatchi church. Aided by a Mr. John Spyker, Sr., a retired builder from Zeeland,

FIGURE 24 Jacob Bosscher, Leonard P. Brink, Herman Fryling, Edward Becenti.

Michigan, who had volunteered to oversee the construction of the church after reading Brink's *Banner* articles, the building was completed and dedicated at Thanksgiving, November 24, 1910. Preaching to more than two hundred attenders, Brink based his message for the day on Psalm 122:1: "I was glad when they said unto me, 'Let us go unto the house of the LORD.'" Following Brink's sermon, native worker Edward Becenti addressed the congregation in the Navajo language, praising God with them for this advance in the Christian mission at Tohatchi.

Making Room

In the mid nineteenth century, U.S. Army officer Richard Henry Pratt was given charge over a number of captured Indian warriors. The warriors, who had been taken prisoner in the various armed conflicts which the U.S. Army was waging at that time, were interned in a prison at St. Augustine, Florida. Faced with the task of watching over these warriors, Pratt decided that rather than being a kind of passive prison warden, he would try to accomplish something constructive with these "savages."

Being a military man, Pratt decided to do what he knew best: structure people's lives according to military-like discipline and regimens designed to make his charges respectable, industrious, and "safe" for life in American society. Thus was born what, by the end of the century, would become a common institution sponsored by the U.S. government: the Indian boarding school. The first such school, based on Pratt's St. Augustine prototype, was established in Kansas in 1879, and others quickly followed. By 1900 there were twenty-five such schools in thirteen states and territories.

Taking their cue from Pratt and his military model, these schools were designed to immerse the Indians in the "pure" waters of white culture and hold them under until they were soaked with it through and through. If such cultural immersion meant that the inner Indian drowned, so much the better. As noted earlier, many Americans in the nineteenth century believed the Indian race was dying. Among the more noble intentions which lay behind the establishment of these schools was the desire to preserve the Indian race.

Unhappily, the only way to preserve the Indian, it was thought, was to stamp out all vestiges of the vile Native American culture which was pulling the Indians down. In its place the Indians would be given the gift of the white man's "superior" culture and ways. Since many believed that "the only good Indian is a dead Indian," the boarding schools worked to "kill" the inner Indian, leaving a shell which could be filled up with the white man's culture.

It soon became apparent to Pratt and his disciples that the best chance one had to produce such results was to start with

children as young as possible, who were still impressionable. Therefore, they reasoned, children needed to be taken away from their parents and their corrosive native influence to be whisked away to boarding schools where the children could be "civilized."

Upon arrival, the children would receive a new (white) name, a haircut, and a military-style uniform. They would also be told that the exercise of native customs was strictly forbidden and that the speaking of their native tongue would lead to corporal punishment. The children would then be taught to march in formation, to join military-like bands, and — in a trade-school setting — to do gender-specific skills like sewing and cooking for girls and farming and industrial arts for boys, the latter especially necessary in a society in the throes of the Industrial Revolution.

Soon assimilation into the white man's culture became official government policy toward the Indians. Boarding schools were the means to that end. These "schools for savages," as some termed them, would transform "wild Indians" into "good Indians" by making Indians over in "the white man's image."[12] That cut hair was a sign of mourning and death to most Indians, that family ties were considered of the utmost importance to most tribes, and that there might be anything at all of value in Native American culture were considered irrelevant by the promoters of these new schools. What mattered was that the "Indian problem" be solved by removing the differences between the culture of the white man and the culture of the red man through eliminating the "inferior" Indian culture.

FIGURE 25 Rehoboth students marching to church.

When in 1903 the Christian Reformed Church established its mission boarding school at Rehoboth, New Mexico, just outside of Gallup, it had, therefore, a model to follow. However, it may have followed the Pratt model too closely and uncritically. When asked what differentiated the Rehoboth school from more secular government schools, many former students and even some teachers admit that the only difference was that government schools taught students to march to the dining hall and to classrooms, whereas Rehoboth taught students to march to the dining hall, the classrooms, and to church.[13]

FIGURE 26 Boy students at Rehoboth in military-like uniforms.

FIGURE 27 Andrew Vander Wagen conversing with Zuni Indians inside a Zuni home.

Though Rehoboth Christian School has produced many fine graduates, though everyone who worked in the school sought to do so in compassionate Christian ways, and though the Rehoboth school had by the late 1970s become a more typical Christian day school, the fact is that for much of its nearly one-hundred-year history, Rehoboth bore striking resemblance to government schools, whose primary goal was the Indians' assimilation of white culture and an active stamping out of Native American culture. Though Rehoboth's primary goal was to evangelize the Navajo, it was commonly believed at that time that a stamping out of native culture was a natural part of the Christianizing process.

By the early 1900s, Christian Reformed missionaries in New Mexico and Arizona had clearly experienced the frustration of tracking down the Navajo in the huge area over which they were scattered. Frustrated by the large distances to be traveled between Navajo camps, Andrew Vander Wagen already in 1897 had moved his mission efforts to the Zuni pueblo, where there was already a very large concentration of Native Americans who were easily accessible. But even among the Navajo, the missionaries had from the outset been focusing their efforts on those few places where the Native Americans were already concentrated, namely, government schools in Fort Defiance and Tohatchi. So it is no surprise that when the opportunity arose, many mission workers and board members believed that creating their own Christian Reformed school would be a great advantage. Now they could work among Navajo who were wholly under their sway from dawn to dusk nearly year-round.

Given the denomination's long history of and commitment to Christian education in day-school settings, this particular move seemed wholly legitimate and natural. Already in 1888, in one of the denomination's earliest mission statements, synod had declared "that through the building of schools, as well as the preaching of the Gospel to old and young, the work [of missions] should be carried out." As it became clear that the work at Fort Defiance was deteriorating because of the difficulties mentioned above, another field of endeavor was being sought. Herman Fryling recalled that the board instructed the missionaries "to look for a suitable location for an industrial institution where we would be able to colonize our future converts and provide means and ways for them to enjoy a Christian life."

In 1903 they found Smith's Ranch just outside Gallup. The ranch was a spacious tract of land on which to develop a new, distinctly Reformed mission outpost. Since it was the largest land purchase the CRC had thus far made in the Southwest, it was christened *Rehoboth,* from the Hebrew word for "room," as recorded in Genesis 26:22. When the patriarch Isaac had at last gained a foothold in the Promised Land of Canaan through the purchase of some property, "He named it Rehoboth, saying, 'Now the LORD has given us room and we will flourish in the land." (Even today the sign at the entrance to the Rehoboth campus is inscribed with this Scripture verse.)

When one sees Rehoboth today, it is difficult to envision how remote and "roomy" the area must have appeared to those missionaries who first came to inspect the site. Today Rehoboth is situated just south of Route 66 and the busy superhighway Interstate 40. Gallup's sprawling commercial business district has crept to within sight of the Rehoboth campus, and a large oil refinery lies just to the northeast. But in 1903 Smith's Ranch/Rehoboth was all by itself, nestled in a hilly area flanked on all sides by soaring red mesas and

FIGURE 28 Sign at the entrance to Rehoboth in 1995.

dwarfed by the big sky which stretches over the New Mexico landscape. Remote though the site was, it was clearly replete with possibilities for the Lord to help the missionaries at long last "flourish in the land."

The original plan for the Rehoboth property was the creation of an industrial site at which to train the Navajo in various vocational and trade skills. But financial constraints and general opposition from many churches to the idea of conjoining missions with business practices led the missionaries to abandon the idea in favor of founding a mission boarding school similar to government-run schools elsewhere around the country. Such a school, intentional in its efforts to assimilate Indians into the white man's culture, seemed the perfect solution to the Indians' "problems" that had been noted by many Christian Reformed observers in their nine years in the Southwest.

FIGURE 29 Cocia Hartog.

A number of missionaries as well as some visitors to the area had long noted with disgust the way the Indians lived. Navajo hogans were described by *Banner* editor Henry Beets as "little shacks or shanties ... [with] no stoves, no chairs, no bed worthy of the name. Not even a chimney. Just a big hole in the so-called roof .. and no door except for a blanket." Some missionaries likewise clearly judged the Indians to be wild and uncultured, having little if anything to offer the white man.

Reverend John Dolfin, a Home Missions pastor, claimed that Indians were generally "sluggish, indifferent and without the slightest ambition to be prosperous in life." He also lambasted the Indians as

being devoid of culture — culturally the Indians were "a blank." [14]

Others were equally uncharitable in their assessments. In a booklet entitled *Indian Mission Sketches*, mission worker Cocia Hartog noted with great appreciation the tender way in which the Navajo tended their sheep as well as the fact that the Navajo seemed generally honest and trustworthy. She even pointed out there were great love and loyalty between Navajo parents and their children. Still, she went on to claim that, overall, Navajo mothers did not know how to give a child "proper care." [15] She also lamented the lack of morals among the Indians — particularly the practice of polygamy: "It is not fitting that a book of this kind should enter into the details of the immorality practiced. Suffice it to say the Indians are vile." [16] Despite having earlier noted with satisfaction the love and loyalty between Indian children and their parents, Hartog — like so many others — saw parental influence as generally undesirable for the Indian children. She and others at Rehoboth had heavy hearts when they observed the children going home for school vacations, knowing that they would face much "immorality and filth" in their parental home environment.[17]

But Hartog also noted with satisfaction that the U.S. government was doing much to raise the moral standards of the Navajo. And indeed, it was precisely this kind of civilizing or assimilation into the white culture which in part fueled the work done at Rehoboth. Missionary Mark Bouma, writing in the fiftieth-anniversary book *Navajo and Zuni for Christ*, noted that the only way to make Indians into "worthy" American citizens was to make them Christians:

"[M]ost of us have seen too often that an educated

FIGURE 30 Henry Beets, John Dolfin, and Meindert Vander Beek.

Indian without the fear of God in his heart ... is a drawback to his race and a liability to our nation. Many a politician and civil service man will testify that most of the Indians that really make good are products of Christian training." [18]

The solution to these perceived problems, the means by which to civilize the Indians, was indeed Rehoboth. There the Indian children would be away from the bad influence of their parents and could be re-named, re-clothed, and re-oriented toward the Christian life-style which, it was then readily assumed, comported perfectly with the ideal American life-style. That this alignment of Christianity with the white man's culture — which had been so harmful to Native Americans for so long — might make many Indians leery of accepting Jesus as their Lord apparently did not occur to most missionaries of the early twentieth century.

In fairness to these early Christian Reformed missionaries and observers, it should be noted that these attitudes were merely typical of the day. Christians all across America assumed that "Christianizing" equaled "civilizing." This was also an era of official paternalism toward Native Americans. In the late-twentieth-century environment of politically correct thinking and speaking, it is hard to believe the things which were said eighty years ago. For instance, in a 1914 speech to a Native American delegation to Washington, D.C., President Woodrow Wilson unabashedly referred to himself as the Indians' "Great White Father," who graciously gave tracts of land and other good things to his Indian children.

It should also be remembered there were even some Native Americans who shared many white assessments of the Indian life-style and who therefore welcomed Anglo help.

One of the most famous Navajo ever to be associated with the Christian Reformed Church was Jacob C. Morgan, later a tribal chairman of the entire Navajo nation. Born in 1879, Morgan became a product of boarding schools of assimilation at Fort Defiance and at the Hampton Institute. In

Sage, Sand, and Silence

Renzina Stob stepped off the train in Gallup, New Mexico, one early morning in October of 1916. A native of Chicago, she had traveled to the Southwest to start a small school at Toadlena, a small Christian Reformed Church mission outpost in New Mexico.

Met by missionary Reverend L.P. Brink, she soon found herself immersed in a land and world that would define her life for the next fifty years. In subsequent decades she would be considered one of the saints among the Navajo. Her name would become almost synonymous in the denomination for dedication to an often grueling, sometimes discouraging cause.

But those first days were among the most amazing for her. Immediately after getting off the train, she began to learn about a rugged land that was vastly different from

FIGURE 31 Renzina Stob.

the Midwest, where she was raised and taught to be a teacher. "I had a lot to learn, and there was so much to see," she once said.

On that first day on the mission field, she rode to Toadlena with Reverend Brink on a one-seat spring wagon. She recalled, "As we jogged over unpaved roads, through arroyos and over mountain passes, there was time to see prairie dogs and coyotes, to learn firsthand what hogans, mesas, and pinons were. It was truly a land of sage, sand, and silence."

She stayed in Toadlena for nearly three years, educating missionary children and local residents, including Indians.

"In 1919 I left Toadlena to go to Moody Bible Institute; but after two months I was urgently requested to teach at Rehoboth to fill in for a teacher who had to leave because of illness," she recalled.

In 1925 she became principal of the school. She later taught seventh and eighth grades. She also was a leader of the girls Gleaners Club and the boys woodcraft and leather-work groups and served as a Sunday-school teacher for pupils at the Fort Wingate government gchool.

When she moved to Grand Rapids after her retirement in 1965, she continued her life of service by sewing garments she donated to needy causes. She died on July 13, 1977.

In the *Banner* article detailing her life and her contribution to Native American missions, Gertrude Haan wrote, "Renzina is one of the last of those well-known pioneers of the Indian mission field who lived and served during the early and difficult years of soil preparation and sowing the seed."

"She was a woman," wrote Haan, "who gave her life to this cause."

his case, however, the reorientation process took hold and significantly shaped his perspectives.

Later in life Morgan became associated with the CRC at Tohatchi and then especially at Shiprock, where he worked with L.P. Brink. Indeed, after Brink's death in late 1936, many felt Morgan would take over the work as a native evangelist for the CRC. But the mission board, refusing to allow a Navajo to

be in a position of leadership, sent instead an ordained white missionary to replace Brink. Morgan then bolted from the CRC, taking a sizeable portion of the Shiprock congregation with him to establish a separate Navajo Christian church. Through the rapprochement of missionary Floris Vander Stoep, relations with Morgan later warmed up, though he kept his distance from the CRC.

FIGURE 32 Jacob C. Morgan.

Strikingly, however, Morgan's own reflections on Navajo life were very similar to the assessments of many whites of the time. In the 1930s, Franklin Roosevelt's New Deal affected the Native Americans in the person of John Collier, FDR's choice to head the Bureau of Indians Affairs. Collier, a great lover of Native American culture, believed that all efforts to assimilate the Indians into white culture should be stopped. Morgan protested this program as vigorously as did any Christian Reformed missionary. Describing the home life of his own people as desperately dirty and unsanitary, Morgan believed the Indians needed the kind of assimilating influence which white missionaries were offering in places like Rehoboth. Morgan praised the Pratt schools for bringing the light of education into the otherwise dark world of the Indians, taming their wildness and making them into a productive and self-supporting people.[19]

Hearing Morgan's voice in such matters is a necessary reminder that Native Americans no more speak with one voice on cultural issues than Anglos do. It is also a reminder that what was done in places like Rehoboth was, even at the time, met

with mixed responses even as the work was often done out of mixed motives. Indeed, many Navajo parents welcomed the opportunity to send their children to a good school, and, though it often was a wrenching experience for the children to be removed from their parents for most of every year, many boarding-school graduates of Rehoboth still speak fondly of the school and of their experience there.

It should also be noted that, despite their adoption of pervasive and questionable cultural attitudes, the early Christian Reformed mission workers in Rehoboth drew from a very deep well of compassion. There can be little doubt about the sincerity and love of such workers, even if some of their central motives or ideas were vandalistic of Native American culture.

Indeed, there is little evidence that Christian Reformed missionaries made any attempts to pick up on admirable aspects of Navajo religion. The Navajo had — and have — great respect for life, for creation, for family, for the spiritual aspects of physical healing — all of which could dovetail nicely with the revealed truth of Christ as Christians have long taught it. Yet, because Navajo religion was bound up

FIGURE 33 The *California Limited,* one of the Santa Fe trains, speeding past the Rehoboth property at more than sixty miles an hour.

FIGURE 34 Rehoboth mission house in 1911 (burned in 1914).

with Navajo culture generally, the larger rejection of that culture and its ways naturally led to a nearly wholesale dismissal also of Navajo religion and all its views.

What was needed, the missionaries believed, was not a sifting of Navajo cultural and religious ways but a wholesale replacement of them with Anglo (Christian) culture and religion. As Reverend Henry Beets put it in 1904,

FIGURE 37 Rehoboth school and post office in 1912.

As our Navajo converts multiply, the pressing question will be more and more: "What shall we do for them and with them?" We certainly cannot leave them to shift for themselves as well as they can. Religious, social, and natural conditions seem to forbid this. [20]

The Christian Reformed answer to the "What next?" question came to fruition in 1903, when the school opened its doors to its first six students. That number would grow to 38 in 1910, 50 in 1911, and 101 by 1920. The enrollment would continue to rise steadily each year. In fact, in some years students had to be turned away because the school could not accommodate the number who applied for admission.

FIGURE 35 J.C.K. Moore.

The story of Rehoboth is one of rapid development and innovation. At the same time that the school was opening and beginning to prosper, the denomination also established its first organized church (1906) in the Southwest, located on the Rehoboth campus. Its first full-time ordained pastor was Reverend John W. Brink, who served from 1912 to 1925. (So far removed was Rehoboth CRC from the rest of the

FIGURE 38 John W. and Mrs. Brink in 1919.

denomination that the nearest classis to which the church could belong was Classis Pella, centered in far-away Iowa.)

In 1910 Rehoboth expanded its efforts still further with the establishment of a hospital and medical dispensary. The denomination hired Dr. J.C.K. Moore and a number of nurses to begin ministering to the physical needs of the children in the school as well as to their parents in the surrounding area. By 1912 the hospital work was going very well. Despite Navajo wariness of the white man's medicine and despite open hostility from the Navajo medicine men, the work proved almost more than the staff could handle. In one year's time the hospital gave 150 medical treatments to Rehoboth students and had 90 inpatients and 355 outpatients. In addition to this work on the campus, Dr. Moore traveled more than 1,140 miles by horse and buggy to administer medicine to Navajo in more than a hundred different hogans tucked away between the surrounding mesas.

FIGURE 36 Navajo boys rolling down slope in old tires in front of the hospital building.

FIGURE 39 Rehoboth church built in 1923.

FIGURE 40 Rehoboth teachers and pupils circa 1910.

Meanwhile, the Rehoboth campus buzzed with all the work and activity necessary for a self-contained campus community. The laundry service operated six days a week to take care of all of the children's bedding, towels, uniforms, and other laundry. The Mission House dining room prepared three meals a day for the children, drawing some of its foodstuffs from the campus's own chickens, sheep, cattle, and vegetable gardens. In the dormitories matrons saw to the physical and moral development of the children by providing a loving, quasi-parental presence in their lives. Of course, the school proper offered students a fairly standard curriculum in math, science, history, literature, and social studies as well as Bible and catechism classes. The school's specialized Industrial Department also taught the boys and girls the vocational skills and trades they would need to make it in society following their graduation.

All of these campus activities were strictly regulated and rigidly disciplined. The school's principal also served as official disciplinarian, making certain that in chapel services and at mealtimes good order and decorum were maintained. A key component was to teach the children how to march in neat formation when going from one building to another. One school worker described the thrice-daily rituals:

Our boys and girls take their meals at the Mission Home, which is a frame building, at some distance from the dormitory. Thither they march and back again three times a day. These daily trips are oft far from pleasant. When the rain comes down in a drizzle or in torrents, when the cold nips the nose, ears, and fingers, it is no fun. Especially not for the little ones, who sometimes shed tears on the path as they run along trying to keep up with the procession. Oft, too, one of the matrons will carry one of the tots. [21]

FIGURE 41 The section at left served as a workshop for the school's Industrial Department; the rest was used for laundry.

The school year at Rehoboth was long: ten months, from September 1 to July 1. The children were permitted to go home only during the summer months of July and August and for one week at Christmas. The school's officials were very candid about telling the parents that, during the course of the school year, the school would have sole supervision of the child, including during times of illness. During the early years the school offered a six-year course of study, generally accepting students at age eight and keeping them until they reached age fourteen. (A high school was added in the 1940s.)

FIGURE 42 Parade passing Gallup railroad station in 1918.

Weekend visits by parents were permitted, in part because of the opportunities such visits provided to invite the parents to Sunday worship to teach them more about the Jesus whom their children heard about every day. One of Herman Fryling's Fort Defiance converts, Zah Tso (later the wife of J.C. Morgan) helped to teach a Sunday-school class in the Navajo language for children and their visiting parents. A number of missionaries through the years noted the Navajo's love of oral narratives and biblical stories and so quickly recognized that the telling of these stories was the way to the Navajo heart. The missionaries also discovered, however, that the Navajo ability to adapt such stories into their Navajo world and life view meant that even when they expressed appreciation for or assent to a story or set of stories, they were not necessarily ready to become baptized Christians. Still, a steady number of Rehoboth students did

FIGURE 43 On November 21-22, 1931, Rehoboth experienced one of the worst snowstorms in its history. At least two feet of snow fell; some other areas received forty inches.

become Christians, and, to the joy of the staff, they frequently were able to reach their parents with the gospel.

The Rehoboth campus continued to grow over the years, including through the building of many Dutch-style homes for the teachers and other support staff. For more than forty years the campus was superintended by Jacob H. Bosscher, who arrived in Rehoboth in late 1909 as a single man of just twenty-three years of age. He remained there until his

FIGURE 44 Marie Vander Weide, dorm matron, telling a bedtime story.

retirement in 1952. During Bosscher's tenure and for another twenty years thereafter, the school's operation remained largely unchanged: the students were still boarded in the dormitories, the kitchen made all their meals, the laundry washed all their clothes, and the hospital met all their physical needs. [22]

By the 1970s, however, changes began to occur. The school slowly made the transition to a day school, busing its students to and from the campus first every weekend and then, finally, by the early 1980s, every day. The hospital closed its doors in 1970. Following a joint venture with the Luke Society — a Christian medical organization — the Rehoboth hospital finally merged with the McKinley General Hospital in 1984 to form what is now the Rehoboth-McKinley Christian Health Care Services in Gallup. The original hospital building on the Rehoboth campus was razed, and the current Rehoboth, New Mexico, United States Post Office and an administrative building took its place.

The transition to a day school, however, began to reveal some of the drawbacks of the school's seventy-year-old methodology. Once they began to go home regularly, the school's children discovered how very disconnected they were from their native culture and from their peers who had not attended Rehoboth. Worse, they found how little they knew

Navajo Nurse

Riding horseback to far-flung portions of the Navajo reservation, Catherine Hood was able to mix her Christian faith with nursing the sick.

Born at the turn of the century, she learned her skills under the tutelage of Dr. Lee Huizenga, a pioneering physician on the New Mexico mission field. She enrolled at age six in Rehoboth Christian School. After ninth grade she transferred to Rehoboth Hospital, located on the campus of the school.

Once she had learned nursing, she often took to horseback and rode with Dr. Huizenga to treat Indian people in their homes.

FIGURE 45 Catherine Hood Whipple.

"It was easier to ride horseback. There were some places a wagon couldn't go. Besides, I loved to ride horses," she recalled in an interview in August of 1988.

She even taught other staff members at the hospital to ride.

While working at the mission hospital, she married Henry Whipple, a childhood classmate. They eventually moved to Crownpoint, where she worked as a nursing assistant at a small community Indian Health Service hospital.

At Crownpoint she saw hundreds of people die from a flu epidemic.

"It was a terrible thing to see," she said. "We fell short of hospital beds, and we had to place patients on the floor. Soon even the floors got crowded, and they had to open the boarding school and dormitories for the incoming patients."

FIGURE 46 Left to right, John W. Brink, William Mierop, Lee Huizenga, Herman Fryling.

Probably the first Navajo Christian nurse to make house calls in New Mexico, she also recalled the serious injuries she often had a hard time treating. In addition, she witnessed several outbreaks of diphtheria and measles.

"There were no immunizations back then, and a lot of people died," she said. "Some would barely make it to the hospital, and a few days later they would die."

FIGURE 47 Aerial view of Rehoboth.

their own parents. Some felt orphaned, despite the fact that both of their parents were still living. Another drawback was revealed in the various mission churches which had been founded over the years.

Because the Navajo children had been at Rehoboth ten months out of every year, the congregations discovered they were not equipped to minister to young people, some of whom were unresponsive to what the churches had to offer them.

In the midst of all these recent changes, the Rehoboth school, its staff, students, past graduates, and the surrounding churches have been forced to wrestle with these and a number of other complex issues. The early missionaries believed that God had "made room" for them to flourish in the land — and in many ways they did just that. Rehoboth graduates have long been recognized for the outstanding education they received, and a number of graduates have risen to prominent posts of leadership in the Navajo nation. As the school approached the century mark, however, some

FIGURE 48 Students at Rehoboth.

in the denomination began to ponder whether Rehoboth in fact takes up too much "room" and whether its hefty annual price tag should continue to be paid through Christian Reformed Home Missions.

By 1996 and the centennial year of Christian Reformed missions in New Mexico, however, a new plan was proposed to ensure the continuance of the Rehoboth school and campus. Following much deliberation during 1995, the Board of Home Missions approved a plan which would deed the entire Rehoboth facility over to a consortium of the school, its board, and Classis Red Mesa. The Rehoboth school would thereby continue to operate under the direct supervision of those closest to it. If successful, there is good hope that the Rehoboth school will continue to "flourish in the land."

FIGURE 49 Busing students to and from Rehoboth.

FIGURE 50 Zuni village with Towayalane Mountain in distance.

The Zuni

Driving through the Zuni pueblo, one encounters a number of signs warning tourists not to photograph any religious ceremonies or activities. Of course, what the signs don't say, according to Zuni CRC pastor Reverend Mike Meekhof, is that at many times of the year in Zuni, *all* of life is religious, so a tourist is best off not photographing anything. Even activities as innocent looking as a woman barbecuing meat on a backyard grill may have a very vital and deep religious significance, the photographing of which would likely incur the wrath of the village disciplinarian, who patrols the narrow pueblo streets in his seven-foot-tall traditional costume. The presence of the disciplinarian, as well as the danger of even accidentally photographing a religious rite, is evidence of what Christian Reformed missionaries to the pueblo have known for nearly a century: the Zuni Indians are a highly religious people, many of whom remain firmly in the grip of ancient fears, superstitions, and even black magic.

Situated forty miles south of Gallup, the Zuni pueblo leaves an impression very different from that left by any Navajo sites farther to the north. Unlike the more nomadic Navajo, the Zuni have long clustered together in villages. The Zuni pueblo has now sprawled out into a much larger area than it had when Andrew Vander Wagen made his first visit in 1897. Bisected by the Zuni River and ringed by mesas, the pueblo exists in the shadow of the towering Towayalane or "Corn Mountain" mesa, which is the most sacred site in the Zuni religion, having been the high ground to which the Zuni fled for safety during the Great Flood of their mythology. Historically, this is also the mesa to which the Zuni fled whenever they were threatened by the Navajo, the Apache,

FIGURE 51 Traditional cooking with adobe ovens.

the Spanish, the white man. On several occasions, the pueblo essentially relocated to the top of the mesa until the current danger had passed. (The people eventually began to grow corn on top of the mesa to sustain themselves during these self-imposed exiles; hence the name Corn Mountain.)[23]

The pueblo itself, at least in its older sections, still closely resembles its turn-of-the-century appearance. Despite the presence of pickup trucks and television antennas, walking around Zuni today gives one a feeling of stepping back in time. The traditional Zuni home, which one still encounters, is a multilevel adobe structure of smooth mud walls punctured by small square windows. Since there are no interior staircases, access to the upper stories still requires wooden ladders, the tops of which peek over the roof of nearly every house. Outside of most of the closely clustered houses, smoke billows from the beehive adobe ovens still used by

FIGURE 52 Zuni mother and child.

FIGURE 53 Bridge over the Zuni River in need of some repair after the approach was washed out.

many women for baking bread and cooking food in the traditional way.

If the visitor feels a sense of history in the pueblo, there is good reason. The Zuni have occupied this general area of New Mexico for as long as eight hundred years. The Zuni, along with other tribes like the Hopi, are known collectively as "Pueblo Indians," the name given to them by the Spanish conquistadors because, unlike many Indian tribes, the Zuni and Hopi gathered in villages (*pueblo* in Spanish). Indeed, in the early sixteenth century it was the Spanish, led by such famed leaders as Coronado, who "discovered" the Pueblo Indians. The discovery caused great excitement among the Spanish, for it was widely believed that these Indians may have been inhabiting the fabled "Seven Cities" of medieval lore. The "Seven Cities of the Antilles" were believed to have been founded by seven bishops who had fled the Moorish invasion of Spain in 734. The myth held that these cities contained enormous riches. Hence the Spanish, including those sailing with Christopher Columbus, had been seeking them for centuries (indeed, Columbus thought he had discovered the cities in the Caribbean; hence the present-day designation of the Greater and Lesser Antilles in the eastern Caribbean).

Animated by the mythological treasure of the Seven Cities, the conquistadors made conquering the pueblos, in the land the Spanish called "Cíbola," a priority in their northward push from Mexico. One of the first villages the Spanish encountered was the Zuni village of Hawikuh. Despite valiant Zuni efforts to repel the invaders, the village fell. The Spanish victory was soon soured, however, when it was discovered that the pueblo harbored no hidden riches. In subsequent months Coronado would discover the same was true of the other pueblos as well. This was not the fabled land of plenty. Still, it was a good land in which the Spanish could one day settle and quite probably prosper.

Forty years later the Spanish returned, this time led by a large number of Spanish missionaries and Franciscans. Numerous Spanish missions were established in the various pueblos, including among the Zuni. Although coexisting peacefully with the Spanish for many decades, the Zuni did stage a rebellion in 1632 after a Franciscan friar had forcibly tried to drag the Indians into the mission for a Catholic mass. Angered at this mistreatment, the Zuni killed friar Fray Francisco Letrado and subsequently assassinated and scalped a number of other Spanish clergy as well.

Fearing a Spanish military reprisal, the Zuni fled to the top of Towayalane, where they remained for three years. Although peace had been established again even before the Zuni returned to their pueblo, relations with the Spanish would remain tense at best. In the decades and centuries ahead, the Zuni steadfastly refused any wholesale acceptance of the Catholic Christianity which the missionaries proffered. But the Catholics continued to make their presence felt, most especially when they erected Our Lady of Guadalupe Church right in the center of the pueblo around 1780. (When Vander Wagen arrived in 1897, this church was in complete ruins and was on the verge of structural collapse. By the 1990s it had been fully restored, even to the colorful, though syncretistic, murals on the walls, which combine traditional Zuni lore with Christian symbols.)

Despite various armed conflicts, Spain's influence remained in the region until 1821, when Mexico won its independence and took over the territory of the Pueblo Indians. However, Mexico's rule of the area was short-lived — only twenty-eight years later the Americans would take over. Whereas the Zuni were largely left alone by the Mexicans,

the same would not ultimately be true of their encounters with the white Americans. However, unlike more nomadic tribes like the Navajo or Apache, the Pueblo Indians fared comparatively well with the white man. Because the Pueblo Indians rather clearly demarcated their territory and because the pueblos were viewed as evidence of a more mature kind of civilization than could be seen among other, more "savage" tribes, the United States government took steps early on to ensure the rights and freedoms of the Pueblo Indians.

This fact did not mean, however, that the Zuni and other Pueblo Indians would be spared the painful loss of land through the encroachment of the white man. But it did stave off the more brutal and deadly armed conflicts with the United States Army which had occurred with many other tribes. Still, the white man continued to move into the area, even into the pueblos themselves. By the late nineteenth century the Roman Catholic Church, frustrated after centuries of resistance and lack of progress, had largely pulled out of the region. Protestant denominations soon saw an opening and took advantage of the pueblos' concentrations of Indians to found their own missions.

At Zuni, the Presbyterians established a Protestant presence in 1877 through the founding of a mission church and day school. The Presbyterians soon found it tough going in Zuni, however. Since the government was helping financially to underwrite the day school, some regarded the missionaries with suspicion, believing them to be government officials in dis-

FIGURE 54 A Zuni on a donkey.

FIGURE 55 Our Lady of Guadalupe Church.

FIGURE 56 The Zuni pueblo with Zuni River in foreground.

guise. The Zuni themselves, according to historian C. Gregory Crampton, were also adept at resisting the Christian religion in favor of quietly continuing their own native rituals and ceremonies:

Since the Zuni people were themselves thoroughly religious — ceremonialism and ritual permeated their daily lives — they found no compelling reasons for changing any of their beliefs or adding the alien dogma to their very large body of religious knowledge.[24]

Mr. Van

One day shy of the first anniversary of his arrival in the Southwest, Andrew Vander Wagen rode into the Zuni pueblo to begin a new branch of the Christian Reformed Church's Indian mission effort. His arrival came at a troubled yet auspicious time. Beginning in 1889, the Presbyterian day school had been headed up by Miss Mary E. De Sette. De Sette believed that her calling to the pueblo was to do more than merely instruct — she also felt responsible to keep tabs on the pueblo's general affairs, including seeing to the prosecution of criminals. In 1897 she reported to the government that several Zuni men had recently lynched a suspected witch, and she demanded that the authorities deal with these murderers.

The government responded not only by sending the sheriff to arrest the men but also by dispatching U.S. Army troops from Fort Wingate to help the sheriff should there be any trouble from the locals. Although a standoff was avoided, the pueblo was in something of an uproar when Vander Wagen trotted into town on his faithful horse, John the Flyer. The uproar that day was something of a foreshadowing of the years ahead, when Vander Wagen would himself be the cause of some uproars through his fiery denunciations of the traditional religion of the Zuni Indians. [25]

But Vander Wagen's arrival also came at an auspicious time because it coincided with a decision by the Presbyterian Home Missions Board to pull out of the Zuni pueblo and close its mission. The timing seemed providential indeed; the Christian Reformed Church was able to move in as the sole Protestant presence in Zuni. For nine years that Protestant presence would be embodied in just two people: Andrew and Effa Vander Wagen.

The Vander Wagens had arrived in

FIGURE 57 Andrew and Effa Vander Wagen.

New Mexico along with the Frylings on October 10, 1896. A Netherlands immigrant, Andrew had come to Grand Rapids, Michigan, where he joined the Coldbrook CRC and became a student at Calvin College. But he never completed his college studies, nor did he attend the Theological Seminary, as had been his plan. The lure of being a missionary to the Far West was too great. Always an animated man of considerable drive, energy, and enthusiasm, Vander Wagen, when he heard that the Heathen Mission Board was sending Herman Fryling to the Southwest, appealed to the board also to send him and his wife. Despite his lack of theological training or credentials, the board was moved by Andrew's contagious enthusiasm and so agreed to send the Vander Wagens along with the Frylings (apparently the fact that Effa was a registered nurse was an asset for Andrew in getting this appointment approved).

Once at Fort Defiance, however, Vander Wagen became somewhat frustrated at the great distances to be traveled to contact the scattered Navajo people. Still, for a number of months "Van," as he was known, traveled untold miles on his horse, earning himself a reputation as "the cowboy preacher." But when he was told about the Zuni pueblo and its more accessible Indian population, Vander Wagen jumped at the chance to become the denomination's first missionary to the pueblo Indians.

Shortly after arriving, Vander Wagen purchased the present-day site of the Christian Reformed mission on the south side of the Zuni River. According to one story, Vander Wagen was told that for a mere $100 he could purchase a piece of property the breadth of which would be determined by how far he could throw a stone. Judging from the sizeable plot purchased, Andrew must have had a pretty good arm! [26] The property secured, Vander Wagen quickly set to work constructing the first mission house.

But Zuni suspicion and Vander Wagen's hellfire-and-brimstone style of preaching did not help the work get off to a pleasant start. The Zuni were occasionally openly hostile to Vander Wagen, and some even threatened him with physical violence. It was not until after the winter of 1898–1899 that the Vander Wagens were better

accepted in the pueblo. That winter a severe smallpox epidemic raced through the village, giving Effa Vander Wagen ample opportunity to put her nursing skills to work. Although 250 Indians died that winter, the Vander Wagens were able to minister to the other 650 afflicted Zuni, apparently earning the missionaries a place in many people's hearts.

Vander Wagen himself labored not only to construct physical facilities but also to prepare himself for the task of evangelization. Within a year of his arrival, with the help of his interpreter, Mr. Nick Tumaka, Vander Wagen had compiled a working dictionary of more than 2,300 words (the Zuni language is considerably less complex than the Navajo tongue, so Vander Wagen could expect speedier progress on the linguistic front than L.P. Brink could accomplish among the Navajo). His language gains enabled Vander

FIGURE 58–59 Shalako ceremonies.

Wagen to begin more active teaching and preaching among the Zuni people.

When he preached, Vander Wagen's normally animated manner became fiery, forceful, and often denunciatory. One of the reasons for Vander Wagen's stern and urgent preaching was the fact that the Zuni were very obviously religious in the service of what Vander Wagen viewed as a most vile pagan religion. After one look at the Zuni's elaborate annual Shalako ceremonies — which included many rituals and dances during the month of December — Vander Wagen was convinced that the Zuni tribe was quite probably "the most idolatrous and superstitious race amongst the red men of today." Seeing himself as working in a "stronghold of Satan," Vander Wagen was uncompromising in his call to conversion.

But like the Roman Catholics and Presbyterians before him, Vander Wagen found the work slow going and frustrating. Vander Wagen succeeded in establishing a visible mis-

A Witch Finally Finds His True Fate

Nick Tumaka was a Zuni sword swallower, a reputed witch, and a Christian.

First informed about the way of Jesus Christ at the turn of the century, Nick served as Andrew Vander Wagen's first interpreter. He translated portions of Scripture and listened attentively to the white man's message of eternal salvation.

But Nick didn't want to join this strange Christian Reformed faith. Instead, he held fast to his Zuni ways — for a while.

"He prided himself on being a sword-swallower, one of the medicine-group that claims not only to heal bodily ailments but also bring snow in the winter," writes the author of *Zuni Also Prays*.

Sword swallowers thrust slabs of wood a dozen inches down their throats as part of a ritual dance.

Although he didn't name himself as such, his fellow tribesmen labeled him a witch. They said Nick Tumaka's ways were strange; he did not fit into the Zuni pattern. He was an individualist; he didn't conform to a community that is based on mutual dependence. He broke the pattern and told a different story.

After he admitted under torture that he was in touch with the evil spirits and a conduit for their power, his people stopped worrying about him. They believed his revelation removed his spirit power. His popularity waned for a time, but then it rose again, and he became governor of his tribe. But he remained unsure; something continued to tug at his soul.

In 1927 Nick Tumaka began to investigate the teachings of Christianity more thoroughly. Fear had started to haunt him, and he needed the solace that belief in Christ could provide.

That fall he grew ill.

"Now I want to be baptized," he said.

As light from a lantern flickered and his Christian friends hovered nearby, he finally joined the church that so many of his fellow Zuni shunned. Soon after, he died.

He is buried among his Zuni brothers and sisters in a graveyard that is home to thousands of others who have died over the centuries in and around the Zuni pueblo. Among their bones are his.

On his marker is written

Ex-Governor Nick Tumaka,
Died Nov. 28, 1927
'I am the Resurrection and the Life.'
John 11:25

FIGURE 60 C. Hayenga with Kawaite on his left and Nick Tumaka on his right.

sion in Zuni, including the 1905 dedication of the Ebenezer Chapel. Although he was heartened by the progress the Zuni were making in terms of becoming more civilized (he noted with approval the increase of "American clothing" and "American furniture [which] has taken the place of their crude and simpler manner of furnishing"), he could not report much progress in gathering a Zuni congregation of Christians. Despite daily catechism classes in the chapel with a regular attendance of around eighteen, Sunday-school classes, and Sunday-evening worship services at which he would preach, as much as possible, in the Zuni language to the fifty or so people who gathered each week, by 1906 Vander Wagen could report only one convert — Nena

Halean, a young girl who had accepted Christ some years earlier. Writing in *The Banner,* Vander Wagen urged readers to pray "that our Zuni desert may yet become a well-watered garden, and Satan's stronghold a tower of gospel light." [27]

Within a year of writing those words, however, Vander Wagen himself would no longer be working as a Christian Reformed missionary in Zuni. In 1906 the Heathen Mission Board approved a proposal of Vander Wagen's to open an industrial school. Having purchased the Z.I. Ranch just outside Zuni for that purpose, Vander Wagen was to be the superintendent of the school, and so the need for another mission worker in the pueblo proper opened up.

The board elected to send none other than Herman Fryling. When the Fort Defiance work had closed, Fryling had accepted a call to pastor a congregation in Pease, Minnesota. After only one year, however, Fryling discovered that his heart was still very much in the Southwest, so he accepted the call to Zuni and was installed to this new post at a special service in LaGrave Avenue CRC in Grand Rapids on November 6, 1906. Remarried in June of 1898 to Miss Jennie Janssen of Zeeland, Michigan, Fryling now was the father of two children, Sophia and John, who accompanied their parents to Zuni shortly after the installation service in Michigan.

Despite their long friendship, a conflict soon arose between Vander Wagen and Fryling over what constituted the best approach to the Zuni Indians. Vander Wagen preferred a no-holds-barred hellfire approach to spur the Zuni to conversion. More than once Vander Wagen had been chided by the Zuni tribal council for his threats of fire and brimstone. On at least one occasion his life had been threatened. But Vander Wagen saw such attempts to intimidate him as evidence that he was on the right track. The offense of the gospel, he believed, needed to be acutely felt by anyone living without Christ.

Fryling, however, offered a milder, though no less firm, approach to evangelization and was not convinced that a frightening message of damnation was the best way to bring about conversion to Christ's gospel of love. Never a man to compro-

FIGURE 61 Ebenezer Chapel was built with adobe bricks on the Zuni River in 1904-1905 at the cost of $800.

FIGURE 62 Mr. and Mrs. John Spyker and Herman and Jennie Fryling, circa 1912, standing in front of the Hemenway building, which served as Zuni's missionary parsonage.

mise his principles, Vander Wagen promptly resigned from his post and withdrew to his newly purchased ranch just outside the pueblo — a ranch which would never become Vander Wagen's hoped-for industrial school. (Whatever differences may have existed at that time, Fryling and Vander Wagen remained friends. When Fryling died on August 15, 1947, Vander Wagen gave the graveside prayer of committal at the funeral.)

FIGURE 63 Trading store at Two Wells.

With his mission work at least temporarily at an end, Vander Wagen decided to go into the trading business, bartering with the Zuni for pelts, livestock, coffee, tobacco, matches, and various manufactured goods like camp stoves, ropes, and harnesses. As Indian scholar C. Gregory Crampton notes in his history of the Zuni,

[T]he Christian Reformed missionary turned trader ... was somewhat more successful trading with the Zuni than converting them. He opened up shop on the south side of the river in [the] "Hemenway House." [28]

Trading with the Indians became not only Vander Wagen's life after he resigned from the mission board but also something of his legacy. Traveling between Gallup and Zuni today, one passes directly through Vander Wagen, New Mexico — a tiny village consisting mainly of a post office and, of course, the Vander Wagen Trading Post. The current shop is run by the Vander Wagens' children and grandchildren, who, like Andrew and Effa, have remained near the Zuni reservation.

The denomination's pioneer missionaries to the Zuni did formally reenter Christian Reformed mission work for a brief time in 1928, when a small hospital was opened in the Zuni parsonage. Andrew served as overseer for the hospital, and Effa once again practiced her medical skills among the people.

Although Andrew's tactics could be offensive at times, few doubted his love of the Zuni people. The couple remained in or near New Mexico until their deaths. Effa died suddenly at Zuni in 1947. Following her death, Andrew traveled quite extensively to visit old friends and his family. He died December 5, 1953, while visiting his son in California. The couple are buried in the shadow of Towayalane in the Zuni cemetery on a knoll just outside the village. A Midwestern-style white picket fence surrounds their graves — a symbolic reminder of the Dutch couple who moved from the Midwest and into Zuni one October day in 1897 with an urgent desire

FIGURE 64 Herman Fryling driving past the Zuni parsonage.

to help the Zuni people, some of whom would one day call Mr. and Mrs. Van their friends.

New Workers

Herman Fryling worked in Zuni from his arrival in 1906 until 1925, when he transferred to nearby Blackrock to begin working in a new government school there. (By 1929 Fryling took early retirement to Zeeland, Michigan, because of the declining health of Jennie, who had become by then an invalid.) During his nearly two-decade tenure in the pueblo, Fryling oversaw many key developments of the ministry, chief among which was the development of the Zuni Christian day school. Begun in 1908 largely as a solution to the schooling needs of the Fryling children, the school would see a steady rise in enrollment until, by 1946, it would enroll over 150 pupils annually.

The first teacher was Miss Nellie De Jong, who in the first year of the new school had a comparatively easy task as the student body numbered only six children: the Fryling children and four Zuni boys and girls. Although the Zuni school was not a boarding school (the children of the pueblo, of course, all lived in close proximity to the school), De Jong still sought as much as possible to bring a "civilizing" influence to the children. She frequently noted that while the Zuni school had the advantage of being able to educate the children without taking them away from their parents, this could also be a disadvantage:

One of the greatest drawbacks is irregularity of attendance, tardiness included. The indifference for instruction by the parents … and attraction for their religious ceremonies are the cause of this irregularity. Another great problem is cleanliness. [29]

Thus De Jong, in addition to her ordinary teaching tasks, also took pains to bathe the children and to sew and wash their clothing. By 1910, with the enrollment of the school up to about one dozen children, an assistant, Miss J. Nyenhuis, was hired to meet the practical and physical needs of the children.

The enrollment at the Zuni school did not rise as rapidly as had been the case at Rehoboth, however, partly because of some competition in the pueblo. In 1916 the Roman Catholic Church decided to return to the pueblo to open its own day school. By 1923 the enrollment at the Christian Reformed school was thirty-five, whereas the Catholic school had garnered forty-eight students. But John Collier's New Deal effect on the Native Americans meant, among other things, the closing of a number of government boarding schools. As the students of such schools flocked back to places like the Zuni pueblo, mission schools like the Zuni Christian School saw a quick spike in enrollment.

The increases in the school's student body, as well as slow but steadily increasing attendance at worship services, eventually necessitated an expansion of the mission's physical facilities. By the early 1920s a YMCA building had been erected in cooperation with the Christian Reformed mission board. The new facility was headed up first by Meindert Vander Beek and then, starting in 1922, by Bert Sprik. By the time Reverend C.G. Hayenga took over from Fryling in 1925, the school's enrollment of sixty students prompted the building of not only a new school but also a whole new mission complex, complete with a new chapel. The Spanish-style stucco structure was formally dedicated on March 18, 1927.

By the late 1930s the work at Zuni was greatly enhanced through the work of the Zuni evangelist Rex Natewa. When Reverend George Yff arrived in Zuni in the fall of 1938, he discovered in Natewa an invaluable resource for interpretation and translation. By 1941 Natewa had translated the entire Gospel of John into the Zuni tongue with other translations soon to follow. But more than a language resource, Natewa also became the linchpin in evangelizing his own people. In future years, working as an evangelist for the denomination, Natewa would reach out to the pueblo through several avenues, including a weekly gospel radio program preached in the Zuni language. Natewa would also teach classes in the church and in the day school, thus providing invaluable assistance for Christian Reformed missionaries until his death in 1966.

FIGURE 65 Nellie De Jong.

FIGURE 66 Herman and Jennie Fryling with students at the Zuni school.

FIGURE 67 Missionaries and their families, with guests, Zuni 25th anniversary, 1921.

1. Helen Bosscher
2. Beatrice Bosscher
3. Jay Bosscher
4. Arthur Bosscher
5. Christine Brink
6. Jessica Mierop
7. Donald Mulder
8. Wilhelmina Mierop
9. John Fryling
10. Herman Fryling
11. Jennie Fryling
12. Bertha Guichelaar
13. Herman Guichelaar
14. Mrs. L.P. Brink

15. Leonard P. Brink
16. Mrs. Van Wyck
17. Mr. Van Wyck
18. Mrs. Barney Steen
19. Barney Steen
20. Johannes Groen
21. Ada Bosscher
22. Jacob H. Bosscher
23. Nellie Bosscher
24. Kathryn Rosbach
25. Hattie Beekman
26. Mary Denetdele
27. Andrew Vander Wagen
28. Effa Vander Wagen

29. J.D. Mulder
30. Gladys Mulder
31. Mrs. William Mierop
32. William Mierop
33. Nellie Baker
34. Mrs. J. Bolt
35. Rev. J.W. Brink
36. Mrs. Brink
37. Dena Vander Wagen
38. Effa Vander Wagen
39. Jennette Lam
40. Marie Vander Weide
41. Rezina Stob
42. Alice Bush

43. Ann Havinga
44. Sophia Fryling
45. Winnie Schoon
46. Nellie Lam
47. Jennette Vander Werp
48. Fannie Vander Wall
49. Jacob Bolt
50. Hugh Denetdele
51. Edward Vander Wagen
52. Cornelius Lucas
53. John Swets
54. Bert Sprik
55. Mark Bouma

Indeed, following Yff's departure in 1944, the Zuni mission field was without an ordained pastor for nearly six years. During this time Natewa carried on the work as the sole Christian Reformed missionary worker in the pueblo.

Perhaps it was Natewa's native influence which helped the Zuni church begin to see more and more baptisms and conversions. On Easter Sunday 1942, Reverend George Yff was thrilled to baptize the entire Louis Chavez family. By late 1944 Rex Natewa's wife, Agnes, and their four children would likewise decide to follow Jesus and so were baptized by Yff shortly before his departure from the Zuni mission field. Fifty years later, an aged Agnes Natewa remembered the cost of her decision to follow "the Christian way."

Having been initially exposed to Christianity through the Catholic St. Anthony's school in Zuni (where Agnes was baptized as a child), Agnes eventually met Rex after he returned to the pueblo from an Albuquerque boarding school. Neither Rex's nor Agnes's family approved of their Christian, church-going ways, however, and the young couple were warned against joining "the white people's religion." But once they did and were baptized on November 5, 1944, they were ostracized from their families for turning from the Zuni way. (With a gleam in her eye, Agnes wonders what will happen to her in that she was "two times baptized"!)

But the cost of her second baptism and earnest profession of faith continues to be felt by Agnes even late in her life: she still receives few visits as she lives alone in the home Rex built for them in 1940. Once they were associated with the religion of the white man, Zuni purists no longer associated with them. But as a true believer, Agnes knew she had to follow the way of Jesus Christ, the traditional Zuni ways no longer holding any answers for her. In turn, Agnes reports feeling the love of the Lord to whom she gave her life on that November day. "[Jesus] love me; he take care of me. When somebody comes in here and says, 'My, you are lonesome here by yourself, Agnes,' I'm not by myself — the Lord is taking care of me. That's what I tell them." [30]

Zuni Also Prays

Although there would be numerous personnel changes over the years, the work in the Zuni pueblo continued to make steady, though sometimes slow, progress. Through the efforts of Natewa and his successor evangelist, Rex Chimoni — along with the Anglo missionary pastors — a congrega-

FIGURE 68 Louis and Margaret Chavez and family.

FIGURE 69 Rex and Agnes Natewa and family.

FIGURE 70 Agnes Natewa, 1971.

A Week at Crownpoint

Reverend Jacob Bolt and his wife, Cora, served on the New Mexico mission field for many years. Here are excerpts from *A Week's Work,* a pamphlet Reverend Bolt wrote in the 1930s describing their labors among Native Americans in and around Crownpoint.

Sunday 9 a.m.

The bell tolls on the campus of Crownpoint Boarding School. One hundred of the smaller boys file into the school auditorium for Sunday School. They sing:

> Into my heart, Into my heart,
> Come into my heart, Lord Jesus.

Sunday 11 a.m.

A group of white children gather about Mrs. Bolt for an hour. Bright, promising youngsters. During the hour, I am visiting the sick in the hospital.

Monday 6 p.m.

After singing a number of songs, Mrs. Bolt goes to the little girls' building, although there are a number girls in this building who are quite advanced. They have already started their meeting. They have had prayer together and are singing gospel songs. Meanwhile I am with the boys.

Tuesday

We are on the road early. Another school is awaiting our visit to give Bible instruction. It is Baca Day School, thirty-five miles east, on the highway that leads to Albuquerque and Gallup. The moment we enter, the children are ours for an hour.

We then go on to Albuquerque School, and a number are in the Sanitarium. It is a treat for them to have us visit them, at least so they act, and so they tell us.

Wednesday 8 a.m.

We are on the road again. A busy day lies ahead of us. Three schools are looking for us. We pass White Horse Lake and go on to Pueblo Pintado Day School, forty miles from home. After instructing the children there (generally there are some older Indians present also, and they too come in to listen), we go on still further to the northeast.

Thursday evening

We have all our pupils for Bible instruction. We divide them into four groups.

Friday and Saturday

There is housework for Mrs. Bolt. There is the place to look after, and we do not have a handyman around to do manual labor, nor a girl to do the housework …. Scarcely a night that we don't retire much before midnight.

Postscript:

After twenty-two years of labor here hundreds of young people have been under Christian care. We count these years the happiest of our lives ….

Heart-breaking cases we have seen. But our joy is that the Lord knoweth them that are His, and not one of these shall be missing in the great home coming ….

Do we not grow tried? Yes, tired and weary often. But it's not the physical weariness that is hardest to bear. Rather the burden laid on the heart has tormented. But we have found rest and contentment in the assurance that we are serving our Lord and Savior.

FIGURE 71 Traveling between missions.

FIGURE 72 Rex and Betty Chimoni and family.

Organized as a formal congregation in 1987, the Zuni CRC now has nearly 150 members. Under the leadership of Reverend Mike Meekhof since 1989, and with the ongoing efforts of Chimoni, the church is making inroads into the pueblo, even into the heart of the traditional Zuni religion, through the conversion of several medicine men (a key current leader in the Zuni congregation is a former medicine man). Sensing the same thing which the pioneer missionaries felt nearly a century earlier, Meekhof believes that the devil has had a firm grip on Zuni for many centuries — and he is not letting go easily. [31]

FIGURE 73 Cornelius and Martha Kuipers.

tion was gathered, sometimes from the graduates of Zuni Christian School and from the Blackrock school, where, for many years, missionaries like Cornelius Kuipers worked to witness to the students and teachers.

On April 17, 1971, disaster struck the mission work when the entire chapel and school mission complex went up in flames. The fire, said by some to have been of suspicious origin, essentially burned the 1927 mission to the ground. Because the building complex had served the pueblo for over forty years and had been the site on which so many students had been educated and so many Christians baptized, the loss was grievous for many. But the determination of the mission board, along with the generous gifts of many throughout the denomination, allowed a new, more modern facility to be constructed later in that same year. With well over one hundred students in the school, the need for a speedy recovery was obvious, and the new facility was quickly put to good use.

In recent years there have been a number of demon possessions among the Zuni people, some of which have been so frightening that even the stalwart medicine men have fled in terror. With the

FIGURE 74 Before the fire. The left part of this building housed the church, the right portion was the school, and the mission home was situated between.

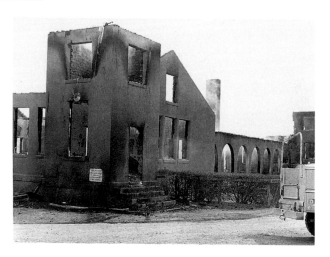

FIGURE 75–76 The fire and its aftermath.

traditional support structure of their own religion gone, a number of the families of these possessed persons have called upon the Zuni CRC and Reverend Meekhof for help in getting rid of these dark forces. Clearly, although times and circumstances have changed considerably since 1897, the head-on spiritual confrontations begun by Andrew Vander Wagen are continuing with Vander Wagen's missionary heirs on the front lines of the battle. The old hellfire-and-brimstone "cowboy preacher" would no doubt approve.

Criticisms

By the mid 1940s, as the mission work in the Southwest approached its fiftieth anniversary, the modest effort begun by Fryling and Vander Wagen had burgeoned into the denomination's largest and most expensive mission outreach. The Rehoboth and Zuni schools were boarding and educating around three hundred children, and new mission outposts had been opened at Toadlena in 1910, Crownpoint in 1912, Farmington in 1925, Naschitti in 1926, Gallup and San Antone in 1928, Two Wells in 1929, Tohlakai in 1930, Shiprock, Red Rock, and Teec Nos Pos in 1933. Although synod turned down the request, the work had even progressed far enough that in 1934 the mission board petitioned synod to form a Classis New Mexico (the actual forming of the new Classis Red Mesa would not take place until 1982). The denomination's 1946 *Yearbook* reports 859 Navajo members in New Mexico churches (that number may have been inflated through the counting also of students in the schools).

Although the Christian Reformed Church had begun in the 1920s to send missionaries abroad to places like China and Africa, by 1950 the Indian mission field was commanding over sixty percent of the denomination's overall mission budget. As is nearly always the case when something costs that much

FIGURE 77 The present Zuni Christian Reformed Mission School, built after the fire.

James Nakhai

James Nakhai served as a Code Talker in the First Marines during World War II. He worked as postmaster in Tohatchi and served twelve years as a Navajo tribal councilman. He was baptized a Methodist but became CRC after meeting his wife. Born in Red Rock, Arizona, in 1924, Nakhai now lives in Tohatchi.

FIGURE 78.

The Navajo religion has its own ways. A lot of us compare, and we see a better future in the CRC religion. There is the promise of eternal life in Christianity. There is hope there. We are taught by the CRC that we are all sinners, but the Lord died for us. He forgives our sins. I believe that.

I believe in what the Bible says. Jesus is the only God. There is no other. I have to put away the Navajo religion. There is another religion and another God.

If more of our people start believing this way, we will have a bright future. But it is hard because a lot of the young Navajo people are still too much with the world. It is hard to turn them around. I think that they will turn around. The Navajo religion will live for awhile, but it will eventually go because a lot of the old men are dying and are taking with them the ways and ceremonies of the old religion. They aren't revealing its secrets.

The CRC effort has been good, especially at Rehoboth school. They have graduated many students there who are faithful to the church. Some of them have attached themselves to good jobs. But today a lot of the children who go to the school come from low-income families who can't pay the price. Heretofore the church helped kids like that. Now I hear they want to take that help away.

The CRC has been blessed with all kinds of things. I wonder why they are cutting back now. I wonder if there is no more love for the people here. We are wrestling with it. We don't know what to do yet. I believe, though, the CRC will stay with the people down here.

Ray Slim

A graduate of Calvin Theological Seminary, Ray Slim serves in the Sanostee area, northwest of Gallup.

I first heard the gospel from Pastor Van Bruggen back in the 1950s, when I was a student at the boarding school in Crownpoint. I was about ten years old at the time. But then I drifted away from the gospel for a long time. I eventually came

FIGURE 79.

back and served as an interpreter for Pastor Van Bruggen.

I attended Reformed Bible College in 1979 and stayed until 1982. Then I came back to work in New Mexico. I was working for some of the time as a draftsman and in the engineering department for my tribe. Then I enrolled at Calvin Seminary and just finished in 1994.

I'm now working as a minister for four churches. I serve about two hundred people. We are very distant out here. It is a real struggle because most of the people I see are involved in the Native American Church, the peyote church. This is a church which is a mix of the Mormons and Navajo traditional religion.

We all worship the same God and Lord, but they have very different thoughts in that other church. They use peyote to get hallucinations that they say show them the Spirit. They contact God through peyote. Also, they are so confused because they say the mountains are God and the earth is God. They don't make the distinction between creation and the Creator. I am married to one God. But they are married to many different gods, and that makes them crazy.

I know I am one of the few Native Americans who are leaders in my church down here. The harvest is great, but the workers are few. I think some of that is because Native Americans have not been encouraged to become leaders. When the missionaries first came, they presented salvation to us right off. Instead of doing all of the work, we just sat back. When it was time for us to work, we didn't know what to do. I know that Jesus Christ is Lord and Savior. But we only learned the Savior part, not the part about him being Lord and asking us to be responsible for our own lives.

money, a controversy began to brew over whether this allocation scheme was just and, by extension, whether the mission methodology being financed was an appropriate one. Since maintaining the Rehoboth campus was the largest single budget expenditure, it was Rehoboth which came in for the largest share of the criticism.

In 1949 missionary Harry Boer, then working on the African mission field, published a scathing booklet severely critiquing the Indian mission field and its approaches to evangelization. The immediate cause for his complaint was clearly the disproportionately high percentage of mission monies flowing from Grand Rapids to the American Southwest. But he was also distressed that in the proposed 1950 mission budget, hundreds of thousands of dollars were being earmarked for the expansion of the Rehoboth campus and similar educational facilities in Zuni. Boer's pamphlet was actually the outgrowth of a growing number of complaints by people who had been appealing to synod to reassess the methodology being employed in New Mexico.

Boer asserted, among other things, that the medical work being carried out in Rehoboth did not properly belong in the category of evangelization:

The preaching of the Gospel carries its own conviction, imparts its own power, and does not stand in need of luring people by free hospitalization and tender care to get them to a place where they cannot refuse to listen to the solicitous evangelist.[32]

But Boer's most stinging critique was that the school had become so enormous an enterprise unto itself that it was engulfing the larger mission effort in New Mexico and had actually become a hindrance to what should have been the true goal of the Indian mission, namely, the establishment of an indigenous native church. This last bit of criticism cut close to the heart of the entire Native American mission program, touching as it did on the whole issue of paternalism and whether the CRC was truly developing mature Navajo and Zuni church leaders or was instead keeping the Indians under the white man's thumb through insisting on white-only leadership in the schools and churches.

Boer wondered whether it had occurred to the denominational mission workers that "the Indian is as human as we are."[33] He also lamented the fact that, to the best of his knowledge, there were no missionaries then on the field fluent in either the Navajo or Zuni languages (he did not make mention of the massive linguistic work done by L.P. Brink or the ability of Zuni workers to speak at least some words in that language). This lack of language skill was, to Boer, a primary indicator that the Christian Reformed Church was not dealing responsibly with the Navajo culture and its ways but was instead ignoring it in favor of imposing the white man's culture. Boer also pondered why, after over fifty years, there were still no native evangelists employed full-time by the denomination. Why weren't Christian leaders rising from the ranks of the native peoples?

In conclusion Boer recommended that the denomination cut personnel by over half and slash its expenditures in the Indian field accordingly. He further recommended a complete restructuring of the educational programs and a cessation of all building projects. Finally, he felt the denomination should tell the Indians that they must develop their own leaders to take up the work because "we will [not] be responsible for the blood of their brethren if they will not find among their own number evangelists and teachers for the

conversion and education of their people." [34]

The Board of Foreign Missions (under whose auspices the Indian mission work would continue until 1964, when it was finally transferred to the Home Missions Board) was stung and angered by Boer's public allegations against its most cherished mission enterprise. Responding to Boer in a pamphlet of its own, the board admitted the struggles

FIGURE 81 Harry Boer.

Loren Tuscon

A Zuni Indian, Loren Tuscon lives in the pueblo of Zuni. He has worked at various jobs, including serving as an alcohol- and drug-abuse rehabilitation counselor. He is helping to translate parts of the Bible into his native tongue.

I'm a recovering alcoholic. Becoming a Christian has not been easy. I've become an outcast from my family. They look at it like I have turned my back on my culture and the Zuni religion. So here I am very much alone. It is not so hard for those who are Catholics. They can mix their religion and the old religion, which has the Katchina dancers.

FIGURE 80.

I grew up here in Zuni. I went to the Christian Reformed school here and heard the gospel then. But I did not become a Christian. I was caught in the old religion. I was ten or eleven years old at the time when I was initiated into the Zuni medicine-man society. All of my life I was a medicine man before this. Being a medicine man is a lifetime commitment. There is no way out. They expect you to be involved in it for the rest of your life.

In Native American religion we worshiped our forefathers, herbs, roots, bears, cougars, mountain lions. But somewhere in the back of my mind there was this conflict, a battle, as to the truth. Ever since hearing the gospel, I wanted to know more.

It was the awesome grace of God that finally converted me and took me away from that about four years ago. Back then, I was still drinking and ended up in a hospital. I tried suicide. I wanted to die. Before that could happen, I had a vision. It was a confusing dream. But I do remember a most outstanding thing from it. I remember these words: "Lead your people. Love them." In the dream, I was in Zuni heaven, the place where we go when we die. Someone brought me back from there, though. It wasn't my time.

It helps me to keep sober to think about what the Lord revealed to me in that dream. That was my turning point. I gave up. Pastor Mike [Meekhof] was my friend. I would visit him at night while I was still drinking. A while after I got sober, I came to his church. I made sure I came early. I sat in a back seat and put my head on a chair in front of me. I prayed, "Father, I have come home. I'm so tired. Help me."

I didn't stay sober the whole time after that. I was feeling much spiritual warfare inside of me. I still feel like the evil one is attacking me. I still feel pain because I have lost my family. I'm very hopeful my family, through prayer, will come to know and accept the Lord. The Bible says who is God. Even if I have lost my family, those are the consequences if I want to serve the Lord, my new master.

in the Indian field but defended the worthy nature of the overall work. They pointed out that in fact persons like Edward Becenti, Zah Tso Morgan, Edward Henry, and others had been converted to Christianity and had been subsequently involved in outreach to their own people. They also reminded readers that it was synod itself which, in 1888, had declared the establishment of schools to be a desirable form of mission outreach.

Regarding the medical-care issue, the board pointed to the fact that the work of the hospital had previously been wholly authorized by synod and that, in response to various criticisms prior to Boer's pamphlet, synod had done some investigation of the work and had concluded that it truly was a desirable outreach arm of the larger Indian mission. Besides, the board claimed, a Christian denomination would hardly be compassionate if, in laboring in the midst of a people with a staggering infant and child mortality rate of fifty-two percent, it did not do something to minister also to the physical needs of those same people.

But the issue of native leadership was a bit more difficult, and it continues to be so today. Whereas the board was able to defend itself against Boer's critique by pointing to the Navajo evangelist Edward Henry, who had taken over the work at Naschitti in 1949, it could certainly not point to any grand-scale movement toward greater native participation in the mission effort. A 1942 synodical report did recommend the reorganization of New Mexico churches to move toward greater native participation, but the board readily admitted having difficulty in achieving this ideal. The linguistic, cultural, and social obstacles were not easily surmounted, the board claimed. It also pointed out that the Christian mission was frequently caught up in the larger cultural conflicts between the Indians and the government. In a statement which showed uncharacteristic insight into the difficulties faced by Native Americans, the board wrote,

Our Indians, subject to an American government with changing Indian policies, have been perplexed for many decades. Pushed around by one administration, pampered by another, they are confused and bewildered. Romanticists urge them to retain their "beautiful religion and culture," while missionaries of every cult ardently advocate as many brands of religion. Exploited, robbed, slaughtered in the past century, once belittled as "stupid, dirty, hardhearted" by those who did not know

them, frequently bested even today by unscrupulous exponents of our supposedly superior culture, is it any wonder that they view with suspicion every white approach? And is it any wonder that even the Christian Indians often distrust our proposal of the indigenous church as another white man's invention which may add to his frustration? [35]

The rejoinder made by the board was largely accurate and, as far as it went, true. But it was also true that the board had

FIGURE 82   Agnes Natewa, left, Marian Roskamp, center, and Maria Roskamp.

Marian Roskamp

Marian Roskamp, daughter of Agnes and Rex Natewa, one of the first native evangelists on the New Mexico mission field, works as a bookkeeper in the public school in Zuni. She and her husband have three children.

I grew up in a Christian home. I haven't known any other way. Being from a Christian home, I get ridiculed, but I don't face as much criticism as some people. My mother has been hurt by the talking. They call her the "Jesus lady." It is kind of hard for me.

When you are Zuni, you belong to many clans. But I don't know my relatives. So I consider my church my family. We belong to God, not the Zuni way. Christianity is not just a white man's religion.

I know that Home Missions sometimes wants us to change down here. I ask them to go slow, to have patience with us. We will change, but not in white man's time, or even in Indian time, but in God's time. God is working in my home, in my mother's home, and in Zuni.

Marla Jasperse

Having grown up in a Navajo family near Chaco Canyon, Marla Jasperse tries to weave the traditional ways of her forefathers into her modern life as a wife, mother, and graduate student in health education.

I was born way out there on the north side of Crownpoint during the time that a lot of Navajo still lived way out there. A lot of times when people talk about Navajo, they just talk about the Navajo they see in Gallup and about all the drinking. In real life there is more to Navaho than that. The Navajo are a tribe so strong in their traditions. They are rich in their teachings and proverbs.

It was very traditional where I grew up. My grandfather was a local medicine man who did singing and the summer and winter dancing. I saw him praying every morning. I feel I grew up in an extended family system. There was always someone teaching me and talking to me.

I had to leave my family when I went to the Crownpoint Bureau of Indian Affairs boarding school for first through eighth grade. I was four years behind because my mother held me back after I had hurt my hip. Mostly, it was all Navajo kids who spoke their own language who went there.

For high school my mother wanted me to go to Rehoboth. I didn't want to go so far from home. She took me to Gallup and drove me around. She showed me some of the Indians who were living a drinking life-style. By having me observe this behavior, she was asking me if this is how I wanted my life to be.

I went to Rehoboth. It was an eye opener. A big shock to me. Kids weren't as willing to help out at Rehoboth as they were at Crownpoint. It was hard for me to be fluent in English. The freshman year was the worst. In my sophomore year, it got better when I decided to be who I really am. School then became a big growing experience for me.

I never thought of going to college. In the Navajo way of life, you are in good standing when you have a husband, kids, a house, a way to travel. I had to decide which way to be. Then I knew there was no in-between because I didn't want to get married. I wanted to work. My coun-

FIGURE 83 Marla and Joel Jasperse.

selor at Rehoboth said I should go to college. I went to the University of New Mexico in Albuquerque in the summer right after I graduated from high school. My uncle took me there and showed me the city for a whole day. I was so naive. He even had to show me how to cross a busy street. He left and I stayed on.

At first I wanted to be a nurse, but I didn't like that. I was too emotional working with the patients. When I finally found health education, I realized that is what I wanted. I graduated in that and got a job as a family-education director in Window Rock. I really enjoyed the work. Realizing that I wanted to help plan and evaluate programs, I went back to school for a master's degree. Then I was able to work with the tribe at the chapter level, planning projects for people in need on the reservation.

I also got married to Joel, who was a teacher at Rehoboth. I knew him at Rehoboth, but we didn't really meet until I was in college in Albuquerque and he was in law school there.

When I think about Rehoboth, I realize that is where the foundation for all of my later schooling came from. I'm now finishing my Ph.D. in health education. The teachers at Rehoboth did a great job. They spent a whole lot of time with me. They cared about students.

Even though I went to the CRC school and am a member of the CRC denomination, I still honor traditional ways. The problem I see is that, in order for the church to survive, the native people have to feel that the CRC is their church for their families, their children, and for future generations.

The church must be made relevant to the culture of the people who are worshiping in it. Don't force foreign things on us. So many missions people come and try to make you lose your way of life. That doesn't have to happen. I believe you can use the traditional fetishes and ceremonies and redirect them to God.

I had a Laughing Ceremony for my two children to celebrate the first time they laughed. When you laugh, that is a sign that you are ready to be part of society. I will have a puberty ceremony for my daughter when it gets to be that time. I will pick an ideal woman who I know will talk to my daughter. Much of native thinking is close to the basic teachings of the Bible. You don't have to strip everyone of their possessions to become a Christian.

often shown reluctance in hiring native workers. The incident with J.C. Morgan in 1936 was one particularly bitter episode in which a qualified native worker was passed over in favor of an ordained white one.

In the coming years, there would be an increase in the number of native evangelists. Rex Natewa and later Rex Chimoni would labor side by side with Christian Reformed ministers in doing church and school work in the Zuni pueblo. But despite the 1942 Native Church Plan, synod remained reluctant to recognize predominantly Navajo congregations as full members of the denomination. Churches made up primarily of Native Americans were for many years relegated to an "associate" status. This second-class rank-

FIGURE 84 Mike Meekhof.

ing was finally dropped in 1956, when the largely Navajo Bethany Christian Reformed Church in Gallup was organized as a formal congregation in the denomination. (The only organized congregation in New Mexico prior to 1956 was Rehoboth CRC, but it was a predominantly white church made up of the mission staff living on or near the Rehoboth campus.)

Today there remains some resistance to accepting Navajo and Zuni Christians as Navajo and Zuni, having their own heritage and their unique ways. Mike Meekhof reports that the third- and fourth-generation Zuni Christians are now struggling to strike a balance between who they are as Zuni Indians and who they are as Christians. But the older Native American Christians are offended by the idea that one can still be identifiably Zuni *and* identifiably Christian. The older Zuni were taught that the two are simply incompatible.

Present-day Navajo leaders like Stanley and Sharon Jim, Johnny and Lois Harvey, and Jerome and Lolee Sandoval likewise are trying to articulate what it means to be Navajo in touch with the good parts of their heritage (including their religious heritage) while also being Reformed Christians. Navajo are now pondering whether they can build their own uniquely designed church buildings, have their own style of church music, and harvest the useful parts of their native religion. These are all issues being addressed by a generation of Christians no longer willing to become essentially Anglo in order also to be practicing Christians.

The struggle of many lay Christians to combine their faith and their heritage is magnified for would-be Navajo and Zuni church leaders. Paul Redhouse believed that he was being called to the ordained ministry in the 1940s. Yet, when he applied to become a student at the Reformed Bible Institute in Grand Rapids, he at first kept his plans a secret. "I knew my missionary would say no. And when I did go, he told me that he felt it'd be too much for me." [36] Redhouse did complete his studies and subsequently worked for many years as an evangelist, radio minister, and finally as a full-fledged pastor after his ordination in 1963.

As late as the 1970s, Navajo leader Edward T. Begay, then serving as a delegate to the Board of Home Missions, discovered that the board's official policy included two pay scales — a higher one for Anglo workers and a lower one for Native American workers — even if the Native American worker had more experience and training and even if he was doing the same work as an Anglo. When Begay pointed out the inherent injustice and racism of such a policy, the board was disgruntled and also reluctant to adopt a single pay scale based on work and not race (though it did eventually make the change). [37]

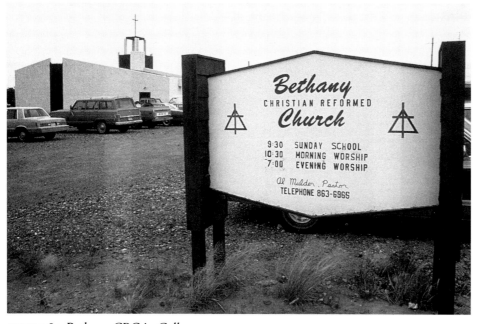

FIGURE 85 Bethany CRC in Gallup.

Stanley Jim

Reverend Stanley Jim spent time as a member of the Navajo church, the peyote church. Coming from a broken home, he found Christ as the answer to his troubles. He graduated from Calvin Theological Seminary in 1995.

Most Navajo who are middle-aged come from their own traditional religion, their ceremonial traditions. We are taught to respect the land, the people, our belongings and possessions, and to do whatever we do in the holiness of the mind.

I grew up in Teec Nos Pos. All summer I was in the mountains with the sheep, either by myself or with my brothers. I learned to survive that way. I loved running and ran three years of cross-country in the state finals.

I first heard about Christ when I was a child and Reverend Corwin Brummel would bring a hand-cranked phonograph to our house to play 78-speed records of Navajo singing hymns. In fact, I taught myself to read Navajo by studying the CRC hymnbook. I still think that when L.P. Brink translated the oral Navajo language into a written one he made a huge contribution to our culture.

But I didn't become a Christian back then when I heard the records. I brushed it off. It wasn't for me.

Early in life, in junior high at a boarding school, I started drinking. About that time my mother left our home. That made me feel unloved and rejected. My whole life shifted downhill from there. The drugs and alcohol did in my career in running. My dad had showed me a lot of love. Whatever he shared, I really took to heart. But he was away a lot working on the railroads and in the uranium mines.

My struggles really came when I was nineteen and out of high school. I was in the mountains. I was feeling no love at all. I put a gun to my head. That is when I remembered Corwin Brummel's words. He had said that if you ever get to the end of your rope, call on God. So I prayed: "God, if Mr. Brummel is right, if you are there, let me put the gun down." And I did. When I opened my eyes and looked around, I felt a tingling come over me.

It was a different situation after that. I stopped drinking. I stayed way out in the boonies, but I went to church. First it was to the Native American Church, where they take the cactus plant. It was a struggle for awhile, but I left that church and went to a Christian church. That was the therapy for me. I found that my needs were met in Christ. I hung on to it. I was so young in the Lord. I went to Reformed Bible College for one year and came back and worked eleven years for the natural-gas company. I went back to RBC in 1989, finished, and then went to Calvin Seminary, where I graduated in 1995.

I see that I am a new pastor here among my people. The older pastors are the ones who make all of the decisions. But that is disappearing. I am not here to make all the decisions. I may be educated, but in life experiences many of the people are more educated than I am. I learn from them. We trade off on learning and teaching.

It is time for Christianity to transform the culture here, to make it new in Christ. The music has to change to become true to who we Navajo are as a people. Churches down here have been seen as being "missioned." That has to change. Instead of being on the receiving end, we have to be on the giving end. We've become too dependent on the old government-handout concept.

My vision down here is to build and plant churches. I'd also like to better equip pastors and help them in their theological reflections. I want to teach other Navajo about our church and our church about the good things in Navajo culture.

I'm a peacemaker. I try to be as neutral as I can be so I can make a difference without hurting either side.

FIGURE 86 Stanley Jim.

Keith Kuipers: Locker-Room Missionary

The talented group of white and Navajo basketball players from Rehoboth Christian High School had been on the gym floor for a little over four minutes when a wash of yellow paper flowers began to pour from the stands. Upset by the emotional show of support by Rehoboth fans from across northwestern New Mexico, opposing coach Gerald Lee called time out. Lee's team, the Bulldogs from the tiny, dusty town of Weed, were already behind 14–2 in the March 13, 1977, Class A high school championship game.

Once the paper flowers had been swept from the shiny court in Albuquerque University Arena, the embattled boys from Weed returned to the floor. They tried their best to catch the lanky, dazzlingly quick players from the school founded in 1903 by the Christian Reformed Church. But it did no good. The Rehoboth Lynx, led by long-time coach Keith Kuipers, took the championship 90–64. In the process, a no-name school that had not even been ranked at the start of the season came out on top.

After the game a huge grin was plastered on the face of the quiet, normally low-key man who had masterminded the state championship for a group of young men

FIGURE 87 Keith Kuipers.

from the school outside Gallup. Among the reasons for the big win, Kuipers told a sports reporter, were the enthusiastic fans who drenched the court with flowers.

"Though we're a high school of only ninety students, we always seem to have many more fans with us than the other team," he said.

Years later Kuipers would sit in the living room of his modest home on the outskirts of Gallup and recall that victory as a highlight in a long career. Before coming to Rehoboth, he had been a coach at a Christian school in Kalamazoo, Michigan.

But it wasn't for himself that he sang praises. It was for the boys he coached, for the fans who supported them, and for the God who was there through it all. As enjoyable and gratifying as coaching was, it never overwhelmed him or clouded his vision of himself and what is important.

"The kids worked hard. For some of them, basketball was their life," he said. "But I tried to tell them that there is much more to living than just playing sports."

He made a point to emphasize this philosophy when he was selected by the National High School Coaches Association as the 1991 National Basketball Coach of the Year. By then, this son of CRC missionaries to the Zuni Indians had retired from coaching. Learning of the honor, he said he was very happy, but once again he put the game in perspective:

"Basketball was not a top priority in my life," he told reporters who asked his reaction to winning the honor. "My family, my church, and my job are a higher priority. Basketball is just a game, and I had fun with it. I enjoyed it."

Born in Gunnison, Colorado, he spent much of his youth playing with Indian children in Zuni and learning the mysterious, often esoteric ways of the Zuni religion. He graduated from Wasatch Academy (a high school) in Utah in 1944, after a three-year break during World War II, when he served in the U.S. Navy.

He earned a bachelor's degree from Calvin College in 1950 and a master's from Western Michigan University in 1956. An athlete himself, he taught English and Latin and coached at Kalamazoo Christian High School, where he put together championship teams before moving on to Rehoboth to teach and serve as superintendent.

Decorating his home in Gallup are many mementos from his years as a coach and educator. Some of his most prized possessions are blankets, paintings, jewelry, and other artifacts given him by his Native American friends.

Showing a visitor his gallery of memories, he makes it clear that it is the vast, often serene American West and its high-desert solace that have shaped and formed both his personality and his faith.

After he won national recognition as coach of the year, players and students spoke about him as a man who is devoted to his faith and who never became angry or critical when something went wrong on the court.

"He liked a real fast game, which we all liked, too," said one player. "He taught us how to play that way and control it. And he never yelled at us, even in our worst games."

Ronald Kamps, a friend and colleague, said Kuipers "was even-tempered and he didn't over-coach."

In some ways, Keith Kuipers was a locker-room missionary. But he didn't preach from a pulpit or even in team huddles. Wearing an ever-present suit coat and tie and sporting a brush cut, he let his example guide his players — among them many Native American boys for whom the sport was a chance to make a mark, however small, on a wider world.

In a poem Kuipers wrote and dedicated to his 1977-1978 championship team, he sums it up:

Some people consider life only a game to achieve
To win all they can and try to believe
That life is much better.
But Christians experience quite a different thing.

In losses or suffering, they learn giving and sharing
And God's blessing in all.

In December of 1995, the gymnasium at Rehoboth was named after Kuipers. Elmer Yazzie, an art teacher at the school who formerly played basketball for Kuipers, created a logo for the program renaming the gym.

"In it you see the figure of a man whose feet are active," said Arlene Kuipers, the coach's wife. "The entire logo has no border — as Keith's work goes on even in his retirement."

FIGURE 88 Keith Kuipers and the 1977-1978 championship team.

By the 1980s a number of Navajo were attending Calvin Theological Seminary to receive training for the ordained ministry. By 1996 — the centennial mark of the Native American mission — several Classis Red Mesa congregations had been served by Native American clergy, among whom were Anthony Begay, Paul Redhouse, Edward Henry, and Sampson Yazzie.

In addition, several Navajo and Zuni ordained evangelists are working in the Native American churches, as are Reverend Stanley Jim and Reverend Ray Slim, who labors in several congregations at once as a kind of latter-day circuit rider.

Despite many years of hope that the Rehoboth and Zuni schools would raise up native leaders for the schools and churches of Red Mesa, it has become clear that somehow this still has not taken place on any grand scale. Curiously, even some Native Americans themselves tend to resist the leadership of their own people, preferring Anglo leaders and pastors:

some of the seminary's Navajo graduates have frequently been passed over for calls to Red Mesa congregations in favor of Anglo graduates. Some feel that after decades of being reduced only to "helping" and assistant roles, many Native Americans today seem not to trust their own people in leadership roles, preferring the Anglo style of leadership over the unique style of Navajo or Zuni church leaders. [38]

FIGURE 89 Edward T. Begay.

By 1995 the mid-century issue of finances for Rehoboth Christian School had surfaced once again as the $1.6 million per year price tag led the Board of Home Missions seriously

FIGURE 90 Elmer Yazzie.

to consider selling the entire 125-acre Rehoboth campus (the board's financial support for Rehoboth has consistently represented up to ten percent of its total budget). As noted above, in the 1970s, Rehoboth had begun moving toward becoming more of a day-school operation. By 1996, although fifty-six percent of the student population are Native Americans, only about twenty of the 340 students now live in the on-campus dormitories.

Efforts to make Rehoboth a parent-run, self-sustaining operation have generally met with resistance, however. A 1970s Parent Advisory Board eventually gave way to a full-fledged school board. Still, many of the Native American parents are not yet willing to take primary responsibility for the school even at a time when the Board of Home Missions in Grand Rapids is moving toward greater local ownership of all its ministries. Many Navajo parents and former Rehoboth graduates are pleading with mission leaders to have patience to allow the seed planted by the CRC in 1903 to come to fuller fruition, even if it does take more time. For the Christian Reformed Church to pull out now, they claim, would send a bad signal of abandonment to the Navajo people and could very likely spell the end of Christian education among them. A new plan, referred to earlier, to deed the school over to a consortium of the school and the classis may, however, offer hope for the school's continued operation.

Conclusion

Navajo artist and Rehoboth Christian School graduate (and now teacher) Elmer Yazzie uses his art to depict the Navajo way. A key characteristic of the Navajo is their desire first to learn, to listen, to experience life, beauty, other people. Educators who wish to "see" Yazzie's art curriculum laid out on a syllabus of typed pages are disappointed. He does not have a formal one, for, Yazzie claims, if a person wants to

know who he is and what he teaches, that person needs to spend time with him, hear what he says, see what he does, experience him and his world and life view. Only through this avenue of personal experience and quiet listening — and not by reading a cold set of factual data on paper — can one know who he is and what he will teach. For the Navajo, one should not presume to speak in instruction until and unless one has first spent time in silence, listening and learning and experiencing in respect and humility.

For much of its first one hundred years among the Native Americans of New Mexico, the Christian Reformed Church often reversed this order — as "civilized" Anglos, many missionaries came to New Mexico with answers and solutions in hand, and they began to teach those answers immediately. Though some missionaries were clearly more sensitive to Native American concerns and viewpoints than were others, often the learning and the listening were expected to be done only by the Indians. That the Navajo or Zuni world and life views might have something to teach Anglo missionaries did not often enter the minds or methodologies of many missionaries.

As the Christian Reformed Church enters its second century of work in the American Southwest and as the third and fourth generations of Navajo and Zuni Christians struggle to hold onto both their native heritage and their Christian faith, perhaps the time has come for Anglo missionaries to follow Yazzie's Navajo advice: they must first listen and learn from Navajo and Zuni people so that they may truly know and understand Native American people — who they are, what they have experienced, where they have come from, how God is directing them in their lives. Then, perhaps, Anglos and Native Americans together can more effectively communicate to future generations what it really means to be Navajo and Zuni for Christ.

Chapter Two

A Chosen People

Mission to the Urban Jew

For I could wish that I myself were cursed, cut off from Christ
for the sake of ... the people of Israel.

Romans 9:3–4

Few struggles in Christian history are as long-standing or as tortuous as the struggle to comprehend Christianity's relationship to Judaism. How are Christians to understand themselves in relation to the Jews? What should the Christian's overall attitude be toward Jewish people? Are Jews close kinfolk in the faith, hostile enemies of the faith, or perhaps a danger to the faith? How should Christian missionaries bring the gospel message to people with whom they already have so much in common?

As far back as New Testament times, even the apostle Paul agonized over such queries. In Romans 9–11 Paul plumbs the depths of God's mysteries as he tries to decipher what would ultimately become of God's chosen people, given their rejection of God's chosen Messiah. At one point Paul goes so far as to say that he'd go to hell himself if he thought it would help save his Jewish brothers and sisters.

After all, Paul points out, it was the Jewish family tree which finally bore the fruit of Christ. The children of Israel are, therefore, surely worthy of Christian attention.

But the question of the Jews is desperately hard, and even

Paul seems at times rather confused as to how or whether the Jews will be saved. At about the point when his argument seems the most tortured and complex, Paul simply stops, leaving several loose ends, and concludes his speculation by singing a doxology to the God whose mysteries are unfathomable, whose judgments are unsearchable, and whose paths are untraceable.

Paul's confusion and pathos provide something of a preview for the millenia to come. For Christianity's history with Judaism has been equally confusing and distressing. Unhappily, it has often also been depraved. In the Middle Ages the church decided to launch a series of Crusades to retake the Holy Land from the Muslim "infidels." In their long march from Europe to the Middle East, some of these devout Christian warriors decided they might just as well slaughter also some Jews along the way, since the Jews were, after all, guilty of murdering Christ. By the time they were finished, these Christian Crusaders had slaughtered up to 100,000 Jews — approximately one-third of the Jews in Europe at that time.

In later years the Inquisitions would likewise tip the Christian church's anti-Semitic hand, even as in this century much of Christian Europe quietly approved of Hitler's pogroms. According to the gospels, when Pilate washed his hands of the innocent blood of Jesus, the Jewish crowd beneath his balcony declared, "Let his blood be on us and on our children." Apparently many Christians in history have concluded, "So be it."

But many theologians have more acutely and thoughtfully wrestled with the very conundrum that so pained the apostle: How do Jews stand in relationship to the gospel message of Jesus Christ? Answers in history have varied widely. Many have concluded that Jews do not receive credit just for being descendants of God's chosen people. If Jews reject Christ, they are as far outside the kingdom as the most godless pagan. Others have believed that God's chosen people remain chosen and that nothing can cut them off from God's kingdom.

> ## *"Are you doing anything for them?"*
>
> — Reverend Jan Isaak Fles

Indeed, in this current age of relativism, many Christian writers seriously question the need to witness to Jews at all since, they assert, Jews already possess a perfectly legitimate belief system. Any effort by Christians to claim that Christianity supersedes or fulfills the Jewish faith is now shunned by many as being an insult to Jews. Indeed, some Christian writers are going so far as to eschew the designations Old Testament and New Testament because this distinction smacks of arrogant Christian superiority with respect to the Jews. Clearly, the questions which plagued Paul are far from settled.

It is an irony of Christian Reformed history that, at a time when the denomination was itself quite young and when precious little missionary activity of any kind was taking place, one of the earliest mission interests would be a mission to the Jews of America. Indeed, mission work among the Jews is one of the oldest outreaches of the Christian Reformed Church, second only to Native American missions both in terms of its start-up date and its duration of active work.

Given the slowness with which overall mission consciousness arose in the CRC, it seems odd that the Jews, hardly the most obvious among potential targets of evangelism, captured the imagination of the denomination.

But actually this may not be as strange as it appears at first. Several factors explain the CRC's early mission interest in the Jews. First, the Jews in America, like the Dutch, maintained a fairly strong immigrant mentality — the burden of being strangers in a strange land. The Dutch, who lived in their own ethnic enclaves, knew firsthand something of the average Jew's experience in the Jewish ghettos of major cities like Paterson and Chicago, therefore feeling a kind of kinship between themselves and the Jews.

But one ought not to underestimate the Continental history of Hollanders with Jews. Unlike much of Europe down through the ages, the Dutch had traditionally been very hospitable toward and accepting of Jews. Many of the Dutch Christian Reformed immigrants doubtless had family memories of Jewish friends and acquaintances in the old country, memories which gave them an equal interest in the Jews of the New World. (In fact, it is no coincidence that it was the Netherlands, more than most other countries, which did so much to harbor, hide, and protect Jews from the Nazis in World War II. The Dutch who risked their lives to protect Jews from Hitler's Holocaust were acting consistently with their long-standing history of amicable relations with Jews.)

Thus, among the earliest Christian Reformed voices calling for increased mission activity were those agitating to reach out especially to the children of Israel. As we will see, active work among the Jews dates back to the late nineteenth century and continues until the late 1960s. Unhappily, however, despite the zeal, dedication, sincerity, and hard work of many people over a span of nearly seventy-five years, the story of Christian Reformed missions to the Jews is not a story of success by any objective measure.

Perhaps one reason for the lack of success is that the primary means by which the CRC targeted Jews over the years was the institutional approach of establishing a kind of community center or mission house in the heart of heavily populated Jewish areas and then trying to hook the Jews with the gospel through offering various programs, services, and Bible studies. But in the end this method of targeting Jews was wide of the mark. Indeed, when the Christian Reformed synod officially abandoned its last organized Jewish mission house in 1966, its summary comment on nearly seven decades of such outreach was a dismal one: "[W]e judge that the Mission House method has no useful place in Jewish Evangelism."[1]

What led to such a conclusion? Was it valid? And even if it was, who were the dedicated people who, despite consistently poor results, labored so long and so lovingly among Jews in places like Paterson, New Jersey, and Chicago, Illinois? While the story of Christian Reformed efforts at Jewish evangelism is not a wholly happy one, it is surely one worth telling.

Early Interest

Like their Dutch counterparts, the Jews in America also saw a sharp spike in their numbers because of massive late-nineteenth-century and early twentieth-century immigration. Census figures reveal that in 1880 there were only

250,000 Jews in the United States, but that number jumped staggeringly to three million by 1914 — a twelve-fold increase in just thirty-four years. Like so many Europeans from the earliest colonial days, what Jews found appealing about America was its religious freedom. Unlike many European countries, America offered the chance for Jews to be both citizens and active practitioners of their faith.

Ironically, however, the move to America entailed some accommodations to the American scene that altered the very faith some Jewish immigrants had come to practice. Soon a more liberal Reform Judaism came to characterize many Jews in America, a movement which stripped away or downplayed many of the ancient rituals and laws. Over time Reform Jews came to outnumber more conservative Orthodox Jews, with a concurrent drop in the numbers of those active in religious life. In fact, the percentage of Jews who were active members of synagogues fell to as low as twenty-five percent by the mid 1930s. [2]

As mentioned earlier, the long-standing Dutch history with Jews in the Netherlands and a shared immigrant status attracted the Christian Reformed Church to Jewish missions. But it was perhaps also this massive influx of Jews, along with an atrophy in active religious practice, which caused some Christian Reformed members to sense that the Jewish communities in America were fields ripe for harvesting.

Already two decades before the first formal work began among Native Americans, people like Henry Vander Werp (1846–1918) were urging the Dutch to reach out in mission to the people of Israel. In 1872 the denominational periodical *De Wachter* featured articles by Vander Werp in which he tried to fire Christian Reformed enthusiasm for Jewish missions.

Another significant early voice advocating work among the Jews was Reverend Jan Isaak Fles (1842–1921). Fles, a Dutch immigrant, was of Jewish descent — indeed, his father, Isaak Jacob Fles, had once been the rabbi of a synagogue in the Dutch village of Aalten. While out for a walk one wintry Sunday in the mid nineteenth century, Rabbi Fles passed a Protestant church and was intrigued by the singing he could hear. Wandering in to listen to the music, the rabbi stayed for the sermon, based on a text he knew well: Isaiah 53. Through the preacher's words that day, Rabbi Fles became a Christian. [3]

When this former rabbi's son Jan Isaak immigrated to America in 1873, he became a Christian Reformed pastor who made it his mission repeatedly to place Jewish evangelism at the forefront of Christian Reformed mission efforts. Fles, along with Reverend William Heyns and Mr. S.S. Postma, were appointed by the 1892 synod to form a committee to find ways of supporting and fostering mission efforts directed toward the Jews.

Meanwhile, however, the work among the Navajo Indians had already begun at Fort Defiance, Arizona, in 1896, but this mission effort distressed Fles. In an 1897 *De Wachter* article Fles lamented that the CRC was zeroing in on a mere 20,000 Indians in the distant Southwest while ignoring the 250,000 Jews in New York City and the 100,000 Jews in nearby Chicago. "Are you doing anything for them?" Fles pleaded. [4]

For many years the most Fles and his committee could manage was the collection of funds to be distributed to existing non-Christian Reformed mission outposts to the Jews. The amounts collected were never large; what little they had was thinly spread out to Jewish missions in Chicago, New York, Boston, Cleveland, and even to overseas efforts in the Netherlands. In 1898 it was finally decided, however, to focus the support on the Chicago Hebrew Mission in the hopes of generating more enthusiasm by highlighting the work of a comparatively "local" agency. [5] Similarly, in 1910 the

FIGURE 1 From left are Walter L. Dunning, Mr. Bornstein, Henry Bregman, and nurse Johanna Veenstra inside the first dispensary at Paterson Hebrew Mission.

Johannes Rottenberg: A Love for His People

Reverend Johannes Rottenberg never lost his childlike faith in Jesus even as he faced death in a Nazi concentration camp in Austria.

A convert from the Judaic faith of his forebears, the pioneer CRC missionary to the Jews sincerely believed that a heavenly reward unlike any other awaited him when he died. As a result, he ignored the Gestapo when they ordered him not to hold worship services inside the camp at Buchenwald. In secret he continued to spread the good news of the gospel to his fellow Jews and to gentiles.

Once they discovered his defiance, the German soldiers ordered him to Mauthausen, along the Danube in Austria, where he was forced to carry sacks of snow for hours without rest. Soon his health broke, and Nazi henchmen dumped him in a mining pit, where he died.

"I remember my father as a man of great commitment and courage. He believed God would take care of him," said Reverend Isaac Rottenberg, a Reformed Church in America pastor, who was in his early teens when his father died in June 1942. "It didn't surprise me that he would continue his work in the concentration camp no matter what would happen," he added.

FIGURE 2 Johannes Rottenberg.

Johannes Rottenberg no longer worked as a missionary to the Jews at the time of his arrest. Even so, his courage and calm in the face of death arose out of a faith that was nurtured years before as a CRC-trained outreach worker among Jews in Paterson, New Jersey, and Chicago, Illinois.

"What a heritage! I have experienced it myself," said Mitch Glazer, executive director of Jews for Jesus, the New York City-based evangelization effort that sprang, at least in part, out of the activities of Rottenberg and others like him. "The hearts of these people, Reverend Rottenberg included, were so burdened for the salvation of Israel."

Rottenberg was born in 1890 in Dombrowa, Poland, where his father, Izaak, served as a rabbi. Even in his youth Johannes had a curious, questioning mind. He couldn't accept his father's Orthodox faith without testing it. This seemingly innate desire to ask questions arose in part out of the community in which he was raised. He grew up in a part of Poland where people were allowed, for a time, to worship as they pleased.

Despite his early probing of his father's faith, Johannes, an only son, still showed every intention of becoming a Talmudic scholar. He trained for several years to be a rabbi.

But the grace of God, Rottenberg later said, intervened and took him off the career path down which his father had earlier walked.

Rottenberg's conversion to Christianity began in Basel, Switzerland, where he had gone to finish his rabbinical studies. It was there that the young man, then in his late teens, overheard a conversation among several Jewish students about Jesus of Nazareth. That experience, though it seemed minor at the time, ultimately transformed his life. It took him eventually to Rotterdam in the Netherlands for further inquiry into Christianity. It also led to his baptism in Rotterdam in 1912. And it took him to the United States and then to Calvin College, where he trained to be a minister.

"My father's conversion to Christianity meant that he died in the eyes of my grandfather," said Isaac Rottenberg. "Once my father became a Christian, they never saw one another again."

While he was in this country from 1914 until 1928, Rottenberg was ordained to the Christian ministry as a Presbyterian pastor and began his evangelistic work among American Jews, first in Paterson, New Jersey, and then in Chicago.

By his own account, the business of trying to win his Jewish brethren for the Lord was a difficult, sometimes dangerous business. He frequently spoke to crowds, mainly Jews, on street corners, in parks, and in storefront churches. Small in stature, he had a powerful voice. His preaching sometimes stirred the crowd to jeer, swear, and throw bottles and wadded papers at him.

"Your presumption that there are discouraging and disappointing features in Chicago, Illinois, is very correct," Rottenberg wrote from the Chicago Jewish Mission, later the Nathanael Institute, to Reverend Henry Beets, then editor of *The Banner*. "But from my own experience I have learned to regard our disappointments as His appointments, and times of trial as times of great and peculiar blessings," he added, describing his work as superintendent of the mission.

As much as he loved the hurly-burly job of trying to bring his Jewish brothers and sisters to Jesus, Rottenberg longed to return to Europe. He felt compelled to preach among the Dutch Jews.

"He felt himself committed to the Reformed Church [in Holland] as the 'historically grown church of the Reformation' .... What he visualized when he came to Holland in 1928 was to make this church aware of its responsibility [to the Jews]," writes S.P. Tabaksblatt, a contemporary of Rottenberg's, in a slender biography of the evangelist.

Back in Europe Rottenberg steadfastly, earnestly, and with characteristic good will and passion preached the gospel. As the clouds of war began to gather, he worked mostly in the Netherlands, but he visited other countries with his message as well. When he wasn't expounding on the relationship between the Old and New Testaments to crowds, he was writing books and articles discussing his love for and understanding of Christ.

"Sunday after Sunday he stood in the pulpits of churches, and boldly presented the Gospel of Jesus Christ as the only means of salvation for the people of Israel and the whole world," comments Tabaksblatt.

Rottenberg's zeal eventually drew the attention of the Gestapo. Warned that arrest was likely if he didn't keep quiet, Rottenberg forged on. He met privately with Jews streaming through the Netherlands in flight from Nazi persecution elsewhere on the Continent, and he continued to write, preach, and seize any opportunity to preach Christianity to his people.

On January 17, 1942, he was taken from his home to the nearby prison in Scheveningen. Soon after, the Nazis shipped him to the concentration camp at Amersfoort and from there to Buchenwald in Germany.

The horrors of the infamous death camp and abuse at the hands of his captors didn't stop him. He continued to defy Nazi orders and held worship services in secret until he met his death in the bottom of a mining pit in Mauthausen.

Tragic as his death was, Rottenberg's thoughts had never been anchored solely in this world from the time of his conversion. For him, Jesus Christ was more than a historical person. He was the very personal, life-transforming Messiah.

A decade before the Nazis killed him, Rottenberg wrote about the change that Christianity brought to his life: "It has been more than twenty years, but the miracle of his grace has never lost any of its reality. What am I saying? It has revealed itself to my soul in increasing glory!"

> *"Sunday after Sunday he stood in the pulpits of churches and boldly presented the Gospel of Jesus Christ as the only means of salvation for the people of Israel and the whole world."*
>
> — S.P. Tabaksblatt

Christian Reformed Church began tying into another established interdenominational effort in Paterson, New Jersey.

Unhappily, however, many in the denomination remained very wary of ecumenical efforts and found the operating constitutions of both Hebrew missions to be doctrinally weak and hence dissatisfying to their strictly Calvinist minds. Over time some voices recommended either that the denomination take over these mission houses or that it withdraw its cooperative efforts from Christians with such dubious theological credentials. Despite having deep and secure roots in the Reformed tradition and despite its stalwartly held, well-articulated theological doctrines, the CRC throughout its history maintained an abiding fear of theological contamination through contact with those of "weaker" doctrinal tenets.

By 1912 those calling for a distinctively Christian Reformed mission to the Jews won out, and when an opportunity to take over the Paterson Hebrew Mission arose, it was seized upon.

Ongoing support for the Chicago Hebrew Mission also drew fire from those who feared that its methods and theology were unacceptable. In 1918 Classis Illinois overtured synod to establish an independent and distinctly Reformed mission, a goal which was realized in 1919 with the Christian Reformed takeover of the Chicago mission. This work, christened "the Nathanael Institute," began operating out of the basement of First CRC in Chicago but was moved in 1927 to a newly built structure on South Pulaski Avenue.

Despite this early interest in Jewish missions and despite organized efforts as early as 1913, there were early on some crosscurrents and tensions which did not bode well for the future success of Jewish evangelism. In what turned out to be a prescient comment, Reverend Enno R. Haan wrote in 1897 that a hearty interest in Jewish missions characterized the few, not the many, and that the denomination as a whole was doing nothing to further this mission cause. Haan believed that efforts

FIGURE 3 Herman H. Schultz.

FIGURE 4 Martha Rozendal.

should be focused on local congregations rather than on centralized mission houses, reasoning that such outposts would always be at a remove from the rank and file members of the church.[6] In future decades it would be precisely this problem which would prevent Christian Reformed Jewish mission efforts from ever being as successful as might otherwise have been the case.

The Paterson Hebrew Mission

By 1913, just four years after an ecumenical ministerial association in Paterson began an outreach to the Jews living in that area, a desire for an independent and distinctly Reformed mission approach led the Christian Reformed Church to take over the mission. The denomination would maintain this control until the mission closed in 1957. By 1915 a three-story building had been purchased at 48 North Main Street, which housed the mission's offices, provided living quarters for the superintendent as well as space for gospel meetings, Bible studies, and classes under the pioneering leadership of superintendent Reverend Herman H. Schultz (1886–1937).

By 1917 a converted rabbi named Bregman became a missionary worker in the Hebrew Mission, and it was his suggestion to expand the work to include a medical clinic. In 1917 such a clinic was opened under the direction of Dr. Walter Dunning, who would serve in this capacity for the next thirty years. The purpose of the clinic, in addition to ministering to physical needs in Christ's name, was to forge personal contacts with the Jews living in the area. The Jews who came to the Hebrew Mission for medical care provided

a good opportunity for mission workers to speak about nonmedical matters such as the gospel of Jesus Christ.

The work of preaching, personal visits, Bible classes, and the medical clinic continued solely at the North Main Street location until 1939, when the mission was forced to branch out because of an exodus of the Jewish population from the North Main Street neighborhood. For nine years the Hebrew Mission operated a satellite mission house at 306 Hamilton Avenue, but finally, in 1948, the entire operation was moved into a new building at 253 Hamilton Avenue.

Meanwhile, superintendent Schultz had died in 1937 and had been succeeded in his post by Reverend John Rozendal (1899–1982), who would continue working in Jewish missions all his life. Beginning in Paterson in 1937, Rozendal would later move to Chicago, where from 1951 through 1961 he would serve as superintendent of the Nathanael Institute. In his later years Rozendal served as a kind of missionary at large to foster local congregational efforts at evangelizing Jews.

But the work in the Paterson Hebrew Mission, like the work in Chicago, was never easy, and it rarely bore visible fruit. As early as 1927 many voiced a concern that the work of the mission houses in both Chicago and Paterson was showing very few results. Writing in the March 4, 1927, issue of *The Banner*, editor Henry Beets asked, "In view of the small attendance [at Jewish missions] and the very little fruit, are we really justified to go on with the work?"

Superintendent Herman Schultz responded to such criticisms by claiming Christians are obligated by Scripture to carry on this work and called for a renewed determination and enthusiasm for this outreach, not a growing chorus of pessimism. In general Schultz was an eloquent voice in advocating Christian love and compassion for Jewish brothers and sisters. In a 1931 article in *The Banner* Schultz wrote,

To say that we love Jesus but hate the Jew is a direct contradiction. Jewish missions cannot and may not be separated from the Christian faith — we must look at Israel with an eye of love. Love is the only key which will unlock a stubborn heart.[7]

As John Rozeboom commented, "Apparently Schultz saw mission, faith, and life with [a] clarity granted to few others then or afterward."[8]

Sadly, however, for all his loving eloquence and obvious sincerity, Schultz, like the rest of the denomination's efforts then and in the future, was locked into an institutional mission house approach to Jewish evangelism. In the long run, however, this approach proved ineffective in terms of garnering converts. Although many mission workers defended the method as being a proven and effective way of witnessing to Jews, there was little by way of objective results to back up that claim.

By 1953, when Reverend David B. Muir, an Orthodox Presbyterian minister, took over the Paterson Hebrew Mission

FIGURE 5 John Rozendal.

from Rozendal (who had left Paterson to go work in Chicago), attendance at mission-sponsored events was very low. John Rozeboom reported that already in the mid 1940s attendance at Saturday-evening gospel meetings hovered around ten people and weekday Bible classes at half that. By the mid 1950s matters worsened until it was reported in 1955 that only one Jewish person was attending weekly Sunday gospel meetings.

Finally, in 1957, the Paterson Hebrew Mission was closed, its buildings were sold, and its last director went to serve a congregation. For some years long-time mission-house worker Miss Martha Rozendal, who had worked as a nurse and Bible teacher since 1923, continued to stay in contact with Jewish acquaintances of the mission. For the most part, however, the Paterson Jewish mission, which had been dying slowly for many years, expired definitively in 1957.

If, as was just alleged, it was the institutional missionhouse approach which largely contributed to this decline and fall, then what is this approach, and why did it fail? By way of a long answer to that short question we now turn to tell more fully the story of the Christian Reformed Church's Chicago mission to the Jews.

FIGURE 6 Staff and Jewish friends gather for Social Night at the Paterson Hebrew Mission on North Main Street.

New Teeth, Tracts, and Prayer

Not long after World War II, as the nation started to return to some sense of normalcy, mission work began with renewed energy at the Nathanael Institute, the CRC's outreach to the Jews. Excerpts from a notebook containing minutes of the Workers' Meeting — a regular gathering of those who labored at the mission — reflect the issues and concerns confronting workers as peace returned, for a time, to this country.

The first entry, dated October 25, 1946, details a conflict that had been facing the institute since it began fifty years before. It had to do with what the relationship should be between gentiles and Jews. Just how close should they be? Specifically, what was the best evangelistic approach to take to win Hebrew souls for the Lord? In this case, the debate was over allowing gentiles to mix with Jews in Monday-evening gym classes.

"There are many problems involved," writes Wilhelmina Tuit, the board secretary. "When a class of boys are all Jews, they unitedly oppose Christianity, and sometimes make it impossible to teach them. Rev. Zandstra is trying to find out whether the presence of Gentiles in the class is a hindrance to bringing the Gospel to the Jews."

On November 8, 1946, the issue was more or less resolved. "Rev. Zandstra reported concerning the boys' work that he told the Gentiles in his Monday night class not to come, with the result that neither the Gentiles nor the Jews are coming now."

On December 13, 1946, a discussion ensued about a heartfelt but apparently misguided request from a ladies' society in Minnesota that wanted to adopt a Jewish infant from birth until the child reached college age. "None of the Jewish people we know are in special need of this kind," reports Miss Tuit. "Perhaps the plan as such is not the best. We decided to suggest to this society that they do what they can in the way of clothes or financial help, or both, for an institution such as Bethany Home."

FIGURE 7   Jack Zandstra.

According to a February 21, 1947, entry, it looks as though it wasn't just gentile and Jewish males who wanted to play basketball in the gym: "A group of girls — Jew and Gentile — appeared one evening [in the gym] and Mr. Huisjen told them there was no open period for them this season."

In July of 1947, after months of preparation, the annual daily vacation Bible school was held for children in the neighborhood of Nathanael Institute. Whether all the children were Jewish is not clear from the July 18 minutes. But it is apparent the summer event was not too busy: "The average attendance at D.V.B.S. was nineteen-plus. The picnic was attended by sixteen children who are enrolled plus two who are not enrolled."

Attendance at the institute's Yom Kippur meeting, September 23, 1947, was not particularly high either. "There were eight Jewish people present, including the speaker, and twenty Gentile Christians. Rev. Nathan Stone was the speaker. Mr. J. Meekma and Mr. and Mrs. Siebert Stob rendered musical numbers. Offering amounted to $9.52. This was placed in the children's fund."

Numbers were up, however, for a Monday-night, December 22, Christmas program: "About sixty young people were present. The Christmas story was read by Rev. Zandstra and then the girls played a volleyball game. After that the boys and Vets' team had a basketball game."

On February 6, 1948, there was news about some of the neighborhood residents. It was reported that Mr. Gordon, a man who frequently attended Institute classes and functions, had died. At the same time, there was talk about some ill feelings: "Miss Van and Rev. Zandstra reported on having visited Mrs. Fink. She had a grievance against us on account of us not giving her financial aid."

For the better part of three years, the board financially supported a Mrs. Gladstone. References to her appear in many places. They bought her false teeth, purchased gro-

The Nathanael Institute

The Roaring Twenties was, in many places, a decade of experimentation and innovation. Prohibition turned many formerly law-abiding citizens into clandestine outlaws tippling their gin and whiskey in speakeasys where alcohol lubricated the salubrious conversations of daring, short-skirted flappers and limbered up muscles for riotous dances like the Charleston. In 1920, Warren G. Harding, a man "of slight intellect, who much preferred the camaraderie of the golf course and the poker table to the world of serious critical thought," [9] was elected President. While such a person might be sharply lampooned and criticized in other eras, President Harding's personality and style well suited Americans of the 1920s. His

relaxed, almost nondescript leadership, like that of his successor, Calvin "Silent Cal" Coolidge, allowed many Americans in the Twenties to cut loose and enjoy themselves.

For the Christian Reformed Church, however, it was a decade of theological consolidation, of circling the wagons against the multiple threats of the modern world. Holding the theological line of tradition, Calvin Seminary dismissed Professor Ralph Janssen in 1922 for his liberal European views of Scripture. Herman Hoeksema's rejection of the doctrine of common grace eventually led to an ugly schism in 1924, when Hoeksema and his followers were squeezed out of the CRC (giving birth to the Protestant Reformed denomination). Finally, in 1928, synod took a firm stand against "worldly amusements" by declaring gambling, dancing, and theater (movie) attendance out of bounds for Christian Reformed members.

In the midst of all this furor and change, the steady advance of Jewish mission work in Chicago went largely unnoticed. Yet in only a few short years the modest effort begun in 1919 had expanded to the point that by 1927 a new $45,000 building had been constructed, complete with a medical dispensary, gymnasium, chapel, reading room, and classrooms. The new facility, modeled after the Chicago Presbyterian Jewish mission, the Peniel Center, was the new home of the Nathanael Institute, so named to avoid titles like Mission House or Evangelism Center, which were known to scare off Jews wary of past Christian methods of mission and evangelism.

The work in the new building continued what had been started already in 1919 under the leadership of Reverend John H. Beld (1876–1932), who had worked out of First CRC on 14th Street in Chicago. Through distribution of tracts, open-air sermons in Jewish neighborhoods, and personal meetings with Jewish families in their homes, Reverend Beld and his wife attempted to bring the gospel message to any Jew who would listen.

After Reverend Beld moved to Iowa in 1921, the Nathanael Institute called as its superintendent a man eminently qualified for the task: Reverend Johannes Rottenberg. A 1921 graduate of Calvin Seminary, Rottenberg had been born into a Polish Jewish family in 1890. Having disillusioned his family by becoming a Christian, Rottenberg fled their scorn and took up resi-

FIGURE 8 Ralph Janssen.

---

ceries, paid doctors' bills, tried to win her an old-age pension, and quizzed a son about an insurance policy that had been hers. At the May 6, 1949, meeting it sounded as if the efforts had borne fruit: "Mrs. Gladstone has expressed a desire to be baptized."

On May 13, 1949, it was mentioned that Reverend Zandstra had met several times with Mrs. Gladstone. But it was unclear if she actually was given the sacrament. On October 7, 1949, the name of the elderly would-be convert came up again: "Mrs. Gladstone can not get along financially and would appreciate getting a little more money. It was decided to give her $2 a month more."

Throughout the early and mid 1950s, workers found the neighborhood around the mission changing. They discussed regularly whether they ought to move. They also began to get rumblings from the church bureaucracy that their future was uncertain. At the December 18, 1956, meeting, it was reported, "There was discussion of our meeting with the [denominational] Home Mission Board. It was decided to ask the local Home Mission Board to meet with us. As there are several things we did not like."

The final, undated entry doesn't mention any of the problems plaguing the mission. Instead, it speaks of the institute's ongoing effort to evangelize the Jews in its area: "We discussed about visitation work and canvassing the neighborhood. Rev. [John] R. Rozendal [the superintendent] suggested we all go individually. Miss Van and Miss Van Mersbergen think it better to go together. There will be times when each goes alone due to class work and other activities. No definite decisions were made. Miss Van Mersbergen closed with a prayer."

FIGURE 9 The gymnasium.

FIGURE 10 The chapel.

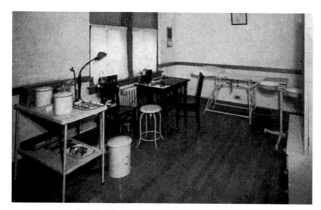

FIGURE 11 The dispensary.

FIGURE 12 The reading room.

FIGURE 13 Building built in 1927, complete with medical dispensary, gymnasium, chapel, reading room, and classrooms.

dence in Rotterdam, the Netherlands. He emigrated from Holland in 1914 and later enrolled in Calvin Seminary. Rottenberg accepted the 1921 call to the Nathanael Institute and served as superintendent until 1924, when he returned to the Netherlands to work in Jewish missions there. Rottenberg remained in Holland until he became a victim of the Nazi Holocaust during the 1940s.

As a convert from Judaism, Rottenberg was exceedingly well qualified to lead the denomination's Jewish mission, but his departure after so brief a tenure may indicate some disillusionment with the direction of the Institute. Colleagues recall that before returning to Europe, Rottenberg frequently expressed concern that the CRC was too heavily in favor of an "institutional approach" to Jewish evangelism to the exclusion of more grass-roots efforts in congregations. As Enno R. Haan worried already in 1897, so Rottenberg also believed that the work of outreach to the Jews would too soon become the concern of a few professionals and not of the CRC in general.[10]

Although the testimony of a former Jew, Rottenberg's concerns seemed to have disturbed few of those involved with the Chicago work. Indeed, only three years after Rottenberg's departure, the newly built Nathanael Institute on South Pulaski Avenue was dedicated as a monument to the very institutional approach Rottenberg felt would be ineffective in the long run.

After the departure of Rottenberg, the work of the Nathanael Institute continued under the direction of Mr. Albert Huisjen (1889–1979), who would continue to be a key figure at the Institute, as well as in Christian Reformed Jewish missions generally, until his retirement in 1956. Huisjen, a native of Holland, Michigan, was not a Calvin Seminary graduate and would never be ordained as a minister (he once listed the University of Hard Knocks, Chicago, as his place of education). But through courses taken in the College of Jewish Studies, he became very knowledgeable in Old Testament studies. Huisjen was in fact so fluent in Yiddish and so well versed in Hebrew Talmudic studies that people occasionally mistook him for a Jew (a few Jews even admonished him to renounce Christianity and return to his Jewish roots).[11]

Other staff workers at the Institute during the 1920s included the medical staff: nurses Henrietta Stek, T. Delis, Marie De Bruin, and Dr. William Yonker. Among those who taught Bible studies were Miss Wilhelmina Tuit, Miss Cora Elhart, and Miss Edith Vander Meulen, who worked among the Jews of Chicago virtually without interruption for fifty years, until her death in 1971.

The dedication of such workers cannot be questioned — a dedication all the more admirable and lovely when one realizes how little there was in their work to encourage them or goad them on. But what was true of all such workers at the Institute was that they seldom ventured very far from a solidly institutional or mission-house method of evangelizing the Jews of Chicago.

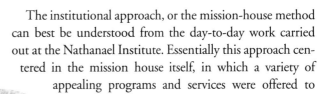

FIGURE 14 Albert Huisjen.

The institutional approach, or the mission-house method can best be understood from the day-to-day work carried out at the Nathanael Institute. Essentially this approach centered in the mission house itself, in which a variety of appealing programs and services were offered to catch a Jewish person's eye so that — it was hoped — they might eventually catch his soul.

In essence the Institute used a kind of carrot and stick approach. For instance, one featured service of the Institute, perhaps taking its cue from the Paterson Hebrew Mission, was the medical dispensary. Dr. William Yonker (also a graduate of Calvin Seminary), one of the Institute's medical missionaries, described this aspect of the work as an attempt to reveal the compassion of the Great Physician himself:

Many [Jews] avail themselves of this medical care. They come early, usually before 8:30 o'clock, and are given comfortable seats in the waiting room. During the next half-hour, one of the missionaries brings them a message in word and song, sometimes addressing them in Yiddish and sometimes in English. After that they are examined in the order in which they arrived, and are provided with the medication needed. We might add that all, no matter how poor, contribute a small fee for this care. While waiting to be examined, the missionaries [sic] have an opportunity to mingle with them and to plead the cause of Christ.[12]

FIGURE 15 William Yonker.

FIGURE 16 Marie De Bruin.

FIGURE 17 Henrietta Stek.

Like inner-city soup kitchens, so also at the Nathanael Institute: If you wanted to receive the service, you had to listen to the sermon first. But there is no doubt that the medical workers saw all of their work bathed in a very spiritual light. While perhaps straining her analogies a bit, nurse Marie De Bruin described in 1944 the ways in which medical work could parallel spiritual work:

Many people [who come to us] have ulcers. An ulcer eats away the flesh, leaving a raw, painful area. So also sin eats away the inner man so that he is no longer able to walk side by side with his Maker. To those suffering from severe anemia, a blood transfusion may be necessary, and as one can see new life and strength flowing into their veins, the opportunity presents itself to show how Christ on Calvary gave of His blood for those who are spiritually anemic. [13]

Similarly, the new facility's gymnasium allowed the Institute to offer sports programs for Jewish young people. But, again, if young peope wished to use the gym, they were required later to attend Bible-study classes. William Yonker wrote in 1928 that the Institute "aims to build boys physically, morally, and spiritually .... All slang and profanity is prohibited. 'Honesty' is our watchword; 'Excelsior' is our motto." [14]

Other classes for adults, and especially for women, were also offered, and a Reading Room was always stocked with Christian periodicals and books for neighborhood Jews to peruse at their leisure. Through all of these efforts the workers at the Institute forged contacts with and made the acquaintance of many of the Jews living in that heavily Jewish sector of Chicago. Such contacts would be followed up by visits to their homes, distribution of tracts in the neighborhood, and hospital calls when they became ill.

In short, the work was fairly wide in scope and quite aggressive. Although something of a carrot and stick approach, there was never any attempt to be deceptive or to hide what their goal was, namely, propagation of the gospel of Jesus Christ, the true Messiah, for whom the Jews had always been waiting.

The work at the Nathanael Institute continued in the 1930s under the leadership of Albert Huisjen. Amazingly, by 1930 the Institute employed no fewer than nineteen mission workers and support staff operating under an annual budget of $24,500. [15] But the economic Depression took its toll on the work as synodical monies were simply not forthcoming. Therefore, the medical work was sharply curtailed, and a number of workers were let go.

Yet the work went forward, and the Institute survived the Depression to enter into the 1940s with high enthusiasm. Reverend Jack Zandstra (1904–1984) succeeded Huisjen as superintendent in 1943 and continued in this post until 1949. Since there was

FIGURE 18 Boys in gymnasium.

FIGURE 19 Wilhelmina Tuit.

FIGURE 20 Edith Vander Meulen.

no one to take Zandstra's place in 1949, Albert Huisjen returned as superintendent for two years until Reverend John Rozendal came to Chicago from the Paterson mission in 1951, thus beginning what would be a ten-year stint as director of the Nathanael Institute.

Meanwhile, the work of the medical dispensary continued under the care of Dr. Yonker (who served until 1951) as did the work of Bible-study classes, gym activities, neighborhood and hospital calls, and tract distribution.

Obstacles and Controversies

By the late 1940s, however, new breezes of change were blowing in the Windy City and in the overall approach to Jewish missions. While the dedication and enthusiasm of the missionaries at the Institute was doubted by none, the lack of results fueled a controversy that perhaps the mission-house approach was simply not feasible.

A sampling of records and reports throughout these years reveals a depressing lack of effectiveness. In fact, in the materials, articles, and reports of the Institute, the line "We're sowing the seed; only God in eternity will know the fruit of our labors" becomes a continual refrain, the simple fact being that there were precious few converts as tangible evidence that this method of evangelism was changing hearts and transforming lives.

Already in 1944, after twenty-five years of such efforts, the authors of an anniversary pamphlet admitted,

We would like to point to a large number of men, women, and children who had found the Christ through the mission efforts of Nathanael Institute. But we can't. The number of those who by the grace of God have become Christians ... is small indeed. Should this discourage us? Not in the least. The seed of the gospel has been sown. [16]

Of course, numbers should never be the bottom-line measure of "successful" evangelism or witness. Scripture calls believers to be faithful to the message and

FIGURE 21 Ben Tabachnick, a Jew who accepted Christ.

not merely to count heads. Nevertheless, while the lack of results did spur a reassessment of the work, the basic methods of the Nathanael Institute remained largely untouched by such reassessments.

Staff-meeting minutes from the late 1940s reveal that the tasks of visiting people in homes and hospitals, distributing tracts, holding daily vacation Bible school in the summers, offering medical care, and providing Bible studies continued. But it was all done virtually in isolation from the larger Christian Reformed Church and its members.

An October 25, 1946, minute reveals, quite by accident, what was a key source of controversy in the mission-house method. Staff secretary Wilhelmina Tuit noted that Reverend Jack Zandstra was grappling with whether to allow "Gentiles" to remain in his Monday-evening gym/Bible class. Although the staff was uncertain as to whether the presence of such non-Jews was a help or a hindrance, it was noted that it had been a long-standing policy of the Nathanael Institute to allow only Jews in its classes.

But it was precisely the separation of the Jews from the gentiles which, over time, made the work of mission houses like the Nathanael Institute just what Haan and Rottenberg had feared years earlier, namely, work done by a few professionals and not by the average churchgoer, thus separating the work from the

FIGURE 22 Staff photo, 1956. Left to right, Betty Wesseling, Everett Van Reken, Edith Vander Meulen, John Rozendal, Julie Van Mersbergen.

church at large and the average Christian Reformed member. The simple fact was that most Christian Reformed congregations, including those in the greater Chicago area, were not an active part of the Jewish mission effort.

Hence it was not surprising that, on those rare occasions when someone was converted through the Institute (and many years later one worker would estimate the total number of converts over the span of sixty years to have been as few as eight), a suitable Christian Reformed church home for the new Christian could not be located. After twenty-five years of work in Chicago, the 1944 souvenir pamphlet lamented that converted Jews generally felt like strangers in Christian Reformed congregations.

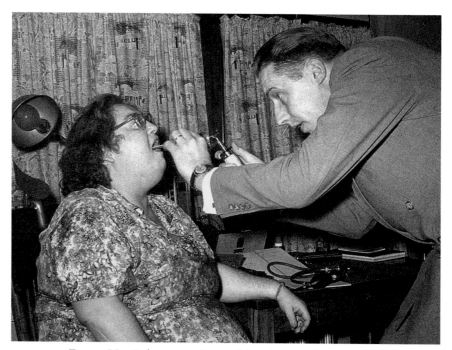

FIGURE 23 Everett Van Reken attending to Mrs. Attaway in 1956.

Interestingly, however, rather than trying to change the local congregations into being more aware of Jewish evangelism efforts and thus more accepting of Jewish converts, the mission board instead decided to work toward the establishment of an all-Jewish Christian Reformed congregation (a goal which was never realized and which was actually never very realistic, given the handful of converts over the years).

In addition to the obstacles which were encountered within the CRC, the workers at the Institute also encountered a fair amount of active Jewish opposition, suspicion, and scorn. The long and often ugly history of Christians with Jews did not give the Chicago Jews reason to trust workers in places like the Nathanael Institute. Rumors circulated in Jewish communities that the doctors at such places would probably make a Jew kiss a cross or, worse, actually burn a cross onto the Jew's skin! Children were scared away by being told that Jewish children were actually killed inside the Institute, and older attendees were sometimes threatened with physical harm from their peers unless they stopped attending Institute meetings.

Many Jews were also suspicious of any efforts to convert them, as this tended to conjure up a cloud of coercion and fear. Some resented any effort to pry them or their children away from their ancient faith, to such an extent that some parents, to the consternation of the Institute workers, would warn their children away from the Christian mission houses.[17] (Of course, one wonders whether Christian missionaries to the Jews ever paused to ponder how they would feel if a Muslim mosque decided to set up a community center in

a Christian neighborhood for the purpose of targeting Christian children for conversion to Islam. A significant number of Christian Reformed parents would probably warn their children to steer well clear of such a place, too.)

But there were also some problems in providing services like cheap medical care to Jewish people who were, for the most part, rising in affluence. Already in 1933, on a return visit to the Institute, former superintendent Johannes Rottenberg commented that the medical dispensary was very nice "but not needed." In 1957 a leading authority on American efforts to evangelize Jews claimed that, to his knowledge, the Christian Reformed Church was the only Jewish mission agency which still employed a medical dispensary.[18] Although by the 1940s there was general agreement that the Jews of Chicago were doing very well financially, some services continued to be offered as though the Jews were among the needy of American society.

Eventually, however, these various cross-currents, combined with a growing controversy over the effectiveness of the institutional approach, led to a reevaluation of Jewish evangelism efforts. By the mid 1940s there were many who believed the institutional approach needed to be buttressed by and perhaps actually replaced by a parish approach.

A New Approach

Among those advocating the new parish approach was former Nathanael Institute superintendent Albert Huisjen. In 1947 Huisjen began advocating a move toward parish Jewish missions, wherein the task of evangelizing the Jews in an area would be taken up by local congregations. So Huisjen began

FIGURE 24 Jewish ladies picnic, 1955.

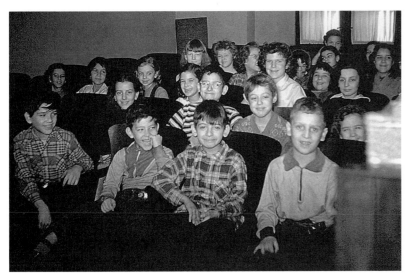

FIGURE 25 First Christmas program at Pulakski Road building.

an effort to educate Christian Reformed members in the basics of the Jewish faith and the best ways to witness to Jewish neighbors and acquaintances. By so doing, it was hoped, the work of Jewish missions would no longer be relegated to the fringes of the denomination, and Jewish converts to Christianity could be assimilated into local churches with greater ease, having been brought in by the friendship of existing church members in the first place.

So Huisjen, who appears to have spearheaded this new approach almost single-handedly, began publishing a quarterly newsletter entitled *The Shepherd's Voice* to aid local congregations in reaching out to Jews in their areas. He also traveled to a number of congregations in an attempt to widen the circle of those engaging in the mission work to which he had dedicated his life.

A January 1, 1956, report on his work reveals his dedication

and drive. In the nine years since he began the parish approach in 1947 (except for a two-year hiatus in 1949 through 1951, when he was tapped to be the interim director of the Nathanael Institute), Huisjen had contacted nearly a hundred congregations all across the United States, helping them find the names of all Jews living in their neighborhoods and providing resources to help these churches approach and forge relationships with these Jewish neighbors.

Sadly, his final report demonstrates that a good many of these congregations showed only mild interest in reaching out to local Jews, and, in many cases, as Huisjen reported it to the 1956 Synod, the churches with whom he had made contact had not responded to his recent correspondence. By 1956 declining health combined with his age (Huisjen was then 67) forced Huisjen to retire. Apparently, however, no one was available to pick up the banner of the parish approach, so the work essentially ended with Huisjen's retirement.

Meanwhile, in Chicago the work of the Institute continued even though the area around the Institute, which had been so heavily populated with Jews in the 1920s, was rapidly changing. Upwardly mobile Jews were moving to the north side of Chicago, and African Americans were becoming the primary ethnic group around the Nathanael Institute. Since the mission-house method depended on offering services in the heart of Jewish sections of a city, it was increasingly clear that the current location of the Institute was no longer viable for carrying on the work.

Therefore, in 1957 the 1927 structure on Pulaski Road was turned over to the local classis for use in inner-city outreach to African Americans, and the work of the Nathanael Institute was then moved to Chicago's north side near Rogers Park, where it operated for seven years out of two adjacent rented stores on Devon and Leavitt streets. The new location, however, was hardly a boon to the work. Even when the Institute had had its own highly visible edifice, the numbers it attracted were never large. Now that it occupied some rather nondescript storefronts, it became even more difficult

Hunted Down by the Hound of Heaven

Donald Levy heard the name of Jesus many times as he was growing up as one of the few Jews in an Irish-Italian neighborhood in Chicago.

Not an observant Jew, he nonetheless was very leery of anything connected with Christianity.

"What I knew is that throughout history Christians in the name of Christ did horrible, horrendous things to Jews," said Levy, a Grand Rapids, Michigan, adult-education English teacher.

Because of the deep-seated cultural animosity he felt, Levy found it startling — almost miraculous — that he turned to Christ for help following a painful divorce in 1989.

Living in West Michigan at the time his marriage of eighteen years collapsed, Levy had thought of seeking relief from the grief and loss by turning to alcohol and sex. As he tried to sort through the debris of his daily life, he imagined going to a bar to find female companionship.

FIGURE 26 Donald Levy.

"I don't drink or go to bars or pick up women. That's not my style," he said. "But it seemed I was getting drawn in that direction."

Something happened, however, to convince him that bar hopping was not the answer. He knows now it was God's grace that intervened. Instead of seeking solace in a smoky tavern, he found himself drawn — moved by God's spirit — to the Mel Trotter Mission, a shelter for homeless men, in the Heartside neighborhood of Grand Rapids.

In need of a home following his separation, he moved into the mission started many years before by evangelist Mel Trotter, a reformed alcoholic. Living for free, Levy was able to keep his job as an English teacher and to send most of his money to his former wife to help support her and their three sons.

"I moved in with all of the bums off the street. It was great. I really liked it," he said.

Being in the company of other men — many of them alcoholics or social outcasts in other ways — was not the only thing he enjoyed. Almost immediately upon arriving, Levy heard that name once again. It was the name of Jesus,

a name that took on a pleasant sound and was soon to have enduring significance for him.

"They were preaching the Word. They were talking about Christ and how he heals. And somehow it didn't bother me this time," he recalled.

As if to test what he was hearing in the mission chapel, Levy decided late one night at the mission to have a conversation with his deceased father. Having harbored rage for many years over the ways in which his father had treated him, Levy arranged an empty chair in front of himself in an upstairs laundry room.

As a sense of peace and strength filled the room, Levy spoke to his dad. He let the anger, the sadness, the disappointment pour out.

"When I started to talk, Christ was there somehow. His presence was in the room," he said. "I cried, embraced my father in my mind. All of the anger came out of me. I knew even then it was a great healing. I had forgiven him."

A week later he took another step that brought him closer to Christ.

Levy went to a Protestant church. He'd been to Catholic mass with his former wife, but he'd never stepped into a Protestant church on his own. The God-appointed moment was a Sunday in the fall of 1989 at Madison Square Christian Reformed Church in Grand Rapids.

"It was powerful, unbelievable, wondrous. Christ was there as soon as I sat down. This was something I couldn't ignore," he said.

Sitting in the fourth row at Madison Square, he listened to the choir joyfully belt out songs of praise. He watched as church members swayed and smiled and waved their arms in time with the music. He listened to the minister lay out a plan of salvation that made absolute sense and filled him with hope.

Another thing happened as well.

"As I was sitting there, I saw all that I had done to my kids. I saw how I just wasn't emotionally available to them," he said.

Surrounded by Madison Square church members, he began to weep. More pain, anger, and guilt flowed from out of him. As it did, he felt relief and forgiveness, he said.

"It was like Jesus, somehow from above, reached down and forgave me," he recalled. "I sat there feeling dumb and happy and, even though I was a sinner, saved."

That experience in the pew, he now believes, was the critical portion of a conversion process.

First came the inner conviction that living at the mission, instead of cruising the bars, was best for him. Next was the post-midnight meeting with his father's memory in the laundry room. Then there was his explosion of sobs and the subsequent experience of God's grace pouring over and into him in the pew at Madison Square.

"Since then, I've been a different person. Christ empowers you," he said. "He does it in one moment, and from then on the Holy Spirit steps in and empowers you to make progress the rest of your life."

The following Wednesday Levy acknowledged his faith to Donn Rainbolt, a minister at Mel Trotter. A man who once believed Christ and Christians were his enemies had undergone a transformation. For him it was a change of heart and mind that came through no formal evangelistic effort to the Jews. The Hound of Heaven had hunted him down.

"If I hadn't felt all of that cultural resistance, I might have truly listened when I first heard the Christian story when I was in church with my wife," he said.

because any day now we would baptise [sic] her and make her a Christian. The other children said they did not believe I would do that." [19]

Despite such resistance and such meager turnouts, the dedication of the staff remained high. In the 1957 annual report on their work Rozendal and Vander Meulen reported that a total of 1,725 visits had been made in the course of the year, sizable monthly mailings of Bible literature had been sent out, and weekly Bible-study classes for children and adults had been held.

But by 1957 it was clear to many that it was time for a thorough study of the issues germane to Jewish missions. With the retirement of Albert Huisjen, the closing of the Paterson mission, and the relocation of the Nathanael Institute, many felt the time was ripe for a systematic synodical study. But the report, commissioned in 1956 and issued early in 1958, did not back off from the institutional approach of the mission house.

Although it reviewed the overall biblical basis for doing Jewish missions and surveyed the CRC's history in such endeavors, the committee still advocated the establishing of "mission stations in the heart of Jewish communities," making use of "the service approach," which had already been happening in Paterson and Chicago for the better part of fifty years. It also recommended that the parish method, as advocated by Huisjen, be reorganized (although there is little evidence that this was done).

FIGURE 27 Gerrit Koedoot.

Since the 1958 report did not step away from the mission-house approach, the Nathanael Institute continued its work virtually as it had been doing for the past forty years. In September 1960, the Institute staff was joined by a Calvin Seminary intern, Mr. Gerrit Koedoot. In seminary Koedoot had demonstrated much interest in Jewish missions, his 1960 paper "God Is Able to Graft Them in Again" earning him the Jewish Evangelism Prize.

Following his graduation from the seminary in 1961, Koedoot was ordained in Des Plaines (Illinois) Christian Reformed Church and then succeeded John Rozendal as what would turn out to be the Institute's last superintendent. In the five years that Koedoot led the Institute, he and Edith Vander Meulen carried on the work of visitation and holding classes. In 1963, a new site was purchased on Devon Street, and a new Nathanael Institute building, without a

to generate interest. In short, the Institute was forced to begin all over again.

Records of that era indicate that most Bible classes were quite poorly attended, often as few as three to six people in morning and evening classes. The kindergarten class of the mission typically attracted anywhere from two to five children on the two days per week it was offered. But between the two of them, mission workers Rozendal and Vander Meulen continued to make upwards of eighty to one hundred calls per month, some of which tried to locate Jews with whom they had formerly had contact in the area around the Pulaski Road Institute.

Resistance to their efforts remained, however. In a June 1958 report Edith Vander Meulen lamented losing a young girl from one of her Bible classes after the child "told the other children her mother said she could not come anymore gymnasium or medical facility, was erected in 1964 at a cost of $60,000.

Despite the move to a new location, Koedoot sensed from the beginning a lack of support. After taking a call to be a missionary to Japan in 1965, Koedoot wrote a final report in 1966, in which he lamented that, when he had accepted the call to the Institute, many had told him he would be wasting his time because Jewish missions were worth neither the time nor the money. In terms of the CRC generally and the mission board specifically, Koedoot wrote, "Our denomination was not exactly bubbling over with enthusiasm for our Jewish Mission program."

Opposition from the Jewish community itself also made life difficult. Shortly after the opening of the new facility, a new class for boys was begun. But soon all of the boys stopped coming due to parental opposition to their being witnessed to by Christians. Although Koedoot labored hard to pump new life into the program (including a more direct, up-front approach to evangelism), the work in the new location and neighborhood proved to be no more fruitful than had been the case in the past fifty years. Attendance in classes remained generally fewer than six persons.

Finally, in 1966, a scant two years after laying out $60,000 for the new building and in the wake of superintendent Koedoot's heading for Japan, the mission board decided to pull the plug on the institutional approach. A February 1966 report to synod at last faced the hard reality which had been painfully obvious for some time: "[W]e judge that the mission house method has no useful place in Jewish Evangelism." Accordingly, the report recommended that Koedoot not be replaced and that the denomination's last Jewish mission house be closed and the property sold. With the retirement of Edith Vander Meulen in early 1967, the Christian Reformed Church's last salaried mission worker to the Jews was gone as was its organized Jewish evangelism program.

Dedicated Workers

Although the overall story of Christian Reformed Jewish missions is not a happy one and the results of the nearly five decades of such work are not

impressive, the devotion and drive of the Nathanael Institute's workers and of those who labored in Paterson should not be minimized. The monthly reports and correspondence of people like Herman Schultz, Albert Huisjen, Jack Zandstra, John Rozendal, and Gerrit Koedoot give a glimpse of missionaries whose love for their Jewish brothers and sisters was real and deep.

There can also be little question that their knowledge of the Jewish faith, including their awareness of Jewish holidays and practices, was very complete. Over the years both the ordained and lay workers of the Institute frequently made use of national conferences on Jewish evangelism in order to keep themselves up-to-date on current theories and practices. Pamphlets and other publications of the mission houses also demonstrate a keen awareness of Jewish history, of Christian anti-Semitism, of Jewish character and piety, and of Jewish fears. Though much of the institutional method may have been, in the last analysis, wide of the mark, it was not due to a lack of effort, knowledge, or sincerity.

FIGURE 28–30 Edith Vander Meulen and Gerrit Koedoot with children.

Of all the workers who labored so hard and so lovingly among the Jews, one stands out in particular: Edith Vander Meulen. "Miss Van," as she was known, began her work among the Jews of Chicago in 1921 and, with the exception of a few periods of illness, continued this work well past her retirement in 1967. Records over the years reveal that, both in terms of classes taught and home/hospital visits made, she consistently did nearly as much work as did the ordained workers like Huisjen and Rozendal. For the most part, however, Vander Meulen did this work quietly and without a great deal of public recognition. Her salary over the years was never very large, and, unlike the male ordained employees of the Institute, for whom houses were bought, Vander Meulen rented her own apartment all along.

Through all the personnel changes over the years, Vander Meulen remained a constant presence in all the various incarnations of the Institute. When Gerrit Koedoot departed for Japan in 1966, Vander Meulen became the last Christian Reformed Jewish missionary active on the field. In a tragic final chapter in the Nathanael Institute story, however, Vander Meulen also became the victim of a dreadful oversight.

Although she had been there forty-five years and remained active at the Institute throughout 1966, submitting monthly written reports on her work to the board, when the mission board decided on December 29, 1966, to close the Institute effective January 1967, not only was Vander Meulen not a part of the decision-making process, but also no one even notified her of the decision. Several weeks later, when the board's minutes were reprinted in *The Banner*, Vander Meulen read for

the first time that her job had been eliminated and that she had been emeritated two weeks earlier!

In a letter dated January 27, 1967, she wrote the board:

I was so surprised and shocked when I read the resume of the Minutes of the Board Meeting held December 29, 1966, saying that all our classes and meetings were to be discontinued on January 15th … and that I was to be advised to retire as of January 1, 1967. As I had not received any letter or word from the Board I certainly felt very hurt about it. [20]

A bit later in the letter she unnecessarily tried to soften her anger by writing, "I'm sorry that I let this upset me so. No doubt, it was not done intentionally but an error some place." [21] Indeed.

But a friend of Vander Meulen's, in a letter of her own to the retired Dr. Yonker, did not hide her own anger at the way this indefatigable worker had been treated in this incident as well as over the years. She wrote that Edith

was so upset and planned to call Grand Rapids on the evening of the day she saw the [Banner article]. She was so terribly provoked, however, that she waited until a few days later for fear of saying too much. She contacted the board while they were in session, but was transferred from one to another. She asked what they wanted her to do with the classes she had scheduled. It took a while before she got an apology for the shabby treatment. [22]

This letter also reveals that Vander Meulen, while never remunerated for what she was worth to the mission, once worked for four years without any pay. At other times, because of insufficient help and support from local board members, Vander Meulen was forced to make repairs, board up broken windows, and (well into

FIGURE 31 The Nathanael Institute building on Devon Street.

her sixties) shovel the snow around the Institute all by herself. Given her nearly fifty years of hard work and loving service, the board's proposed pension of $50 per month also struck many as woefully inadequate. As her good friend summed it up, "No other worker ever worked more conscientiously for the cause than Edith." [23]

That conscientious work continued in an official capacity throughout 1967 and, informally, right up until Vander Meulen's death. Although not required to do so, she continued to correspond with the Board of Home Missions until the early 1970s. Her letters reveal the heart of a woman deeply devoted to the salvation of the Jews and lovingly in touch with a good many of the Jewish friends and acquaintances she had made over the many decades of her service. These letters make clear that while converts to Christ had been few over the years, warm and genuine friendships had been plentiful.

When Jewish holidays such as the Jewish New Year or the Passover came around, Vander Meulen sent cards to as many as forty-five acquaintances, receiving back from them calls and letters of gratitude and friendship. Although increasingly plagued by bronchitis and pleurisy, Vander Meulen continued the Christian Reformed mission to the Jews long after the Nathanael Institute had locked its doors.

FIGURE 32   Edith Vander Meulen.

In the last recorded letter from Vander Meulen to the Board of Home Missions, dated September 29, 1971, she reflected on her declining health (she was 71 at the time) but also said,

Our Jewish friends are having their Holy Days now. In fact tomorrow is their Day of Atonement, I sent out about 50 cards with a short message reminding them of the only way in which they could have an atonement for sin. And pray the Lord will open their eyes that they may see and believe that Jesus truly is their Messiah. [24]

In her love, devotion, empathy, and concern, Edith was clearly an heir of Saint Paul.

Though this chapter of Christian Reformed North American missions is in many ways a disappointing one, the work of people like Edith Vander Meulen gives one cause to rejoice even where visible results were lacking. For many years, against long odds and despite a discouraging lack of fruit, the workers in Jewish missions insisted that they labored on because, in the end, God asks for our faithfulness to his Great Commission. Few embodied that kind of biblical faithfulness better than his servant Edith Vander Meulen, truly an unsung heroine of the Christian Reformed Church's mission story.

Conclusion

In the years following the closing of the Nathanael Institute, there has been no organized CRC work among the Jews of North America. The 1971 Synod adopted some mission guidelines which included reaching out to Jews through local churches. Indeed, some congregations have endeavored to include Jews in their neighborhood evangelism programs, and many churches have also become acquainted with the organization Jews for Jesus. Ten years after the closing of the last mission house, Home Missions minister of evangelism Wesley Smedes continued to raise awareness and prick the conscience of the denomination with regard to Jewish missions.

But such efforts have generally been sporadic at best. Despite its long-term ineffectiveness, it appears that the heyday of the mission houses in Paterson and Chicago represents the high-water mark for Christian Reformed outreach to the Jews. That the work never achieved its lofty intentions is perhaps best demonstrated by what could be seen as a final ironic metaphor for this chapter of the story: the last Nathanael Institute complex, built on Devon Street in 1964, is now a Jewish synagogue.

Home Missions in Canada

Dominee James Holwerda made the exhausting four-hundred-mile trip over a narrow-gauge railroad from Manhattan, Montana, to Lethbridge, Alberta, in early May of 1905 to bring the Christian Reformed Church to Canada.

Called to "come over and help" by the early Dutch settlers, the hardy turn-of-the-century preacher stepped off the train and then rode a wagon across an unbridged river into a community that was hungry for the Word and the administration of the sacraments.

"It was realized that something had to be done to promote the spiritual life of the Dutch-immigrant families in Alberta," writes Reverend Tymen E. Hofman, a retired CRC minister, in *The Strength of Their Years*, a history of that first church and its community. "There was an urgency about the matter for the settlers had not heard the Word preached for nearly a year, nor had they celebrated the Lord's Supper."

On Sunday morning, May 11, 1905, Holwerda offered prayer and preaching for forty-five men, women, and children gathered in the home of John Postman, one of the early immigrants. Holwerda was a pastor stationed in Manhattan, Montana, at the time of his visit to Alberta. He stayed in a community northwest of Lethbridge for more than a week, visiting families in their homes and connecting the settlers to a church whose ethnic history mirrored their own.

When he left, he took with him a signed petition asking the church back in Grand Rapids to send a full-time Home Missions minister to oversee their growing spiritual needs. The church responded by sending, in November

FIGURE 2 James Holwerda.

1905, a home missionary to investigate, and soon the Montana church was urged to organize the Canadian petitioners into a new Christian Reformed church. Ministers and home missionaries from the states of Montana and Washington would continue to serve the fledgling church as best they could.

"The story of the Canadian church is inextricably linked to the story of denominational Home Missions," said Hofman, who was born in Alberta in 1922. "Out of this work eventually came almost one-fourth of our denomination. This is one of the most successful operations the CRC has ever undertaken."

The work that began in the small Alberta community did not, however, quickly spawn other efforts. Nonetheless, it was through the work of the Home Missions board, directed from West Michigan, that the denomination slowly but surely gained a foothold in the United States' neighbor to the north.

FIGURE 1 The Lethbridge train station, with horse-drawn cabs waiting for passengers.

FIGURE 3 Jan (John) and Janna Postman family.

FIGURE 4 "The old prophet" Menno Borduin and his wife, Trientje.

The Home Missions heroes who helped forge the Canadian church are many. Following is a look at a few of them, as well as a sketch of the phases of Home Missions' involvement in Canada.

"The Old Prophet"

One of the first of the saints was Menno Borduin, a home missionary for Classes Pella/Pacific. He came to the Fort Mc Cleod area in 1907. Affectionately known as "the old prophet," he was the outstanding man in the life of the first congregations in Alberta. His "devotion and faithfulness made him the epitome of the selfless servant," said Hofman.

The old prophet was one of the circuit riders who came out of Montana to help establish worship and fellowship in a scattering of Canadian communities.

"A large portion of his time was spent traveling from one church to another, in all sorts of weather, finding his lodging in generally overcrowded pioneer homes," said Hofman in his history of the era. "His possessions were meager; his clothing was not always warm enough; on trips in winter he often wore newspaper under his coat to keep out the cold."

Sadly, the opportunity to take up a permanent ministry for himself in Canada eluded the old prophet. He finished second in the congregation's voting for its first minister. "While Borduin was dearly loved and highly respected for his devotion and service, it seems the people were not impressed with his overall performance," said Hofman.

Even so, the old prophet devoted his energies to making sure Hollanders in this new country had a chance to learn about and live the Reformed faith.

Beginning the Work

Another of the early personalities on the Canadian front was John R. Brink, a legendary Home Missions worker. In his memoirs, Brink recalls how in June of 1925, Dr. Henry Beets, CRC secretary of missions, decided that someone ought to look into the report that "some 50,000 Hollanders had come to Ontario." Until then, the conventional wisdom held that only a handful, a few hundred, Dutch men, women, and children had moved to Canada.

Brink was the person called upon to check out reports of an influx of immigrants from the Netherlands into Ontario. Beets chose him because he was a church-planting veteran who had already opened several mission fields in his thirteen years as a home missionary.

First off, Brink contacted the editor of *De Wachter*, the CRC Dutch weekly, to find out if there were any subscribers in this province that encompassed 41,382 square miles. He found the name of only one man, who lived in Burlington. In a letter, the man invited him to stop in for a visit.

So on a hot day in July of 1925, Brink arrived in Burlington and made his way to the address he was given. But there were problems right off.

"I found no shades or curtains or furniture in the house," he recalled in his autobiography. "I asked a Canadian neighbor if these people had moved. She said yes. They moved to Pickering."

Undaunted, he asked the woman if there were any other newly arrived Dutch folk in the vicinity. She told him there were, just down the street. Brink thanked her and then called on this couple, who happened to be from Dokkum, Friesland. They spoke in Dutch. One thing led to another, and Brink organized the first CRC service in that part of Canada. Later he recalled that "they were real glad at the prospects of getting a Holland service in Burlington."

Brink eventually moved on to Toronto and other Ontario cities, bringing the Dutch people a taste of the gospel in their native tongue. He rode wagons with whiskey-drinking farmers, preached in kitchens, held services for Hollanders who considered themselves atheists.

"How those people appreciated the services .... Some of them came great distances to attend services," he recalled. "It is a great blessing that the Lord opened the doors for us in Canada."

Growing Numbers

Building on such early efforts as those of Borduin and Brink and others, the CRC developed a permanent presence in four of Canada's provinces. There were thirteen CRC churches in Canada when the Second World War broke out in 1939. None was large, none impressive, but all had come through tough times with help from the denomination and the Home Missions board, said Hofman. "Those tough times included prairie pioneering, the western dust bowl of the 'dirty thirties,' and the Depression," he commented.

But the church was small. The real growth came out with the onset of European emigration after the war, in 1945. Canada at this time opened its doors to outsiders because it

FIGURE 5 Peter J. and Hattie Hoekstra.

FIGURE 6 John R. Brink.

was in need of people to help build its agriculture and industries. As for the Dutch, they "were particularly attracted to Canada because the Canadian Army had a major role in the liberation of the Netherlands" said Hofman.

As a result, he added, this "was the window of opportunity through which Home Missions launched a major ministry in Canada. Therein lies an exciting story and one marked with outstanding success."

Reverend Paul De Koekkoek, an American pastor of the First CRC of Edmonton, Alberta, got the ball rolling. The visionary preacher saw the great needs as well as the opportunities involved in bringing thousands of his fellow Reformed Hollanders across the sea to a new life. He launched his crusade for a denominational outreach and ministry to these immigrants in 1945 in *The Canadian Calvinist*, a mimeographed two-page single sheet which he put out monthly and financed by personal gifts, said Hofman.

The initiative spearheaded by De Koekkoek led the Synod of 1947 to establish, under the auspices of Home Missions, the Immigration Committee for Canada. And it was this bureaucratic tool that served valiantly to smooth the tumultuous transition into Canada for many newcomers from the Netherlands, said Hofman.

Three members of the Immigration Committee symbolize the heart of the ministry carried out by the CRC to the newcomers. It was headed up by Reverend Peter J. Hoekstra, a southern Alberta pastor who himself became a home missionary, along with John Vander Vliet, who served as its secretary and became a fieldman, and home missionary-at-large John M. Vande Kieft, who was the Board of Home Missions' presence on the committee.

"Hoekstra caught the vision very early and led in the formation of a partnership in ministry," said Hofman. Hoekstra

FIGURE 7 Ralph Kooy, Sr., and family and others arriving from the Netherlands.

served as the only president of the committee and as home missionary from 1949 until his retirement in 1962. "He was one of a corps of about twenty home missionaries, each of whom ministered to both the physical and the spiritual need of the people in their care."

"They transported families to the Sunday services which they conducted in makeshift meeting places. They preached in Dutch (though most of them were born in the U.S.) and in Dutch and English mixed to assist in the process of moving to English services. Their parsonages, often marginally adequate, served as emergency hotels in which their wives served countless meals," said Hofman.

Looking After Needs

Shouldering much of the burden of helping the growing tide of immigrants were the fieldmen, of whom John Vander Vliet, the friendly, dedicated secretary of the Immigration Committee, was the leading figure.

"He helped organize the placement of the first postwar arrivals," writes Albert Vander Mey in *To All Our Children,* a book detailing the Dutch move into postwar Canada.

"He did field work himself. And during the ensuing years, when the trickle (of newcomers) became a flood, he seemed to be everywhere — meeting boats in Halifax, visiting with newly arrived families in rural areas, meeting with Canadian officials, and looking after the affairs of the committee."

Vander Vliet, himself an immigrant from the Netherlands, knew from experience the needs of the newcomers. He spent the last part of his life in this work.

FIGURE 8 Bernard Nieboer, far right, with immigrant family in Iron Springs, Alberta, on a Sunday morning circa 1950.

FIGURE 9 Classis Pacific, October 1951.

1. C. Vos
2. R. Haan
3. R. Postuma
4. W. Hekman
5. L. Sweetman
6. T.E. Hofman
7. Bill Potts
8. Harry Van Dyken
9. A. De Jonge (FM)
10. Paul De Koekkoek (HM)
11. J. Steigenga
12. J.K. Van Baalen

13. C. Schooland
14. P. Spoelstra
15. A. Koning
16. G. Kingma
17. J.M. Vander Kieft (HM)
18. J. Weidenaar
19. W. Vander Griend
20. P. Kooy (FM)
21. J. Betten (HM)
22. C. Vander Ark
23. Peter Eldersveld
24. Elko Oostendorp

25. John Hanenberg (HM)
26. John Olthuis
27. John De Jonge
28. J.R. Van Dyke
29. J. Brouwer
30. Peter Van Dyk
31. Wm. Vanden Acre
32. John Schuurman
33. John Verbrugge
34. P.J. Hoekstra (HM)
35. C.T. Withage
36. J. Groen

37. Pete Hofman
38. Gerard Van Laar (HM)
39. Herman Wierenga (FM)
40. Carl Toeset
41. Evert Tanis
42. Klaas Tiemersma
43. Herman Kuiper
44. Anno Nieboer
45. Nick De Vries
46. R. Vander Woude
47. John Stap
48. George Monsma
49. J. Elenbaas
50. H. Waslander
51. A. Breen
52. M. Vander Griend
53. R. Dykstra
54. G. De Koekkoek
55. E. Lampers
56. T. De Jong
57. C. Katte
58. H. Slotemaker

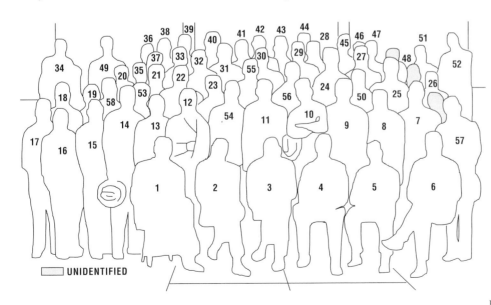

UNIDENTIFIED

(HM) Home Missionary
(FM) Fieldman

The Fieldmen

The actual hands, eyes, ears, and hearts of the immigration committee were evident in the work of the fieldmen, who worked to bring sponsoring farmers and immigrant families together.

Some fieldmen served full-time, some part-time, and some volunteered their services. Bernard Nieboer, Herman Wierenga, and John Vellinga were the most prominent figures of those who served full-time. Wierenga gave his life for the cause, dying in an automobile accident while on duty.

As the numbers of new arrivals swelled, fieldmen, often joined by missionary-at-large John M. Vande Kieft, met each immigrant ship docking in Halifax or Quebec. "They would welcome all the newcomers, minister to their needs, even of those not specifically designated for the CRC," said Hofman.

The fieldman would ride on trains with the immigrants to reach the far-flung communities where their sponsoring farmers and businessmen lived. Fieldmen lent money, taught rudimentary English, and shared their own stories of facing the hardships of life in this sprawling, alien world. "The fieldmen gave their service far beyond the requirements of duty," wrote H. Ganzevoort in "A Bittersweet Land: The Dutch Experience in Canada."

Fieldmen often brought immigrants home with them, fed them, housed them, found them jobs. "Some saw their work as a simple response to human need, others as an extension of their personal faith; a very few regarded it as a means of building congregations and extending the work of their particular church," said Ganzevoort.

Settling In

Dutch immigration to Canada began to ebb by 1959. The ministry of the fieldmen, as well as that of the committee, was no longer crucial. The business of building churches and making them an enduring part of the everyday fabric of Canadian society and culture had now begun in earnest.

"As a result of about fifteen years of work by Home Missions and the Canadian Immigration Committee, the membership of the CRC grew by about thirty percent, and the number of Canadian congregations grew from 13 to 170," said Hofman.

The job wasn't easy, and it didn't occur without clashes. Immigrants from Europe were often more liberated in their life-style than their established CRC "brethren." Most of the missionaries promoted a way of life that many Reformed Dutch considered legalistic. On the other hand, the members transferring from the Gereformeerde Kerken in Nederland brought a new and vibrant Calvinism that insisted on immediate involvement in the establishment of Christian schools and other kingdom organizations. But overall the transition went smoothly for many who saw Canada as a land of opportunity following the devastation of the Second World War.

"The new Canadians served the CRC well in the important and formative years that preceded the move to the multicultural and greatly diversified ministries of the CRC," said Hofman.

Chapter Three

The Electronic CRC

The Back to God Hour Ministry

"… you will be my witnesses in Jerusalem, and in all Judea and Samaria,
and to the ends of the earth."

Acts 1:8

Viewers of the TV series *The Waltons* recall the dominant image of the show's weekly opening sequence: to the great excitement of the entire Walton clan, Pa Walton pulls up in front of the white clapboard house and carries to the front porch the family's newest possession — a radio. In the course of this series, set in the Depression years of the 1930s, the family often gathered around the radio to escape their troubles through popular shows like *Amos 'n' Andy* or *Fibber Mc Gee and Molly*. Sometimes they also sought to be reassured in their economic woes by the soothing tenor voice of FDR in one of his famed fireside chats.

But for Grandma Walton, it was the lovely religious broadcasts which made the radio worthwhile. She was not alone. Indeed, by 1938, religious music and preaching programs were so popular and well-established that songwriter Albert E. Brumely could, in all seriousness, copyright a Christian song entitled "Turn Your Radio On":

> *Come and listen to a radio station*
> *Where the mighty hosts of heaven sing,*
> *Turn your radio on.* [1]

During those early years of radio in America, a great many Christians were indeed daily and weekly "turning their radios on" to get in touch with God through the various religious broadcasts then being aired. By 1939, listeners could select from a spectrum of options — everything from the broadcast of local church services to the more professional, nationally syndicated shows which featured the preaching of well-known radio pastors. In fact, though Congressional legislation in the late 1920s had caused a reduction in the number of Christian radio stations and broadcasts, a surprising number of religious programs were still on the air.

The growth of the so-called electronic church is a story almost as amazing as the growth of the radio industry in general. America's first public radio broadcast was transmitted on November 2, 1920, originating from station KDKA in Pittsburgh. For the first time in history any American with a radio (about 50,000 at that time — though the number of sets would explode to 600,000 by a year later) could hear instantaneously the results of that day's national Presidential elections. Radio listeners that November learned that the

Republican ticket of Warren G. Harding and Calvin Coolidge had defeated by a landslide the Democratic ticket of James Cox and Franklin D. Roosevelt.

A scant two months later, on January 2, 1921, what could be considered the first religious broadcast took to the airwaves when station KDKA carried live the worship service of Pittsburgh's Calvary Episcopal Church with a sermon delivered by Dr. E.J. Van Etten. How many listened to this broadcast is unknown, but at least the Herron Avenue Presbyterian Church of Pittsburgh did — since they were without a pastor, they placed a radio in the front of the sanctuary and worshiped through and along with the broadcast of Calvary's service, even receiving an offering during the offertory segment of the broadcast service.

In the next few years similar local broadcasts of church services continued. More significantly, Christians began setting up and operating their own radio stations and syndicating their own all-religious programming. In 1922 Paul Rader set up station WJBT (Where Jesus Blesses Thousands),

FIGURE 1 The cathedral of the air.

which broadcast each week the evening worship service from Rader's Gospel Tabernacle in Chicago. Rader's fiery, charismatic style caught the attention of many listeners, thousands of whom began coming out on Sunday evenings to hear him in person.

Rader's successful use of this new medium caught the attention of many other ministers, churches, and denominations. Ironically, despite their world-shunning ways, it was especially the Fundamentalists who seized on radio ministry with a vigor lacking in many of the larger mainline denominations. One estimate claims that by 1932, Fundamentalist churches and broadcasters accounted for 246 of the 290 weekly religious broadcasts then being aired. [2]

But some mainline denominations did get in on the action. In 1924 Walter Maier opened station KFUO, from which he broadcast his own brand of religious programming. In 1934 the Mutual Network contracted with Maier to conduct a program which became known as *The Lutheran Hour.* By 1939 *The Lutheran Hour* was on 178 of the Mutual network affiliates and was hailed by *Time* magazine as "radio's most popular religious broadcast," possibly even exceeding the popularity of *Amos 'n' Andy.*

Another household name was Charles E. Fuller, who

began broadcasting two weekly Bible lessons from Los Angeles on station KJS (operated by the Bible Institute of Los Angeles). In 1934 he purchased an evening time slot on "The Voice of Hollywood" station KNX for his *Heart to Heart Talk.* His success, including a surprising level of financial support from listeners in those Depression years, allowed Fuller, like Maier, also to affiliate with Mutual to begin *The Radio Revival Hour.*

By 1939 Fuller's show, now called *The Old Fashioned Revival Hour,* had a sixty-percent share of the radio market and was being heard on 456 stations nationwide. Five years later, operating under a staggering wartime budget of $1.6 million, Fuller was being heard by as many as twenty million Americans, making him the premier voice of religious broadcasting. This fact is especially remarkable because, as Quentin Schultze points out, the show was utterly simple and free of glitz. Each show featured Fuller's low-key, straightforward Bible lesson, a few very familiar songs, and the reading of letters from listeners.

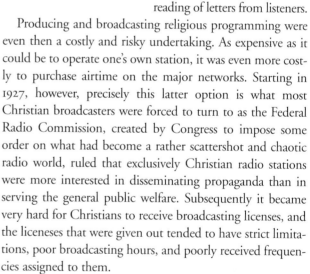

Producing and broadcasting religious programming were even then a costly and risky undertaking. As expensive as it could be to operate one's own station, it was even more costly to purchase airtime on the major networks. Starting in 1927, however, precisely this latter option is what most Christian broadcasters were forced to turn to as the Federal Radio Commission, created by Congress to impose some order on what had become a rather scattershot and chaotic radio world, ruled that exclusively Christian radio stations were more interested in disseminating propaganda than in serving the general public welfare. Subsequently it became very hard for Christians to receive broadcasting licenses, and the licenses that were given out tended to have strict limitations, poor broadcasting hours, and poorly received frequencies assigned to them.

Although most networks were more than willing to have Christian shows purchase airtime, the new industry was costly (see the figure cited above for Charles E. Fuller). It was not unusual for networks in the late 1930s to charge up to $10,000 per half-hour of broadcast time. But because such broadcasts could reach literally millions of people at once, most were convinced that this new medium was more than worth the cost and effort.

Among those who were so convinced were a number of people in the Christian Reformed Church. Their efforts culminated on December 17, 1939, when the Christian Reformed *The Back to God Hour* took to the airwaves. That broadcast was actually the result of over ten years of efforts to get the Christian Reformed Church on the air — efforts which, for various reasons, were repeatedly stifled or shelved but were never abandoned by those convinced that radio ministry was a wave of the future which the CRC simply had to catch.

A Gift of God

Sunday afternoons in many Dutch Christian Reformed homes were generally quiet and relaxed intervals between the morning worship service and the upcoming evening one. But beginning in 1927 radio listeners in the Grand Rapids, Michigan, area could fill up some of that time by listening to a radio program called *Vesper Hour*. Organized and hosted by Reverends R.B. Kuiper, Henry Verduin, and James Ghysels, this pioneering effort of the Christian Reformed Church was generally received warmly by local listeners.

But it was only a *local* effort, benefiting a comparatively small number of people in an urban area known for its heavily religious atmosphere and dominant Christian Reformed influence. Some forward thinkers began to consider the benefits which might accrue if the whole denomination would back a more concerted radio effort beamed to a much larger and hence more diverse listening audience. In 1928 Classes Grand Rapids East, Grand Rapids West, and Illinois urged the church's highest ruling body to recognize radio "as a gift of God" perfectly suited for the task of preaching the gospel in fulfillment of Christ's mission command.

But Synod 1928 concluded, "… the interest in Radio preaching [is not] so general as to warrant the placing of the entire denomination under financial obligations." [3] Still, it recognized sufficient merit in the project to encourage local initiative in organizing and broadcasting local programs and allowed the

FIGURE 2 Henry Verduin.

FIGURE 3 William B. Eerdmans, Sr.

formation of a Radio Committee to investigate ways by which this could be carried out and to give future synods updates or recommendations in this area of ministry.

That committee, consisting of publisher William B. Eerdmans, Sr., and Reverends Henry Verduin, James Ghysels, Leonard Trap, and Isaac Westra, quickly went to work in the hope that, despite the discouraging conclusion in 1928, it might approach synod once again with a more complete recommendation. By June 1930 the committee was ready to submit to synod a thorough report urgently recommending that radio preaching become a denomination-wide ministry. It argued that America was in great need of the kind of positive world and life view which the Reformed heritage could bring and that it was the CRC's solemn and holy responsibility to deliver this needed message in the face of widespread materialism and shallowness of character. "The radio reaches millions, and to bring our message to the masses in the best and most efficient way we can think of, would be a worth-while missionary work." [4]

The committee also recommended that any such radio program be a preaching program of no more than thirty minutes, centered in the Chicago area, where a number of powerful stations were available. It also sounded a note which would recur again and again in the next fifteen years, namely,

FIGURE 4 Leonard Trap.

Opening-Morning Jitters

Helen Brondsema Opperwall rose early on that brisk Sunday in December of 1947. She got dressed, ate a quick breakfast, and then walked the few blocks from her home to the Hekman Chapel on the Calvin College campus.

Reverend John Hofman also rolled out of bed soon after the sun rose on December 7 of that year. He was nervous. The day, he knew, would be hectic. But he was eager and ready to make radio history for the Christian Reformed Church.

By eight a.m., Opperwall, Hofman, and other members of the newly formed Radio Choir of *The Back to God Hour* had arranged themselves for a quick rehearsal on risers in the Seminary Chapel.

FIGURE 5   Radio Choir in 1949–1950.

"We knew there would be no cuts or retakes once we went on," Hofman would recall nearly fifty years after that memorable first morning. "We had to go on for better or worse. The anxiety level was pretty high."

From an inconspicuous beginning in 1939 on a single station, the radio voice of the CRC expanded its broadcast that December day to cover the nation on the Mutual Broadcasting System.

Suddenly, with that broadcast, the church's missionary outreach over the radio waves could be heard on seventy stations by an estimated listening audience of three million people. Before December 7, 1947, the Chicago-based *The Back to God Hour* was heard on only a smattering of stations, mostly in the Midwest.

"We were a small church and thought it was really something to be heard over Mutual," said James De Jonge, the Calvin College music professor who organized the Radio Choir.

Standing before his singers prior to the maiden voyage into live radio evangelism, De Jonge was still a little surprised at the fairly quick pace of what brought them all to the small, high-ceilinged chapel.

Only a few months before, *The Back to God Hour* had been asked to join Mutual. Wanting to link with the large

network as soon as possible, the CRC's Radio Committee had had to send a letter seeking approval to do so to every consistory in the church because there wasn't enough time to petition the synod for permission. Responses, De Jonge recalled, were quick and almost unanimous. The rest of the church was solidly behind this venture. On with the show, church members said.

Meanwhile, as part of the expanding *Back to God Hour* program, radio minister Reverend Peter Eldersveld wanted music. Which is where De Jonge came in. In the fall of 1947, Eldersveld asked him to form the choir. Advertisements posted in visible places across the Franklin Street Calvin campus put out the call. And several singers answered.

"It was a new medium through which the gospel could be brought," said De Jonge. "It was a very exciting time."

So there the choir was that first nervous morning, facing the empty rows of pews.

After running through a quick rehearsal, De Jonge suggested to choir members that they envision a family member or friend when they sang into the large microphone that would carry their voices into the station of nearby WFUR. From WFUR, their songs were to be beamed to WGN in Chicago and then out across the country. "I always thought it would be easier for them to think of someone to sing to as they stood there in that otherwise empty chapel," he said.

Also present on the morning of that first live broadcast was Caroll Marts, radio executive for Mutual's Midwestern division, on hand for the sendoff, who gave the choir these words of encouragement: "More people will be listening to you within the next half-hour than ever heard Enrico Caruso, the world-famous Italian tenor, in his entire lifetime."

Not exactly soothing words for a trembling, college-age choir. But the radio executive's words did put into perspective the significance of the moment. For seven subsequent years, fifty-two weeks a year, the Calvin Radio

Choir would sing hymns live over the radio. After 1954, technology would allow James De Jonge to tape music beforehand for later use on the denominational radio broadcast.

But that was the future. Until 1954 it was show time live. "We knew we couldn't flub anything," said Lucile De Stigter Poel, a junior at Calvin at Christmas time of 1947. "We felt we were part of a much larger enterprise."

Soon enough that morning, the engineer in the front of the chapel gave word to announcer Gordon Kibby that it was time. On cue, De Jonge raised his arms and led the choir in a flawless rendition of *Psalter Hymnal* 169, "Lord of Hosts, How Lovely."

Following the music was the Scripture reading of Luke 2:11: "For unto you is born this day in the city of David a Savior, which is Christ the Lord."

A verse from Matthew 2:9 came next. Then Peter Eldersveld, there for the inaugural performance, gave his message. The following week he was back in Chicago, preaching from his pulpit at WGN. "Whenever anything in the world becomes a channel to convey the Word of God, that thing immediately is enhanced with a new importance," he spoke over the air. "Beginning today that can be said about this half-hour period on a large number of radio stations which have been made available to carry our broadcast across the country."

Either that moment or later that day, listeners in Kalamazoo, Michigan; Billings, Montana; Spokane, Washington; Fremont, Nebraska; New York City; Holyoke, Massachusetts; and many other cities would hear the CRC's radio evangelist discuss the significance of this effort in electronic evangelism.

"But let it be said on the other side that there is today no greater channel for preaching of the gospel, and there is no means placed at the disposal of the church which gives so large an opportunity to reach millions of starving souls with the bread of life [as radio]," he said.

When the minister completed his sermon, which went on to discuss the significance of Christmas, the choir sang again. This time it was *Psalter Hymnal* 342: "O Come, O Come, Immanuel."

The twice-a-week practice sessions had paid off. Nervous as they were, the choir had performed without a spoiled note.

By a couple minutes after nine a.m., they were finished. They climbed down the steps, congratulated one another, buttoned up their coats, and went back out to continue their day. Some had to work. Others to study, to help fix dinner, to attend additional church services.

"I think now that those broadcasts were probably like an oasis in the wilderness for some people out there listening," said Elaine Ryskamp Hofman, whose then boyfriend, Leonard Hofman, the denomination's future general secretary, also sang with the choir.

For James De Jonge, the first successful performance was only the beginning. He would direct the choir, and eventually take singers on tour across North America, until 1972. Still, that first morning remains clear in his memory. "I don't see how we were able to do it," he said. "Thinking back, I have to think that the whole venture of our church going into radio was quite something."

FIGURE 6 Radio Choir visits WGN studios in Chicago in 1948.

FIGURE 7 Various logos used for *The Back to God Hour.*

that as soon as possible the CRC should find and call one person to host this program from week to week.

Although the committee reassured synod that raising the necessary money ($5,000–$6,000) would not be difficult, that assurance could not alter the fact that the 1930 Synod met under the dark shadow of Black Tuesday — the stock market crash which had plunged the nation into the Depression only eight months earlier. Synod once again refused to adopt so expensive a denomination-wide program, encouraging only local initiative in radio. If radio was indeed "God's gift," as the 1928 overtures to synod had claimed, it was a gift which would have to remain unused for the foreseeable future.

The Reformed Hour?

As the Great Depression sank its roots into the American landscape during the early 1930s, it became evident that the economic conditions which had been partly responsible for the 1930 synodical rejection of radio ministry would not soon improve. Still, even during those dark years, religious programs like *The Lutheran Hour* and *The Radio Revival Hour* experienced a rapid rise in popularity. Those in the Christian Reformed Church who were convinced of radio's usefulness witnessed such success in official silence. Barring local broadcasts, nothing was proposed again on a denomination-wide basis until the 1938 Synod.

By the late 1930s, when many Americans began to see an end to the Great Depression, synod received a proposal for a more concerted, larger-scale effort in radio ministry. This time, at last, the effort met with synodical success: synod approved the formation

of a Radio Committee to explore a *Reformed Hour* radio program. The report presented to Synod 1938, which actually came by way of an overture, reveals some interesting views on how a radio ministry would function for the CRC.

Curiously, a primary target audience highlighted by the overture was

the upper class in our nation. Our emphasis on sound biblical preaching by an educated ministry should be a powerful asset in seeking to touch this forgotten class. Preaching of the Reformed evangelistic type is admirably adapted to have a strong appeal, with God's blessing, for the cultured and educated. [5]

The overture also claimed it was comparatively easy to get into the homes of the poor because they welcomed the helping ministry which local congregations could provide. But because the upper classes had no such physical or monetary needs, they were more difficult to contact. The radio, therefore, would be a natural way to enter the living rooms of those whose homes lacked other points of entry. How much impact the CRC's radio ministry eventually had on such "upper classes" may be hard to gauge, but it is interesting to note that reaching this group was a key selling point to the 1938 Synod.

Whether this angle on radio ministry was decisive or not, the fact is that the synod did give the go-ahead, and a new Radio Committee was formed (the other having long since disbanded). The committee, consisting of Reverends Dick Walters, Edward Pekelder, Benjamin Essenburg, Henry Baker as well as Mr. Jacob De Jager and Mr. Mark Fakkema, quickly went to work. By 1939 it presented to synod a proposal for beginning a half-hour program entitled *The Back to God Hour.* It further proposed that attempts be made to secure airtime on stations with a large broadcast range and that, as soon as possible, one man be hired to be the denomination's radio minister because "All successful radio broadcasts center about a personality." [6]

Recognizing the financial worries of past synods, the committee was also careful to research just what such a proposed broadcast would cost. It conceded that any national network hookup was not financially feasible, because of exorbitant costs. A 50,000-watt station like Chicago's WMAQ would cost $324 per half-hour, whereas broadcasting over a chain of stations, as did *The Lutheran Hour,* would cost nearly $100,000 for a twenty-six-week broadcast season. It would be much more realistic, the committee concluded, to use a smaller station like the 20,000-watt WJJD in Chicago, which would cost about $1,118 for a thirteen-week broadcast season and which would still cover most of the United States except for the states in the far East or West.

The proposed method of broadcasting, which would be followed for many years, was not a live broadcast but rather a recorded program transcribed onto a record, which could then be sent from station to station for broadcast at different times. Such a transcribed recording would cost approximately sixty dollars per program and would have the advantage of being usable a number of times.

But perhaps one of the strongest points made by the 1939 Radio Committee, and one which would be repeated for years to come, was that it was high time the little-known Christian Reformed Church became more widely recognized as promoting a world and life view which was desperately needed to combat America's multiple ills of materialism, humanism, and watered-down liberal religion. Synod 1939 obviously agreed and so gave its approval to broadcast *The Back to God Hour,* perhaps as early as October of 1939. Radio ministry in the Christian Reformed Church was born.

Penetrating Power

On December 17, 1939, as the shadows of war were lengthening in Europe and worldwide, *The Back to God Hour* took to the air as Reverend Henry Schultze (later president of Calvin College) opened with this prayer:

Almighty, omnipresent, and loving God and Father, we are fervently grateful to Thee this afternoon that Thou art permitting us to begin a season of broadcasting the truth that can make men free from sin and its enslaving power. We acknowledge Thy divine Providence and incomparable grace for the privilege of employing such far-reaching and penetrating power to proclaim the whole counsel of God to a needy generation.

We beseech Thee, O Spirit divine, that Thou wilt accompany us as we work through the season now begun so that the messages brought today and on the Sundays that follow may cheer and comfort those in sorrow, may sustain and guide those in affliction, may strengthen and encourage those that are weakly stumbling along life's pathway, may fill the hearts of the faithful with joy and peace, and may move men everywhere to a renewed consciousness of the great glory of our God. [7]

Carried over Chicago station WJJD, *The Back to God Hour's* first season lasted fourteen weeks, from December 17,

FIGURE 8 Henry Schultze.

1939, to March 24, 1940. Other speakers in the inaugural season included Reverend H.J. Kuiper (then editor of *The Banner*) and Reverends Herman Kuiper, William Rutgers, Gerrit Hoeksema, and Benjamin Essenburg.

The Radio Committee's report to Synod 1940 brimmed with enthusiasm as it reported receiving 553 pieces of "fan mail" from throughout the Midwest and from as far away as West Virginia, North Carolina, Georgia, and Mississippi. While the majority of the letters were from Christian Reformed members, 157 pieces of mail came from people not affiliated with the denomination. A total of 622 printed radio sermons were mailed to meet listener requests for them.

The committee was also pleased to report that the $3,275 it had received in gifts from listeners and offerings from churches was actually more than the $2,277 it had disbursed for that season. All in all the committee was mightily encouraged and so requested that synod authorize another season in which to continue the work already begun and change those things that had not gone well.

The committee readily admitted that inexperience with this new medium and its restrictions led to, among other things, some run-ins with the Musicians' Union of Chicago, which disallowed the singing of many of the hymns the committee had wished to air. It also admitted that some of the ministers' inexperience in speaking on the radio had resulted in messages which did not play well over the air and that having different speakers from week to week detracted from the overall unity of the broadcast.

This last problem, the committee believed, would be instantly solved if a regular weekly radio minister could be

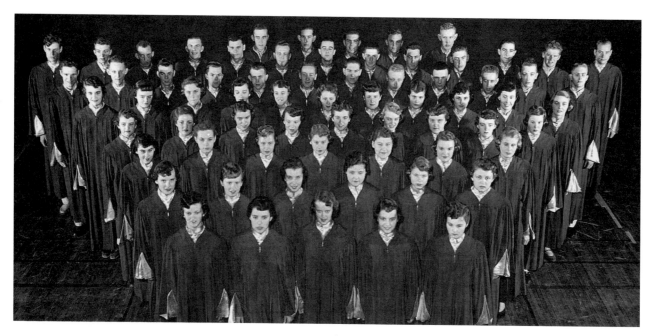

FIGURE 9-10 The Calvin College Radio Choir.

hired. Since that was not yet feasible, a committee of three ministers was to be selected who could work more closely in coordinating their messages and refining on-air techniques of preaching for the second season. Synod agreed to all the Radio Committee's requests, thus launching the 1940–1941 broadcast season.

Over the ensuing years synod would continue to renew the work of *The Back to God Hour,* virtually without hesitation. After more than ten years of opposition to denominational radio work, once the decision to broadcast was made, synod seems never to have looked back. This fact is the more striking in light of how rapidly the work expanded, especially in terms of its budget. In the 1939–1940 premiere broadcast season, the Radio Committee expended just under $3,000 on its fourteen broadcasts. The second season would increase the program's coverage from only one station (WJJD Chicago) to six stations, covering the area from New York City to Sioux Falls, South Dakota. But the budget would increase accordingly to $5,585. Stunningly, by 1944 the budget would increase eightfold over the first season to just over $17,000 and would quintuple from there to $87,000 three years later for the 1946–1947 season. These increases would continue each year until, after only ten years on the air, the annual budget of the *The Back to God Hour* would be well over $300,000.

But the reason why synod would again and again approve such large expenditures is clear: *The Back to God Hour* was an unqualified success with a rapidly expanding listening audience. During the second broadcast season, the program also expanded musically by making use of the Calvin College choir (under the direction of Seymour Swets). The choir, despite ASCAP restrictions on what could be legally sung on the air, provided lovely and appropriate musical selections to go along with the Calvinistic world and life view preaching, which continued to be the centerpiece of the program.

By 1942 *The Back to God Hour* expanded to a twenty-six-week broadcast season under the preaching leadership of a team of speakers (since a single speaker had not yet been found). Transcribed recordings continued to be the most economical method to broadcast over the nine stations then carrying the program (although it was freely admitted that such transcriptions "lacked the personal touch" and could occasionally seem less than up-to-date because they needed to be made three or four weeks before the actual broadcast date). By 1943 the chain of stations increased to thirteen, including stations in New Mexico and California.

By the mid 1940s *The Back to God Hour* had become a fixture of the Christian Reformed Church's mission outreach to North America. Having used a pool of speakers for its first six seasons, the Radio Committee finally found one person who was willing to be the speaker for a full season; it was the same man who had opened the program in 1939: Calvin College President Henry Schultze, who somehow managed to fit recording the program into his already hectic schedule.

Perhaps as a result of this more unified approach, the radio staff found a marked increase in the number of requests for printed copies of the radio sermons. During the 1945–1946 season a staggering 700,000 copies were distributed. The staff was also now receiving close to 5,000 letters and cards per season from the listening audience, most of which came from non-Christian Reformed listeners.

These successes were sufficient to embolden the Radio Committee to suggest expanding *The Back to God Hour* to a year-round program which would continue to be led by President Schultze and a few other substitute speakers until a full-time radio minister could be secured. Synod agreed to this request, which more than doubled the operating budget but which would also, it was hoped, double the effectiveness of what had already proven a wildly successful venture. The "penetrating power" for which Henry Schultze thanked God on the 1939 inaugural broadcast was reaching farther and wider than even the most optimistic and ardent radio proponent could have hoped a mere eight years earlier.

FIGURE 11 Peter Eldersveld.

A Remarkable Man

Despite the program's rapid rise in popularity, each year when the Radio Committee reported to synod, it included a reference to one nagging deficiency: the lack of a full-time radio minister. Already in the 1920s and again in the decisive proposals of the late 1930s, the need for such a person was expressed as being a key ingredient in all successful radio programs. Although *The Back to God Hour* would always steer away from creating a personality cult, the need for consistency and unity and the listening audience's desire to identify with the same voice from week to week made obvious that such a person had to be found. By the mid 1940s Charles E. Fuller and Walter Maier had become household names. Although it was their radio programs which made them so well-known, their renown in turn fed into making their programs even more popular. Though not thinking they could duplicate this level of success and popularity, the Radio Committee certainly desired something of the same synergy for its own already successful program.

Beginning in the early 1940s, the name of Reverend Peter Eldersveld began to appear in *The Back to God Hour* reports and literature. Born in Kalamazoo, Michigan, in 1911 and a 1936 graduate of Calvin Seminary, Eldersveld also went on to do graduate work at the University of Michigan, where he earned a master's degree in speech prior to his being ordained a Christian Reformed minister in 1938. Following his ordination, Eldersveld served a congregation in Holland, Iowa. In Iowa, Eldersveld shared with some other ministers in the area the hosting duties of a fifteen-minute weekly radio program on KFJB in Marshalltown. Some time later, when KXEL in Waterloo developed a half-hour weekly program entitled *Call of the Cross,* Peter Eldersveld was invited to be the program's regular host and preacher. [8]

After taking a call to serve a congregation in South Holland, Illinois, Eldersveld again found his way onto the radio when his congregation's evening services were carried by a local station. It was through this involvement that Eldersveld's name was noticed by the synodical Radio Committee, of which he became a member in 1944. Soon his on-air speaking skills got him included in the pool of speakers for *The Back to God Hour* and as the program's regular announcer.

Eldersveld's involvement with *The Back to God Hour* came at precisely the right time. As the program prepared to enter its eighth season, the committee was more determined than ever to hire a full-time radio minister. Although several names were considered, the choice seemed clear: Peter Eldersveld would be granted a one-year leave of absence from his congregation so that he could devote his full-time energies to the task of broadcasting sermons on the now weekly *Back to God Hour* program. Following the one-year trial run during the 1946–1947 season, synod extended a call to Eldersveld to become the denomination's first full-time radio minister, a call he accepted at the 1947 Synod.

The wisdom of this appointment soon became clear. For years the Radio Committee had claimed that a consistent speaker would greatly enhance the program and establish it firmly among other, similar radio programs. The accuracy of the committee's judgment was confirmed during the summer of 1947. While in Los Angeles, Peter Eldersveld learned of an opportunity to purchase a half-hour weekly time slot on the Mutual Broadcasting System. Although the cost was higher than the current budget would permit, Eldersveld saw a rare opportunity which he did not wish to slip away. Furthermore, he learned that Mutual favored *The Back to God Hour's* buying the time slot because Mutual considered it a high-quality program much superior to many similar broadcasts then available.

The negotiations yielded fruit, and an agreement was signed with the result that on December 7, 1947, *The Back to God Hour* was heard on 70 of the Mutual Broadcasting System's largest stations. By March 1948 it would be on 235 Mutual stations nationwide. This first-time national exposure marked the opening of a new era in Christian Reformed broadcast history, and it was largely due to the presence and efforts of Peter Eldersveld, just the man for whom the Radio Committee had been searching for nearly eight years.

The prospect of this new affiliation with Mutual also prompted the formation of a new Calvin College Radio Choir under the direction of Professor James De Jonge. The Radio Choir provided live music for *The Back to God Hour*. Its sound was transmitted by the telephone from the Calvin Seminary

FIGURE 12–13
James De Jonge and the Radio Choir record album.

Chapel to Grand Rapids station WFUR, from where it was further transmitted by phone to station WGN in Chicago. This live feed was then incorporated into the Sunday morning's broadcast so smoothly that it was as though Eldersveld and the choir were in the same room. The choir's rendition of "Unto God Almighty" (the last stanza of the hymn "By the Sea of Crystal") became the program's signature lead-in, and "The Lord Bless You and Keep You" closed out each week's broadcast for decades.

The Radio Choir itself became a very popular part of the program. Listener requests to hear more of the choir resulted in the production of a record album of hymns, which was released in the spring of 1952. The choir was also honored when some of the Mutual stations began to request the use of its recordings for other programs. The choir continued to provide high-quality music live to *The Back to God Hour* until 1954, when taping facilities in Calvin College's auditorium allowed the choir to record its music in advance (no doubt a relief to the choir members and to Professor De Jonge, who, for years, had been assembling early each Sunday morning to rehearse and prepare for the live broadcast at eleven a.m.).

Under Eldersveld's leadership *The Back to God Hour* hit its stride by the late 1940s. The office staff, by then headquartered at 11106 South Michigan Avenue in Chicago, mailed out 30,000 radio sermons per week, processed the voluminous listener mail, sent out nearly 3,000 Daily Manna calendars annually, and began to put together a newsletter to keep churches informed of their activities and ministry. Meanwhile, the program itself reflected exactly what Eldersveld desired it to reflect: the Reformed heritage.

Eldersveld was convinced that if all *The Back to God Hour* aimed to do was present the simple gospel and call people to conversion, its efforts would be superfluous; dozens of radio programs were already doing the same thing. But Eldersveld was certain that there was a definite niche which only *The*

Back to God Hour was filling: the broadcasting of Calvinism — of what he would later call "militant Calvinism." Eldersveld once wrote,

[B]y putting Calvinism on the air we are taking a public place amidst a great Babel of confusion. The radio listener is tossed to and fro between Fundamentalism, Romanism, Modernism, and some other forms of religion which almost defy description. We of the Reformed faith have always maintained that Calvinism is the one thoroughly intelligible and respectable conception of historic, orthodox Christianity. We have said that it organizes the life of the individual in relationship to God; that it simultaneously satisfies the intellect, governs the will, and expresses the emotions; that it brings order out of chaos in the soul of man. The simple, objective fact is that our response from radio listeners abundantly substantiates that contention. In this matter of radio response God has been gracious beyond our expectations. [9]

To the task of presenting this unified and intelligent world and life view Eldersveld brought sizable gifts of communication. His rich baritone voice seemed perfectly suited for broadcast over a medium such as radio. His training in speech at the University of Michigan taught him how to use

FIGURE 14 Peter Eldersveld at the giant memo that stood for many years near Mt. Vernon, Washington.

that voice to the greatest effect, for there he learned the value of careful advance preparation for all speeches.

Although the crucial timing of a radio broadcast required that Eldersveld always use a written manuscript, when preaching from a pulpit, his preferred method of preparation was carefully to craft a well-written manuscript (written more for the ear than the eye), memorize it, destroy or at least put aside the written copy, and then deliver the speech extemporaneously (according to friend and choir director James De Jonge, Eldersveld would sometimes write, destroy, and rewrite a speech or sermon up to eight times before feeling ready to deliver it publicly). With the written speech firmly implanted in his mind, Eldersveld was freed up to apply his efforts to smooth delivery, careful enunciation, and forceful vocal punctuation of key points. [10]

Listening to recordings of Eldersveld's sermons, one is impressed by his excellent diction and enunciation. On the radio Eldersveld's style was a fitting blend of conversational cadences with firm (but not fiery) oratory befitting a sermon. The result was a smooth, clear, yet utterly poignant presentation which was engaging and easy to listen to.

Eldersveld's illustrations also provided relevant, up-to-date, and vivid buttressing of his messages, clearly indicating that, while firmly planted in God's Word, Eldersveld was more than a little aware of what was happening in the world to which he was preaching.

But always the main point of Eldersveld's preaching — the thread which wove through all of his sermons — was "Jesus Christ and him crucified." During an age in which Eldersveld was convinced people were focusing on "man and him glorified," he sought repeatedly to call the modern world back to the changeless Savior and the truth of his cross. Indeed, Eldersveld's first published booklet of radio sermons (from messages which he had preached while on the radio in Iowa) was entitled *The Call of the Cross.*

His style and skill did indeed enhance the listening audience of *The Back to God Hour.* It also earned him wider recognition. On June 6, 1960, Eldersveld delivered the commencement address at Capital University in Columbus, Ohio, at which time he was also awarded an honorary Doctor of Divinity degree. At the ceremony Eldersveld was hailed as a renowned spokesman for historic Christianity as well as a "vital evangelical preacher, keen critic of our social order, [and] trusted guide for thousands of searching hearts." [11] Eldersveld also became the subject of student research papers at various seminaries around the country and was invited in 1955 to join other religious leaders at the third annual White House Prayer Breakfast with President Dwight Eisenhower.

Meanwhile, in addition to being mailed out by the tens of thousands to listeners each week, Eldersveld's sermons were gathered into five anthologies. His presence at *The Back to God Hour* also greatly sharpened the listeners' appetite for other printed materials. While for some years the Daily Manna devotional calendar had been mailed to those requesting it, by 1950 the staff believed that something more could be offered. Thus, beginning in 1950, a daily-devotional booklet entitled *The Family Altar* went to press. By 1951 it was being mailed to 45,000 homes, the majority of which were not Christian Reformed. The circulation of this devotional would continue to rise over the years. By 1952 it was being mailed to 60,000 homes, increasing four years later to a total of 80,000 homes by 1956.

Obviously many lives were being affected by the Christian Reformed Church's radio ministry, now being carried on 315 stations. By 1951 *The Back to God Hour* staff was being buried by over 70,000 cards and letters annually — an average of nearly 270 pieces of mail each working day. It became increasingly obvious that some more aggressive follow-up work would have to be considered. The time and effort which Eldersveld needed to devote to the broadcast proper prohibited his being able to travel or even to arrange any concerted follow-up efforts, so in 1950 the Board of Home Missions appointed Reverend Harold Dekker as assistant to the radio minister. His responsibilities would include the production of new listener literature, Bible courses, on-site follow-up in places without local Christian Reformed churches, as well as preaching during the two summer months when Peter Eldersveld took vacation.

Through Dekker's efforts a number of new churches were planted, new fields for home missionaries were opened, radio rallies were held in various locations, and local pastors were apprised of *Back to God Hour* listeners in their area who would doubtless welcome a pastoral visit. Dekker continued these follow-up efforts until 1954, when he accepted an offer to become dean of students at Calvin College. After two years, he became professor of missions at Calvin Seminary. Meanwhile the denominational home-missions office pondered along with *The Back to God Hour* staff how best to conduct follow-up to the pro-

FIGURE 15 Harold Dekker discusses publications and follow-up with Peter Eldersveld.

FIGURE 16 *Back to God Hour* support staff at work.

gram. It was decided in 1954 that this all-important work would become a joint venture of The Back to God Hour Committee and the Board of Home Missions.

New Fields

The 1950s were a fertile era in which a program like *The Back to God Hour* could readily grow and expand. Led by Dwight Eisenhower's "faith in faith," America experienced a sharp increase in religious interest and a large-scale return to houses of worship. Even the circulation of *The Family Altar* was doubtless aided by common 1950s slogans like "The Family That Prays Together Stays Together."

But the 1950s also saw the rapid rise in popularity of another phenomenon: television. Though most Americans did not yet own a TV set at the beginning of the 1950s, before that decade was over, television sets would be almost as common a fixture in American homes as radios. Already in 1951 The Back to God Hour Committee made reference to this new broadcast medium, noting that it "has, to some extent, invaded the radio audience generally." But while possible forays into this new area were being studied, the committee assured synod that it was far from ready to propose any active work in this new field.

Still, one year later the committee came back to synod with a proposal that a fifteen-minute pilot television program of *The Back to God Hour* be produced in order to test the viability of this new market. Noting that much of the religious

programming then on TV was "little more than entertainment and showmanship" and that it remained to be seen whether TV would ever be a fitting place from which to preach the gospel, the committee still sensed enough interest in the new medium to warrant giving it this small test. The plan was approved. But even before this pilot was filmed, WGN-TV Chicago offered *The Back to God Hour* three free half-hour time slots. Programs to fill these slots were produced, and then four similar programs were also run on a New York station.

The results were sufficiently encouraging that the 1953 Synod approved a plan to produce thirteen fifteen-minute pro-

FIGURE 17–18 Peter Eldersveld on *The Back to God Hour* set for the second series of programs produced in 1956.

Preaching the Word over the Air Without Flair

Dressed in a tasteful charcoal-gray suit, white shirt, and colorful teardrop-pattern tie, Reverend Joel Nederhood gave the TV camera a serious, no-nonsense stare. In the last months before he retired as TV evangelist for *The Back to God Hour/Faith 20,* the silver-haired Grand Rapids native was speaking about the Lord's Supper. As he had for the past thirty years, Nederhood was using his electronic pulpit to offer a simple biblical message: "We are people desperately in need of redemption." He spoke directly to an audience who would eventually include thousands of viewers around the world. "We must come to the Lord's Supper in humility, with contrition. We abhor ourselves because of our sins."

The half-hour segment he was taping this spring day in *The Back to God Hour*'s Palos Heights office would be aired within the next month on stations across North and South America and Europe.

On the same morning that Nederhood gave his catechism lesson on Holy Communion, Reverend David Feddes worked in his office down the hall to put the final touches on a radio sermon. Feddes, son of a Montana rancher, would have his words recorded shortly after noon for later broadcast over *The Back to God Hour,* the original radio broadcast of the Christian Reformed Church.

Combined, Nederhood and Feddes were the main English-language voices of radio and TV for the electronic media outreach throughout the early and mid 1990s. Working out of a modest brick complex outside Chicago, they maintained a decidedly low profile as they tried to bring Christ-like values to a complex, sometimes indifferent society. Nederhood retired in late 1995.

Once he had delivered his TV message against a backdrop that looked like a pastor's study, Joel Nederhood slipped into a bathroom to remove the makeup from his face. He would later have his face powdered again for a TV interview with an evangelist from the Philippines.

Returning to his office overlooking a road leading into the sedate campus of Trinity Christian College, Nederhood took in a deep breath of air. He rubbed the side of his face as he tried in a short interview to put into perspective thirty years of preaching for his church.

"Back in the 1960s, when I first came, we used to speak against the movement of liberalism in American Christianity," said Nederhood, who even after official retirement from his TV pulpit planned to stay for a time as host and main minister on the *Faith 20* program.

But liberal Christianity, with its emphasis on the rights of women and gays and minorities and its less literal reading of Scripture, took a back seat in the 1980s and 1990s to a different foe, he said. "These days we speak against a more general backdrop of the broad rejection of Christian doctrine in the West," he commented.

Day after day, week after week, Nederhood stepped before the cameras in the studio and dug into the Bible for quotations and interpretations that, he hoped, would stir viewers out of their spiritual lethargy. "Relativism is the reigning orthodoxy these days," he said. A lack of passion for anything spiritual and a culture-wide belief system that has no firm moral base were topics he addressed often in his sermons.

Paradoxically, he blamed the very medium on which he preached for the decline in values and widespread indifference to God. "TV is more dangerous and transforming than people think," he said. "It is terrible what I've seen it do. The images you see can be so easily manipulated to make you think, feel, and respond in a certain way."

The bulk of TV, religious programming included, falls into this category. By playing to the audience with colorful settings, emotional situations, and pitches for audience sympathy, TV has become a monster that gobbles people's minds and even steals their hearts, he said.

Believing as he does in the essentially insidious nature of TV, Nederhood has been careful how he portrays the gospel before *Faith 20* viewers. Unlike many other media ministries, the show he hosted never made a pitch for money. The bulk of the program itself took place in a simple, relatively unadorned setting. There were no glitzy outtakes, no fast switches from camera to camera and scene to scene.

"We are niche broadcasters," he said. "There is no way we can fit into the TV scene broadly. We don't do flamboyant, audience-manipulative things."

In fact, *Faith 20,* is mainly a radio show on TV. The Word, and words, have remained more important than visual images, said Nederhood, who started out as the preacher on *The Back to God Hour* radio program.

Though the CRC's TV effort may change as the twentieth century comes to a close, the radio outreach is likely to keep its same format, Nederhood said.

On this sunny spring day in Palos Heights, Illinois, Reverend David Feddes had a very personal, even painful sermon to deliver over the radio. Sitting in front of the microphones in the padded recording booth, the Calvin Theological Seminary graduate awaited his cue to go on.

"Grandma was over ninety years old, and she still lived in her own house," he said as the tape started to roll. "She had some help with yard work, but other than that, Grandma handled things herself."

Although the sermon started out with rosy reminiscences about his grandmother, it quickly moved to darker memories. Feddes recalled how his own twin girls had to be attached soon after birth to machines to help them breathe. One of his children was kept alive and thrived. The other got sicker and died.

The message he wrestled from the experience is that life is sacred and cannot be terminated on human whim. "God is in charge, and he created each of us in his image," Feddes preached. "Decisions about life support are important, but we need to keep this all in perspective," Feddes said at the end of this sermon on euthanasia. "The most important part of preparing for death is that you be ready and eager to meet the Lord."

The show he taped this afternoon would be shipped out and heard within the next few weeks over nearly three hundred stations around the world. Copies of his sermon — "Life Support" — would be printed and mailed to more than thirty thousand people.

Still the flagship program of the CRC's radio missionary work, *The Back to God Hour* has not changed much in more than fifty years. There is music, a sermon, more music, and it's over.

Growing up in a Montana home where there was no TV, Feddes thought early of becoming a minister. "As a little boy, I often preached to my sister and her dolls, and afterward we would eat bread and drink Kool-Aid together," he recounted in *Soundings,* a newsletter sent to supporters of the ministry.

But his preaching aspirations diminished at Calvin College, where he excelled in mathematics and computer technology. He won a state math competition and started to envision a career using those skills.

The problem was, he said, that he continued to experience a deeper longing to serve as a minister. He fought it. After all, speech class was one of his least-loved courses in college. "It was a hard decision, but I eventually yielded to what God wanted me to do," he said in an interview. "I remember I wept when I realized I would have to switch my basic direction in college."

With a mind for math, he excelled in philosophy and theological investigation at Calvin Theological Seminary. He married his wife, Wendy, in 1986, and he served a congregation in Strathroy, Ontario, before becoming a broadcast minister.

Although back on the cattle farm he did daydream about becoming a preacher, he never imagined preaching over the radio. "Coming to *The Back to God Hour* was not something I actively pursued," he said.

But by 1990 Feddes was hired by *The Back to God Hour,* and in 1992 he replaced Nederhood as English-language radio minister.

In the tradition of his predecessors, Feddes views the electronic ministry with some skepticism. He is comfortable sitting before the microphone and, unseen, delivering messages of salvation. He sees himself as preaching especially to those who say they believe in God and yet are not committed to their faith.

After Nederhood's retirement at the end of 1995, he planned to continue the simple give-it-to-them-straight approach.

"Religious broadcasting is important, whether you like it or not," he said. "Many people at least pay attention to it, and many others are deeply affected by it."

FIGURE 19 The fiftieth anniversary of *The Back to God Hour;* left to right, Henry Bruinooge, Aaron Kayayan, Juan Boonstra, Joel Nederhood, and Bassam Madany.

grams of preaching. The result was a TV series on "Law and Love," in which Peter Eldersveld, situated on a set designed to resemble a pastor's study, went before the camera to explicate and preach on the Ten Commandments. The program was run on 180 stations around the country and may have been viewed by as many as three million people. The viewer response was sufficiently encouraging that by 1956 another series, this time on the Lord's Prayer, was produced, though with less encouraging results. Competition for television air time was by then fierce, resulting in fewer programmings, and, hence, fewer responses, for this second television venture.

Rather than try to compete in the costly world of television, *The Back to God Hour* instead began focusing its innovative efforts on the field of foreign and foreign-language broadcasts. By 1957 *The Back to God Hour* was being broadcast around the globe through various short-wave hookups. The program was now being heard throughout Europe, in the British West Indies, the Philippines, Liberia, Panama, and — via powerful station HCJB in Ecuador — throughout the Pacific. In fact, it was the generosity of an anonymous donor which made possible some of these foreign hookups, including especially the 30,000-watt signal of HCJB (Heralding Christ Jesus' Blessings).

But these were still English-language broadcasts in foreign lands. *The Back to God Hour* had yet to enter the field of international broadcasting with foreign-language programs produced solely for that purpose. But that changed in the late 1950s with the arrival of Reverend Bassam Madany. A native of Syria and an ordained minister in the Reformed

Presbyterian denomination, Madany was living in Canada when he first heard the broadcast of a Peter Eldersveld sermon. Having been frustrated in recent attempts to preach in Middle Eastern countries due to hostility and persecution, Madany began to see in radio a way to cross closed borders and enter hostile countries with the gospel message after all.

After joining the Christian Reformed Church and receiving additional training at Calvin Seminary, Madany was approached by a radio station in Liberia to preach to the Arab world in Arabic. But before accepting the appointment, Madany approached Eldersveld and The Back to God Hour Committee, setting into motion a sequence of events which, by the summer of 1958, resulted in Madany's becoming the denomination's first foreign-language radio minister. Hosting a program entitled *Saatu'l Islah (The Hour of Reformation)* Madany blanketed the Middle East with the Reformed message of faith and hope in Christ.

Madany's pioneering effort would become the first of many such foreign-language broadcasts. Beginning in 1961

FIGURE 21 Bassam Madany.

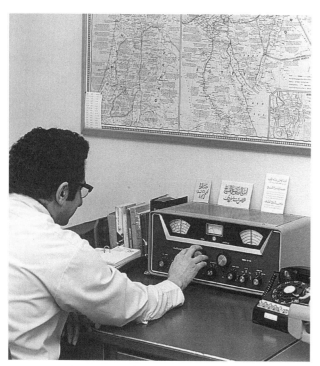

FIGURE 20 Bassam Madany at the short-wave radio.

Argentina-born Juan Boonstra began assisting in Spanish translations of *Back to God Hour* broadcasts, becoming in 1965 the denomination's Spanish radio minister. Given the widespread use of Spanish throughout Mexico and Central and South America, the potential impact of a Spanish radio ministry was readily apparent. In the coming years Boonstra's broadcasts would become a source of assistance to missionaries in the field as well as the first step in the opening of new mission fields. When the Mexican government lifted its ban on foreign-language broadcasts in 1966, Boonstra's program was the first to take to the Mexican airwaves.

By 1979, *The Back to God Hour*'s fortieth-anniversary year, the success of Boonstra's efforts was demonstrated by Reforma '79, a radio and television blitz centered in Tegucigalpa, Honduras. When people were invited to attend a series of radio rallies in a local baseball stadium, the response was overwhelming. People came from all over Honduras to fill the ten thousand seats for three separate meetings at which Boonstra preached a message of renewal through Christ. Interestingly, this entire effort, like the first HCJB broadcast in the 1950s, was financed by a single North American contributor who wished to see *The Back to God Hour*'s message take hold in Latin America.

Foreign-language broadcasts soon became a standard part of *The Back to God Hour*'s larger operation. These efforts received a major boost in 1969, when *The Back to God Hour* was given the opportunity to broadcast over Christian network Trans World Radio's newest broadcast facility on the Caribbean island of Bonaire. Located just fifty miles north of the Venezuelan coast, Bonaire is a twenty-four-mile-long island whose license-plate slogan "Divers' Paradise" highlights the island's one claim to fame: exceedingly pristine coral reefs. Yet this little island's TWR towers, which had begun operating in 1965, packed a wallop — their multiple five-hundred-foot transmitters would blanket the entire Western Hemisphere with a 260,000-watt short-wave signal, which could be picked up as far away as western Europe and even portions of the Far East. [12]

While it was clear that such an offer needed to be accepted, the costs involved were considerable. To meet such costs, a new association — RACOM Associates — was formed with the sole purpose of raising funds to finance projects like the TWR-Bonaire hookup. Through the efforts of RACOM members (many of whom were savvy businessmen), the needed funds were raised for *The Back to God Hour* to be hooked into one of the world's largest and most powerful Christian broadcast networks. Ironically, the island of Bonaire is a former colony of the Netherlands, and its official language remains Dutch. But by hooking up with this island's broadcast facilities, the Christian Reformed Church was able to broadcast its message to millions of people far beyond the Dutch ethnic boundaries which had once defined the denomination.

By the late 1950s televison threatened to eclipse the prominent place which radio had formerly occupied in the United

FIGURE 22 Juan Boonstra.

FIGURE 23 Juan Boonstra speaking at Reforma '79.

FIGURE 24 Extending Peter Eldersveld congratulations on his twenty-fifth year in the ministry are Bassam Madany, James De Jonge, Joel Nederhood, and Lambert Beré, president of the denominational radio committee.

States. Yet it was at this very time that *The Back to God Hour*'s foreign and foreign-language broadcasts began beaming their radio programs to other countries where televison had not yet made an impact. Thus, despite some decrease in radio listening at home, the wise moves made in the direction of foreign-language broadcasts ensured that the denomination's radio ministry would not decline but actually increase.

End of an Era

Without question, Peter Eldersveld was the most famous Christian Reformed minister of his day — perhaps the most well-known Christian Reformed pastor ever. By 1965 his voice, and twice during the mid 1950s even his televised image, had been entering people's homes regularly for nearly twenty years. Even listeners who had never met him felt that they

FIGURE 25 Joel Nederhood discussing program ideas with Peter Eldersveld.

knew him personally. But many actually had met Eldersveld as he traveled and preached around the United States and Canada with great frequency. (On the cover page of his sermons, many of which are now in the Calvin College archives, Eldersveld carefully listed all the places in which he had preached a particular sermon. The list on many of his sermons includes up to thirty different congregations.)

When, at the age of 54, Eldersveld died suddenly of a heart attack on October 14, 1965, the news spread quickly as a wave of shock and grief washed over the entire denomination.

Many expressed their deep sorrow even as others questioned why God would allow the career of so key a figure to end so prematurely. Eldersveld's heart difficulties had actually begun when he was in his mid forties. His first heart attack, in 1955, had taken him off the air for four months, and that was followed by another episode in the summer of 1958. But when he actually succumbed to a third attack, the denomination and the entire *Back to God Hour* radio audience mourned the loss of a friend.

Newspaper articles and obituaries hailed Eldersveld as "an

internationally known" speaker who oversaw and helped make possible the remarkable growth of *The Back to God Hour* from 1946 until his death. Indeed, when Eldersveld was selected as the denomination's first radio minister, the program was being heard on twenty-two North American radio stations for an annual budget of $87,000. By the time of his death the program was being broadcast each week on over four hundred stations in seventy-five countries on an annual budget of over half a million dollars. Replacing Peter Eldersveld would not be easy.

Meeting in emergency session two days after Eldersveld's death, The Back to God Hour Committee immediately took up the question of a replacement for Eldersveld to ensure that the program Eldersveld had dedicated his life to build would suffer no interruption. Had Eldersveld died in the late 1950s, the task of finding a successor would likely have been exceedingly difficult and would have consumed many months. But in 1960 *The Back to God Hour* had welcomed to its staff Dr. Joel Nederhood as associate radio minister. Since that time Nederhood had already established himself as a very thoughtful, very competent radio minister who assisted Eldersveld in almost every area of production and had become a regular substitute speaker for the program.

It was, therefore, clear to the board that in God's providence a successor to Eldersveld was already in its midst. Nederhood was appointed as the denomination's second English-speaking radio minister, a position he would hold for the next thirty years, until his retirement in 1995.

Nederhood also delivered the sermon at his mentor's funeral. He praised his friend's utter love for the church of Christ, his indefatigable devotion to the pure gospel, his courage in calling all people to faith in Christ, and his vision for the possibilities of communicating that gospel by the gift of radio technology.

But, despite Eldersveld's stunning achievements and praise-worthy legacy of gospel communication, Nederhood reminded the congregation on that October afternoon, their friend was not saved because of those accomplishments but only because of

the grace of God in Christ. Sounding again Eldersveld's life-long theme of the cross of Christ, Nederhood said,

[W]e remember with joy this afternoon that he was among those who stood astonished at the cross of Calvary, who was impressed with the fact of Christ's sacrifice above all other facts. He trusted in him, and thus we know that he is now with our blessed Lord because Christ has cleansed him from all his sin. [13]

To this gospel message of grace through the cross Eldersveld surely would have added his own "Amen."

Worlds Beyond

Listeners who tuned in to *The Back to God Hour* following Eldersveld's death were struck by the similarity between Eldersveld's voice and that of the new radio minister, Joel Nederhood. Indeed, far from intentionally imitating his mentor and friend, Nederhood possessed very naturally an excellent radio voice and presence. More important, however, he also shared Eldersveld's vision for radio communication and the kind of message which should be presented, partly, no doubt, owing to the fact that Eldersveld, knowing the frailty of his own health, had been grooming and preparing Nederhood to take over his beloved broadcast in the event he died or was forced to retire.

That grooming paid off as Nederhood took over *The Back to God Hour's* microphone with sincere conviction, a stalwart Reformed message, and the same kind of warm, personal

> "*He is now with our blessed Lord because Christ has cleansed him from all his sin.*"
>
> — Reverend Joel Nederhood

FIGURE 26 Nederhood preparing a sermon.

FIGURE 27 The International Communications Center

presence through which Eldersveld had made the program so successful for so long. But Nederhood's skills and gifts went beyond Eldersveld's grooming. A 1957 graduate of Calvin Seminary, Nederhood had previously served for two years in the Army, including a tour of duty to the Far East. Following his seminary graduation, Nederhood was honored with a Fulbright scholarship for graduate study at the Free University in Amsterdam, where he earned a Ph.D. in the study of missions in 1959.

By 1960 Nederhood had returned to the United States to enter the ministry for which he had been trained. After a brief stint as guest pastor of a mission church in Florida, Nederhood received a call from The Back to God Hour Committee to become the denomination's first associate radio minister.

In the years that followed, Nederhood frequently spoke on *The Back to God Hour* as guest speaker. Behind the scenes he also worked closely with Eldersveld on every

aspect of the broadcast ministry so that, by the time he took over as director of ministries in 1965, Nederhood was well poised not only to continue the vital work of *The Back to God Hour* but also to oversee a period of rapid growth and substantial expansion.

During his first fifteen years on the job Nederhood helped the broadcast to open several more foreign ministries through the efforts of Bassam Madany and Juan Boonstra. He also oversaw the development of Project Bonaire, the formation of RACOM Associates, and the hiring of a number of new foreign-language radio ministers to Japan, Indonesia, France, and China.

On May 29, 1976, *The Back to God Hour* also dedicated its new International Communications Center in Palos Heights, Illinois. Since its inception, *The Back to God Hour* had made do in buildings converted into makeshift broadcast facilities. But the new multimillion-dollar facility had been specifically designed for broadcasting and recording and so was free of the problems which had been experienced in previous facilities. More important, the Communications Center would make possible a serious journey into an area which had been only briefly and tentatively explored in the 1950s: the world of television.

A key component of the new building was a three-camera color-TV production and editing studio. Recognizing the dominant role of television in American and Canadian cultures and, like those pushing for radio ministry in the 1930s, recognizing that others were already using television to promote their religious viewpoints, many began to prod *The Back to God Hour* toward producing an ongoing televised version of the program.

As had been the case with radio networks of the 1930s, so also TV network programming was enormously and prohibitively costly.

FIGURE 28 Bassam Madany, Joel Nederhood, and Juan Boonstra.

Purchasing large-scale time slots was impossible. Therefore, like the transcribed recordings for radio in the early 1940s, so also *The Back to God Hour*'s television efforts would be recorded onto video cassettes and distributed to independent and local stations around the United States and Canada. Though the costs would still be comparatively high, they would be much more affordable than any larger-scale efforts.

A few short television programs were produced by the denomination in English and Spanish in the early 1970s, but CRC-TV became a reality only after Synod 1976 approved a plan to go forward with the production of a regular TV series. Aided by communications specialist Jerry Vreeman, Nederhood and *The Back to God Hour* staff entered the highly competitive world of television in 1977 with a program entitled *Faith 20.* The goal of this program was articulated by Nederhood:

> *Each CRC-TV presentation is to present the Lord Jesus Christ, using relevant elements of creation with proper respect to the testimony of both the Old and the New Testaments, as the person through whom the blessings of God's covenant can become a reality in the lives of all those who are united with Him by faith, that is, by acknowledging their own sin, confessing the atoning significance of Christ's sacrifice, and turning to Him in repentance and trust.* [14]

The resulting *Faith 20* program, set in a pastor's study like Eldersveld's two series in the 1950s, was very much the television version of the long-standing radio program. Using the same low-key, conversational, yet poignantly forceful style which Eldersveld and he had always used on radio, Nederhood effectively presented the message of Christ to the TV audience. *The Back to God Hour* staff recognized the need for high-quality professional productions if it was to be taken seriously in the competitive world of television, but what it would not do in the name of competition was imitate the glitzy, high-powered, entertainment-oriented productions of many other televangelists then on the air.

Indeed, *Faith 20* took to the airwaves just as televangelism was reaching its zenith and just before it saw its darkest years, during the 1980s. Writing in 1979, Ben Armstrong enthusiastically predicted that the 1980s would see bigger and better things for broadcasters like Oral Roberts, Jimmy Swaggart, Jim Bakker, Jerry Falwell, and Pat Robertson. He scorned the idea that any of them were in it just for the money even as he laughed off as ludicrous the suggestion that some of these televangelists might actually be setting their sights on political goals like becoming President of the United States. [15]

By the end of the 1980s the picture would be very different: several televangelists had grabbed for political power (including the power of the Presidency), and several formerly successful religious broadcasts had been reduced to ashes in the wake of sexual and financial scandals — scandals which angered and disillusioned many viewers.

Evaluating the world of televangelism in 1991, Quentin Schultze highlighted the features of television which made such missteps altogether too likely if not inevitable. Television, Schultze points out, is an audience-driven medium to which people turn to be entertained. For a program to be successful on television, it needs to give viewers what they want (irrespective of what they might need) and must do so in the most engaging way possible. The result is an emphasis on drama and dramatics, on powerful personalities around whom the TV empire can be built, and on the medium of television itself and all the wondrous, heart-tugging, eye-popping spectacles it makes possible. Finally, of course, all of this costs money — a lot of it — so many televangelists need to beg for funds, often making such pleas the linchpin of their broadcasts. [16]

The combined force of these currents and eddies proved disastrous for a number of televangelists. Even those programs which did not fall into public scandal often presented a gospel which, in the opinion of many commentators, represented something more like an American idealism than like

FIGURE 29 Joel Nederhood and Jerry Vreeman on the CRC-TV set.

a biblical world and life view. In short, when *Faith 20* took to the airwaves, it was entering a field with at least as much potential for ill as for good.

But under Nederhood's leadership, *Faith 20* resisted many of the trends and pressures which had corrupted other religious programs. Nederhood himself criticized the "crassly commercial and abrasively secular" ways by which they solicited money as well as the personality cults which rose up around TV preachers. He also decried the fact that many of these powerful TV preachers were not properly accountable to ruling bodies such as synods or councils or boards. [17]

By contrast, *Faith 20*, like the radio component of the ministry, remained very much a ministry of the whole Christian Reformed denomination. The program never solicited money on the air, relying instead primarily on church offerings to meet *The Back to God Hour*'s overall budget of nearly $10 million. Nederhood also made clear his desire to connect his viewers with local churches in their own neighborhoods. Call-in lines as well as other follow-up efforts over the years worked hard to make sure that *Faith 20* would never become a substitute for established congregations but rather a help to them.

Aware of the emotional manipulation to which TV is liable, Nederhood resisted on-air flamboyance, tear-jerking stories, and showmanship in favor of straightforward Bible lessons, practical applications of the Christian faith to a complex world, and occasional interviews with guests. Nederhood even avoided praying on the air, stating that "a prayer on television is not a prayer." [18]

Like his predecessor, Nederhood earned a wide respect and recognition for his excellence in communication and thoughtfulness of content. In 1977 he was the recipient of the National Religious Broadcasters Association Award of Merit, presented to him at a banquet in Washington, D.C. In 1987, as the Soviet Union began to open up under Mikhail Gorbachev's program of *glasnost* and *perestroika,* Nederhood was invited to conduct a preaching tour through portions of the Soviet Union, where he discovered a number of Soviet citizens who knew of *The Back to God Hour* through its Trans World Radio broadcasts.

The Next Generation

For the first fifty years of its existence, *The Back to God Hour* ministries had a remarkable continuity of staff, but by the mid 1990s the last formal connections to Peter Eldersveld's generation began to fade as figures like Juan Boonstra,

Bassam Madany, and finally Joel Nederhood entered retirement. By 1992 Reverend David Feddes, a 1987 Calvin Theological Seminary graduate who had come to *The Back to God Hour* in 1990, had taken over the weekly radio program. Meanwhile, Nederhood continued to host *Faith 20,* airing weekly over hundreds of local and cable stations. *The Back to God Hour* ministries also now print over 400,000

TODAY™
The Family Altar   March-April 1996

copies of the daily devotional *Today* (formerly called *The Family Altar*) and estimates that as many as one million people are touched by this devotional outreach each month.

Now under the leadership of the new director of ministries, Reverend Calvin Bremer, the staff at the International Communications Center processes over seventy thousand pieces of correspondence annually, including responses from the overseas ministries. Following the collapse of the Soviet Union, *The Back to God Hour* expanded to include Russia in its overseas broadcasts with the program *Vozvranshcheniye k Bogu — "Back to God."*

Through all of the history-shattering changes which have taken place since 1939, *The Back to God Hour* radio and television ministries have endured and, indeed, have prospered. Though radio does not occupy the prominent place it did in the era of the Waltons, *The Back to God Hour* program continues to minister to people around the world. Though televangelism may never be what it was in the early 1980s, *Faith 20* is as steady and reliable in its ministry to viewers as its message is faithful to Scripture.

As a new generation of radio and television preachers prepares to take over *The Back to God Hour* ministries, it remains to be seen just what shape the programs will take in the coming years. But if the past is any predictor of the future, then it appears quite likely that these new leaders will continue — like Peter Eldersveld, Bassam Madany, Juan Boonstra, and Joel Nederhood — to be the answer to Henry Schultze's earnest prayer on that December afternoon in 1939, a prayer that the broadcast efforts of the Christian Reformed Church might "move [people] everywhere to a renewed consciousness of the great glory of our God."

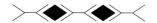

Chapter Four

Going to School

Campus Ministry

"'Love the Lord your God with all your heart and with all your soul
and with all your mind.'"

Matthew 22:37

In *The Soul of the American University* George Marsden traces the nearly Copernican revolution which American universities have undergone in the last two hundred years. [1] Since their beginnings as officially Christian institutions of learning, American universities have shifted to the point that now the mere thought of striving for a distinctly Christian public education would strike most as patently absurd.

Yet the soft-pedaling of Christianity in the circles of higher learning is actually a very recent phenomenon. Marsden's survey of nineteenth-century history demonstrates that, for most people of that era, there was no question about *whether* schools like Harvard, Yale, or Princeton would be Christian — it was simply assumed. The only debatable issue was how to be Christian institutions without also being sectarian (that is, unduly influenced by any one denomination).

Indeed, Marsden reminds readers that as recently as 1951 William F. Buckley, Jr., assailed Yale University for being insufficiently Christian. Far from laughing off such a charge as irrelevant, however, the university was so stung that it commissioned a blue-ribbon panel to study the issue. The panel's final report defended Yale's integration of faith and learning, even going so far as to say with pride that "religious life at Yale is deeper and richer than it has been in many years." [2]

But, as Marsden also notes, despite this comparatively recent report, active religion in the halls of academe has been in slow retreat since at least the mid nineteenth century. As confidence in the objective methods of science grew and as colleges became universities designed to train people for professional careers ranging far beyond the institutional church, religion was more and more marginalized. Indeed, theology became the bailiwick of separate seminaries and not, as had previously been the case, of the whole college or university.

Very early on, the Dutch Reformed in America also had an intense interest in a relationship between Christianity and education. But rather than entering the wider public fray over whether or how Yale, Princeton, or the University of Michigan was Christian, Dutch Calvinists instead began establishing their own distinctly Christian, distinctly Reformed, distinctly Dutch schools. Fueled by Dutch patterns and nourished by the teachings of the Dutch theolo-

gian Abraham Kuyper, the members of the Christian Reformed Church decided from the beginning that nothing less than thoroughly Christian and Reformed schools would suit the educational needs of their children.

Even before the 1857 schism which led to the Christian Reformed Church, the Dutch Reformed had transplanted to America the Netherlandic pattern of establishing separate church schools. The theologian Abraham Kuyper mightily influenced Reformed believers by claiming that there ought to be no division between the sacred and the secular — every square inch of the planet is of proper Christian concern. Ironically, however, although Kuyper called for no sacred/secular divisions, he did call for the founding of separate Christian organizations through which to learn about and then also influence the world outside the institutional church.

The members of the fledgling Christian Reformed Church took this message to heart. It took many decades before the CRC began active mission work, but such was not the case with active Christian-school planting. Already by 1861 many churches were running their own Christian schools in the Dutch language, and all other congregations were encouraged to do likewise.

In 1876 the denomination formally established its Theological School in Grand Rapids, Michigan, branching out from this in 1898 to form the John Calvin Junior College (a reversal of the larger American trend in which colleges had given birth to seminaries). By 1900 the CRC had set up seventeen Christian schools, had graduated ninety-four men from its Theological School, and could boast an enrollment of seventy-two at its newly formed college. [3]

During the first sixty years of its existence, the Christian Reformed Church kept a fair amount of daylight between itself and the United States (indeed, articles in the denominational weekly *The Banner* would refer to the United States as "the country of our adop-

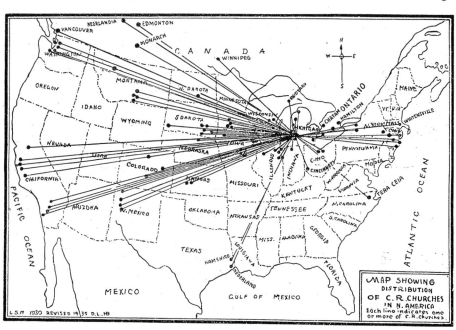

FIGURE 1 Abraham Kuyper.

tion" until well into the 1940s). While not all of its children attended distinctly Dutch Christian schools, over half of them did. Also, the majority of congregations still worshiped exclusively in Dutch, and many regarded early twentieth-century efforts to introduce worship in English as a subversive attempt to erode the Reformed heritage by blending in too conveniently with the larger nation.

Slowly, however, a process of Americanization began to take hold. As James Bratt notes, many of the Dutch near the turn of the century were able to agree with those who believed America was a Christian nation. Compared to the European countries with which the Dutch were the most familiar, America appeared to be comparatively free of the Enlightenment thought which had turned Continental Christianity in a more liberal direction. [4]

Still, the overall attitude of Dutch Reformed immigrants toward America remained ambivalent at best. In general the CRC felt content and secure within the separate religious fortress it had constructed for itself, staying away from the materialism and immorality which were gripping some segments of the country. But World War I and II forced the Dutch out of their isolation as their young men were drafted and their own patriotism was cast into doubt by their fellow Americans.

Indeed, the anti-German sentiment which raced through

FIGURE 2 Map showing distribution of Christian Reformed churches in North America in 1935. Each line indicates one or more churches.

the United States during World War I spilled over to affect the CRC as some Americans confused the words *Dutch* and *Deutsch* ("German"). This linguistic misfortune, combined with the facts that the Dutch maintained separate schools and that some Christian Reformed ministers refused to allow the American flag to be placed in the sanctuary, fueled suspicions that Dutch Christians were pro-German. Thus many of the Dutch found themselves harassed in one way or another, and, in one extreme incident, an Iowa Christian Reformed church and Christian school were burned to the ground by patriotic American zealots. [5]

As it was forced into the mainstream, the Christian Reformed Church began coming out of its isolation. Perhaps in an effort to snuff the idea that the Christian Reformed Dutch were anti-American and pro-German, the 1918 Christian Reformed Synod sent a telegram of support to President Woodrow Wilson and even joined the national (and liberal) Federal Council of Churches in order to be able to conduct ministry in the Army camps which had become home to many Christian Reformed young men. Although the 1920s and 1930s would see a return to the fortress mentality, the seeds of American acculturation had been planted. By the end of World War II the CRC was well poised to participate in the civil religion which so characterized 1950s America.

Among the fruits of this at first enforced contact with the broader society was the increasing number of young men who began choosing secular universities for their college or postgraduate educations. By the late 1930s it could no longer be assumed that Christian Reformed young people would all attend Calvin College in Grand Rapids. Indeed, so many of them were enrolling in the University of Michigan in

FIGURE 3 Leonard Verduin.

Ann Arbor that a fraternity for Reformed and Christian Reformed students was formed (Phi Alpha Kappa, or the Dutch House, as it was affectionately known). At the request of the students themselves, Reformed religious services began to be held on campus.

It was precisely this situation in Ann Arbor which began the denomination's ministry on university campuses, though denomination-wide sponsorship of campus pastors would wait until the late 1960s. Until then the story is restricted to a local effort focused on the University of Michigan.

The Ann Arbor Story

According to Reverend Leonard Verduin, the denomination's first campus chaplain, "From its inception the campus chapel was something of a novelty in the framework of the Christian Reformed Church. Perhaps it would be right to say that from the beginning it was something of an experiment." [6] Indeed, although not officially under the auspices

FIGURE 4 George Goris.

of the denomination's mission committee, the establishing of the Ann Arbor Student Evangelical Chapel in 1940 represented an innovation in Christian Reformed outreach.

Four years earlier the 1936 Synod had reorganized the denomination's mission program, formally establishing a General Home Missions Committee, whose revised mission order included evangelistic outreach to "the unchurched of America" (not just to the *Dutch* unchurched or to unique groups like the Jews or the Indians as had previously been the case, but to ordinary Americans of all backgrounds). Shortly after this time the denomination saw increased expansion of its urban ministries as well as the 1939 founding of *The Back to God Hour* radio program, both of which targeted a wider audience.

The campus ministry in Ann Arbor, though not under the larger denominational umbrella, may also have resulted at least in small measure from this broader outlook. But actually the roots of the new ministry had taken hold already in the 1920s as an increased number of Christian Reformed students began attending the University of Michigan.

The earliest indication of a need for campus ministry came from the students themselves, who, not finding local churches to their liking, began occasionally to hold their own lay-led services in the Arboretum, located just off the Ann Arbor campus. Soon they began to petition Michigan Christian Reformed churches to provide them with ordained clergy to lead these services. Their request in turn led to the formation of a committee whose task it was to oversee periodic worship services in Ann Arbor. Eventually LaGrave Avenue CRC and Classis Grand Rapids South took charge of

A Ministry to the Heart and Soul

Their heads bent into the brisk winter wind, Kevin Thompson and Randy Dik marched along the snowy sidewalk on the campus of the University of Michigan in Ann Arbor. Members of the Christian Reformed Church Campus Chapel at the U of M, the two were on the way on this January night to learn more about what was to them a foreign religious tradition. Along with a handful of other CRC students, they had an early evening meeting with some Roman Catholics.

"This is a test run," said Dik, a 22-year-old public-health student from Kalamazoo, Michigan. "We've brought along our grappling hooks and are storming the ramparts of the papacy."

Actually they were participating in a Wednesday Evening Roundtable program whose focus was on other traditions and other faiths, one of many similar educational projects launched at the Ann Arbor Campus Chapel. The trip to the nearby Catholic chapel was only one of several the students would take that winter semester.

"I guess we're going there because we want to know more what is going on religiously on this campus," said Thompson, a 22-year-old engineering student from Monroe, Michigan.

The Campus Chapel is the oldest campus ministry of the CRC. Surrounded by the large secular university, it is a place that helps people more powerfully live out their faith.

"We are here to help enhance the religious life of the people who come to our church," said Lisa De Boer, a graduate student in art history and the chapel's student-ministry coordinator, as the group approached St. Mary's Chapel, the center for Catholic activities on campus.

Once they'd reached their destination, the Campus Chapel members situated themselves in chairs and couches in the meeting room at St. Mary's. Here to learn more about the Roman Catholic Church and to explain things about their own denomination, the students at first seemed nervous. But soon the discussion became lively.

"I've always wanted to know," said one of the Catholic

FIGURE 5 Donald Postema.

students. "What is a Calvinist? My ignorance is very huge when it comes to other Christian religions per se."

After gazing at her students, De Boer fielded that one. "Our church is a very small splinter of other large Protestant churches," she said. "John Calvin is one of the founders."

Audry Brosnan, the Catholic chaplain, then jumped into the discussion. "What's this concept of total depravity? We always hear that Calvinists believe that. What is it?"

Andy Kaufmann, a 28-year-old biology graduate student from Ravenna, Illinois, explained that it's a view that human beings are sinful by nature. "I guess we believe that everyone is really, really bad and you can't do anything to save yourself."

His answer drew a few laughs, from both sides of the denominational divide.

Established in 1940, the Campus Chapel is not a CRC church. It is, according to campus pastor Donald Postema, a ministry that exists on the far edges of the larger church and of the university.

The visit with the Catholics, he said, is an example of the chapel's approach. Always, from its beginnings, this chapel has challenged its members to reflect on their faith and how it fits within the larger framework of the U of M campus and the world beyond.

"Our redemptive task is to reach out to the university," said Postema, a barrel-chest, bearded man with an infectious smile and clear, probing eyes.

Before he sent members of his chapel out to interact with the Catholics, Postema said he sees his task as training young people to be church members. But beyond that, he said, is the need to help students see how their religious beliefs can affect and even shape the work they do in the classroom.

"We are here to support the university in its search for truth and to criticize it when we see that it is speaking falsely," said Postema, who came to the Campus Chapel in 1963, shortly after graduating from Calvin Theological Seminary

this task, arranging for speakers and soliciting funds from other congregations.

By 1939, however, the task and the need had become large enough to warrant the students' request for a full-time pastor to minister on the campus and to lead their now weekly services. Many of the students expressed a desire for consistent leadership and preaching to help them find their way as Christians through the maze of competing philosophies, world views, and religions which they inevitably encountered on an international campus of 13,000 students.

In order to test the waters, the LaGrave committee appointed Reverend Dr. George Goris of Fuller Avenue CRC in Grand Rapids to spend three months living and laboring among the students in Ann Arbor. After his term Goris reported to the LaGrave committee and to several Michigan classes that a vital ministry was nascent on the U of M campus — one which would be enthusiastically embraced by the Reformed students living and studying there. Although he had been in Ann Arbor only briefly, Goris's work set the tone for what would follow as he poured his energies into leading the Sunday worship services, establishing a counseling service for students, creating social and fellowship programs, and calling on people in the hospital.

Goris reported that each of these areas contained enormous potential for growth and that, again, the students themselves were the ones requesting just such programs and ministries. Reverend Goris was followed by two other ministers, each of whom likewise performed a three-month interim ministry: Reverend E.J. Tanis and Reverend J.M. Vande Kieft, both of whom echoed Goris's enthusiasm for the potential on-campus ministry in Ann Arbor.

Classis Grand Rapids South passed a motion on January 10, 1940, to form a campus ministry. By March other Michigan classes concurred with this decision, agreeing also to call a full-time ordained person to serve as the denomination's first campus pastor. After two unsuccessful efforts with other candidates, the committee extended a call to Reverend Leonard Verduin, who, following a one-month exploratory visit in late 1940, accepted the call in early 1941.

Verduin, a 1929 Calvin Seminary graduate who had since

and the Free University in Amsterdam. There is a direct ministry here to students, faculty, and Ann Arbor residents who attend services on Sunday. There is also an outreach to the university itself.

In October 1994, for example, the Campus Chapel helped sponsor "The Role of Religion and Ethics in Transforming the University," a conference "to explore the place of religion, spirituality, and ethical and moral values in the life and mission of the university."

"In the university, you achieve and produce, and then you are somebody," said Postema. "We say to the university that you are someone before God before you ever get that degree."

In even more practical terms, the outreach to the university over the years has entailed Campus Chapel involvement in protests on matters of social justice. For example, Campus Chapel goers were active in criticizing the U of M's investments in South Africa under apartheid. Postema himself has taken to the streets to criticize racism and protest the war in Vietnam. The church council has written various overtures to the CRC synod, among them calls for the ordination of women.

"I believe campus ministry ought to be Word and sacrament, along with programs, Bible studies, and protests," said Postema.

Postema has been transformed by his time at the Campus Chapel. In viewing the deep spiritual hunger experienced by students, he glimpsed the need for a wider, prayer-based renewal in the church itself. As a result of his experiences at the university, he saw that intellectual knowledge of God wasn't enough. So he started a retreat and writing ministry that has taken him around the world. With groups of all sizes he discusses the powerful desire humans have for reflection, meditation, and prayer. He speaks about ways of connecting with God on all levels. But it all came from his job as a campus minister.

"What I've tried to offer is a ministry to the mind and to the heart," he said. "I ask people to pay attention. I ask them to have the courage to search for truth wherever they can find it."

A search for pieces of that truth, he said, took some of his chapel members to the Catholic center on this blustery winter night. Gathered in a circle, Catholic and CRC students spoke about their religious beliefs for more than an hour. They talked about grace, sin, predestination, Reformation-era heresies, the role of women in the pulpit, and their differing views of the Eucharist.

When it was over and they were walking back to their church home, several students said they had received exactly what they had been looking for — a better understanding of what separates and also what unifies their denominations.

"It was good," said Kyla Ebels, a freshman from Grand Rapids. "They had a lot of wrong ideas about us, and we had the same about them."

FIGURE 6 Sketch for the chapel.

FIGURE 7 Building on the U of M campus.

lism which seeks refuge in obscurantism. I have been greatly encouraged by the fact that our young people here do not stumble at the preaching of the Cross. It must also be said, however, that the acids of modernity do have a tendency to corrode the ancestral faith of the student in this environment. Whoever works at Ann Arbor will have to reckon with that type of unbelief which keeps men from appropriating the Truth subjectively because it questions the objective validity of the Christian thesis. [7]

From the outset Verduin's campus ministry — to be supervised by a committee consisting of representatives from six area Christian Reformed classes in Michigan and Ohio — aimed primarily at nurturing the faith of Reformed young people in a rather liberal, world-wise atmosphere. An early motto of the Ann Arbor Campus Chapel was "The Old Faith in the Idiom of Today," clearly a statement of the desire to communicate historic Christianity in a way which would neither ignore nor fail to take account of the obviously modern milieu of a major university.

Toward that goal Verduin poured his energies into intelligent Sunday worship services and sermons. Within three months, attendance at the services, held at first in university-owned buildings like Lane Hall and the Women's League, had doubled, drawing not only the Reformed youth of the campus but a number of Christian young people from other Protestant traditions as well.

Verduin also secured an on-campus office in which to do individual counseling, offered catechism and Bible-instruction classes, set up social programs, and made numerous hospital calls every week. A 1942 article reported the rewards of this work:

The hospital work is unlimited ... the patients called on are from every denomination, and some patients have no church connections at all. But the work is especially appreciated by people who come from Reformed homes and suddenly find themselves in an entirely different environment. When they see one of their own ministers, they often weep for joy. An opportunity to teach a Bible class was also given to the minister and this too was an opportunity with far-reaching influence, for in this class was a Chinese student and a Russian minister present regularly. This Russian minister had belonged to a liberal group and had lost his courage to preach, because he felt that he had no message.

his graduation been pastoring a church in Corsica, South Dakota, was an intelligent, stalwartly Reformed, uncompromising advocate of the historic Christian faith — precisely the type of candidate most people felt was needed for ministry in so heady an academic environment. Even before accepting the call to Ann Arbor, Verduin's December 19, 1940, report to the Ann Arbor Committee revealed something of his character, of his approach to the modern world, and of his goals for the campus ministry he was contemplating:

The students respond quite readily to a message from the ever-living Word of God, something "by which a man can live" as one of their number put it. Speaking generally the students are quite nauseated by the milk and water thing that is called preaching in our days. Nor are they exactly satisfied with a frothy evange-

Through the work of the Bible class and the services, together with the influence of God's Spirit, he was brought back into the ministry with a real message. [8]

In fact, the services and other work were so well received and attended that in less than a year the Ann Arbor Committee began to solicit funds to build its own on-campus chapel. Despite the high enthusiasm for the new ministry, practical considerations — chiefly the economic constraints of World War II — delayed the actual building of the chapel until 1948, when the new facility at the corner of Forest and Washtenaw was dedicated.

Although the Ann Arbor Campus Chapel began as an attempt to minister to Christian Reformed young people — and although that continued to be the ministry's primary focus — Verduin and the classical Ann Arbor Chapel Committee early on sensed the potential to have a wider impact on the U of M academic community and, through that, on the broader society. In its initial 1942 request for funds, the Ann Arbor Committee pointed out that perhaps more than any other then-current ministry, the CRC's presence in Ann Arbor gave it a unique opportunity to "disseminate our precious Reformed heritage .... In no other single field can this be better accomplished than at a great university of some thirteen thousand students, most of whom will be leaders in some field of endeavor." [9]

Looking back over his twenty-year ministry in Ann Arbor, Verduin fondly recalls just such opportunities to meet, interact with, and preach to students and visitors from far and wide. One week shortly after the end of World War II

Verduin welcomed to a worship service the daughter of Japanese Emperor Hirohito. On another occasion, when the queen of the Netherlands was receiving an honorary degree, Verduin was tapped to offer a prayer in the Dutch language. In general, Verduin believes his relationship to the University of Michigan and its staff to have been "entirely pleasant." [10]

Verduin also used his position to advocate a place for religion in the modern university. Already in the 1950s Verduin sensed the growing opposition to allowing a distinctly Christian voice on a public campus (the very trends George Marsden recently traced). In a 1952 memorandum Verduin lamented to the Campus Religious Council of the University of Michigan the ways in which the modern university was attempting to be "neutral" and "commitmentless" in terms of morality and a religious world view.

Verduin pointed out that, although a university should not favor any one religious viewpoint, it could not completely ban religion from the campus or curriculum without thereby subtly endorsing the viewpoint of "a-religion." He then pleaded passionately to allow religion its proper place on the university campus, including the offering of courses which — while not seeking to win souls — would fairly present the viewpoints of various religions such as Christianity and Judaism. [11] Clearly Verduin made every effort to let his voice be heard on the campus which was his mission field.

While all of this work was being carried on, a debate was being waged as to the exact status of the Ann Arbor Chapel. As Verduin himself recognized, the establishing of a chapel was something of an innovation in the CRC. Because its con-

FIGURE 8 Students at Ann Arbor Campus Chapel in 1942.

Kent State "Massacre"

Reverend Henry Post was on his way to Malone College in Canton, Ohio, when the news came on his car radio: Four students had been shot and killed and nine others wounded by National Guard soldiers patrolling the campus of Kent State University.

Post found it hard to believe. The Christian Reformed Church campus minister had just left the school in nearby Kent an hour or so earlier. There had been tension, but he never dreamed the difficulties would explode into bloodshed.

Later news reports would inform him that the National Guard soldiers, hot and tired and scared themselves, had started shooting when it seemed that the rowdy anti-Vietnam War protesters were going to attack them.

"It was a shock to have this sudden awareness that human lives had been taken in the community in which I lived," recalled Post of the early afternoon of May 4, 1970.

One of a handful of CRC ministers working on campuses during that turbulent antiwar era, Post completed his trip to Malone, a Quaker college in Canton. Malone, along with Kent State, was among the half-dozen schools to which he was assigned.

But he didn't stay long. He felt compelled to return to the university, which had already shut down and would stay that way for the rest of the spring and summer.

"I wasn't at Malone an hour when the grief hit me and I had to go back home," he said. "Kent State was the last place in the world where I would have thought something like this would happen."

The violence at Kent State capped five years of increasing dissatisfaction on United States college campuses over the role America was playing in the war in southeast Asia.

During this time students took over university buildings from one coast to the other, marched in the streets, burned effigies of school officials and political figures, and generally called into question the actions of those who ran the "military-industrial complex."

In the midst of some of this unrest — both before and after Kent State — CRC campus ministers tried to bring the healing power of faith into the turmoil of angry rhetoric and emotions.

> *"It was a shock to have this sudden awareness that human lives had been taken in the community in which I lived."*
>
> **— Reverend Henry Post**

"I took it upon myself to give the students during that difficult time a philosophy and interpretation of Christianity," said Reverend John Schuring, a campus minister from 1968 to 1972 at the University of Minnesota.

While discussing the sovereignty of God with students, Schuring and his wife, Gladys, also tried to be peacemakers. Sometimes they saw it as their job to stand between the students and the authorities.

"Some people saw me back then as a Jesus freak who brought Christ's message of love to the streets," said Schuring, who went on to finish his career as a foreign missionary and pastor of various churches.

Henry Post wasn't entirely sure before the violence at Kent State what his role as a campus minister should be. On loan to Inter-Varsity Christian Fellowship, he saw himself initially as an evangelist, calling students to conversion. But the deaths of the students changed him.

"I broke away from the more evangelical posture and awakened to the fact that our culture was in transition," he said. "The event at Kent State radicalized me."

As a result, his approach to campus ministry became less structured. In essence, he started to involve himself more deeply in the lives of students. He realized that he had been too passive before the shootings.

"I reassessed my Calvinist upbringing," he said. "I realized my role as a campus minister was not just to help students get ready for heaven. It was also to help them reconstruct their culture."

In the months following the Kent State incident, Post spoke with the families of the slain and injured students over the phone. He offered them solace born out of his religious beliefs. He helped draft a letter that was published in the *Akron Beacon Journal.* The letter itself reflected his change of heart as well as the remorse he felt.

"We ask the forgiveness of God and our fellow men for the passive role we played in the tragedy we suffered at our university," he wrote. "We ask you [the public] to consider whether any one of us is really innocent of the shootings at Kent State."

When the students returned in the fall following the violence, Post met with them one-on-one, helped them prepare worship services, and conducted gatherings at which they discussed Christian forms of antiwar protest.

"I tried to help the students recognize that God still ruled the world even after the kind of sacrifice made by the students who were shot," he said.

Other CRC campus ministers across the country also found themselves facing angry students who wondered where God was in all the chaos enveloping colleges.

Reverend Henry Pott, a chaplain on the UCLA campus, wrote in *The Banner* about a black man who had just returned from a three-year stint as a demolitions expert in Vietnam. Then serving as defense minister of the Black Panther Party at UCLA, the former soldier had wondered, "Can I get to know God, too? Can I ask him into my life? And become a Christian …?"

Pott told him that of course he could. He then went on to inform the veteran of how Christ could work in his life as well.

Reverend Daniel Bos, then at Purdue University, told *The Banner* that he was deeply concerned about the tough moral decisions about the war that graduating seniors faced. Should they allow themselves to be drafted into the service or not? he asked.

Reverend Earl Schipper reported that nearly a thousand students were arrested during one massive protest at Ohio State University. He was in the middle of the fray.

"After answering the question about Christian ministry in this situation, I spent my time dodging tear-gas canisters and trying to calm people down. We opened a first-aid station to help the gassed, injured, and disturbed."

Also on the campus at this time was Reverend Roger Van Harn, then serving as pastor at a CRC church in downtown Columbus, not far from the university.

Van Harn, senior pastor at Grace CRC in Grand Rapids in 1995, recalled spending many hours as a chaplain to students at Ohio State.

Campus ministers, said Van Harn, provided support for the students before, during, and after the "Kent State massacre."

"I tried to provide reflection times on what was going on," he said. "After an evening of protesting, I would gather the students and go the the chapel." Van Harn did not join the marches across the campus himself.

Actively involved in the affairs on secular campuses, campus ministers were able to touch the lives of students who were otherwise floundering in an academic world that only infrequently made room for a Christian perspective.

Dennis Hartin, a Foxboro, New York, real-estate salesman, is a man whose life was substantially changed through his contact with a CRC campus minister. In his case, it was the ministry of Roger Van Harn at Ohio State that made the difference.

Reared in the Congregational church in upstate New York, Hartin brought a highly intellectual approach to religious belief when he enrolled at Ohio State in 1973.

Interaction with Van Harn, especially in that introspective period in his life, brought a new understanding of what it means to be Christian into Hartin's heart and mind.

Chapel services, discussion groups, and lengthy sessions with Van Harn helped to form a way of thinking and feeling about God that remains with him today, he said.

"College was a great environment in which to explore," said Hartin, who attended a Lutheran seminary following graduation from Ohio State. In 1995, a husband and the father of two children, Hartin was training to be an English teacher.

"I would be profoundly different today if it weren't for my experience with CRC campus ministry back in the seventies," he said.

FIGURE 9 John and Gladys Schuring.

gregation was in some measure transient (student turnover created a new congregation every four years) and because many believed the Campus Chapel to be made up of individuals and not families (when in reality the chapel did minister to many families of former students who had remained in the Ann Arbor area after graduation), the Campus Chapel was not viewed by many as an emerging, established church which was headed for formal organization. Questions arose as to how and whether the sacraments could be administered in a nontraditional church setting, who would provide on-site supervision of Verduin's ministry, what to do with memberships of those who were permanent residents in Ann Arbor, and so forth.

FIGURE 10.

FIGURE 11 Donald Postema.

Although the CRC would later adopt policies regulating chapels and chaplains, in these early days of the Ann Arbor Chapel the matter remained rather ill defined. To solve some of these dilemmas, there eventually was a move to organize an established Christian Reformed church in Ann Arbor, either supplementing, replacing, or working in conjunction with the existing chapel. Eventually it was decided to establish an organized Christian Reformed congregation which would work alongside the on-campus chapel and its unique congregation. Hence, the Ann Arbor Christian Reformed Church was organized in 1955, at least temporarily alleviating a few of the practical issues, though still leaving unresolved the exact nature of a chapel.

Verduin continued his work on the Ann Arbor campus until his retirement in 1962. He was succeeded in 1963 by Reverend Donald Postema, who, following his 1960 graduation from Calvin Theological Seminary, went to the Free University of Amsterdam to pursue a degree in pastoral psychology. Since 1963 Postema has carried on the campus ministries begun under Verduin, adding his own unique imprint. A deeply spiritual man, Postema was much influenced by his mentor, Father Henri J.M. Nouwen (who would write the preface to Postema's 1983 book on spirituality, *Space for God*). In his writing and in his campus work, Postema has brought together the deep piety and intellectual resources of his Calvinist tradition with the deeply spiritual writings of Nouwen, Thomas Merton, and the Desert Fathers.

Postema has also been a catalyst for numerous other programs and ministries — ones which not only ministered to the students but also gave students an opportunity to minister to one another and to the wider university community. During the turbulent decade of the 1960s Postema participated in and organized antiracism and antiwar protests. The Ann Arbor Chapel community also produced the "Household of Peace" overture to the Christian Reformed synod. This document became a key component in the 1975 guidelines on war and just-war theory adopted by the synod.

Under Postema's leadership the Ann Arbor Chapel also innovated a coffee-house ministry as well as a "basement ministry" for dropouts and homeless people who live near the campus. Appropriate to the university setting, it has been a citadel of reflection on subjects connected to the liturgical reform and renewal movement. Additionally, even as Verduin had forged contacts with the broader university community, so Postema also encouraged ecumenical endeavors through participating in the Association of Religious Counselors, the Council for Ethical, Spiritual, and Religious Dialogue, and other committees related to the university.

For over fifty years the Ann Arbor Chapel has provided a Reformed presence on the U of M campus. Though it took nearly thirty years to do so, the merits and benefits of such a mission outreach eventually captured the imagination of the broader denomination and its home-mission leaders, resulting in the comparatively recent move toward official establishment of Christian Reformed campus ministry.

FIGURE 12 John and Jacqueline Kennedy on the campaign trail in Harlem, New York, in 1960.

The Ministry Expands

The theme song of John F. Kennedy's 1960 presidential campaign was "High Hopes." Indeed, following the deeply religious and comparatively calm decade of the 1950s and beginning with the elan and elegance of Kennedy's Camelot, most Americans entered the new decade with high hopes. But before it was over, Americans would be shaking their heads in disbelief at the violent, turbulent, bloody decade that was the 1960s. Few decades in American history had been more explosive. From the assassinations of JFK, Robert Kennedy, and Martin Luther King, Jr., to the Vietnam War and the race riots in the streets of nearly every major city in the land, America was shaken to its core at how easily "the land of the free and the home of the brave" could rattle into disarray.

Among the epicenters of that decade's turbulence and violence were college and university campuses. Under even comparatively ordinary circumstances, a campus is often the locus of experimentation, questioning of the past, new ideas, novel trends, and the forging of new patterns for new generations. But the circumstances of the 1960s were anything but ordinary as an almost bizarre confluence of cultural streams created a roaring river of rage and discontent.

FIGURE 13 Campus scene in the 1960s.

Experimentation with drugs and sexuality, simmering anger over a war fought in a nation few had even heard of five years earlier, a perceived "generation gap," and a growing distrust of anyone in a position of authority made college and university campuses ripe for riots, rallies, sit-ins, love-ins, dropouts, hippies, and yippies. All such events were, of course, calculated to get the attention of, shake up, and anger the adults who, in the minds of many young people, were responsible for the mess the country was in. In this the counterculture succeeded, and the result was many ugly and at times brutal confrontations between the old and the young, the establishment and the counterculture.

Queen's University: Kingston, Ontario

University campuses are designed to be places which encourage innovation, creative thought, and expanding horizons. Ministering to the students and faculty in so unique an environment likewise requires innovation, creativity, and a willingness to expand into unchartered areas of mission. An examination of one present-day campus ministry in Kingston, Ontario, reveals the unique and varied types of ministry which can result through such an engagement with an academic community. It also provides a working model for precisely the kind of ministry envisioned by the 1967 synodical report.

Queen's University in Kingston is one of Canada's largest and most prestigious universities. With a student body of over twelve thousand and with separate colleges for law, medicine, and business, Queen's is clearly a research university well-known for its excellence in scholarship.

Since 1974 the Christian Reformed Church has had an on-campus presence there, at first through Reverend Bill Dykstra, who worked as a campus pastor until 1982. During those eight years Dykstra maintained a busy schedule, which included preaching, supervision of a "students' club," teaching a Greek class, assisting in Inter-Varsity meetings, and conducting a weekly Tuesday-morning Bible study.

After Dykstra took a call to pastor a church in Chatham, Ontario, the work was picked up by Dr. Willis "Bill" Van Groningen. Van Groningen, who holds a Ph.D. in philosophy, would not be ordained until 1988 but threw himself into the work immediately upon his arrival in October of 1982. Since that time Van Groningen has labored diligently to make the Queen's University campus ministry into the kind of honest, unstinting, intelligent engagement with an academic setting which the Board of Home Missions envisioned when it first proposed such a ministry in the early sixties.

Despite some initial discomfort and resistance from local Christian Reformed churches which were unclear as

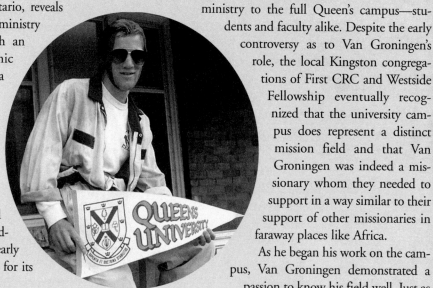

FIGURE 14   Student at Queen's University.

to the nature of the campus work, Van Groningen succeeded in carving out a clear identity for himself. Rather than try to split his time between the campus and other local congregational work, Van Groningen established himself as specifically and exclusively a *campus* pastor who would be immersed in, and hence well-suited for, ministry to the full Queen's campus—students and faculty alike. Despite the early controversy as to Van Groningen's role, the local Kingston congregations of First CRC and Westside Fellowship eventually recognized that the university campus does represent a distinct mission field and that Van Groningen was indeed a missionary whom they needed to support in a way similar to their support of other missionaries in faraway places like Africa.

As he began his work on the campus, Van Groningen demonstrated a passion to know his field well. Just as foreign missionaries might study native languages and take courses on the foreign culture in which they would be working, so also Van Groningen studied the history of Queen's University, became acquainted with its various faculties, attended philosophy and other departmental colloquia, and "hung out" with the students in their favorite gathering places. Only then did Van Groningen develop a plan and vision for ministry to Queen's University which aimed to establish a Christian community within the larger university community — a place where students and faculty could be together not only as Christians but also as students and scholars, a place, as it were, which was in the university but not of it.

Early on Van Groningen also availed himself of ecumenical opportunities to participate in larger campus ministries, thus giving himself entree into ecumenical worship and baccalaureate services, campus-wide orientation programs, panel discussions, retreats, and membership on various campus-wide committees which oversee various ministries. Clearly, Van Groningen, while firstly wishing to minister to the Reformed and Christian Reformed young people on the campus, also aimed to influence the wider university and, through that, the wider world — which also was precisely one of the early goals of the Ann Arbor Chapel as well as Home Missions' move toward campus ministry.

For the first few years Van Groningen had to be content with office space provided to him by the university in the Student Affairs Center, which was sometimes called "the Gay House" because it was the place where the university placed all of its "deviant" groups such as the Green Party, the Womyn's Centre, gay-support groups, and the like. Desiring to carve out a distinctive, more mainstream identity, in 1987 Van Groningen secured the rental of an on-campus facility and also christened the campus ministry as "Geneva Fellowship," thus giving the mission an identifiable name and presence on the larger campus. The ministry remained in this space until 1994, when a house at 182 Frontenac Street was purchased. This new house, situated on the edge of the campus proper, is very accessible and visible to the student community.

Over the years Van Groningen and his Campus Committee have succeeded in making Geneva Fellowship a real presence at Queen's. Geneva Fellowship now sponsors numerous programs, retreats, Bible studies, and even an endowed lecture series which brings Christian scholars like Nicholas Wolterstorff to the campus to discuss issues related to faith and learning in an academic setting.

In addition to the Tuesday-morning Bible study, Geneva Fellowship now also sponsors an evangelistic Bible study, faculty-led study groups, and a Graduate Colloquium on Christianity and Scholarship, in which graduate students present papers related to their major fields of study with an emphasis on the interaction of their scholarship and their Christian faith. They then discuss their ideas and insights with other graduate students and professors.

The Reformed tradition has always stressed that mission is the task of the whole church and not merely of individuals within the church. Thus the local churches in Kingston remain active in this mission in terms of their supervision of Van Groningen (and he is regular in reporting to them) but also through interacting with the Queen's University students. Regular fellowship suppers are held with local church members, which give an opportunity for the students to have some contact with an established church. Since Geneva Fellowship does not sponsor weekly worship services, weekly potlucks provide a church home away from home for the Christian Reformed students who attend Queen's.

In general, the Geneva Fellowship at Queen's University is a living embodiment of the type of ministry

FIGURE 15 Bill Van Groningen, second from right, with students at Queen's University.

envisioned in 1967. Van Groningen and his fellow campus pastors across the United States and Canada are good representatives of the Reformed tradition and its desire to see all of life under Christ's Lordship. The Reformed tradition's love of scholarship and esteem for learning are also highlighted through campus ministries, which seek to engage not only a few select Reformed students but also the wider academic community, including professors and administrators.

The need for and success of such a ministry are perhaps best captured in a letter sent to Van Groningen in which a student wrote, "Although I was already a believer when I came to Queen's, it is likely that I would not have graduated as one were it not for the opportunity to struggle through difficult questions about our faith." Indeed, as campus pastors know, if Christian students and professors cannot learn to love God with heart, soul, *and* mind, it is all too likely that they may end up not loving God at all.

FIGURE 16 Geneva House on Frontenac Street.

It is an irony of recent history that precisely at the time when this turbulence was climaxing, the Christian Reformed Church formally moved to establish a widespread presence on university campuses across the United States and Canada. Known for its long-standing isolation from the mainstream of American cultural and ecclesiastical life, the CRC and its new campus ministers would suddenly find themselves in the eye of one of this country's most violent national storms.

Although the University of Michigan campus ministry had begun in 1940, the denomination as a whole had never been involved in the work (indeed, the Ann Arbor Chapel remains to this day an independent ministry of area classes) and had never imitated the work on a larger scale. But following World War II and the G.I. Bill, an increasing number of Christian Reformed young people were attending secular universities and colleges. As the baby-boom generation of the late 1940s and 1950s began to come of college age in the 1960s, once again the CRC witnessed an ever-increasing on-campus population of its young men and women.

Thus, in 1964, the Christian Reformed synod commissioned a study committee to investigate whether the Board of Home Missions should engage in on-campus work and to draft a set of statements and guidelines to establish the parameters for any such future mission work. The report presented to Synod 1965 (and distributed to the churches for study) highlighted the enormous opportunity which campus ministry represented — an opportunity which the church ignored to its own peril. Echoing many of the same points raised thirty years earlier in Ann Arbor, the 1965 report stated that because the leaders of tomorrow were to be found on college and university campuses and because many foreign students also now lived on American campuses, the church had a rare opportunity to touch the future in many lands by ministering to such young people.

The report also urgently noted that the Christian Reformed men and women now attending secular colleges and universities were being bombarded by academic, social, and vocational decisions with which a Reformed campus pastor could help. To meet the unique needs of a campus environment and college and university students, the report recommended that a new campus ministry be tailored to provide the following: counseling to help students sort through complex intellectual, academic, and vocational issues and choices; a ministry of Word and sacraments; social programs both to attract students to the ministry and also to provide more wholesome alternatives to the sometimes dubious social opportunities available in fraternities and sororities; a home-away-from-home environment in which faith could be nurtured even as the secular world and its views were encountered and taken seriously.

A key concern of the 1965 report was the relationship of the broader church to this new ministry. Basically the report encouraged established churches to reach out to local colleges and universities either through existing staff or through hiring additional pastors whose sole task would be outreach to the campuses. However, if a local church was not present to reach out to a particular college or university, the report recommended that a campus pastor be called through Home Missions to establish a Christian Reformed presence on that campus. Another key recommendation was that wherever a campus ministry was begun, contact should be made with the on-campus religious organizations and, especially, that a good working relationship should be established with the on-campus chapter of Inter-Varsity Christian Fellowship (the Christian Reformed Church had previously recognized IVCF as a worthy Christian association for which it also periodically collected funds).

This report was studied by the churches, was amended after the 1966 Synod (based on various recommendations from congregations and classes), and was finally adopted by Synod 1967. In summary it gave the following main guidelines:

1. There is a great opportunity and an urgent need for the Christian Reformed Church to be engaged in campus ministry both for the sake of the many Christian Reformed young people now on secular campuses and for the future leaders of this country and of many foreign lands.

2. The church's ministry on campus will be a ministry of the Word and sacraments, a ministry tailored to and relevant for an academic environment and the students within it. Students will be urged to develop their faith in that context so that they can go on to assume active leadership roles in the campus ministry and, one day, in the larger Church of Christ.

3. Existing local churches should find ways to branch out their ministries to local colleges and universities, but where this is not possible the Board of Home Missions will seek to call and place a chaplain or religious worker on the campus who will be encouraged to cooperate with existing ministries and religious organizations. [12]

Following the adoption of these guidelines, the Christian Reformed Church saw a fairly rapid proliferation of on-campus ministries. Whereas for years the denomination was informally connected to only one campus ministry in Ann Arbor, by 1971 the CRC's on-campus ministry had mushroomed to encompass no fewer than twenty-three campuses. By the 1980s that number had grown to over thirty campuses in twelve states and two provinces of Canada.

In the first few years following the 1967 go-ahead for this new outreach, campus pastors were, as noted above, forced to deal with the acute crises of the times. By 1970 reports of campus pastors were focusing predominantly on their efforts to provide a sane and compassionate Christian presence in the midst of the ferment and furor of their campus mission fields.

FIGURE 17 The Campus Chapel logo was created by Chris Stoffel Overvoorde when he was a student at the U of M and a chapel member.

FIGURE 18 The Campus Chapel in Ann Arbor.

FIGURE 19 Donald Postema with Chapel Council, 1992.

Beyond the issues plaguing the wider society, however, campus ministers also had to grapple with issues within their own denomination. Already in 1971 sufficient questions had been raised about campus pastors and their work that the periodical *The Reformed Journal* noted,

[The CRC] made a serious approach to the campus on a wide scale only a short five years ago. Already there are quivers of fear within the denomination about the work it is doing. One wonders if this denomination is sufficiently mature to carry on a ministry on campus or whether it, too, will gradually back off from the work so recently begun. [13]

A series of articles followed in which campus pastors attempted to address some fears and answer some questions. Among the concerns about campus ministry was the concern that on-campus worship services were very often nontraditional in format. In an effort to meet the unique needs of students, as well as to reach out to students already disenchanted with the style of their home churches, students were often invited to participate in planning and leading liturgies, writing litanies, and the like. The result was, predictably, a very nontraditional, contemporary, and informal style of worship.

Reflecting the kind of feedback which campus chaplains received on such nontraditional services, Michigan State University chaplain Reverend Alvin Hoksbergen wrote in 1971 that it could be very discouraging when a campus pastor "learns that his Christianity is called into question and that he is threatened by withdrawal of all support because he had made some changes in the format of worship." [14]

Recognizing the crisis in authority of that era and the desire of many students to move away from anything which smacked of the older generation, many pastors did attempt to tailor a worship experience which, while not denying the central tenets of the faith, sought to bring them alive in a less formal environment. Hence, informal "dialogue worship" was implemented in some places in an effort to proclaim traditional truths in a way which would involve the students in a worshipful way while also engaging their minds and hearts by giving them opportunity to express ideas and share experiences. When some in the larger church expressed their disdain, campus pastors pleaded for tolerance. Given the spirit of the times, they claimed, the campus pastor had all he could do to keep students from leaving the faith altogether because they categorized even the Christian faith as one more oppressive piece of the adult culture so much under suspicion in those days.

Christian Reformed campus ministers also soon discovered that their presence on major college and university campuses forced them to deal with issues that pastors in other places could almost ignore. When the 1967 report stated that a vital part of campus ministry would be to provide Christian guidance on social and academic issues, it probably did not immediately foresee that such counsel would have to answer urgent student questions like these listed by Reverend Marvin P. Hoogland in October 1971:

Should we not in conscience and on Christian principle be opposed to all war? Is homosexuality (and the homosexual) to be condemned? Are pre-marital sexual relations necessarily wrong?

Should not abortion laws be abolished and abortion even encouraged in many cases? Is there any usefulness to a second formal worship service on Sunday? Do we need an ordained, full-time clergy? Do we even need an organized church? [15]

When a few short years earlier the Christian Reformed Church had decided to pursue campus ministry, it did so in order to make clear the claims of Christ over all areas of life. The campus pastors who in those difficult years tried to accomplish that goal deserve enormous credit. In a time when routine appeals to authority (including, for many students, the authority of the Bible and of the Christian tradition) were insufficient to answer probing queries like those listed above, campus pastors had to do some significant creative, critical thinking, which doubtless tested them and, by extension, their denomination far beyond the narrow bounds and confines within which the CRC had traditionally existed.

FIGURE 20

Another expansion of CRC outreach came through its increasing association with Inter-Varsity Christian Fellowship. As envisioned in the 1967 guidelines, the denomination did indeed begin cooperative ventures with IVCF on various campuses. Since 1938, when IVCF had first come to North America, it had been a vital spiritual presence on numerous campuses across the United States and Canada. Informally the CRC's relationship to Inter-Varsity began with Leonard Verduin, who, over the years in Ann Arbor, had developed a friendly working relationship with the U of M Inter-Varsity chapter.

In the first year of the CRC's formal endeavor in campus ministry, a seminary intern, Richard Sytsma, was loaned to IVCF to work on the Wayne State University campus in Detroit, Michigan. As the relationship continued, the Christian Reformed Church would also loan even ordained clergy to work under IVCF's umbrella, thus tying in with a mainstream influence in campus ministries while also availing itself of Inter-Varsity's substantial resources in publishing, training seminars, and student mission conferences

such as the Urbana conference, which typically attracts tens of thousands of students.

The relationship between the Christian Reformed Church and Inter-Varsity Christian Fellowship was formalized in 1977 by a study-committee report in which the Board of Home Missions formally endorsed and recognized the legitimacy of loaning Christian Reformed pastors to IVCF, of participating in joint campus ministries with IVCF, and of IVCF's training and supervision of Christian Reformed campus pastors and workers.

The Future?

Despite the proliferation of Christian Reformed campus ministries since 1967, the exact future of campus ministries and their relationship to the Board of Home Missions has been in dispute since 1987. As the board began its major push of *Gathering God's Growing Family,* it began pouring its energy and money into new-church planting and into helping established churches grow through new evangelism programs, alternative-style worship services, and the like. The result was that some programs which had for many years been funded directly through Home Missions (and hence through the larger denomination) were told that they would now receive only grant monies, on a declining basis over a period of years. The board communicated that this financial arrangement would keep ministries from becoming unduly

FIGURE 21 The original Ann Arbor Campus Chapel sign, which was stolen.

dependent and would also foster local ownership of various ministries like those of campus pastors.

The decision shocked many campus pastors and led to a storm of protest. Many felt the move reflected less a desire for local ownership of ministries and more a desire to focus only on ministries which "count," that is, ones which can garner new members for the CRC and hence fulfill the then-stated Home Missions' numerical objective of "400,000 by 2000." Since campus ministry does not generally result in much numerical growth for the denomination, some campus pastors felt this was the real reason for their being cut off from direct funding. Though the Board of Home Missions made clear that this was not the case, the fact remained that the new funding model imperiled many campus ministries.

One of the results of the controversy was the formation of a Campus Ministry Task Force with a mandate to look into the future of campus ministry in the light of proposed changes by the board. New vision statements were drafted and adopted, and on May 1, 1991, the Christian Reformed Campus Ministry Association was founded. The new association, which would continue to have formal contact with the Board of Home Missions, now seeks to promote the cause of campus ministry within the CRC and to provide its campus pastors with seminars, professional-development opportunities, collegial and financial support, annual conferences, and a liaison with Home Missions and the wider church.

Though the Christian Reformed Campus Ministry Association is still in its early stages, it is seeking to further

the vital ministry of campus pastors begun in Ann Arbor in 1941 and in the wider denomination in 1967.

Even as the new organization was being founded, however, the shifts in funding begun in 1987 resulted in the closing of several campus ministries, including those at Arizona State University, Ohio State University, the University of Colorado, Western Michigan University, UCLA, and Kent State University.

Through the efforts of former campus pastors like Reverend Bill Lewis (who served at Ohio State University from 1976–1993), a new task force was established in 1994 to find ways to solve the perceived crisis in campus ministry in the wake of new funding models and the demise of several ministries. [17] New plans made in 1995 proposed making campus ministry a full-fledged agency under Home Missions or perhaps under the Chaplain Committee, recently renamed Chaplaincy Ministries.

Meanwhile, the work of campus ministry continues on over twenty American and Canadian campuses. Under the leadership of dedicated campus pastors, these ministries seek to reach out to those in academia so that they may, as the apostle Paul once recommended, add knowledge to their faith and faith to their knowledge.

Chapter Five

The Great Cities

Urban Ministry

"Should I not be concerned about that great city?"

Jonah 4:11

By the late twentieth century the appearance of new technological wonders seems routine to people in industrialized nations. As recently as the 1960s, a computer was a buzzing, blinking, whirring machine which generally occupied an entire room as it processed cardboard punched cards. By the 1990s, battery-driven laptops contained far more power and capabilities than the behemoth machines of only thirty years ago. In the late 1960s the original *Star Trek* television series envisioned flip-phones, hand-held computers, and fax machines as the stuff of the distant twenty-third century. Already by the 1990s many of these fantastic devices were in daily use, making the stuff of science fiction look quaintly anachronistic.

Whereas late-twentieth-century folks are accustomed to innovation, people of the late nineteenth century experienced technological invention as a new phenomenon which captured their imaginations. Many believed the Industrial Revolution, driven by amazing new machines, was sure to lead to a golden age in which life would be easier and all people happier. It truly was an era of innovation and discovery:

the phonograph, telegraph, telephone, and incandescent lamp were but the headline inventions of the day, for, as historian Winthrop Hudson reports, inventions of every kind were appearing almost daily. Whereas prior to 1865 the United States had issued a total of 62,000 patents, the next thirty-five years would see an explosion of new devices and a stunning 637,000 new U.S. patents between 1865 and 1900. The result was that by 1894 the United States had become the world's leading manufacturer of goods.[1]

But while some saw this period as a golden age of advances, riches, and success, others labeled it a tragic era. Mark Twain called it a "gilded age" — one which looked golden but which, underneath, was corrupt, ugly, and harsh. Indeed, those who see the period between 1865 and 1901 as a glorious era conveniently forget, as historian Sean Dennis Cashman points out, that this period was bracketed and bisected by the assassinations of three presidents: Lincoln in 1865, Garfield in 1881, and Mc Kinley in 1901. The shocking frequency with which America's top leaders were killed testifies to the era's unrest, squalor, and chaos.[2]

Nowhere could the era's unrest be better seen than in America's booming urban centers. As the locus of the Industrial Revolution, the city seemed to hold great promise. Immigrants who came to America's land of opportunity and rural residents weary of the rigors and fiscal disappointments of agriculture flocked into the cities. Between 1860 and 1890 the already-large population of New York City doubled. But other cities grew even more: Detroit's population saw a fourfold increase, Chicago a tenfold increase, and Los Angeles a whopping twentyfold leap.

But for all of its technological wonders and advances, the Industrial Revolution could not keep pace with such urban population surges. The result was widespread unemployment and, by 1893, a severe economic depression. It was not simply economics and employment opportunities that lagged behind, however. Laws to govern the practices of labor and to ensure fair wages also did not keep up with burgeoning factories and sweatshops. Hence the few got exceedingly wealthy (this was also the era of the great robber barons and their monopolistic empires) while the many were beaten down by unfair labor practices, shameful wages, corrupt management, and hideous work conditions. By 1890 a tiny one percent of Americans were garnering twenty-five percent of the nation's income. Yet many persisted in believing that things would get better. As Cashman put it, "During the Gilded Age natives and immigrants alike were more interested in the stars in their eyes than the stripes on their backs."[3]

The church also had a hard time keeping up with the urban world and its numerous problems. Unaccustomed to dealing with cities and social issues, the institutional church found itself ill equipped to minister to the new situation. In fact, very often there were no regular churches to be found in the neediest areas of the inner cities. Partly because of this fact, and partly because of the anonymity of the city, many who had been faithful attenders of churches when they had lived in rural settings found it very easy to break the church-going habit in the city.[4] Thus the population of the inner city became increasingly unchurched even as it became increasingly needy.

FIGURE 1 Looking south from mid Manhattan with the Empire State Building in center.

By the late 1800s, therefore, a new movement began in American churches: the Social Gospel. Founded and fueled by the writings of Washington Gladden, Charles Sheldon, and Walter Rauschenbusch, the Social Gospel reformers attempted to educate the church to the needs of the inner city as well as to the realities of the labor world. Through sheer ignorance many in the church had been siding with management whenever labor disputes arose. The Social Gospel tried to foment sympathy for the workers and a desire to improve their lot. As historian Mark Noll puts it, the Social Gospel "combined a prophetic ideal of justice with a commitment to building the kingdom of God through the power of Christ. [It attempted] to adapt the Protestant tradition of an earlier rural America to the changing demands of a newly industrial society."[5]

The late 1800s also became the era of the rescue missions. Situated in areas which were in dire need of ministry but which were largely without churches, rescue missions were designed "to reclaim the dregs of society — vagrants, alcoholics, former convicts, jobless men, and fallen women."[6] Believing that physical needs took precedence over spiritual ones (at least initially), organizations like the Salvation Army reached out through soup kitchens, clothing ministries, and overnight shelters.

As noted in the Introduction, this was the same era during which the Christian Reformed Church was struggling to establish its identity and groping to find its mission voice. It is not surprising, therefore, that throughout the late nineteenth century and well into the twentieth century the Christian Reformed Church maintained a wary distance from the inner city even as it cast a critical eye on the Social Gospel. Believing that right doctrines took precedence over all else and being very wary of the Social Gospel's association with liberal theology and progressive politics, the leadership of the CRC showed little inclination to cooperate in such inner-city missions and social concerns.

But the denomination was not of one mind on such issues. Indeed, as Christian Reformed historian James Bratt has noted, during the early twentieth century various factions

within the Reformed movement vied with one another in their attempts to shape and control the denomination's perspective and ministry. Some hailed the Federal Council of Churches (at that time largely dominated by Social Gospel leaders and concerns) as evidence of Christianity's forward march and hence as being worthy of Christian Reformed participation. But others were suspicious of such an ecumenical body, being convinced that the CRC could gain nothing by participating in such movements and that, in fact, it could even lose much of its doctrinal purity and distinctiveness.

As Bratt notes, when it came to the larger body politic, "The Reformed were to construct in theory a set of political principles deduced from the Confessions, but in practice they were merely to complain about violations of these, abstain from political action whenever possible in favor of nurturing piety, and participate when necessary in an individualistic, haphazard way."[7] Indeed, in the period between 1900 and 1917 (before World War I forced a measure of participation in American society) there were in Christian Reformed circles so much theological ambivalence about almost every issue in society, so much pondering of issues from every conceivable angle, and so much worry about getting too close to society and its problems that there were few clear lines of action available anywhere on anything. Hence, ministry to the city, though promoted by some, was largely ignored by the broader denomination and its mission agencies.

But some local outreach to cities did take place. Although it would be mid century before the denomination made a concerted effort to reach out to America's larger urban centers of Chicago and New York, churches in places like Grand Rapids, Michigan — where the Christian Reformed denomination was headquartered — did begin to reach out to their own cities through a variety of evangelism methods and programs. Some of these programs would later be imitated when the denomination did at long last target the inner city as a distinct mission field.

Beyond the Dutch Ghetto

Grand Rapids, Michigan, has long been a highly religious place, touting itself as "the city of churches." As James Bratt notes in *Gathered at the River,* a religious history of the city, nearly every denomination eventually was represented in Grand Rapids, from Roman Catholicism to Eastern Orthodoxy to African-American Baptists. Without a doubt, however, it was the Reformed, and more particularly the Christian Reformed, who made the largest impact on the city's religious landscape. As far back as 1837 Dutch immi-

grants had made west Michigan, and more particularly Grand Rapids, a favorite place in which to settle.[8]

The city's first Reformed church was founded already in 1840. A host of other Reformed and Christian Reformed churches would follow until, by 1995, in addition to housing the denominational headquarters for the Christian Reformed Church in North America, the Grand Rapids area is home to over 170 Reformed congregations, 100 of which are Christian Reformed (that number accounting for approximately one-eighth of the entire denomination). The Grand Rapids phone book also reveals a high concentration of Dutch names, nearly 6,500 listings being variations on the Dutch surnames *Van-* and *Vander-*.

Immigrants who came to America's land of opportunity and rural residents ... flocked into the cities.

Although Grand Rapids did not undergo the seismic shifts which cracked the pavement of America's larger cities in the late nineteenth and early twentieth centuries, it was not immune to the decay and corruption which could be seen in places like New York and Chicago. Although the Christian Reformed Church was known as an ethnic enclave which in most places still worshiped in the Dutch language through the 1920s, some Grand Rapids congregations began to see the need to reach beyond themselves to minister to the wider city and its problems. As early as 1909, and then more generally beginning in the decade between 1910 and 1920, Grand Rapids-area Christian Reformed churches began opening mission outposts and chapels.[9]

The establishment of chapels became a favorite way by which congregations attempted to extend themselves into

FIGURE 2   Sketch of first Reformed church in Grand Rapids, Michigan.

new areas. Between 1900 and 1968 no fewer than fifty-two chapels were started in the Grand Rapids area, thirty-one of which would go on to become permanent established congregations. While some of these chapels worked to attract Dutch Reformed people in areas not currently served by another church, many of them were clearly designed to target other ethnic minorities as well as to minister to working-class people who often had great physical and financial needs.

One such ministry was Buckley Chapel, founded in 1949 by Neland Avenue and Bates Street Christian Reformed

FIGURE 3 Buckley Chapel in 1949.

churches. Located near the inner city and near an area with an expanding black population, Buckley sought to bring a healing gospel presence to what was often a troubled area of the city. Established as Grace Christian Reformed Church in 1962, the congregation continues to minister to the Forgotten Corners area of the city, where drugs, prostitution, and crime are altogether too common. Seeing itself as a kind of community center, Grace now reaches out through its clothing center, food pantry, single-parents group, Head Start program, and Bible clubs for all ages. It also plays host to other organizations working in the inner city — Habitat for Humanity, Inner City Christian Federation, and others that network and meet in the Grace facilities. Indeed, Grace is a part of a larger urban renewal in its part of the city as nearly fifty new homes are being built or planned in Grace's immediate vicinity. Grace CRC, pastored for twenty years by Reverend Roger Van Harn, remains the presence of Christ in a needy area — precisely the goal of chapel planting throughout most of the twentieth century in Grand Rapids.[10]

Another Grand Rapids congregation long active in mission outreach is Eastern Avenue Christian

FIGURE 4 Left to right, Henry Washington, Andrew Cross, Luther Ward, Martin Toonstra, William Burress, in 1962.

Reformed Church. Already in 1916 it contracted with Miss Johanna Veenstra to do mission outreach to the street women who spent their days along South Division Avenue. Veenstra, who later became a pioneering foreign missionary to Nigeria before dying an untimely death at 39, worked in Grand Rapids for only one year. But though her stint of mission work was brief, she showed the Eastern Avenue church there was indeed much that could be done. Veenstra's successor, Italian immigrant Abel Del Vecchio, likewise helped people catch a vision for the effectiveness of street preaching and, more particularly, of the rescue-mission format. Del Vecchio's work at the Way of Life Mission in the heart of the city was a harbinger of various gospel halls that soon began popping up in the interior areas of the city.[11]

By 1926 six gospel-hall missions were in operation: Way of Life Mission, Madison Square Mission, Bethel Gospel Mission, Ionia Avenue Gospel Hall, West Leonard Mission, and Hanley Chapel. Though not strictly speaking rescue missions, such gospel halls could not help noticing the city's premier mission, run by Mel Trotter. A former drunk from Chicago — who himself had been converted in a rescue mission — Trotter had helped found the City Rescue Mission on Chicago's Canal Street in 1900. Trotter, who would go on to establish seventy rescue missions throughout the United States, knew how to attract large crowds. His bombastic style and fiery fundamentalist preaching routinely attracted about sixteen hundred people

FIGURE 5 Roger Van Harn.

FIGURE 6 House being built by Habitat for Humanity.

FIGURE 7 Inner City Christian Federation in Grand Rapids, Michigan.

FIGURE 8 Bethel CRC Mission erected this building in 1919.

to his Friday-evening evangelistic services. In addition to such meetings, Trotter also operated a soup kitchen and a clothing ministry and personally called on residents of the inner city.[12]

Similar Christian Reformed mission efforts got a boost in 1929 when the denomination's first city missionary came to town in the person of John Vande Water. Having already worked for years in the Helping Hand Mission in Chicago, Vande Water came to Grand Rapids with high energy, good experience, and a vision for reaching out to the city's downtrodden. Under Vande Water's leadership a new mission soon opened on West Fulton Street, holding its first service on Easter Sunday, March 31, 1929. Although forty children attended Sunday school that day, only five adults came to the service. Vande Water could see he had much work to do.

Over the next fifteen years during which he served as city missionary for Grand Rapids, Vande Water did much to get all the local churches on board for mission work. The need for ministry to the city became the more acute in late 1929 following the crash of the stock market. The economic Depression which followed caused life to go from hard to impossible for many inner-city residents. Already by mid 1930 over twenty thousand Grand Rapids residents were out of work and in need of assistance. A newly formed Industrial Department of the Grand Rapids mission board dispensed thousands of articles of clothing and hundreds of food baskets. The board's volunteers and workers also fixed furniture for and distributed stoves and other appliances to the needy. Meanwhile, to help meet the great needs of the day, a half-dozen other mis-

sion stations opened, including the Baxter Mission (now Baxter Community Center) and the Blodgett Convalescent Home (now Mary Free Bed Hospital).[13]

When the Guiding Light Mission opened on March 8, 1957, the Christian Reformed churches in Grand Rapids formally entered the rescue-mission effort, which had been pioneered in Grand Rapids by Mel Trotter. By providing meals, offering counseling for alcoholics, visiting people in their homes or in hospitals, and leading Bible classes for young people, the mission's first workers, Andrew and Cornelia Vander Veer, helped local congregations provide an inner-city presence by proxy.[14]

During this same time, however, the cherished method of chapel establishment came under fire. Some, like the always fiery Harry Boer (who had earlier raised grave doubts about Christian Reformed mission methods to the Native Americans), believed that chapels amounted to second-class congregations whose members were viewed as not yet worthy of full inclusion in the broader church. Such a de facto segregation, Boer alleged, was improper and insulting to the people involved.

FIGURE 9 Mel Trotter.

Boer's critique led to a reevaluation of the chapel method of doing inner-city mission work. More immediately, the social forces shaping the civil-rights movement and the race riots which ensued also caused a shift in inner-city mission strategy. Indeed, far from needing to establish satellite chapels in other areas, many old and well-established congregations found themselves in changing areas where the population was shifting toward ethnic minorities. Instead of sending out workers to find people in need of ministry, many congregations discovered that they needed to do work in their own backyards: the needy had come to them. Some congregations began to do such work; others followed their constituency into the suburbs, abandoning areas of the city which no longer felt like home.

One indication of the change in Grand Rapids neighborhoods from primarily white, Reformed, Dutch areas to places inhabited by increasing numbers of ethnic minorities came in 1973, when the Grand Rapids Christian School Association decided to close the doors of the Oakdale Christian School no later than 1976. The reasons cited pointed to declining numbers of "tradi-

God's Glory in the Inner City

Reverend Reggie Smith considers himself a "street rat" whose life blood pulses with the beat of the inner city.

Having grown up on the west side of Chicago, the minister is convinced that the salvation promised by Jesus Christ will come first to America's urban areas. Whenever he can, this is what he preaches and teaches to anyone who will listen.

"The city is where the river of life will be," said Smith, who in 1995 was pastor of Roosevelt Park CRC, a congregation located in a predominantly Hispanic and black Grand Rapids neighborhood.

"God is coming, and he will be downtown and in the barrios. When he arrives, there will be a big party in the neighborhoods."

As one of few fully ordained black ministers in the CRC, Smith is committed to bringing God's glory and the hope promised by Christ to the core city. He believes the Christian church has a duty to stay downtown and not flee to the suburbs. He uses his own background as a city kid to bring multicultural ministry to the streets.

"If God is going to be in the city, why can't the church be there knee-deep in the city?" he asked over breakfast in a small diner across the street from his church on Grandville Avenue southwest.

Smith's own congregation is an experiment in change and ethnic diversity. In 1994 Grandville Avenue CRC merged with the congregation from nearby Bethel CRC. Both had grown up in the years before and after World War II as worship homes for mostly white, mostly Dutch residents of the surrounding neighborhood.

As these people began to move away into communities outside the city, both churches began to suffer. Numbers of families declined; income plummeted; programs were cut. There was serious discussion of closing both churches.

But then, with denominational support, a decision was made to combine the churches and to develop a greater focus on serving the needs of those living in homes and apartments on and along Grandville Avenue. Smith was called and ordained as the first full-time pastor of the consolidated congregation.

"I've always been involved in urban ministry. I'm a street rat; it's kind of my thing," he said. "I came here to try to build a presence in this neighborhood. We want to reach people for the kingdom."

The work of Smith's congregation is done through various outreach ministries, including food and clothing banks, Bible classes for area children, counseling programs for adults, and regular worship which emphasizes the rich cultural diversity of this inner-city Grand Rapids area.

"I can see that God is opening the doors here," said Smith. "He is expanding people's vision of what urban ministry is all about."

Smith first came across white Dutch Christians when he and his older brother showed up one day at the gymnasium attached to Lawndale CRC in Chicago. First through sports and later through conversations with members of that church, he glimpsed a wider world that included people of many races.

Smith is one of seven children. His parents met and married in rural Mississippi before moving to Chicago, where his father worked in a steel mill. He attended Culver-Stockton College in Canton, Missouri, majoring in political science. He planned to become a lawyer, certainly not a preacher.

But back in Chicago, even as he prepared for a career as an attorney, a divine prodding nagged him. Conversations with friends, coupled with this inner sense of vocation, led to Calvin Theological Seminary.

"I figured I'd go a semester, realize I hated it, and then come on back home," he said.

One semester led to two and then to summer internships in urban churches, including Lawndale, and eventually to graduation.

Soon after earning his master's degree in divinity, he took a copastoring job with Reverend Stanley Vander Klay in Paterson, New Jersey. At first he thought he would eventually take over from the long-time pastor of the Northside Community Church. But that didn't happen for various reasons, among them the fact that he was called back to the church in Grand Rapids.

Whether in Chicago, Paterson, or western Michigan, Smith envisions his job as remaining close to the streets, surrounded by concrete and the daily busyness of city life.

"God is still getting together a people of every tongue and race for himself," he said. "I believe if we can't get it together down here in the city, we'll make a mockery of ourselves if we ever get to heaven."

FIGURE 10 Harold Dekker.

efforts included a coffee-house outreach in the downtown area through Dégagé Ministries, campus chaplain Harry Lew's ministry to the city's downtown colleges, the Criminal Justice Chaplaincy, and the stimulating of ministries in the city's established congregations, including outreach to newly arrived ethnic minorities like Vietnamese refugees.

By the late 1980s, however, it was clear that ministries to the city increasingly needed to be and were being "owned" by local churches and their classes. Following the dissolution of the Grand Rapids Area Ministries in 1992, the congregations of Grand Rapids faced a situation similar to that of the early twentieth century, namely, one in which they had to, on their own, find creative ways to reach out to those neighbors for whom life in the city is often chaotic, brutish, and spiritually bewildering.

The Other Harlem

By the mid twentieth century the Christian Reformed Church was beginning to hear the mission call of America's major urban centers. Prior to the late 1940s, however, the denomination had not entered large urban centers in any organized way, and there was certainly no formal Christian Reformed presence in the heart of places like New York City. In general such cities looked like a new and yet unexplored mission frontier for the Christian Reformed Church — one which the denomination as a whole had yet to enter.

Not long after the denomination began to investigate urban evangelism, however, it became apparent that the Christian Reformed Church *had* entered many major cities after all: it had done so through the voice of Peter Eldersveld. When *The Back to God Hour* was established in 1939, synod stated its hope that the program would reach especially the upper classes of American society. This neglected class of people, it was noted then, was harder to reach than were the poorer, lower classes in that it was harder to get into the homes of the wealthy. In the absence of physical needs, which a mercy ministry could meet, the rich, unlike the poor, had few reasons to open their doors to mission workers.

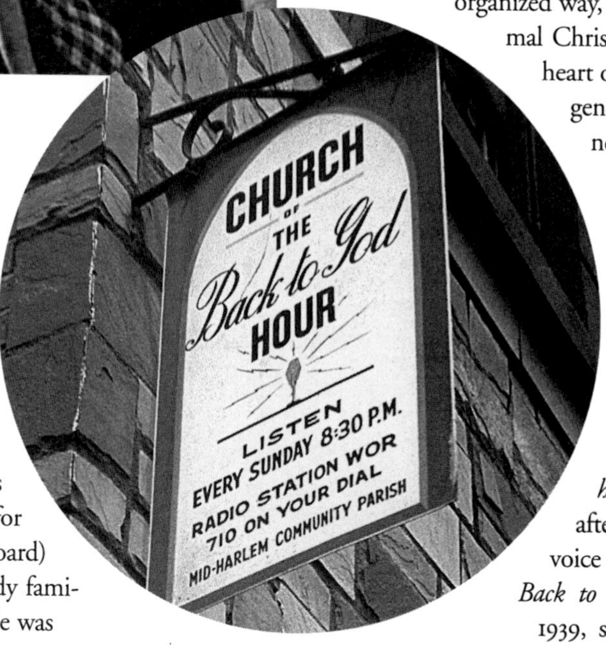

FIGURE 11 Sign on the Manhattan CRC building in New York City.

tional" Christian-school families living in the area, leading to the belief that the school would no longer find enrollees and hence would soon not be a viable enterprise. But as a result of the protests of local families committed to racial integration and through the intervention of Grand Rapids Area Ministries (the new name for the old Grand Rapids Mission Board) and its scholarship fund for needy families, the decision to close Oakdale was rescinded.[15]

The fact that such a decision was contemplated at all demonstrates that city missions in Grand Rapids had clearly shifted from something "out there" to something which needed to be tackled from the inside of congregations which were situated in changed and changing areas.

During the 1970s and 1980s the Grand Rapids Area Ministries, under the creative and energetic leadership of missionary-at-large Reverend Donald Griffioen, continued to found and sponsor outreach agencies. These agencies and

Whether such an impact was ever made on America's wealthy elite may be hard to gauge. What cannot be disputed, however, is the impact the program had on the inner city. By mid century it was apparent that *The Back to God Hour* was being heard regularly by blacks in impoverished places like Harlem in New York City. Indeed, when Second CRC of Paterson, New Jersey, proposed the beginning of inner-city work among nearby Negro populations, it did so in part at the urging of Reverend Harold Dekker as a result of his follow-up work to Peter Eldersveld's broadcasts.

In a letter dated December 20, 1949, Eastern Mission Board secretary Oren Holtrop, then pastor of Prospect Park CRC in Paterson, New Jersey, proposed to the executive committee of the Board of Home Missions that Harold Dekker be appointed to work in New York City both to contact Christian Reformed members already living there and to follow up on *Back to God Hour* listeners, possibly organizing them into catechism and Bible classes in local YMCAs.

By 1951 the follow-up work of Dekker and others had progressed far enough that the denomination was able to appoint its first African-American evangelist: Reverend Eugene St. Clair Callender. A native of Boston, Callender had attended schools in Cambridge, Massachusetts, before

FIGURE 12 Eugene St. Clair Callender.

going on to earn a bachelor's degree from Boston University in 1947. Though born and raised a Baptist, Callender enrolled at the very Reformed Westminster Seminary in Philadelphia in the fall of 1947, the seminary's first black student. By his senior year he was made class president while

also serving as president for Westminster's chapter of Inter-Varsity Christian Fellowship. Following his graduation in 1950, Callender had planned to be ordained in the Reformed Church in America.[16]

Judging the RCA to be drifting in a liberal direction, however, Callender began to look for another denomination to hire him as an evangelist among his own people in the great urban centers of the East. By the fall of 1951 Callender had found his way to the Second CRC in Paterson, a congregation already interested in doing mission work in the Paterson and greater New York City area. At a congregational meeting September 12, 1951, Second CRC agreed to call Callender to perform the task of "Negro evangelization," beginning November 1, 1951. Callender was subsequently licensed to preach by Classes Hudson and Hackensack.

Callender wasted no time. By December 1951 he reported to the executive committee that he had already begun his work in New York, which he described as "*the* great metropolis of our Country" — a city of 8 million people, only 1.5 million of whom already attended church. Additionally, Callender pointed out, New York was a city with "no distinctly Reformed witness" — a fact Callender desired to alter.[17]

In the midst of so large a mission field, Callender narrowed his focus by beginning with those listeners who had responded by mail to *The Back to God Hour*. "*The Back to God Hour*

FIGURE 13 View of New York from harbor.

Life and Love in the City

Mrs. Jacoba Woudenberg, a Dutch immigrant, grew up at the turn of the century in Paterson, New Jersey, America's first industrialized city. In a 1983 interview, Mrs. Woudenberg recalled how her family lived in a brightly furnished second-floor apartment in a beautiful house on Water Street, between Jefferson and Arch. In her youth all the houses and stores were in good repair. The area was heavily Jewish, almost as heavily Dutch, and it also had small numbers of people from other ethnic groups.

"It was very lovely back then," she told Reverend Stanley Vander Klay, pastor of Northside Christian Chapel, a CRC congregation that has been at work in the heart of Paterson for many years.

At the time of Mrs. Woudenberg's interview, the city she had loved as a child had changed. The neighborhood that had been so solid and secure in the early 1900s had grown ugly. Trees had been cut down, buildings boarded up, stores closed, empty lots turned into scrap yards. Drug pushers and prosti-

tutes cruised streets on which she once ran freely as a child.

Mrs. Woudenberg was troubled by the decline, as was Vander Klay, who has devoted more than three decades of his ministry to battling the forces that threaten to destroy America's first true factory town.

"I have to describe the work in this area of the city as ebb and flow," said Vander Klay. "There have been times of great vitality and growth, only to be followed by periods of slippage and discouragement," the minister added.

Despite the struggles, the Christian Reformed Church in the form of the Northside congregation has remained steadfast in its commitment to bringing the message of Christ to this part of Paterson. There are other Christian Reformed efforts in the city, among them the work at Madison Park CRC. But Northside has been one of the toughest. The story of this church reflects the difficulties of maintaining a Christian presence in a changing urban area.

FIGURE 14 Stanley Vander Klay.

FIGURE 15–16 Left, Jacoba Woudenberg's childhood home on Water Street (picture taken during flood of 1903) and, right, the same site in 1980.

"We're still working hard. We're still praying hard, even if what we are facing is yet another generation of children of welfare parents who themselves are babies having babies," said Vander Klay.

Hovering on the eastern edge of the country, Paterson made a name for itself in the 1800s for its sprawling textile mills, its silk-manufacturing plants, and its Colt revolver company. It was in this town that many European immigrants first landed and found jobs.

"The city was begun as a corporation," said Vander Klay. "The people were merely functional, imported to man the machines and produce profits."

The Northside Mission began as a storefront in 1935. By then, the 1910-era neighborhood that had thrived in Mrs. Woudenberg's recollection was well on the way to ruin.

After a time the mission turned into a family-oriented church. It made a journey from one building to another until it found a permanent home after Vander Klay became pastor.

Vander Klay himself never envisioned a career solely as the pastor of a mostly African-American congregation in the poorest section of the nation's oldest industrialized city. He first came to the area during his second summer in seminary. Basically, he came because he wanted to work in the East to be near his fiancee, Barbara, a Calvin student who spent her summers in Massachusetts.

He didn't even think that first summer of ever coming back for good. But a denominational committee which had been reviewing the situation in New Jersey decided it was time to make a commitment to the area. The committee decided to transform the chapel into an officially organized and duly recognized congregation. As a result, the summer intern was eventually asked to become a full-time pastor in the heart of the city.

"And so, the year that began the sixties was one of profound import for us," Vander Klay recalled. "My fiancee and I graduated in the same ceremony, she from college and I from seminary. We got married a few weeks later and in late September moved to Paterson, where I was shortly thereafter ordained."

In more than three decades at Northside, the pastor has been involved in many efforts to bring Christian love to the area — a halfway house for drug addicts; a day-care center; renovation of an old silk mill, which has been transformed into a Christian school, offices for various

FIGURE 17 Northside Gospel Mission at 19 North Main Street.

religious activities, and a gymnasium; lobbying successfully to keep a freeway from being built through the neighborhood; beginning and supporting a popular vacation Bible school; starting a Habitat for Humanity program; and the construction of more than forty homes within a square mile of the church.

"It is fair to summarize by noting that our community's crises have by and large been the crises of the rest of Paterson," said Vander Klay.

As the pastor neared retirement, he kept busy in early 1996 training church members to take over for him. Looking back on the triumphs and setbacks of his time in the city, Vander Klay said he is glad his one-time summer job turned into a career.

"I have remained here both out of the conviction that God wanted me to stay and the never-ending challenge and often-surprising joy of ministering in this place where I have come so much to feel at home," he said.

FIGURE 18 Eugene Callender and V.B.S.

has had a large mail response from New York City. This is especially true of Harlem, the massive, ever-expanding section of New York that is predominantly populated with Negroes," Callender wrote, adding this irony: "As you may observe from the name *Harlem*, this section was the center of the original Dutch settlement."

An Atmosphere of Fear

Based on mail responses, Callender focused his efforts between 116th and 145th streets and Lenox and Eighth avenues — an area in which, Callender noted, "The Christian Reformed Church is conspicuous by its absence." In his first month and a half alone Callender made 127 calls and contacted eighty-five different families. Many of the people on whom he called reported being very impressed by Peter Eldersveld's sermons and by their clarity, variety of topics, and poignance. Some believed, according to Callender, that they "needed more of that type of preaching among Negroes." A few even reported they didn't leave home for their own church services until they had heard Eldersveld preach on the radio. Even though this often made them late for church, "they felt that the message of *The Back to God Hour* is of vital importance to them." [18] Callender also frequently found himself answering questions which were raised by *The Back to God Hour* sermons as well as meeting the spiritual needs of many shut-in radio listeners in Harlem.

Callender had many ideas and plans for the future. Just into his second month of work in Harlem, he recommended a *Back to God Hour* rally in Harlem, to be conducted in part by Harold Dekker. He also noted that some newly planned housing projects would open up a whole new field which he could target, as between fifteen hundred and five thousand people would soon be moving into the newly built apartment complexes. He fervently believed there was enough work to be done to warrant a permanent facility in Harlem, though his reports in future months would regularly express his shock at how expensive even the most dilapidated buildings were.

A modest building in need of much renovation could go for as high as $150,000, an economic reality that made the purchase of such a facility impossible for the CRC and its thus-far modest urban-ministry efforts. Still, Callender urged that a chapel be founded as an identifiable site for the ministry. As it was, Callender was conducting several weekly Bible studies out of local YMCA facilities. Although his initial reports occasionally expressed frustration at the slow pace of the work, Callender soon began using words like "fruitful" to describe his work of conducting Bible studies, bringing *The Back to God Hour* literature to listeners, visiting shut-ins, and getting into the new housing projects.

By the summer of 1952 the Board of Home Missions was impressed enough with Callender's work to formally extend a call to him to become a home missionary for the New York City area. In his letter of acceptance, Callender said,

I rejoice with you in the fact that our covenant God has led us into the field of Negro Evangelism. I am deeply humbled as I realize that the mantle of initiating this task has fallen on me. I know that of myself I am not equal to such a task. Thus, as I accept your call, I request your prayers. [19]

Thereafter Callender continued his work in Harlem and the Bronx, working out of local YMCAs to conduct Bible classes. He also continued doing follow-up for *The Back to God Hour* and, when finding people not yet acquainted with the program, encouraged them to listen, which many did.

But Callender could not escape or ignore the social pressures and prejudices afflicting the people of his mission field. In a report to the board in February 1952 he noted,

The Negroes [in Harlem] live in an atmosphere of ignorance, fear, prejudice, indifference, exploitation, and benevolence created by New York's white majority. It is the white segregation policy which is responsible for the housing situation in which thou-

sands of Negroes are squeezed into vermin-ridden, cold-water flats.... [W]hite avarice is to blame for the exorbitant rates they are charged. It is no wonder the Harlem Negro turns away from the established Church and uses alcohol, the Cult, and the Communist Party as escape mechanisms. I am of utmost certainty that our Reformed way of life with its God-centered, Biblical message and its tremendous social implications can meet the needs of the Harlem Negro. [20]

To meet such enormous needs, by late 1952 it was clear that the ministry would indeed require a permanent, visible site in Harlem. But the costs would likely be near $100,000 to purchase a lot and construct even a modest chapel. Callender urged the denomination to approve such an expenditure because the work was bearing more fruit than could be accommodated in individual homes or at the Harlem YMCA.

The "Y" chapel was small, seating a maximum of thirty for Sunday worship, thus creating routine overcrowding and discomfort for the worshipers. The chapel was also situated above the Y's restaurant, and the clang of silverware, crash of

FIGURE 19 Eugene Callender holding services outdoors at a street meeting.

dishes, and shouting of cooks were not adding anything positive to the Sunday services. Furthermore, the possibilities for work among children, while very great, could not be realized until more regular access to adequate space could be secured.

After numerous study reports and multiple contacts with local realtors, by November 1953 a building at 122nd Street and (then) Seventh Avenue was purchased for the more affordable sum of just over $36,000. The building, however, was in need of extensive repairs and renovation. Previously it had housed several stores, including a butcher's shop, a candy store, a laundry, and several apartments. (Callender once reported that the grease on the butcher shop's floor was several inches thick because the floors had never been mopped, only covered over and over again with sawdust.) The deal for the building, closed on January 4, 1954, established a visible presence and allowed Callender to map out a more defined parish for his ministry. But the work would still be challenging — even the immediate area around the new 122nd Street site contained over thirty thousand people (Harlem's population density in 1950 was nine hundred people per acre, ten times denser than most areas of New York at that time).

Throughout 1954, now operating out of a central location (though the renovation of the building would not be complete until well into 1955), Callender continued making what he termed "incessant calls" on *Back to God Hour* listeners, on friends referred by Bible-study attendees, and on the sick and shut-in. He also conducted classes designed to help people make formal profession of their faith in order to join an established church (though this was a problem in that the nearest Christian Reformed congregations were in New Jersey, twenty miles away). On March 6, 1955, however, several did make the trip into Paterson, New Jersey, to make their professions before the consistory of Second CRC.

Meanwhile Callender had been joined in his work by two lay mission workers: Miss Marjorie Visser of Sumas, Washington, and Miss Elsie Koop of Borculo, Michigan. Both Visser and Koop were 1955 graduates of the Reformed Bible Institute in Grand Rapids, Michigan. Visser's enthusiasm for the work in Harlem was fired when she heard Callender speak to a mission fest in Lynden, Washington, in 1954 (Callender was frequently on the road addressing mission groups throughout the United States). Koop became interested in the mission to Harlem during the course of her education at the Reformed Bible

FIGURE 20 Manhattan CRC at Seventh Avenue and 122nd Street.

FIGURE 21 Building renovations.

FIGURE 22 Gordon Negen, left.

Institute. Both were appointed to serve with Callender in April of 1955 and began their Harlem mission work in July.

With the increased staff the mission was able to sponsor a month-long daily vacation Bible school in July of 1955. The 89 children who attended the program that month encouraged the staff to hold a second Bible school in August, this time bringing in 151 children. By the fall of 1955 follow-up to the summer Bible schools led to increased numbers at all of the mission's activities. The Sunday-school program enrolled 78 children, and an average of 25 adults attended morning and evening worship services.

Callender noted to the board, however, the difficulties involved in getting adults to attend worship. Some already belonged (nominally at least) to other churches; some simply did not wish to come; others resisted worshiping in what amounted to a storefront church. But many others did not attend because, simply put, their lives were riddled with problems. Many in this Christian Reformed parish had *"no zest for living." A whole dimension of their life has left them. The religious dimension is missing entirely. Quite a few live only for the next welfare check, or for the next bottle of beer or shot of heroin. Fear, ignorance, superstition, tension, pressure, and pain permeate their life.*[21]

But matters gradually improved for the mission. By October, forty-six people were attending worship. Midweek activities were also going well, including a junior choir, girls and boys clubs, and various recreation programs. Callender, Koop, and Visser also sought to alleviate the physical suffer-

FIGURE 23 Children lined up to enter Manhattan CRC for vacation Bible school.

ing in this area by distributing clothing (donated by New Jersey congregations) and joining advocacy efforts to get rents lowered in various tenements in the area.

Callender continued his work, slowly but surely gathering a congregation. By the summer of 1956 Calvin Theological Seminary was sending summer interns to assist Callender (seminarians Gordon Negen and Edward Meyer were two of the first such interns, making over sixteen hundred calls on neighborhood families during the summer of 1956). By mid 1956 the building was at long last able to be occupied fully. Attendance at worship was by then over 60, though summer outdoor services in a nearby vacant lot frequently attracted over 200. The Sunday School enrollment was nearing 120 children, and that summer's Bible school attracted 276.

The needs of high-school-aged young people became a matter of increasing concern to Callender and the staff, so in 1956 Ren Broekhuizen was brought on staff. Broekhuizen worked diligently to reach out to the youth, transporting them to and from mission activities and coordinating programs designed to keep them off the streets.

Another program run by the Harlem mission was known as Friendly Town. During the summer months the Friendly Town program placed inner-city children in Christian homes for a couple of weeks. Young people were transported to as far away as the Midwest to spend time on the farms and in the homes of Christian Reformed people. During the summer of 1956 ninety children were placed in homes from Whitinsville, Massachusetts, to Graafschap, Michigan. The program had the dual advantage of giving inner-city children a taste of a radically different environment and giving the members of the denomination a chance to break out of their own isolation by participating in the mission to the faraway and essentially foreign place that was Harlem.

FIGURE 24 Garbage-collection day on 122nd Street.

A Social Gospel

The mission's new auditorium was dedicated on October 22, 1956. Through an emphasis on "kerygma and koinon-

FIGURE 25–26 Participants in the Friendly Town program in 1960.

ia," Callender called people to the worship and service of God. By then attendance at worship had risen to around ninety in the morning and sixty in the evening. Many of the worshipers presented grave spiritual needs but even graver physical ones. Some were among New York's poorest, with families of five often subsisting on as little as $140 per month.

The need for a ministry of mercy was readily apparent. Thus the Mid-Harlem Community Parish, as it was then called, often got involved in bringing sick children to the doctor (and paying the bill), pointing out to the authorities rents which were higher than the legal limit (and getting them reduced accordingly), providing clothing for ill-clad children and their families, and calling building-code violations to the attention of the New York Housing Commission.

To those who questioned the validity of these many and varied programs, Callender stated,

> Our attempts to reach men with the good news of hope and justice and God's love will continue to carry us into non-conventional church activities. We have been using our church and a vacant lot for church functions, undertaking community action campaigns to demonstrate Christ's continuing concern through our Parish for man's soul, health, and welfare, and fighting for justice in the economic and political structures of our world in response to God's redemptive purpose.[22]

> Perhaps the most obvious feature which one can notice in our attempts to relate the Gospel to our community is our awareness of our Social concern. In Harlem we must be aware of the teem-

FIGURE 27 Harlem backyards.

evangelistic task, giving proportionally less of this time to projects of a civic nature."[24]

When a team of church visitors inspected the work of Callender and the mission in January of 1958, the team noted with gratitude Callender's gifts for communication, particularly in public worship. They also felt that while his approach to evangelism encompassed many "social" concerns, these did not unduly impinge on the spiritual aspects of the work. These same visitors noted the somewhat unusual worship practices (a higher, more Episcopal liturgy) but felt conscious effort had been made to make the worship meaningful and that, for this field anyway, the slightly different style of worship should not be viewed as a problem.

Still, there were those who were concerned with the tenor of Callender's work. Callender responded,

ing thousands whose need for a total and most virile ministry cries out from the disintegration of their overcrowded streets. As one sees our Parish actively concerned with the struggle against bad housing and ill-health, various forms of injustice or inadequate education, against the scourge of drug addiction and the loneliness that breeds delinquency, one really does feel that this concern is not being used as some kind of "bait" to attract people in their need to some specially religious event but that it is recognized as an integral part of the gospel of Jesus Christ and the Mission of his Church. [23]

In this work Callender was joined in January of 1957 by Dolores C. Dixon, a member of the Harlem community who, among other things, played the piano and organ for worship, taught Sunday school, made calls on sick and shut-in members, conducted follow-up work, prepared music for the worship services, and ran an after-school class at the parish. However, even as Callender and his staff were wrestling with issues of poverty and social justice, some who were observing the ministry from afar began to worry about other, more theological, issues.

Some began to grow suspicious of the style and content of the worship services Callender was conducting in Harlem. A November 27, 1957, letter from Henry Blystra, secretary for the executive committee of the Board of Home Missions, informed Callender of their "disagreement with the episcopally oriented liturgy ... and vestment of the minister. We ask that the missionary take immediate steps to change this present order of things to conform with the accepted order that obtains in the Christian Reformed Church." They also instructed Callender "to spend a much greater part of his time in the specific spiritual aspects of his

One basic fact must be realized about our Harlem work. That is to restore faith in God, we must restore to the people in this community, whether or not they ever join the parish, a sense of individual worth. Harlem is a microcosm in which the almost unparalleled overcrowding of hundreds of thousands of persons into a few blocks, the sordidness of life, and the de facto segregation arising out of Ghetto living [erode any sense of self worth]. Therefore, the parish

FIGURE 28 Dolores Dixon.

FIGURE 29 Playtime in New York City.

must in its own effort to communicate the Gospel, enter into problems of housing, of the education of children, of race discrimination, of injustice, of violence, of drug addiction, and of the cold impersonality of public service, by sharing these problems and by taking action to meet them. [25]

But Callender also went on to say,

If there is one impression that I have received from all the conferences that I have had with the Visiting Committees, it is this: There is a strong element of suspicion about me and my aims in Harlem. This may stem from the usual suspicion "outsiders" generally receive from the CRC, or it may be that there are basic cultural differences that can never be resolved. [26]

Unhappily, the voices of criticism continued to multiply. Some began to lament that Callender did not appear to be devoting sufficient time to administrative or organizational work. Callender had also rankled some of those supervising him by accepting a weekly preaching assignment at Riker's Island Prison without first seeking anyone's permission. Although Callender stated that the extra income from his Riker's Island work was a great help to him and his family, the mission board eventually asked him to leave the work at Riker's.

By 1959 matters came to a head when Callender and his wife found their marriage teetering on the brink of divorce. Callender's response to the situation, to say the least, did not sit well with those sent to counsel with him on the matter. Callender admitted that a failed marriage was not "ideal." But he did not see it as a hindrance to his work among blacks in Harlem, nor did he understand why the CRC would single out divorce as being singularly disqualifying for ministerial office.

But the executive committee was not happy with Callender's lack of seriousness about what was, to their minds, an utterly serious matter. They recommended that he take a two-month leave of absence from August until September, during which time he had to effect a reconciliation with his wife or be removed from his missionary post. The committee which worked with Callender saw no other options in that, given the situation, "the blessing of the Lord cannot be expected upon the Missionary's labors."

Callender did not wait for his leave of absence to be up,

however. He resigned his ordination and mission post in the Christian Reformed Church, accepting instead a call to the Church of the Master Presbyterian Church a few blocks east on 122nd Street. Having been denied the opportunity to preach a farewell sermon, the denomination's first African-American missionary/preacher ended his Christian Reformed career on a bitter and unhappy note. Second CRC in Paterson concluded that Callender had become doctrinally heterodox even as he personally was living in a sinful state. Such a person, they felt, did not deserve to preach even a farewell sermon.

Meanwhile, already during the leave of absence, another minister had been brought in temporarily to take Callender's place. Reverend Gordon Negen, two years out of Calvin Seminary, had been a preacher in

FIGURE 30 Carrie Goodwyn of Manhattan CRC.

FIGURE 31 Children playing in closed 122nd Street.

Lodi, New Jersey. Negen had long shown an interest in inner-city work, having already worked at the Harlem mission as a seminary intern a few years earlier. Following Callender's resignation, it was decided to offer Negen a permanent position as Callender's successor, the board having previously ruled the color of Callender's replacement to be a matter of indifference.

Interestingly, within six months of Negen's arrival at the Mid-Harlem Community Parish, the church applied and received approval for formal organization in January 1960 and was christened the Manhattan Christian Reformed Church at its formal organizational worship service on March 20, 1960. By the end of 1960 the congregation numbered forty-nine confessing members and forty-five children, for a total of twenty families.

Although Callender's leaving was a great shock to the parish, the work continued to go well under Negen's leadership, including the sponsorship of a narcotics support group led by James Allen, who joined the staff in the summer of 1960. Allen was himself an ex-addict who had found his way to recovery through Callender's narcotics rehabilitation program, which had begun in 1958. By 1964 the addict-recovery program was doing a vital ministry — in that year alone Allen had contact with over 1,800 addicts. If addicts were still active users, Allen steered them toward admitting themselves to a drug-detoxification clinic in the local hospital. Former users who were struggling to stay off drugs were enrolled in classes and support groups at the church in a kind of "aftercare" program which served as a follow-up to their medical detoxification. This program clearly was one of Callender's greatest legacies, typifying the total and comprehensive approach needed for that particular mission field.

The work in Harlem continued, now as a formal Christian Reformed congregation, with a staff which included Duane VanderBrug, who served as minister of evangelism; Bernard Greenfield, who labored among the youth; James Allen, who worked with the narcotics rehabilitation program; and Dolores Dixon, who continued her musical and youth work. The ministry was varied, encompassing all of the normal groups and clubs of other congregations but also meeting the social needs and economic crises unique to that area. Although Callender had been criticized at times for the social and civic focus of his work, under Negen's leadership social issues continued to occupy a

major portion of Manhattan's ministry. Negen himself was deeply committed to the larger civil-rights movement, even participating in a Freedom Ride from June 12 through June 16, 1961 (an action which earned him a fair amount of scorn from many in the wider denomination).

The Manhattan church also launched, largely at the urging of Duane VanderBrug, its own local radio ministry to the New York area — the *Evening Altar* began a once-weekly fifteen-minute broadcast every Thursday, starting on September 21, 1961, over station WADO. Through the broadcast the church was able to send out the message of salvation and to let people know about the church's programs of social outreach and support. Phone lines were

FIGURE 32 James Allen, Manhattan CRC staff member, 1961.

FIGURE 33 Manhattan CRC Council, 1960. Left to right, Clarence Rowe, Torry Brown, Gordon Negen, James Allen, and Dave Cunningham.

An Iowa Farm Boy Comes to Chicago

First, a woman stood and asked fellow members of Roseland Christian Reformed Church to pray for an aunt who had been strangled two days before by a neighbor.

Then, on a sunny autumn afternoon in 1995 in the same south Chicago church, another woman climbed to her feet to thank the congregation for its support in helping her kick a twenty-year drug habit.

Not long after that, a middle-aged man told churchgoers about a vision he had of Jesus. This vision, he said, sustains him as he copes with the death of his son, cut down not long before by gangland gunfire. Pray for him and his dead boy, he asked.

Once the prayer requests had been made, Reverend Tony Van Zanten, the white Iowa-born minister of this predominantly black congregation, bowed his head, touched together his hands, and brought the petitions before God.

"Father God, thank you for your gifts and the names by which you call us," he said in a solemn voice. "We especially thank you for the promise of a new life that we have in Jesus. We ask you, God, for your grace to help us in our many struggles here in this city. We ask you, Father God, as you always have, to remain with us in all the commotion and pain and confusion of our lives."

Heads bowed, eyes closed, many of the people in the pews murmured "Amen."

Fearful and troubled as they were by the violent life that confronted them daily in the nearby neighborhoods, comfort came to the church members this morning in the words their preacher spoke, in the songs they sang, and in the verses of the Bible they read. Fed and sustained at least for a time, they soon filed out of their seats, mingled with one another in the aisles, and then started toward the doors leading out to sunshine.

Later, when the church had cleared, Van Zanten sat at a table in the basement, ate lukewarm spaghetti, and tried to put into perspective almost twenty years of ministry deep in the bleeding heart of urban America. In an hour or so, the preacher would pile several teenagers into the church bus and drive to Indiana for an evening service. But for now, he stayed still, at least for a few moments, and spoke about the importance of his denomination's work in the inner city.

"I don't think it is awkward for the Christian Reformed Church to be here," he said. "For twenty years, through various programs and with a great deal of help from the broader church, we've been able to offer people service, worship, and training — and all in the name of God."

Service, worship, and training in this small, brutal, and yet always acutely human corner of the Midwest has meant much heartbreak and a good deal of sorrow for Van Zanten and his family. At the same time, ministry in the tumultuous, sometimes hopeless, midst of the city has also brought profound rewards, object lessons in grace, and a continuing conviction that God's love is the best and finally the only answer to the problems besetting urban dwellers in the last part of the twentieth century.

"Being here has been very invigorating. There is never a dull moment," said Van Zanten, who worked in Harlem in New York before coming to Illinois. "By and large, I see myself as magnificently blessed to be in this crazy mix of things going on and even once in a while being able to touch and, with God's help, change someone's life."

In a yet unpublished book detailing his experiences in Chicago, Van Zanten recalls the people, places, and events that have shaped his ministry, touched his life, and at times brought him to tears or given him great joy.

He remembers the prostitute who showed up in his office clad only in a ratty trench coat, which she pro-

FIGURE 34 Tony and Donna Van Zanten

FIGURE 35 The congregation outside Emmanuel Christian Reformed Church, October 8, 1989.

ceeded to drop as she tearfully asked for help turning her life around.

There was the man who broke into the church and then, upon hearing the pastor arrive, made a hasty escape through a partially barred window. On the way out, his right middle finger was snagged by a sharp piece of metal. When police arrived, they found no robber, but only the finger dangling there.

And there was the dreary afternoon two men robbed and threatened to kill Van Zanten as he walked from a phone booth near his home. Or there was the older woman who told him she once was such a bad alcoholic that she didn't remember when her husband died, of what he died, or where he was buried. This woman eventually became a good friend.

Perhaps the most devastating event in his career came one Sunday morning in March of 1985 when Ronald Nelson, a history professor at Northwestern College in Iowa, was gunned down outside the Roseland Christian Ministries Center by a heroin addict on a desperate search for money for a fix.

Nelson had been at the service with his wife, Marion, his son, Roger, and Roger's fiancee, Sandi. In the parking lot, as they made lunch plans, evil arrived in the form of the junkie with a gun. After herding them into their car and stealing their money, he shot the professor in the stomach. Although he escaped that day, the killer was eventually caught.

Also involved in the event was Van Zanten's wife, Donna, and son, who was 17 at the time. Both were threatened, although neither was physically harmed.

For a painful time the Van Zantens struggled with whether they wanted to leave the inner-city ministry. But they stayed, in part because members of the congregation had made it clear that they were as shocked and enraged by the murder as the Van Zantens were.

Later, in a devotional booklet, Van Zanten wrote of Ronald Nelson's death:

Why did it happen? I don't know. I do know that his life was laid down in the service of the Lord. I do know that he is a twentieth-century martyr. I do know that he blessed those who persecuted him. I do know that the word of the Lord came to me through him.

In 1995, Van Zanten's congregation met for worship in a former Reformed Church in America church building on State Street just north of 103rd. About half a mile away, on Michigan near 109th, was the 23,000-square-foot structure in which the church's outreach ministry was housed. It all began, in fact, in this cavernous former Ford Motor Corporation dealership in 1976. That was when three Chicago-area classes, the Synodical Council on Race Relations, the Home Missions board, and officials from the Christian Reformed World Relief Committee decided to sponsor an inner-city effort.

Located in a neighborhood begun by Dutch market gardeners, the ministry center was first used as a car showroom and warehouse. Then the denomination's Back to God Hour ministry took it over, followed by the CRWRC. When the CRWRC moved its work to the denominational headquarters in Grand Rapids, the building was available for a ministry providing for the needs of the people in this changing community.

In 1971 there were eight churches of the Reformed persuasion in the area.

Two years later, only one, Emmanuel Reformed, was left. This neighborhood was once called Hope, Illinois, but that had changed a long time before 1976, when Van Zanten arrived and opened the center.

After his lunch of spaghetti, Van Zanten drove to the center to do some paperwork before making the trip to Indiana in the church bus.

In a drafty garage area once used as a gymnasium and now converted to a large, open living area, about fifty men and women, all homeless, sat and watched the Chicago Bears play on a color TV as Van Zanten entered. In the kitchen a dinner of pizza, pasta, and marshmallow salad was being prepared. Many of those watching the football game turned, smiled, and said hello to Van Zanten, who paused to catch a few minutes of the game with them.

"Pastor Tony is something else. He's like a Duracell battery. He just keeps going and going. He's always there. We count on him," said one of the men on the chairs in front of the TV.

On the top floor of this aluminum-sided concrete building is a seventy-five-bed shelter called Midnight Ministries. It opens in early November every year and serves as one of the largest free motels for men in this part of town throughout the blustery Chicago winter. A corporation that provides homes for the needy and a thrift shop are also based here.

The busiest part of the building on this afternoon was the Drop-In Center. While most of the homeless men and women watched football, a few played cards, read the newspaper, or talked. One man sat in a corner, a wild wide grin on his face, his eyes locked into nowhere.

"We're trying to give these people a sense of family," said Shirley Griffin, coordinator of the Drop-In Center. "We're offering them a chance to get off the streets and rest. This is a place of refuge for them."

Dino Artis looked at it that way, too. Without a home and job, he was a regular at the center. Outside, he daily encountered dope deals gone bad, the ravages of poverty, armies of prostitutes, a landscape pocked by decay and arson-set fires. In the center, however, he often found another spirit and atmosphere.

"It's like a social center," he said. "They give you help here. One of the big things for me are the Narcotics Anonymous meetings that they hold."

As halftime approached on the TV, Betty Collins was in the kitchen, just about ready to dish up supper.

Collins lost her factory job in the early 1990s. When that happened, she knew she needed work, but she also needed something deeper and more powerful to soothe the distress that plagued her soul.

"When I walked in here, they made me feel welcome and like I was someone special," she said. "Pastor Tony talked to me. He knew what I needed, and that was that I needed some place to belong."

Just about ready to take the teens to sing at the church across the border in Indiana, Van Zanten said there are days when he wonders if it is all worth it. This is when the drugs take their terrible, predictable toll, when one more family splits up, when yet one more fire races through an apartment building killing children, when one more crook breaks into the church. At those times he questions why a farm boy from Iowa has worked for so long so deep inside an American city.

But then something always happens: someone gets sober, a husband and wife reunite, a prostitute comes in off the street, a home is refurbished, and a family from the projects takes up residence in safety and comfort. Or maybe something funny happens. He hears a joke, sees a smile, gets one more lesson in the gritty beauty of urban life. And as a result, he knows once again that Roseland is exactly where God wants him, as well as his denomination, to be.

"This truth is self-evident," he said. "To be CRC, urban, and black is not a contradiction. I really believe that there is a rhythm, a cadence, and a really good beat to all the work that we are doing down here."

used for people to call in and talk to staff members like James Allen about drug problems and other issues in their lives.

The church continued to grow, reaching thirty-four families by 1963. Negen continued as the church's pastor until 1968, after which he was succeeded by James White, who ministered from 1969 to 1977, and J.K. Boersma, who worked from 1979 to 1983. Following Boersma's departure, however, the ministry slowed, and the church was unable to attract another pastor.

After many years without a pastor to guide the congregation, membership dwindled. By 1992 some long-time members of the Manhattan church began to look for help from its own history by contacting the retired Eugene Callender and asking him to come and once again lead the congregation. Callender consented to do so — on one condition: that the church leave the Christian Reformed denomination. The congregation agreed, affiliating instead with a Baptist storefront church near the former ministry site. The CRC's latest contact with its premier inner-city church came in 1994, when, at Callender's invitation, former minister of evangelism Duane VanderBrug spoke to the congregation once again.

FIGURE 36 Aftermath of the Watts riots in Los Angeles, California.

It was becoming clear to many Americans that the United States was not the great melting pot after all — it had instead become a boiling cauldron of racist division.

The New Nathanael Institute

During the 1960s, Chicago, like nearly all of America's major cities, became the setting for racial strife. The race riots which tore the fabric of American society during that most turbulent of decades frequently erupted also in Chicago's streets, climaxing in the 1968 Democratic National Convention in Chicago. The chaotic images of strife, bludgeoning, anger, hatred, and protest spilled into living rooms around the country even as protestors raged down Michigan Avenue and surged around the Conrad Hilton Hotel. These images far overshadowed anything which took place on the convention floor. By then it was becoming clear to many Americans that the United States was not the great melting pot after all — it had instead become a boiling cauldron of racist division.

By 1970 Chicago and its suburbs had become a focal point also for Christian Reformed race conflict as Classis Chicago North found itself at odds with the synod and with many in the denomination generally. Although the 1960s in Chicago-area Christian Reformed circles ended on a sad note, they had surely not begun that way.

By mid 1955 it had become apparent to the Chicago Mission Board and to the Board of Home Missions that the Nathanael Institute at 1241 South Pulaski was no longer in an area populated by the Jews on whose local presence the Institute depended (the institutional approach, as traced out in a previous chapter, could not function unless there were Jewish neighbors and passersby who could make use of the Institute's various services). So as the Institute prepared to pull up stakes and follow the Jewish population north to Rogers Park, some began to ponder whether the Nathanael Institute facilities could be converted for use in Negro evangelization. The old Institute building was now as perfectly poised to reach out to the area's growing Negro population as it had been to reach out to local Jews when it had been built in 1928.

A June 27, 1955, report written by committee members B. Van Someren, E.L. Haan, J.R. Rozendal, and J.M. Vande

Kieft concluded that there was a great need for the Christian Reformed Church to minister to the blacks living in the area now known as Lawndale. Since many churches (including not a few Christian Reformed congregations) had abandoned this inner-city area in favor of following their constituencies into the suburbs, an ecclesiastical and mission vacuum had been created which a new work in the old Nathanael Institute could meet.[27]

With a new staff, including, it was hoped, a Negro evangelist in the style of Eugene Callender, and with minimal ren-

FIGURE 37 Doris Larken and Louise Buist.

ovation to the building itself, the committee believed there was no reason a new mission outreach could not be started almost immediately after the Nathanael Institute's planned relocation in 1957. (The local mission board knew of the exorbitant real-estate costs which Callender had encountered in New York and recognized the huge blessing of an already-owned building.)

The initial sponsoring agency for the mission work in Lawndale was the Chicagoland Board of Missions. Mr. Clarence Buist, a graduate of the Reformed Bible Institute and a long-time mission worker for Warren Park CRC, was one of the first evangelists to move into the old Jewish mission outpost on Pulaski. For many years Buist had worked out of a storefront at 13th and Karlov streets (very close to the old Nathanael Institute). Now operating out of a highly visible and more complete facility, Buist soon saw the work of the Lawndale Gospel Chapel expand. Already by 1958 the new chapel made it possible for him to hold weekly Bible studies and youth clubs, make routine calls on local residents, and conduct Sunday worship services in the Institute's gymnasium. Although the number of attenders at worship started out very small (some weeks attracting only about a dozen), the Sunday school was regularly ministering to around one hundred children.

Compared to Harlem, the work in Chicago broadened much more quickly (perhaps owing to the more visible and permanent facility which it had from the beginning). By the summer of 1959 over 185 children were enrolled in the chapel's daily vacation Bible school. A number of the parents of these children also began to express their desire to profess their faith and join the Lawndale "church." Thus Classis Chicago North began to see the need to take over the ministry as a classical, and thus more formally ecclesiastical, enterprise.

By March 1959 Classis Chicago North formally approved the work among the Negroes, effective January 1, 1960. By early 1962 the Lawndale Chapel reported fifteen Sunday-school instruction classes enrolling a total of over 200 children, ten weekday Bible clubs and societies, twenty-four confessing members, and 35 baptized children. During the summer of 1962 the vacation Bible school enrolled 335 children and was able to reach a number of new areas through

FIGURE 38 Clarence Buist with the first members of Lawndale CRC; left to right, Anne Owens, Mrs. Robertson, Mrs. Rains, Mrs. Davis, Mrs. Benton, Mrs. Robinson, Bill Larken, and Doris Larken.

backyard story times in various neighborhoods. By the summer of 1963 over 430 children and young people would participate in various programs. Taking a cue from the Harlem mission's Friendly Town program, the Lawndale Chapel instituted the Lawndale Ambassadors program, which likewise sent inner-city children to families in rural areas of Grand Haven, Michigan; Volga, South Dakota; and southwestern Minnesota.

But as the Lawndale church approached formal organization in 1963, Reverend Earl Marlink of Classis Chicago North asked in a September 19, 1962, report,

Are we ready to extend to our Negro brothers and sisters in Christ the full measure of ecclesiastical fellowship? Are we prepared to have them present at Classis? Invite them as members of the covenant to share the privilege of Christian education? We dare not forestall discussion of this problem any longer. May God give us grace to be Biblical in our thinking on the matter, disallowing any past prejudices to cloud our classical boundaries. [28]

Though such questions were in the air, the Lawndale work was going so very well that the Lawndale Christian Reformed Church was formally established in 1963, with Reverend Peter Huiner, who had been working there since 1962 while still finishing his seminary studies, as its first ordained pastor.

The CRC Selma

Unhappily, Marlink's questions proved prescient. Past prejudices hovered like a dark cloud on the horizon of the Lawndale work. Following the church's formal organization in late 1963, the work continued briskly, and the congregation grew steadily. By the mid to late 1960s, as racial tensions erupted in Chicago and across the United States, the congregation had grown sufficiently that many of the church's members expressed a desire for their children to receive a Christian education. The closest Christian Reformed-run elementary school was Timothy Christian School in nearby Cicero, Illinois. Since the white parents of local Christian Reformed congregations sent their children to Timothy, it was natural that black parents do likewise.

In 1965, however, to the shock of the Lawndale staff and the deep hurt of the parents, the Timothy Christian School board ruled that no black children would be allowed to enroll at Timothy's Cicero school. Fearing criticism and violence

FIGURE 39 Timothy Christian Elementary School in Cicero.

from the conservative, all-white Cicero community, the board voted against black enrollment and its consequent desegregation of the Timothy school and, by extension, of the Cicero community.

Thus began what would prove to be many years of pain and frustration as the Lawndale community tried without success to change the board's mind. For its part, the Timothy board claimed the decision was not a matter of believing blacks to be inferior but only a matter of public safety for the students and the school as it feared a violent public backlash from the Cicero community were it to take the step of enrolling black children. The board's minutes explain its rationale:

The board realizes that the children from our Christian Reformed Church in the Lawndale area should be accepted for admission .... However, enrolling them in our schools in the Cicero area ... [involves] dangers that all those in touch with the prevailing racial attitudes are well aware of. [29]

As proof of their ostensible lack of prejudice, the Timothy board pointed to the fact that in September 1966 three black students were enrolled in Timothy Christian High School, located in nearby Elmhurst, Illinois — a community not as opposed to the presence of blacks as Cicero was.

Most in the Lawndale community, however, were not buying the rationale the Timothy board was selling. Many believed there were sufficient law and order personnel in Cicero to ensure protection if it was needed. Many others believed that while opposition in Cicero was no doubt real, there was very little evidence that actual physical harm would be visited on any person or on the school's buildings.

FIGURE 40 Lawndale CRC looking south on Pulaski Road, Chicago.

Indeed, after the Timothy board issued a public statement indicating why it was not allowing black children to enroll — namely, the threat of physical harm to students and/or facilities — the Cicero town council responded by promising "full and complete protection [to Negro students]. We will definitely protect students. We've got to protect everybody whether they're residents of Cicero or not; that's the law."[30] The Timothy board, however, stood by its decision and its grounds for years, defying ecclesiastical, classical, and synodical injunctions to repent of an action, which, as Henry Stob put it, "is calculated to shame us all."[31]

For the first few years of the controversy the Lawndale community poured its hope and energies into various efforts to get Classis Chicago North involved, quietly using its influence and leverage to help the Timothy board see its sin and change its policy and also doing its best to keep this issue out of the public press and media. In addition to being the year that would see the assassinations of Martin Luther King, Jr., and Robert Kennedy as well as various riots in Chicago and elsewhere, 1968 proved also to be a crisis year for what had

become known as the Lawndale-Timothy situation. Synod 1968 weighed in on the issue through a Synodical Declaration on Race Relations, which proclaimed that

fear of persecution or of disadvantage to self or our institutions arising out of obedience to Christ does not warrant denial to anyone, for reasons of race or color, of full Christian fellowship and privilege within the church or related organizations such as Christian colleges and schools ... and that members of the Christian Reformed Church advocating such denial, by whatever means, must be reckoned as disobedient to Christ and be dealt with according to the provisions of the Church Order regarding admonition and discipline.[32]

Despite this firm statement from the denomination's highest ruling body, however, the Lawndale-Timothy situation only worsened. Meeting in special session on July 28, 1969, Classis Chicago North, while advocating yet another committee to work with the Timothy board, refused to mandate that this committee do its work in the light of the previous year's synodical declaration. At its next regular meeting, on September 17, 1969, the classis again backed away from decisive action or witness to the truth when it refused to adopt the recommendation of its committee to "declare to be sinful the present policy of the Timothy Christian Board by which black covenant children are excluded from Timothy schools in Cicero, and to declare that this policy cannot be continued with willful disobedience to Christ."

Through it all, the mission workers at Lawndale were infuriated. Mission worker William "Bud" Ipema (who was a seminarian working under the auspices of Young Life) expressed his frustration in his August 1969 monthly report:

How does one bring the message of a Christ embraced by the Christian Reformed Church to black youth ... when we as a church continue to refuse to rise against the Christ-rending injustice existing in our own church? How can verbal witness of love, acceptance, equality, and unity in Christ be brought by anyone wherever, when the action of the church bringing that witness is totally contrary? Where are the men of action who call themselves reformers?[33]

Likewise, mission worker and seminary intern Karl J. Westerhof informed the Board of Home Missions,

Only God knows the depths of the wounds and the intensity of the frustration among the Christians at Lawndale Church, and it is only in his strength that we continue to stand. Having exhausted every possible route, including a special meeting of Classis and the calling in of the Synodical Commission on the Christian and Race Relations, we believe there are two urgent questions that cannot be avoided: 1) Do black Christians really have an integral part and a meaningful future in our denomination? 2) How can our denomination have an authentic ministry to the urban crisis?[34]

In the aftermath of this crisis, mission workers found it

difficult to look their black brothers and sisters in the eye. The morale of the congregation was also reported to sag, and attendance at some meetings declined. The staff reported embarrassment and a feeling of shame in inviting members into a denomination in which they so manifestly had no place and in which they would quite soon bump into a racism at least as ugly as anything they might encounter in the larger culture.

These problems were somewhat exacerbated by the fact that the Lawndale congregation was at that time without a full-time ordained pastor, the congregation having reluctantly urged Reverend Duane VanderBrug to accept a position with Home Missions, particularly in connection with the newly emerging synodical committee on race matters in 1969, in order that he might promote wider sensitivity to the same urban and race issues with which they were dealing in Chicago. But according to Westerhof, whether the congregation had an ordained minister or not, the simple fact was that "the physical and emotional and spiritual energy of the congregation have been drained into overcoming the resistance of fellow Christians in the classis." 35

The 1970 and 1971 synods both declared Classis Chicago North to be in contempt of synod and ordered it to bring itself into line with synodical declarations on race relations.

FIGURE 41 Cicero city-limits sign: a study in irony.

The classis refused to take any decisive action except for sending a pastoral letter of concern to the Timothy board. By 1972 Classis Chicago North, far from complying with synodical declarations on race, appealed to synod to change its race policies, especially its past statements regarding the Lawndale-Timothy situation.

Matters became even more polarized when, in October 1971, three black families of the Lawndale community, with the financial aid and counsel of the Christian Reformed race committee, filed a lawsuit in U.S. District Court, Chicago. The suit urged the court to issue an injunction forcing the Timothy board to comply with the law of the land in enrolling black children and to take legal action against any citizens of Cicero who would try to block such a move. The families also sought personal damages in the amount of $22,000 and punitive damages amounting to $100,000.

The suit drew a storm of comment and protest as writers across the denomination wrestled with the justice of lawsuits in the light of the apostle Paul's biblical injunctions against lawsuits in the church. More progressive commentators in places like *The Reformed Journal* concluded that in this situation, having exhausted all other means for over six years, the litigants were surely justified. More conservative writers decried the suit as sub-Christian and vigorously protested the use of denominational monies to finance such a legal action.

The suit nevertheless went forward with little difficulty in the courts. On November 23, 1971, Federal Judge Hubert L. Will issued an unequivocal judgment:

It is just as unconstitutional to be discriminatory under alleged coercion or intimidation as it is to be discriminatory enthusiastically and voluntarily. A discrimination isn't discrimination depending on what are the motivations. It is discrimination depending on what your conduct is, and nothing that I read in this complaint ... [is] a justification for unconstitutional discrimination. 36

Despite legal and ecclesiastical injunctions directed against Cicero, most black parents of the Lawndale community began to steer clear of Timothy Christian School, choosing instead to send their children to other schools. One such school, Des Plaines Christian School, had courageously made a stand for racial equality by inviting Lawndale's disenfranchised black children to attend the Des Plaines school. Though this required an expensive and dangerous two-and-a-half-hour daily bus ride over busy highways, thirty-six Lawndale children did attend Des Plaines Christian School.

In future years a Christian school opened in Lawndale itself, thus alleviating some of these difficulties. Meanwhile, the Timothy Christian schools sold their Cicero facilities in the early 1970s, moving their entire school system to Elmhurst. While these developments solved some of the practical problems of Christian education for Lawndale children, a residue of bitterness and suspicion became the unhappy legacy of the Lawndale-Timothy crisis.

Meanwhile, on another front, the Lawndale CRC in 1970 lamented what it termed "resistance" from Classis Chicago North in granting Lawndale full partnership status. The classis seemed to prefer viewing and treating Lawndale as a mission outpost only, not pouring any more money into it than it had to. At least some mission workers felt that it was the black constituency of Lawndale CRC which led to this reluctance — the message to black Christians that they were not worthy of full ecclesiastical inclusion but were therefore relegated to a de facto second-class "chapel" status.

They, like Eugene Callender fifteen years earlier, also noted the official suspicion of anything smacking of a Social Gospel approach. Hence the classis routinely refused to fund certain programs of a social impact or nature. The same forces which led white Christians and their churches to move away from the core city and its problems led to later reluctance to engage that area fully in ministry.

A 1970 Lawndale report noted that within a few blocks of the Lawndale CRC were the former locations of two Christian Reformed churches which had been abandoned when the area's population began to change. Also nearby was the building which had once housed the Timothy Christian School (the building had by then been bought by a black Baptist church), which stood as a grim reminder of the current crisis with Timothy in Cicero.

The results, according to a 1970 church profile, were declining membership, a lack of zeal, a lack of desire to bring in black friends and neighbors, cynicism from teens about the church and about the CRC in particular, and lurking fears that the church may not have a future at all. A 1976 history written by Lawndale's third pastor, Reverend Rich Grevengoed, claims that as the Timothy crisis continued in the early 1970s, energy and time for evangelism were sacrificed to combat the racism in the area and in the school. Grevengoed says,

Needless to say, this was not the best time to conduct a vigorous evangelism program as the energy and the mood were not ripe for this endeavor. The Sunday school was virtually disbanded, church attendance dwindled to 35-40 worshipers, the building became more and more run down, and there was even an

FIGURE 42 The Chicago Civic Commission urging all to attend church regularly.

overture brought to Classis Chicago North to close down Lawndale by having the Classis withdraw its support. Whites were leaving the fellowship and there were few new professions recorded from the community. [37]

Unhappily, the valiant and loving mission efforts of some were, for a time, all but eclipsed by a cloud of racism.

Moving Forward

By the mid 1970s the work at Lawndale began to rebound. Starting in 1973 Barbara Clayton began working at the Lawndale church. Her presence as the first black on the Lawndale staff helped stimulate a new sense of vigor following the dismal decline of the early seventies. Clayton was instrumental in developing black leadership in the church, in reaching out to young people, and in developing programs designed to meet social needs.

Her formal title was director of religious education, and she took care of community-directed projects like the Sunday school, sewing classes, senior-citizen assistance programs, weekday recreational activities, Bible clubs, and the numerous summer programs, including coordination of all SWIM (Summer Workshop in Ministry) participants. By the mid seventies Lawndale was thriving again, with numerous professions of faith, more indigenous leadership and teaching coming from within the congregation proper, up to one hundred children participating in year-round weekly programs, and a large number of non-members attending weekly worship services.

Clayton's innovative thinking in the area of education — she personally developed tailor-made curricula for the children to whom Lawndale ministered — continued to serve Lawndale well until her departure in September 1983. Her ministry was generally considered to be of such an excellent caliber that it served as a model for other inner-city mission efforts.

Today Lawndale CRC is a well-established Chicago ministry and congregation with over 140 members under the leadership of Reverend James Wolff, who came to Lawndale in 1981. Other current staff members include Vanessa Young in charge of educational programs, La Verne Young, who works with youth and evangelism, and Reginald Looney, who heads the church's Employment Plus ministry.

FIGURE 43 James E. Wolff and congregation at Lawndale CRC, Palm Sunday 1996.

Like so many other areas of the country during the 1960s, Lawndale weathered that decade's racial storms, emerging wounded but not dead. If the controversy which swirled around Timothy Christian's Cicero school represents one of the Christian Reformed Church's dimmest periods, the gospel light emanating from the Lawndale community represents a clear, bright spot of Christian compassion and Christ-like love for all people. As such, the Lawndale staff over the years have been transparent to the Savior they serve — the one in whom divisions of gender, class, and race all drown in the waters of baptism, leaving all believers "one in Christ."

The Joshua Generation

According to Christian Reformed Home Missions African-American ministry coordinator Robert Price, if the Christian Reformed Church truly desires to nurture the fruits of its mission efforts in places like Harlem and Chicago, then it must now make room for cultural diversity. According to Price, leaders like Eugene Callender were part of the "Moses generation" — the initial generation of leaders who worked to gather into the CRC a people from among American blacks. But Price and others now see themselves as belonging to the "Joshua generation" of leaders, who must lead these people into a new day — a day which must include the full acceptance which the CRC has promised. But as African Americans become a full part of the Christian Reformed Church, the church needs to make room for their culturally specific expressions of faith, life, and worship.

Price has written,

[B]lack leaders are attracted to [Reformed] theology, but repelled by the Dutch-American cultural environment. Blacks have had allergic reactions to overdoses of Dutch-American culture. Unfortunately, many quality black leaders have left the CRC for cultural reasons. 38

Thus Price and others are pushing for a broader vision of what it means to be Reformed — lengthening the cords and strengthening the stakes of the Christian Reformed Church's expanding tent to make room for a diversity of viewpoints and religious expressions.

The Christian Reformed Church's outreach efforts to African Americans, like so many such past efforts, generally began as the labor of the few on behalf of the many. In the future, however, it will be up to the many to embody the love of Christ in a fellowship broad and inclusive enough to embrace and celebrate ethnic diversity. Forty-five years ago the voice of a white man named Peter Eldersveld blazed a trail into America's black community

FIGURE 44 Robert Price.

by preaching the Reformed message of the gospel. Leaders like Price now remind the CRC that the time has come for the denomination to listen to those distinctive African-American voices which are even now replying to Eldersveld's message.

Doing the Job in L.A.

There were two outs, and the score was tied in the bottom of the fourth inning in the Bible-baseball game between the Saints and the Angels when Selena Moore came to bat.

Sitting nervously on the edge of the chair designated home plate, the 9-year-old inner-city girl waited for Reverend Thomas Doorn to ask the question.

"Are you ready?" asked Doorn, copastor of Los Angeles Community Christian Reformed Church, a distinctly nontraditional CRC congregation located in one of the most gang-ridden neighborhoods in the United States.

Selena nodded.

"O.K.," said Doorn, "recite Colossians 3:20."

As voices rose in the church auditorium, Selena put her fist to her forehead and tried to recall Saint Paul's words: "Children, obey your parents," she began in a halting voice. "Do it in everything because obeying pleases the Lord."

The fans broke out in cheers, and Selena began to smile as Doorn swept an arm through the air and called out: "Home run!"

In a matter of seconds, the daughter of a woman who had come to this church five years before for food had made a triumphant circuit of the bases. She had broken the game wide open.

FIGURE 45 Tom Doorn asking a Bible-baseball question of Selena Moore.

Bible baseball was only one of several activities occurring on the first Sunday of Advent in this church which sits a mile or so from the intersection at which truck driver Reginald Denny was dragged from his vehicle and severely beaten at the start of the 1992 Los Angeles riots.

As the youngsters answered Scripture questions in the auditorium, several adults were upstairs holding a Bible study with Reverend Stan Ver Heul, Doorn's fellow pastor. A dozen teens were attending Sunday school, taught by Ver Heul's wife, Judy. And members of the choir were slipping into their blue robes and running through music with Sam Spann, the minister of music, who once played piano for Reverend Martin Luther King, Jr.

All in all, this would be a typical Sunday morning at a church that sprang to life in the late seventies after members of the former predominantly white CRC congregation dispersed into such suburbs as Bellflower, Glendale, and Long Beach.

For a couple of hours, men, women, and children living in the midst of a virtual urban war zone would have a chance to praise God. Many of them would be able to gather enough grace, hope, and strength from the day's service to go out for another week to face the gritty world beyond the church doors.

"The work that Tom Doorn and Stan Ver Heul have been doing in L.A. just knocks my socks off," said John Rozeboom, executive director of the CRC's Board of Home Missions. "They are working in a tough place. Our entire church needs to look at what they're doing and how they are doing it. They have created a real solid, loving community out there."

It is the pastoral teaching that keeps the church from foundering and helps it remain the community that it is, said Samuel Spann, the music director.

"The teaching is fantastic," he said as he prepared to play piano for the service. "This place has become my family. Community is the right word for this church."

Doorn and Ver Heul are a pair of white pastors who show no fear and a great deal of love as they move among the people in this neighborhood, he said.

"The pastors in this congregation are all up and down the street, doing things," he said. "When someone passes away, they are at the hospital. They don't

FIGURE 46 Left to right, Sam Spann, Stan Ver Heul, and Tom Doorn.

expect anything back. If they were black, the church would be packed."

Al and Linda Mc Cloud, both 34, are still wondering exactly why they have worshiped for so many years in a CRC congregation in their inner-city neighborhood.

On this Sunday both were busy helping with the Sunday school and putting on the worship service. In an interview before the service, they said they had never heard of the CRC before joining this place of prayer. But they are pleased at the support given them by the denomination.

"The people in the CRC really have a vision for ministry in a place like this," said Linda Mc Cloud.

Their church is located in a neighborhood that is a deceiving mix of abandoned buildings and colorfully painted houses with neatly trimmed lawns.

"You can go out to any of the major streets around here and come across some unbelievable stuff. But I feel safe in my neighborhood," said Al Mc Cloud, an air-conditioning maintenance man for the L.A. public schools.

"You put on your battle gear every day and go out there

FIGURE 47 Alfred James and A.J.

and do what you have to do. The good outweighs the bad."

Stable families, single persons, street people, former gang members, the poor, and those with decent incomes comprise the membership of this church. The various personalities and backgrounds always make for an interesting and vital mix on Sundays.

"The church is a physical place where I can assemble with others in the common goal of doing God's work," said Linda Mc Cloud. "It's where I can gain strength for the weekly endeavors of life."

Bible baseball was over, Sunday-school classes were finished, and the main event — weekly worship — had begun in the sanctuary of the church. Arms raised over his head, Stan Ver Heul walked up and down the center aisle, exhorting those in the pews to get ready for songs and prayer.

"Let's praise God. Let's praise him with all of our hearts this morning," said Ver Heul.

Although Ver Heul and Doorn look a little out of place in the predominantly African-American and Hispanic congregation, they are truly at the center of what goes on

FIGURE 48–49 Stan Ver Heul leading in a group prayer. Right, interior of the church.

here, both in church on Sunday mornings and in various ministries throughout the neighborhood during the week.

Doorn is from Kalamazoo. Ver Heul hails from Pella, Iowa. Both are products of the hectic, consciousness-raising sixties. They attended Calvin College and Calvin Theological Seminary in an era when many students were questioning their values and their place in the larger society. Today both hold firm to their Reformed roots. At the same time they have thoroughly embraced and promote a gospel that speaks to the everyday issues facing people.

"This is not a narrowly defined ministry," Doorn said in an interview before the service. "I think we have been a transforming agent in people's lives."

Besides overseeing work in the church, the ministers are part of grass-roots, locally based organizing groups that have been active in L.A. and even in national political issues over the years. Among other things, they helped push assault-weapon-ban legislation through the California state legislature and then through Congress in 1994. They have helped hike the California minimum wage, undertaken a successful campaign to close liquor stores in their neighborhood, and begun a jobs and a housing program for southeast L.A. residents.

But politics wasn't on the agenda this morning. The top item of this day was the Christmas story and its impact on the lives of members of this church.

"When we think of Christmas, we think about the very

special present God gave us in his Son, Jesus Christ," said Ver Heul when the first of the hymns was over.

"Lord Jesus," added the pastor with the silver hair and close-cropped beard, "we thank you for coming at Christmas so long ago. We are thankful you are always with us and are close to us still."

Sitting in the pews and performing in the choir this morning were several people whose personal worlds and relationships have been transformed by the work of this church, which began when Ver Heul was sent here in 1980 by the CRC's Home Missions board. Ver Heul came after members of what was the former First CRC of L.A. voted to disband.

Among those in the pews was Jeanean Evans and her two children, Selena, the Bible-baseball star, and Aleem Taplin, 16, the church drummer. In an interview just before her daughter got her home run, Jeanean said she

FIGURE 50 Aleem Taplin.

had been hooked on drugs and near death when she first made contact with the church five years ago.

"I didn't know who they were and where they were from, but a referral agency sent me to Pastors Tom and Stan to get some food," she said.

One visit to the church led to another. Eventually, Jeanean stopped hanging around the people on the streets and using heavy drugs. She began to see a better picture of what she wanted for herself and her children and how to go after it, she said.

Evans is not alone. Many of the members of this maverick CRC congregation give credit to Doorn and Ver Heul for helping them avoid the despair and desolation so common in this part of California. Graffiti may be scrawled on many of the homes and businesses in the area, but the church itself is sturdy, brightly painted, and intact.

"This congregation is my foundation," said Lynn Sanders, a 42-year-old Air Force veteran who was addicted to crack cocaine and living in back alleys of L.A. before meeting Doorn and Ver Heul and then joining the congregation three years ago. "My rehabilitation is because of my faith in Jesus Christ and the saints living within the walls of this building," he added.

Helping late-coming church members down the aisles and into their seats this morning was Creavessie Chamberlain, an usher who hails from Mississippi and came to L.A. after World War II. Taking a break outside the sanctuary, he recalled how the two white ministers

were right there a couple years back when his daughter, Marci, died in a house fire. Both men stood firmly next to him and his wife, Marcia, in the painful days and months after the blaze.

"Tom and Stan stand way out," said Creavessie, a retired automobile painter, as he gets ready to go back to ushering. "They have been known in the community. They work hard in this mixed neighborhood. They are strong enough to handle whatever happens."

Inside the church, music bounced off the walls and ceiling. People swayed in the pews. And in the front by the altar, Aleem Taplin was pounding the drums. Hair done up in cornrows, the high school junior kept time for the choir and for Spann, the music director, who smoothly tapped out songs on the piano. Aleem had learned to play the drums at a music store a few blocks from the church. Other teens, many of them in the Denver Lane street gang, often made fun of him as he slipped in and out of the shop for his lessons. But he paid them no mind.

Having grown up with many gang members, he could talk with them and let their taunts slip away. And yet he was aware of how another teenage church member recently was shot in the leg by a gang member because he refused to join a gang.

Banging away at the drums, Aleem was also well aware that more than a dozen mostly gang-related murders had occurred within blocks of the church this year. All of it is hard to deal with. But he's doing it, with help from his mother and the two white pastors from the church in Grand Rapids, Michigan.

"I like this church," he said later. "They don't force you into anything. They let us choose how things should go. Most kids my age are into fun, not the Bible. But coming to the church is fun for me. I get into God."

Nearly ninety minutes after it began, the service started to wind down as the ministers blessed home-baked bread and tiny plastic cups of grape juice. It was Holy Communion Sunday here. Church members, at the invitation of the pastors, had crowded into the first few rows.

"If you have room for Jesus," said Ver Heul, "then he

has room for you. Even two thousands years after he was born in that little town of Bethlehem we can remember him." Ver Heul raised the loaf of bread and tore off a chunk. Doorn stood as a sentry over the silver trays containing the juice.

"We break this bread, take off a piece, hold onto it, and then we eat it together as a family," Ver Heul said.

Bread and "wine" were circulated among the faithful. Together they ate and drank. Chewing the bread and sipping the wine, they showed their solidarity. Members of a denomination founded by Dutch people, they worshiped the same God who has room for people of every race and tribe, whose grace is all inclusive. Communion was another way to celebrate the unity of all Christians in Christ.

As the church emptied from the service, Ver Heul got ready to take Communion to a sick parishioner who couldn't make it to church. Doorn was upstairs counseling a mother whose son had started to run with the wrong crowd. Money is tight, time is at a premium, and the issues of the day are many. But Doorn and Ver Heul would stay busy, bringing spiritual light to this part of California, until long after the sun set over the Pacific on this day.

"I have to think that L.A. is the way in which the world is going to go," said Doorn. "There is no majority out here. It is just all minorities, working together to spread God's Word and hope."

FIGURE 51.

Chapter Six

The Reverend Chaplain

Military and Institutional Ministries

The LORD is my light and salvation — whom shall I fear? Though an army besiege me, my heart will not fear; though war break out against me, even then will I be confident.

Psalm 27:1, 3

The United States of America was generally an isolationist nation in the early twentieth century, having little interest in concerns beyond its own considerable borders and hence little desire to enter global politics. Thus, in 1914, when the assassination of Archduke Francis Ferdinand of Austria by a Serbian terrorist in faraway Sarajevo triggered what would be called "the Great War" in Europe, many Americans gave the incident only passing notice, believing the conflict would never involve them.

Within that generally isolationist nation, Dutch Christian Reformed enclaves were isolationist par excellence, being at least one or two more steps removed from the wider global fray than were most other Americans. As was noted earlier in the chapter on campus ministry, the Dutch kept a wary distance from their adopted homeland, generally resisting Americanization in favor of maintaining and nurturing the Dutch ethnicity which many believed integral to the entire Reformed world and life view. Indeed, when some congregations began to worship in the English language in the 1910s and 1920s, not a few Christian Reformed scholars seriously

pondered whether it was even possible to speak English and still be Reformed.

But by mid century two world wars had forced the Christian Reformed Church out of its isolation by forcing its young men out into the world — into its beauties and possibilities but also into its brutality and horrors. When Christian Reformed young men began to be drafted in 1917, the church knew it could do only so much to protect them physically. However, it also knew that it *could* do something to minister to them spiritually, but only if it broke out of its religious fortress and participated in the wider war effort.

Therefore, the 1918 Synod appointed a committee to consult with the Wilson administration's War Department to investigate getting Christian Reformed pastors to work among the troops in France. At that time the committee was told that to receive a passport to work in the Expeditionary Forces in Europe, a pastor needed either to be a Regular Army chaplain or be sponsored by the YMCA or the Red Cross.

The overarching concern of synod in pursuing military chaplaincy was, not surprisingly, to keep contact with and to

provide spiritual nurture for Christian Reformed boys. The *Acts of Synod 1918* reported,

It is the only way in which we can have any assurance of our men reaching our boys. And at the same time we'll be doing our part as Church in serving the general spiritual needs of our overseas troops.[1]

The United States Congress at that time designated the Christian Reformed Church as one of twenty "miscellaneous churches" from which additional chaplains could be drawn to meet the present crisis. Synod opted to take advantage of this ministry need and opportunity by voting to allow Christian Reformed pastors to serve as chaplains through any of the three possible avenues then open — the Army, the YMCA, or the Red Cross.

The War to End All Wars?

When the United States entered World War I on April 6, 1917, there were only seventy-four chaplains serving in the Regular Army and another seventy-two in various National Guard Reserve units. But when American troops actually entered combat, even normally isolated denominations like the CRC saw the need to pitch in and do their part for the country and the larger war effort. Thus, the number of chaplains swelled to over two thousand by November 1918, ministering to the nearly four million troops taking part in the war. Out of all those chaplains, however, only one was from the Christian Reformed Church: Reverend Leonard Trap (1885-1950), who had been a pastor of Third Christian Reformed Church in Zeeland, Michigan, prior to entering the Army as a chaplain in 1917.

As noted above, the United States had never intended to enter the Great War in Europe, President Woodrow Wilson having vowed to stay out of such a foreign conflict. But, as would be true of another war twenty years later, the United States was drawn into the conflict by the very hand of the enemy. Following the torpedoing and sinking of several U.S. ships by the Germans, entering the war in Europe became inevitable. When Congress finally heeded President Wilson's call to help "make the world safe for democracy," it was hoped that doing so would not take long.

But although U.S. involvement was indeed comparatively brief — lasting just nineteen months — as the war ended, the country reeled at its staggering cost in human life. From April 1917 to November 1918 the United States lost over 116,000 men, and another 200,000 were wounded. The Great War,

FIGURE 1 Leonard Trap.

hoped by some to be "the war to end all wars," did not end any wars; but it did end a mind-numbing ten million lives worldwide. The madness of trench warfare surely contributed to this horrific carnage as wave after wave of troops would be sent over the top of the trenches only to be mowed down by the enemy's waiting machine guns. The losses in many individual battles were overwhelming. In one battle the British lost 160,000 lives and gained only seven thousand yards of territory.[2] The Battle of Verdun resulted in a sickening 900,000 casualties. Great Britain's total of over one million men dead and another two million wounded prompted Winston Churchill to write that this was a war whose "victory was bought so dear as to be indistinguishable from defeat."[3]

Having witnessed and participated in this carnage, the United States had seen enough. The isolationist voices in Congress seized the moment once again to build a wall around the United States. Despite Woodrow Wilson's prominence on the world stage during and after the war and despite his leading role as architect of the League of Nations, Wilson got nowhere when he pleaded with Congress to enter this new international League.

The isolationists won the day even as Wilson wrecked his health traversing the country, trying to build grassroots support through a vigorous campaign for the League. By late 1919 the strain proved too much. Wilson collapsed from a paralyzing stroke which would leave him bedridden in the White House for the last seventeen months of his Presidency.

The Christian Reformed Church had seen enough as well. Having previously maintained a wary distance from the public matters of its adopted country, the denomination had been forced to become involved in national and world affairs for a brief time. But with the end of the war, that compelling force ended, and the denomination returned to its earlier isolationist frame of mind. While elsewhere in the wider church world the modernist-fundamentalist battles raged and while the country itself roared its way through the sometimes riotous decade of the 1920s, the CRC withdrew into its religious fortress, becoming as isolated ecclesiastically as was the rest of the country internationally.

Despite a declaration by the 1922 Synod allowing and encouraging Christian Reformed pastors to continue to enter the military Reserve Corps of Chaplains, no one did. After Chaplain Trap was discharged in 1919, no Christian

Reformed pastors would serve in the military again until 1940. Meanwhile, the denomination was occupied by its own internal battles over theological issues, such as the meaning of common grace, and by taking defensive postures against "worldly amusements," finally issuing the 1928 synodical ban on theater attendance, dancing, and gambling/card playing.

It would be the mid 1930s before anyone began to pay attention once again to the possible need for a Christian Reformed presence in the armed forces. Although most Americans remained firmly isolationist in the 1930s and although many fancifully believed that there was no new threat of war in Europe — despite the continued border incursions by Germany's new Führer, Adolf Hitler — a few visionary and world-wise leaders believed differently.

One such leader was Reverend Henry Beets. Beets had long been one of the Christian Reformed Church's most colorful, intelligent, and outward-looking leaders. Unlike most of the Dutch isolationists, Beets was, in Christian Reformed historian James Bratt's words, "downright cosmopolitan," as he became involved in American society (and encouraged the denomination generally in the direction of Americanization), made contacts with other denominations, and pushed for foreign mission work.

Perhaps it was Beets's broader outlook and vision which

FIGURE 2 Henry Beets.

helped him sense impending disaster in the mid 1930s. Perhaps it was for this reason that, as stated clerk of the synod in 1936, Beets took the initiative to crack open his own wallet and pay the Christian Reformed Church's fifty-dollar membership fee in the National Committee on Army and Navy Chaplains, opening the door for more Christian Reformed pastors to serve as chaplains if the coming crisis which Beets feared would materialize.

Thus, when World War II's storm cloud broke over the United States at Pearl Harbor on the day of infamy, December 7, 1941, the denomination was poised to begin a serious ministry to the troops — a ministry which would ultimately also establish chaplaincy as a permanent arm of mission outreach for the Christian Reformed Church.

Minister or Chaplain?

On October 29, 1940, President Franklin D. Roosevelt, seated on the stage of a crowded Washington, D.C., auditorium and speaking into a bank of radio microphones, made a simple and innocent-sounding announcement: "The first number is 158." However, no sooner had the President uttered those simple words than Mrs. Mildred Bell, a woman seated in the audience, gasped and screamed. The number which the President had read was printed on a cobalt-blue capsule which had just been drawn out of a bowl by a blindfolded Secretary of War, Henry Stimson, thus setting into motion the first peacetime conscription in the history of the United States. Mrs. Bell screamed because her 21-year-old son, Harry, had two weeks earlier been one of thousands of young men around the country who had been issued number 158 by his local draft board.[4]

The draft was on, and, in addition to Harry Bell, thousands of other young men would be conscripted in the coming months, including a great many Christian Reformed boys. As they were inducted into all branches of the armed services, the need for ministry to them became apparent once again. Still, prior to 1942, although there were a few service pastors who would occasionally enter military camps to make contact with Christian Reformed young men, only one Christian Reformed pastor was an official military chaplain: Cornelius H. Oldenberg, who became a chaplain in 1940 and was discharged for health reasons just as the war got underway in 1942. But by 1942 many other pastors in the CRC began to heed the government's call for more chaplains.

As was true so often in Christian Reformed history, the transition into this new field was fraught with theological speculation, worry, and controversy. Among the issues debated was the exact ministerial status of a chaplain — without a formal congregation to supervise the life, doctrine, and ministry of the chaplain, where would such a person fit in Reformed church polity? Was the chaplaincy even a legitimate

Ministering to the Bottom Line

Reverend Jack Vander Laan never assumed that his career as a minister would make him pastor to football players, garbagemen, and video-store owners. But that is exactly what happened for this Calvin Theological Seminary graduate who in 1995 was the only CRC minister working full-time as a chaplain in an industrial setting.

On the payroll of millionaire industrialist M. Wayne Huizenga, Vander Laan spends his time bringing the message of the New Testament to employees of Fort Lauderdale, Florida-based Huizenga Holdings.

In his job he meets with members of Huizenga's three professional sports teams — the Miami Dolphins, the Florida Marlins, and the Florida Panthers — and with employees in the corporate office and people who are part of the corporation's other far-flung operations. By 1995 these enterprises included outdoor-advertising, security-system, and various trash-disposal companies.

"Mine is a very dynamic ministry. But I do find people who wonder exactly what it is that I do," said Vander Laan. "What I tell them is that I'm not doing typical parish ministry. My parish is instead the business community."

Vander Laan's journey into the world of business began

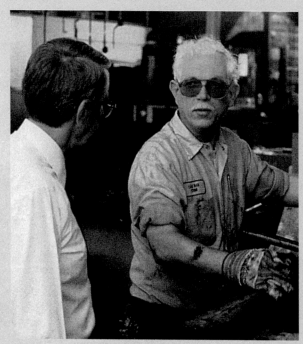

FIGURE 3 Jack Vander Laan, left, served employees of Waste Management Inc.

in the late 1970s, when Huizenga's father, Harry, suggested he do some counseling for those working for Waste Management Corporation, the waste-hauling firm cofounded by Harry's son in the 1960s. Vander Laan was pastor of the CRC congregation in Fort Lauderdale at the time. Seeking a new challenge, he gave this form of ministry a part-time try. Right off, he loved speaking about God's grace and love in a corporate setting.

His first efforts were launched among Waste Management truck drivers, trash compactors, and salespeople.

"I called on people if they were sick, if they had had surgery or an accident. I also called on family members when there had been a death," he said.

Before coming to the pulpit in Florida, Vander Laan had served churches in Michigan, Iowa, and Colorado. When Wayne Huizenga, a member of the CRC, asked him to come to work for him full-time, Vander Laan eagerly accepted.

At first he performed his industrial chaplaincy out of the Chicago area, at that time the headquarters for Huizenga's corporation. The death of his son in an unexplained murder compelled Vander Laan to return to Florida in 1989. He has remained in Florida ever since, in part because Huizenga moved his corporate office back to Fort Lauderdale.

Other denominations have active chaplaincy programs with various companies. But for the most part Vander Laan has been the only one in his church to get paid for mixing the bottom line of the business world with the challenges of the gospel.

"I've helped to plow new ground for our church," he said. "I see this as an important ministry. I have access to people who would never otherwise come to church."

As a minister to professional baseball, football, and hockey players, he strolls through the locker rooms, pausing to speak to athletes about their hopes and fears. Sometimes that means first listening to a tale about bad batting averages or bruised ankles. Other times it means assisting a sports star through a rocky time in a marriage.

"When I introduce myself, they know my background and training," he said. "I'm not hired to convert anyone or to change their religion if they have one."

Much of his time is spent in one-on-one counseling

FIGURE 4
John M. Vande Kieft.

field for a minister to enter at all? Synod 1942 partially solved this difficulty by establishing a Chaplain Committee both to recruit chaplains from among Christian Reformed pastors and to monitor their work. One of the first ministers to be appointed to this committee would also go on to become an eloquent spokesperson for chaplaincy: Reverend John M. Vande Kieft. Himself a former service pastor during World War I, Vande Kieft would reassume that role for a brief time in 1943.

During the years of World War II, Vande Kieft frequently found himself answering questions and addressing concerns relative to chaplaincy ministry. In a series of *Banner* articles titled "The Chaplain Situation," Vande Kieft kept the denomination up-to-date and argued for the proper place of chaplains within the ministry of Christ's church. Through Vande Kieft's and the committee's efforts, the number of Christian Reformed chaplains would rise rapidly until, by the end of the war, twenty-six Christian Reformed ministers were serving as military chaplains, fully ten percent of all Christian Reformed ministers at that time. Calvin College and Seminary would also cooperate with these efforts as both schools instituted year-round courses of study in order to graduate new chaplaincy candidates in less time than was typical for ministerial candidates.

But was chaplaincy really a ministry? These questions continued to arise throughout the war. Writing in the November 24, 1944, issue of *The Banner*, Calvin Theological Seminary professor Diedrich Kromminga tried to answer the question of a reader who was worried about whether or how the ministry and the chaplaincy could go together:

As I see it, the chaplaincy and the ministry can by no possibility be coordinated. There is only one ministry; and the chaplaincy can come into consideration only as a special form which that ministry assumes due to circumstances. And for that reason a man who is called to the ministry is not at liberty to ask himself whether he shall choose the ministry or the chaplaincy. His question must be, whether in addition to his call to the ministry the situation is such as to warrant the entrance into the chaplaincy. If he comes to the decision it is, he may very well be perfectly correct; but the question must be decided on its own merits and may never be settled by the easy reasons: the chaplaincy is equal to the ministry in a church, therefore I choose it.[5]

Among those who shared doubts about the validity of chaplaincy as a ministry was *Banner* editor Henry J. Kuiper. For Kuiper the real red-flag issue, which he raised often, was the issue of restricted or "close" Communion. Throughout its history the Christian Reformed Church had taken seriously the need for the elders to guard the Lord's table against the profane use of the sacrament by unbelievers. The practice of close Communion mandated that only Christian Reformed members in good standing could participate in the blessed sacrament. If, on the Sunday on which Communion was celebrated, there were any visitors in the congregation, they were required to register with the elders before the service and be approved by name before being allowed to partake of the sacrament.

But what would become of this practice in the military setting, where there was no supervisory body of elders and where the Christian Reformed chaplain would be forced to preside over a mixed congregation? Indeed, the issue was of particular importance for naval chaplains because the U.S.

sessions. In the past, when Huizenga owned Blockbuster Video, Vander Laan traveled the country to meet with those who had been robbed or shot during holdups. Or he spent time with persons whose family members were killed in robberies.

"In these cases, I was mostly handling post-traumatic-stress situations," he said. "My faith motivates me to care about people and their needs."

He was a constant, gentle presence for those undergoing the shock of violence, the pain of loss, the confusion of some difficult change in their lives.

Bringing Christianity into the workplace, Vander Laan said, is not easy. It takes backing from the front office. Without Wayne Huizenga's support, he could never do the job.

"Our church hasn't pushed hard to do this on a wider scale," he said. "As a denomination, we're happier with more traditional military- and institutional-based chaplaincy."

Denominational officials say it has been hard finding business people as willing as Huizenga to give a paycheck to a full-time chaplain.

Vander Laan loves his job, which allows him on any given day to share Christ's compassion with short-stops, goalies, billboard builders, security guards, and waste haulers.

"In a way, I'm like an insurance policy for the company," he said. "They don't always need it, but it's good that I'm here when they do."

Navy mandated that its chaplains serve Communion to all sailors who desired it, without regard to their ecclesiastical backgrounds. (The Army gave more latitude in its regulations, allowing a chaplain to perform his duties in accordance with the rules of his own denomination.)

In reply to these concerns, Vande Kieft and other pro-chaplaincy writers in the periodical *The Young Calvinist* claimed that no one was advocating that the CRC change its Communion policy within its churches. The question was whether this principle could be meaningfully applied to the very non-church setting of a military unit in wartime. Vande Kieft and others judged it could not be, seeing Christian Reformed chaplains not first of all as representatives of a particular denomination but as representatives of Christ in and to the larger world. They also reminded those worried about this issue that no branch of the military forced any minister to violate his conscience on such matters but left it up to the discernment and integrity of individual chaplains to administer the sacrament as they saw fit to those they believed to be true believers in Christ.

In the absence of a supervising consistory on the battle-field, in the camp, or aboard ship, therefore, Vande Kieft urged the denomination to trust its minister chaplains to make right, biblical decisions regarding to whom they would give the sacrament. As Vande Kieft said, even in established churches with supervising consistories, "close [C]ommunion does not keep the unworthy from eating and drinking."6 Churches and ministers can only go so far in determining whether those celebrating the sacrament are doing so in a "worthy manner." The same applied to chaplains. In short, the controversy was unwarranted, and the chaplains should be allowed to do their work as trusted servants of God.

While these issues were being debated back home, the ministers of the CRC who had applied for chaplaincy went about their work — not oblivious to the issues but bold in the conviction that chaplaincy was a needed work in God's kingdom during those dark times.

Meritorious Service

In 1940 Franklin Roosevelt was intensely interested in running for an unprecedented third term as President. In an effort not to appear power hungry, however, Roosevelt did not declare his desire openly, hoping that the Democratic National Convention would draft his name into nomination by acclamation. In this way it would appear that Roosevelt

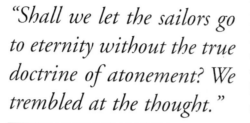

"Shall we let the sailors go to eternity without the true doctrine of atonement? We trembled at the thought."

— Council of Prospect Park CRC

was merely doing the will of the people and not clutching presidential power for its own sake.

Roosevelt maintained so low a profile that he did not even appear at the convention in person, sending his wife, Eleanor, to speak in his stead. In addressing the issue of nominating someone for a third term, Eleanor stated that, of course, under normal circumstances it would indeed be odd to nominate a President for a third term. However, Eleanor reminded the delegates, with a depression hanging on at home and a war raging in Europe, this could not be seen as a normal nomination in a normal time, for, she said, "This is no ordinary time." 7

A similar line of argument was used by those who wanted to open up the Christian Reformed Church to calling and ordaining military chaplains. Following the United States' entry into the war, one of the first Christian Reformed men to enter the chaplaincy was Harry R. Boer. Upon graduation from seminary in 1941, Boer indicated he felt called to this specialized ministry. To facilitate this move at a time when

FIGURE 5 Harry R. Boer.

the exact ecclesiastical status of the chaplaincy was yet fuzzy, Boer was called by Prospect Park Christian Reformed Church in Holland, Michigan, to be an associate pastor with the understanding that he would be performing his ministry off site as a chaplain in the United States Navy. Despite all of the concerns mentioned above, the consistory of Boer's church determined that the abnormal times brought about by the "topsy-turvy" nature of sin allowed latitude relative to the normal rules and procedures of Church Order, ministry, and ordination. It was no ordinary time, not even for the church.

But just in case that argument did not allay the fears of those resisting a Christian Reformed chaplaincy, the consistory also asked, "Shall we leave this field to the modernists?" Noting that in all branches of the service the preaching of the Word was neither restricted nor proscribed, they argued that this was the CRC's chance to proclaim its Reformed gospel heritage to the men whose lives were on the line in the great conflict of the day. Reflecting the utter certainty common to that era that Reformed churches were among the few churches left which still proclaimed the gospel truth, Prospect Park

church defended its ordination of Chaplain Boer by saying, "In the light of the liberty to preach the entire Word of God, shall we surrender this field to the modernists? Shall we let the sailors go to eternity without the true doctrine of atonement? We trembled at the thought."[8]

Once the denomination was able to work through some of these fears and apprehensions, the chaplains were able to go to work. During the war years the United States military indoctrinated, trained, graduated, and commissioned over eight thousand chaplains from its various chaplaincy-training schools, including Fort Benjamin Harrison in Indiana, Harvard University, Fort Devens in Massachusetts, and Fort Oglethorpe in Georgia. At these schools the typical course of instruction included up to seventeen different classes on topics relating to military leadership, military hygiene and first aid, field-service regulations, close-order drill and conditioning exercises, graves registration, discipline and courtesy customs, and military law, as well as courses relating specifically to chaplain duties and the performance of religious ceremonies in a military setting.

FIGURE 6 Christian Reformed chaplains, Harvard Chaplains' School, 1943. From left to right, top row: Dewey Hoitenga, George Stob, Henry Vande Kieft, Cornelius Van Schouwen. From left to right, bottom row: Nick De Vries, George Vander Kooi, Cornelius Holtrop, John Vander Meer, Cornelius Schooland.

Offering Hope in the Valley of Death

Fighting back tears, the middle-aged widow asked Reverend Robert Koorneef if she ought to forgo the upcoming Christmas service at her church.

For the better part of two decades she and her husband had worshiped together and had often sat side by side in the same pew. Since he had passed away from a heart attack a few months before, her world had been ripped wide open and turned on its side. All of their shared rituals, their public and private ways of being together, no longer applied.

On this afternoon in November 1995, she felt empty and sad and anxious. She wanted to know how to best handle the holidays.

"I just can't imagine what it will be like to be in church without him," she told Koorneef, a Christian Reformed chaplain who serves as bereavement director for Hospice of Greater Grand Rapids.

Conducting a seminar on how to deal with Christmas in the wake of a loved one's death, the chaplain leaned forward in his chair, looked at the woman with compassion, and spoke to her in a calm voice.

"You need to be gentle with yourself," he said. "Church services can be a trigger for your grief. Often in church we relax, and then the pain just washes over us."

Serving as pastor to those who have experienced the death of someone they love, Koorneef on that day was consciously trying to let the grace and care of God work through him. He is convinced that the Lord is always there in times of sorrow, but he also believes that some person often needs to be the conduit through which God's solace can be made evident.

"Many people want to smother you and with the best of intentions ask you to do things and go places with them this time of the year," the chaplain explained to the woman, one of twenty people attending the seminar. "If you don't want to go to church this Christmas, fine. Or if you want to go to another church, that's okay, too. Don't force yourself to do things you really don't want to do. The word *no* is a complete sentence."

The son of Dutch-immigrant parents from Hamilton, Ontario, Koorneef came to the chaplaincy later in his career as a minister. He served churches in Belding, Michigan, and Bellingham, Washington, before making the switch.

As supervisor of several social workers, Hospice counselors, and volunteers, he tries to make sure that spirituality plays a role in the lives of those who come to his organization before, during, and after a death. The work is not easy, for them or for those they try to help. Grief, he has learned, has its own logic, consistency, and depth for everyone who encounters it.

Although he had done a great deal of pastoral counseling before coming to Hospice, his nearly twenty years in a traditional church hardly prepared him for the special work entailed in helping people handle the hurts that come when someone close to them dies.

"When I was preaching in those churches, I really didn't realize the depth of people's pain," he said in an interview after the seminar. "I would look out at them and see them, but I really wouldn't see them. I wouldn't see the terrible things many of them were feeling."

As a minister in the Belding and Bellingham churches, he assumed grief hit hard in the days and weeks following a funeral. Soon after coming to Hospice in 1994 following a year's worth of specialized study at Pine Rest Christian Mental Health Services in Cutlerville, Michigan, he learned that the real suffering often doesn't come until long after the memorial service ends, the friends and family go home, the thank-you cards have been written.

It's frequently months later that a huge hollowness opens in a person's life. Anniversaries and holidays especially make the memory and recollections more acute. Now that he knows this, Koorneef makes sure to follow up with persons in the months and even year or so following a death.

"People are very private in their grief," he said. "They withdraw, and I try to get them to talk or to deal with their pain in some way."

And that fact is another of the things he learned after he stepped down from the regular pulpit and entered this other, in many ways more personal, form of ministry. He discovered that each person handles loss differently.

Some people want and need to talk; others want to listen; others clam up and seek no help at all. Some people keep all of the items left behind by a dead friend, relative, spouse, or child. Others throw everything out. Some like to hold special rituals on certain days to recall a person's life; still others want no part of that kind of

FIGURE 7
Dewey Hoitenga, Sr.

After graduating from these various schools, the chaplains of the Christian Reformed Church, like all soldiers and military personnel at that time, began to face all of the dangers and horrors that were the Second World War. Many of these men deserved far more credit for their service than they received at the time. While *The Banner* continued to feature articles with titles like "Should the Christian Reformed Chaplain Administer Open Communion?" and "The Chaplaincy from Its Church Polity Angle," the actual chaplains were entering not a theoretical skirmish but a very real and very bloody war.

Reverend Peter Honderd was one such chaplain, who, by the time his World War II chaplaincy was complete, had endured 280 days in a combat zone. Chaplain Dewey Hoitenga, Sr., served as a troop chaplain aboard transport ships. In the course of the war Hoitenga traversed the Atlantic and Pacific oceans nearly three dozen times.

The dangers to which military chaplains were exposed is highlighted by the tragic fact that during World War II seventy-seven Army chaplains were killed in the line of duty. (Four chaplains died in one day on February 3, 1943, when the *S.S. Dorchester,* a ship taking nearly 1,000 troops to Europe, was hit by a German torpedo. In addition to the four chaplains, 674 others also lost their lives as the ship sank rapidly in the frigid waters of the North Atlantic.) To the joy and gratitude of the Christian Reformed Church, however, none of its twenty-six chaplains died, but some, like Chaplain Captain Richard Wezeman, did have some close calls.

Wezeman was one of many who responded to Henry Beets's 1942 plea for ministers to enter the military chaplaincy. After receiving his training at Fort Benjamin Harrison, Wezeman was ordered to Fort Davis, North Carolina, as chaplain for the 445th Auto Weapons Battalion. On September 23, 1943, while en route to a search-light unit, the plane carrying Wezeman crashed, leading to a three-month convalescence for him. But Wezeman's adventures had only begun. As soon as he recovered from his injuries, he was transferred overseas. In Scotland Wezeman had the rare and odd

remembering. Some place special ornaments on the Christmas tree; some never put up a tree again.

"However people deal with a death, they often become their own worst enemies," Koorneef said.

"There is no one way for everyone to cope with grief. Each person has to discover what works best. Often that means changing habits and paying attention to what you want to do and not what you think you should do."

In his job the chaplain finds many grieving people who are angry with God and/or with the church. Never does he try to evangelize them or to convince them to go to church. His role, he said, is to act as a loving presence, to show by his steady commitment to them that there is hope and healing beyond the darkness of death.

"I used to think what we as ministers say is what makes the difference," he commented. "I now know that it is who we are that really makes the difference."

With those who do embrace a religious faith, the chaplain will pray as a loved one lies dying and during the time of and after the funeral. He lets them know that he believes God remains strong and steadfast with them even in times full of personal devastation.

"We need hope when we are emotionally wounded," he said at the conclusion of the grief seminar on that afternoon before Christmas. "There is nothing easy about any of this. But we can choose to be survivors and not victims. Hope, after all, is the standard equipment of the human spirit."

FIGURE 8 From left, John Verbrugge, Harry R. Boer, and Harold Dekker, stationed together in Saipan in 1944.

opportunity to minister to some German POWs who were interned there. Later he rejoined his old unit, the 445th, now on active combat duty in France. For his efforts Wezeman was awarded the Bronze Star by President Harry Truman,

[F]or distinguishing himself by meritorious service as Chaplain in connection with military operations in Western Europe during the period 24 August 1944 to 8 May 1945 against an enemy of the United States. Chaplain Wezeman's outstanding accom-plishments and performances of duties are in the highest traditions of the military service. [9]

Naval Chaplain Harry Boer likewise faced a variety of dangers, threats, and frustrations. Boer reported that not only did a chaplain have to deal with the horrors of war (Boer was present at the battle of Tarawa, in which many of the Marines on board his ship died) but also with the religious apathy and low attendance at the services he conducted. Though interest in religious matters tended to increase just prior to impending military engagements, many times Boer had to contend with low attendance, snide comments, profane language, and loose morals.

But chaplains also had to deal with death. With grim frequency Boer and other chaplains were asked to conduct funerals for the newly killed. Boer recalled his first such funeral for three Marines killed in action:

[T]he dead were in winding sheets and covered with American flags .... A pharmacist's mate played "Abide with Me" at a portable organ [and] ... the warship's guns and airplanes' bombs boomed and roared intermittently. When it was over, the honor guard carried the bodies to the slide at the railing. The bugler blew taps and the bodies were committed to the deep. From D-Day to

FIGURE 9 Harold Dekker officiating at a funeral service in Saipan.

FIGURE 10 Richard Wezeman survived this plane crash in 1943.

D plus six the march of death went on with one or more funerals nearly every day. The refrain became monotonous, " . . . and so we commit to the deep the body of our departed comrade to await the last day." [10]

After what most of the chaplains faced while at war, it is no wonder, as Reverend Jacob Heerema, current head of the Chaplaincy Ministries, has written, that they returned home with a broader vision, a heightened awareness of human corruption, and an urgent compulsion to minister not just within the ethnic enclave of the CRC but to the wider, spiritually hungry world.[11]

FIGURE 11 Van Schouwen and Corporal Carwell standing next to the tract stand and bulletin board.

One Chaplain's Story

Each of the twenty-six Christian Reformed ministers who served as chaplains during World War II had a story to tell. One chaplain who kept a detailed record of his experiences was Cornelius Van Schouwen. His story and experiences are likely representative of what his colleagues also faced in the various places they served.[12]

During the summer of 1942, Van Schouwen was pastoring his second congregation, in De Motte, Indiana. As he watched the congregation's young men be drafted and as he saw *The Banner* advertisements calling for more military chaplains, Van Schouwen felt he was being led into this new avenue of ministry. By December of that year he mailed in his application to the Chief of Chaplains in Washington; he received his letter of acceptance on January 19, 1943. Commissioned as a first lieutenant, Van Schouwen reported for duty at the Harvard Chaplains' School on March 1, where he would receive six weeks of intensive training and education.

Upon arriving in Cambridge, Massachusetts, Van Schouwen joined eight other Christian Reformed pastors who were attending the Harvard chaplaincy school at that time. Together with two hundred other classmates, they drilled, hiked, and learned other basic skills of soldiering. The chaplains also attended classes in which they were taught the basics of being a military chaplain and some rudimentary skills of warfare like how to sneak up on the enemy, how to survive tear-gas attacks, how to read a map, and how to use a compass. By the time his class graduated on April 3, 1943, Van Schouwen felt ready for his first assignment: being a chaplain at Camp Shelby in Hattiesberg, Mississippi.

FIGURE 12 Cornelius Van Schouwen and wife, Sue.

As he began his work, Van Schouwen decided that inasmuch as all soldiers are trained to "know the enemy," he would make it his goal to help the men know also their true spiritual enemy, Satan and his hosts. Toward that end Van Schouwen determined not only to preach the gospel in Sunday services but also to live and teach the gospel in his conduct among the men, in small-group Bible studies, and in the distribution of tracts and other gospel information.

Van Schouwen also learned that, as an Army chaplain who would one day go overseas, he needed to know how to defend himself against enemies who did not always accord chaplains their Geneva Convention rights as noncombatants. After holding a worship service near the firing range one sunday, Van Schouwen was told by his colonel on the following Monday morning to put in some time practicing with an M-

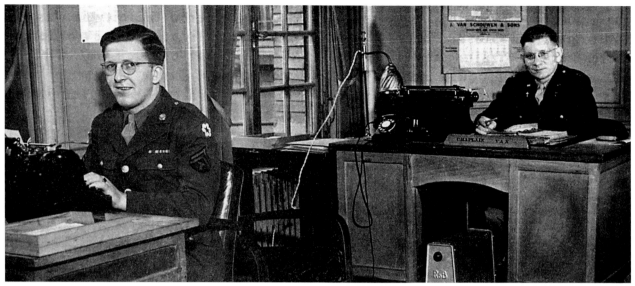

FIGURE 13 Van Schouwen and Corporal Carwell at the University of Paris.

FIGURE 14 Van Schouwen with the 746th Railway Operating Battalion.

1 rifle. When Van Schouwen's first three shots all hit the bullseye, the colonel asked incredulously, "Chaplain, where did you learn to fire a rifle?"

"From one of my consistory members," was Van Schouwen's straight-shooting reply.

The duties Van Schouwen was asked to perform and the situations he encountered were surely far more varied and unusual than anything for which his Dutch background and seminary training had prepared him. In addition to performing weekly worship services, Chaplain Van Schouwen visited the sick in the infirmary, verified and cashed checks for the soldiers, attended AWOL disciplinary hearings, delivered mail, accompanied the soldiers on bivouac, and held many an impromptu counseling session with confused soldiers and with soldiers whose families were enduring great hardship back home. In addition to consoling soldiers who

missed parents, wives, and children, he also had to deal with soldiers who contracted venereal disease.

On one occasion Van Schouwen noted that an officer in his unit, a man whom Van Schouwen knew to be married, was involved with several women. So Chaplain Van Schouwen confronted him, telling him to quit his sinful behavior. Said Van Schouwen, the man

agreed with what I said but refused to mend his ways. He boasted about his virility. I reminded him that the wages of sin is death. A few days later I received a report from the doctor stating that this lieutenant was in the hospital with VD. I went to the hospital and just stood in the open door and said, "I can't believe it! A real virile man in the hospital?"

In his subsequent counsel with the man, Van Schouwen listened to his grief as well as his concerns about how to tell his wife. Van Schouwen encouraged him to be honest, to admit what he had done to his God and to his wife, and to hope in this way to receive forgiveness. But, as with so many men with whom chaplains had contact, Van Schouwen was never able to know if his advice had done any good because the unit's colonel transferred the man to another unit, not wishing to have "his kind" around.

Van Schouwen remained at Camp Shelby until July of 1944, when he was sent to Europe aboard the captured Italian luxury-liner-turned-troopship *The Saturnia*. As part of a twenty-six-ship convoy, *The Saturnia* sailed through the North Atlantic, enduring at least one close call with a German U-boat, finally arriving in Liverpool, England, on August 5.

From there Van Schouwen made his way to southern England and to a transport which landed him on the famed Omaha Beach on August 21. Van Schouwen was to spend many months thereafter working among various units stationed in and around the newly liberated city of Paris, France. Upon arriving on September 17, Van Schouwen observed:

Disorder reigns in Paris. The Germans retreated in a hurry and left everything to itself. Some German soldiers stayed in Paris when the army fled. They kept their guns and there is shooting going on every night. Some of our soldiers have been killed by these German soldiers still in Paris. I do not dare to walk the streets of Paris when it is dark.

While working in and around Paris, Van Schouwen arranged Sunday services wherever he could — hotel lobbies, motor pools, abandoned schools. By March 1, 1945, Van Schouwen observed his second anniversary in the United States Army. He reflected,

When I became a chaplain, I did not know what to expect, but I was rather confident. Romans 8:28 says the Lord gives grace to whatever task he calls us. The blessings I have received for myself thus far are incalculable. To God be all the praise and glory.

Soon thereafter Van Schouwen was assigned to the 746th Railway Operating Battalion and was sent east to begin

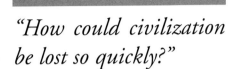

"How could civilization be lost so quickly?"

— Chaplain Van Schouwen

moving into the German territory only recently conquered by General George Patton and his advancing tanks. As he traveled, Van Schouwen was frequently aghast at the devastation in every town and city. But in the midst of the rubble, decay, and fragmentation, he continued to set up makeshift chapels wherever he went. He wrote,

A command car was assigned to me and my assistant did the driving. I placed my field organ and hymnals on the back seat of my car and stopped every place where our men were stationed and held a service there and spent the rest of the day with the soldiers.

Chaplain Van Schouwen was so occupied that when he turned 42 on April 16, 1945, he wrote in his diary that it had been late in the day before he even realized it was his birthday. "I suppose that I was too busy [to notice]."

When the war in Europe ended on May 7, 1945, Van Schouwen was in Marburg, Germany. Two days later he conducted a VE Day celebration and thanksgiving service for 225 soldiers. But later that same day Van Schouwen was reminded of the cost of that victory as he toured Kassel, Germany, noting that because so many civilians had been killed and buried beneath the rubble of the city, many of their relatives could do no more than toss wreaths of flowers onto the rub-

FIGURE 15 Destruction in Nüremburg.

FIGURE 16 Hitler's house in Berchtesgaden after Allied bombing.

ble to mark the general place where men, women, and children had lost their lives in the Allied attack.

As he continued his tour of duty in the now-conquered Germany, Van Schouwen was personal witness to the war's greatest horror — the concentration camps. He personally toured the Buchenwald, Dachau, Nordhausen, Bad Orb, Ziegenheim, and Ohrdruf camps, wondering with the rest of the world, "How could civilization be lost so quickly?" But for Van Schouwen the experience was also grimly confirming in an experiential way of the Calvinist doctrine of total depravity, which he had been taught since his youth.

Before returning to his family on March 20, 1946, and being decommissioned on May 19, Van Schouwen received a commendation from Brigadier General Kimball for his *devoted and untiring efforts extended … during your tour of duty in Paris. This command appreciates the innovation in chaplain's work such as your daily sermonettes, your university discussion groups and your modern down-to-earth Bible classes.* President Truman later awarded Van Schouwen the Bronze Star for distinguished and meritorious service.

Home Again

When the war ended, the Christian Reformed chaplains, like all of the returning soldiers, were welcomed home as heroes. Local churches lauded their bravery in battle and their ministry in Christ, Calvin Theological Seminary offered them refresher courses, and synod even agreed to give them a modest salary, called *wachtgeld,* to tide them over until they received a call back into congregational ministry.

At the 1944 Synod, Chaplain Henry R. Van Til had delivered a stirring address urging the Christian Reformed Church to continue its chaplaincy ministry even after the war was finally finished. "Since compulsory military training may be continued after the war," he said, "we ought to induce some of our younger men to remain in the chaplaincy, and we ought to look forward to making the chaplaincy part of our concern as Church from now on."[13]

Still, when the war ended one year later, most of the CRC's chaplains chose to return to parish ministry, and all but two of the twenty-six wartime chaplains requested honorable discharge from their various branches of the armed services. Though the viability of the chaplaincy as a ministry had been demonstrated in World War II, chaplaincy as an arm of the Christian Reformed Church's ongoing mission outreach was not much exercised for a number of years to come.

After the war, the synodical Chaplain Committee was cut back from five members to three, and only two chaplains remained in the military Reserves: Paul Boertje and Dick Oostenink. By the time the Korean conflict came in the early 1950s, only one Christian Reformed pastor served the military on extended active duty, Chaplain Dick Oostenink, who conducted field services and performed all of the many and varied duties of a chaplain on the Korean peninsula.

Of course, although in this chapter we have focused on wartime military chaplaincy, it must be remembered that except for those tasks unique to a combat zone, the chaplaincy duties described in this book continue to be carried on during peacetime as well. Full-time and Reserve military chaplains continue to perform the work of counseling, preaching, teaching, hospital visitation, and staff meetings along with their ongoing participation in general military training the same as do all members of the armed forces. Many Christian Reformed pastors who serve as Reserve chaplains have the added challenge of balancing their duties as parish pastors along with putting in the required number of military service hours each year. (Indeed, despite this century's grim plethora of armed conflicts, military chaplains have spent more time ministering on bases during times of peace than they have working in the field during times of war.)

Following World War II, the ministry of chaplains also began to expand beyond the specifically military setting into other areas. In the late 1940s Reverend Elton Holtrop, a former Navy chaplain, was one of the first Christian Reformed ministers to enter hospital chaplaincy. In 1947, at the request of the government, Holtrop became the chaplain at a veterans facility in Tomah, Wisconsin, where he ministered to the more than eleven hundred psychiatric patients receiving treatment there as one of 247 Veterans Administration hospital chaplains nationwide.

In a March 26, 1948, *Banner* article Holtrop noted the desperate need for more such chaplains to the more than 100,000 veterans who were hospitalized for physical and psychiatric difficulties in hospitals around the country. Though he admitted that the work was very often depressing, Holtrop noted that these men deserved the presence of Christ in their midst as they wrestled with the mental ailments, alcoholism, and physical handicaps which the war had inflicted on them.

As chaplain in a VA hospital, Holtrop conducted weekly worship services and daily Bible classes, counseled patients and their family members, distributed religious tracts and literature, and spoke in various churches to inform the public about the needs of these sometimes-forgotten ex-soldiers. His own words attest to his wish that the Christian Reformed Church ought to be doing more with chaplaincy in the VA hospitals:

Sufficient has been said to show the many opportunities for spreading the Word and to present our own standards of truth. I wish we had more representatives of our Church in this work.[14]

But for a time there were not many Christian Reformed pastors who joined Holtrop in this kind of work. For his part Chaplain Holtrop would spend the rest of his career in the veterans hospital setting, working in Wisconsin until 1950

FIGURE 17 Dick J. Oostenink conducts services in the combat zone during the Korean conflict.

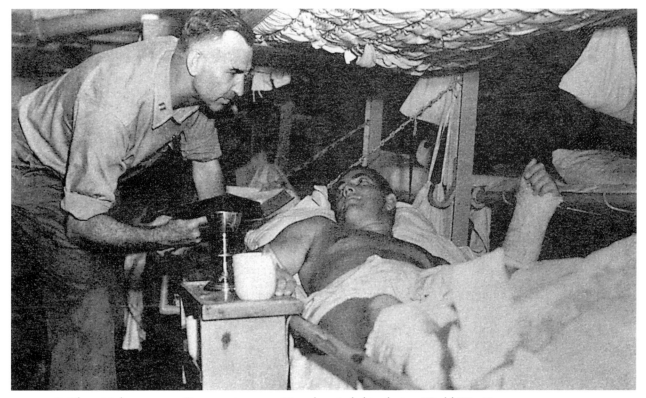

FIGURE 18 Elton Holtrop serves Communion on a Navy hospital ship during World War II.

Not Just a Jail-House Religion

Reverend Ray Swierenga doesn't really mind it when members of the Melanic Palace of the Rising Sun refer to him as a racist white devil. As institutional chaplain for the Muskegon Correctional Facility in Muskegon, Michigan, Swierenga oversees the Sunday-afternoon services of the Melanic group. A mixture of Christianity and Islam, this jail-house denomination is comprised mostly of militant black men. Some of them use their weekly service as a chance to complain.

"It's mostly the younger guys who vent their spleen like that," said Swierenga, a Christian Reformed Church minister who has spent his entire ministerial life as a chaplain. "I don't get too bothered by what they say," he added. "But I do ask them to quiet down when they get a little more carried away than they should."

Testy as the inmates can get some Sundays, Swierenga would never consider prohibiting the Melanics from meeting. A large part of his job, he said, is to make sure that all of the nearly three thousand men in the Muskegon prison have the chance to worship as they choose.

Given the diversity of religious faiths behind the walls of this correctional facility, Swiergena often has to set aside his own Reformed approach to belief. He's more a conductor of religious affairs than a prison preacher. He sets schedules, does counseling, and leaves the evangelizing to others, be they Roman Catholics, tongue-speaking Pentecostals, or mainline, Koran-reading Muslims. For him, it is a faith-filled and highly satisfying way of acting out his calling.

"I see myself representing God and the church in a setting where God doesn't have much formal acceptance," said Swierenga, referring to battles he sometimes has to wage with wardens who see religion as the least of their worries. "I think my presence in the prison helps. I'm not just doing a job. I believe this is a pastoral ministry."

A native of Cicero, Illinois, Swierenga attended Calvin College not knowing what he would do for a career. Near the end of his undergraduate program, he came to believe that nagging inside him was a nudge to the ministry. As a result, he enrolled in Calvin Theological Seminary.

As his stint in theology school came to a close, he was even more convinced that being a preacher was his lot in life. But he also realized he had little desire to find a position as a pastor in a church. He wanted something less formal.

So he joined the U.S. Navy as a chaplain.

"It sounded like an interesting challenge. It was only a commitment for three years," he said.

Three years, however, turned into more than two decades. He served as a chaplain on ships, in ports, on bases, and with a U.S. Marine infantry unit outside of Da Nang during the Vietnam War.

"I just stayed in once I signed up," he said. "The ministry was always interesting. Each duty station was different."

When he was at sea, his work entailed counseling men who, like himself, were away from their families. On shore his was a more traditional ministry. He preached, taught Sunday school, married and buried people. He did all of this not as a CRC pastor, but as a Protestant chaplain.

"It was a very broadening experience. I was exposed to a variety of religions," he said in an interview held in the cafeteria of the Muskegon prison as sunlight glinted outside on rolls of barbed wire used to keep inmates inside the compound

Once he retired from the Navy, he still wasn't interested in finding a church. He attended a one-year clinical pastoral-counseling course at Pine Rest Christian Mental Health Services and then took a job as a chaplain at the Dunes Correctional Facility in Saugatuck.

He learned right off that serving in the prison system was much like his chaplaincy in the military, especially when he was on Navy ships.

"The parishioners are all male. They are separated from their families by no choice of their own, and they aren't happy about it," he said.

Furthermore, he said, prison, like the military, is bureaucratically governed by rigid rules and regulations and overseen by a boss who may have no religious affiliation whatsoever. Prison, in addition, is multicultural and the site for an array of spiritual disciplines.

What's different in prison is pretty obvious: the men are there because they usually have broken the law. In many cases that means they bring to their cells a history of anger and violence missing in the Navy.

First at the Dunes, then at a prison in Ionia, and finally in Muskegon, Swierenga has tried to offer doses of God's grace to murderers, child molesters, robbers, drug dealers, addicts, pimps, arsonists, and habitual drunk drivers.

"There are a lot of religious concerns here," he said.

and then at the VA hospital in Battle Creek, Michigan, until his retirement in 1966. Yet for the first ten years of his work in that setting, Holtrop did not have any official synodical endorsement. It was not until 1957 that the Chaplain Committee recommended to synod that the scope of officially sanctioned chaplaincy ministry be expanded to include institutional chaplaincy.

Despite synod's endorsement of this proposal, by 1958 the committee's report to synod included the names of only six active chaplains: Holtrop in the Veterans Administration and five active military chaplains: Jay Ellens, Harvey Smit, Bernard Dokter, Jay Vander Ark, and William Kosten.

In the years to come, the number of Christian Reformed chaplains would hold fairly steady as new chaplains entered the military and current chaplains sought discharge following their specified time of duty in order to enter the parish ministry or other traditional ministry settings.

Ministering along the Ho Chi Minh Trail

During his retirement years on his ranch in Texas, Lyndon Johnson often told family and friends that he was still haunted by echoes of "that horrible song" which had been chanted at him so often during his Presidency: "Hey! Hey! LBJ! How many kids did you kill today?" Indeed, the Vietnam War, which had driven Johnson out of the White House, would, in the end, dog him all the way to his grave in 1973. According to biographer Robert A. Caro, however, this was a haunting problem which Johnson had created for himself. Less than one year after assuming the Presidency following John Kennedy's assassination, Johnson campaigned to be elected President in his own right. One of his 1964 campaign promises was that he would not "send American boys nine or ten thousand miles away from home to do what Asian boys ought to be doing for themselves."[15] The American people believed him, and Johnson handily won the election over Republican Barry Goldwater.

At the time when Johnson made that campaign promise, there were approximately 16,000 American advisers and noncombatant troops already in Vietnam. Within a month of his 1965 inauguration, however, Johnson so escalated troop build-up in Vietnam that by 1966 more

FIGURE 19 A.J. Dahm shown in cockpit of U.S. Navy aircraft at Quonset Point Naval Air Station while on tour with student chaplains in 1958.

"Prison is an environment that accentuates a person's failure as a citizen and as a human being."

Some prisoners, with his help or with assistance from other persons of faith, experience a close and lasting encounter with God while they are incarcerated. Doing a hitch in prison can often force a man to look hard and long at himself, said the chaplain.

"Each guy has to answer how he is going to do his time. Some guys spend all their free time in the weight pit building their muscles. Others go to the library and do legal research on their case; others turn to religion," he said.

As institutional chaplain, Swierenga schedules all the services and meeting times for the various religious groups. He also leaves his office door open for inmates who want to drop in and just talk.

"I think they feel safe with me. They know they won't get into trouble by telling me what's on their minds," he said.

The chaplain also performs about two weddings a month. He won't baptize anyone, since he believes a man can be baptized when he gets out. But he does consider helping a prisoner tie the knot with his sweetheart as part of the job.

"These men are human beings who have problems and did something wrong," he said. "I help them practice their religion just as they would out in the world. I try to help them make their religious experience behind bars more complete."

Americans had been *killed* in Vietnam than had been there in 1964, when Johnson had promised to send no more troops. By January 20, 1969, when Richard Nixon was sworn into office, 549,000 troops were fighting a war in Vietnam — a war which was looking increasingly unwinnable.[16]

By the time the Vietnam War came along, having ministers serve as chaplains had become commonplace for the Christian Reformed Church. By the time Johnson prepared to leave office at the end of 1968, twenty-two Christian Reformed pastors were serving as chaplains in all branches of the armed forces. A number of these pastors were serving in combat with their troops in the jungles and rice paddies of Vietnam.

Among them was Chaplain Jan Friend, who reported to readers of *The Banner* that on more than one occasion he had had his makeshift worship services interrupted by Viet Cong gunfire and grenades. Friend and the other chaplains who served in Vietnam endured the same hardship and misery that all soldiers experienced during that most trying of wars. Friend reported,

We established a perimeter for the night about 3:30 p.m. It looked as though an hour later might be a good time for a short [worship] service. It's not Sunday, but worship opportunities yesterday did not present themselves. The sanctity of the Sabbath is not respected by war. We worship when circumstances permit. The congregation was small but appreciative. In spite of very little preparation time, the Holy Spirit led to a message that spoke to the needs of fighting men. We chatted until suddenly rifle shots pierced the air and exploding grenades shattered the short silence and we dashed for our [fox]holes and weapons.

It's 11 p.m. now. If only my poncho will keep rain out. The monsoon torrent fills the hammock as though it were a bathtub. No sleep tonight, that's certain.[17]

Other Vietnam War chaplains included Herman Keizer, who was the only Christian Reformed chaplain seriously wounded in the war. When a helicopter in which he was riding was hit by a shell just after takeoff, Keizer was thrown out, breaking his arms and severely bruising the rest of his body. Keizer survived his injuries to continue serving as a military chaplain, eventually being assigned to work in the Pentagon. By 1995 Colonel Keizer had been reassigned to Stuttgart, Germany, to serve as the senior chaplain for the U.S. Army throughout Europe.

Naval Chaplain Herbert L. Bergsma's two tours of duty as a chaplain in Vietnam eventually led him to write *Chaplains with Marines in Vietnam: 1962-1971* as part of his role as official historian of the U.S. Navy Chaplain Corps. Bergsma's book, though not specifically about Christian Reformed chaplaincy, shows the many and varied duties of Vietnam

FIGURE 20 Herman Keizer.

FIGURE 21 Sunday-afternoon field service led by John Hoogland with officers and men of B Battery, 1st Rocket Howitzer Battalion, 9th Artillery, in 1968. "Honest John" rocket in background.

chaplains, from conducting field funerals to celebrating Communion on the makeshift altars afforded by stacked ammunition boxes and the hoods of jeeps.

Starting in the late 1970s, Americans began to gain a keener sense of what went on in Vietnam from movies like *Coming Home, Platoon,* and *The Deer Hunter.* Among the things Americans discovered in these films was the prevalence of drunkenness and of illicit drug use by troops seeking to escape the utter horror of the war around them. According to Bergsma, these were among the many knotty problems with which chaplains had to contend in Vietnam. Another difficulty was the southeast Asian version of the same racial strife that was tearing the country apart back home. Since military units had by that time been desegregated, chaplains frequently needed to act swiftly to head off the divisions of racial hatred.

As is true of all chaplaincy work, Vietnam proved that, perhaps more than ministers in other settings, chaplains need to be flexible, creative, and energetic to deal with the abundance of unforeseen, on-the-spot problems and crises which routinely come up in such nontraditional, atypical ministry settings. As Jan Friend wrote in his diary, in Vietnam "there is no typical day or night."

The Work Expands

During the 1960s, as racial tensions increased at home and the war in Vietnam crept into the American consciousness, the Christian Reformed Church was taking steps to formalize and expand the work of chaplaincy. Already in the late 1950s former World War II Chaplain Richard Wezeman was appointed secretary for active-duty chaplains, a part-time position designed to keep contact with chaplains on a regular and official basis. The 1961 Synod took another step toward formalizing chaplaincy ministry when it declared that, in addition to a consistorial and classical endorsement, new chaplains thereafter would be urged to secure also the endorsement of the synodical Chaplain Committee.

Through the efforts of people like Harold Dekker and Casey Schooland, synod would continue to take steps to make chaplaincy a more official and more widely used avenue

FIGURE 22 Ammunition boxes serve as a makeshift altar as William L. Childers, 9th Marines, conducts services on a jungle hilltop south of Khe Sanh.

FIGURE 23 Worship service held in the field in 1968 by Company K, 3rd Battalion, 4th Marines of the 3rd Marine Division.

of mission service, not only to military personnel but also to people in a variety of institutional and industrial settings. Throughout the 1960s much of this work was advocated and accomplished by Schooland, himself a former World War II chaplain who, after his retirement in 1963, continued to push for more work in chaplaincy ministries of all kinds.

Eventually the value of Schooland's contributions led to the conviction that a full-time executive secretary for the Chaplain Committee would lead to even greater expansion of the work. The synod concurred in this decision, making the Chaplain Committee an official agency of the denomination, eligible to receive denominational monies. The committee's first executive secretary was Reverend Harold Bode, who was hired in 1974 and continued in that post until 1994. Bode, an Air Force chaplain who entered the service in 1962 and moved into the Reserves in 1974, helped to expand the denomination's chaplaincy ministry until, by the time of his 1994 retirement, the denomination could boast nearly a hundred chaplains, or ten percent of all Christian Reformed pastors, as was the case also at the end of World War II.

Among the achievements of the Chaplain Committee under Bode's leadership was the expansion of the work into Canada by the forging of ties with the Ontario Provincial Interfaith Committee on Chaplaincy. A Canadian subcommittee of the denominational Chaplain Committee (consisting of Carl Tuyl, Peter Van Katwijk, and John Van Til) helped to recruit the denomination's first Canadian chaplains, including Reverend

FIGURE 24 Harold Bode, right, visits a helicopter crew at Clark Air Force Base, the Philippines, in 1967, during the Vietnam War.

FIGURE 25 Donald G. Belanus conducts shipboard services.

Siebert Van Houten, who became chaplain to Ontario's Hamilton Psychiatric Hospital in 1979.

In 1994 the Chaplain Committee welcomed its second full-time executive secretary, Reverend Jacob Heerema. Heerema, who had previously served as a chaplain for Pine Rest Christian Hospital in Cutlerville, Michigan, now oversees a Chaplain Committee with an annual budget of close to half a million dollars. Siebert Van Houten in 1995 became the first full-time director of CRC Canadian chaplaincy. The combined American-Canadian Chaplain Committee consists of twelve people, who oversee a Christian Reformed cadre of chaplains consisting of sixteen active-duty military chaplains, sixteen Reserve and National Guard chaplains, twenty-two chaplains in acute-health-care settings, twenty-three institutional chaplains in organizations such as Hospice, nine prison chaplains, two industrial chaplains, and a dozen full-time counselors.

By 1996 the one hundred Christian Reformed chaplains work throughout the United States and Canada as well as in places as far away as Germany, Panama, and Hong Kong. A recent denominational restructuring plan placed the work of Heerema and the Chaplain Committee (now called Chaplaincy Ministries) under the broader auspices of the new Pastoral Ministries agency. But through their many and varied tasks, the men and women now serving as chaplains do far more than pastoral work: they also do the work of missionaries, expanding the work of God's kingdom into many new and needy settings, thereby proclaiming the Lordship of Christ over all of life. One suspects that Henry Beets would see such work as a mind-bogglingly good return on his original fifty-dollar investment.

FIGURE 26 Harold Bode.

FIGURE 27 Richard E. Ferris is shown reading his Bible on a five-minute break after hiking for three hours during Operation Prairie near the Demilitarized Zone during the Vietnam War.

Chapter Seven

The Backyard World

Ministry to Ethnic Minorities

There is neither Jew nor Greek, slave nor free, male nor female,
for you are all one in Christ Jesus.

Galatians 3:28

The United States has always been a land of immigrants — an ostensible melting pot of people from all backgrounds and nationalities. Still, when the French presented the United States with the Statue of Liberty in 1886, the "huddled masses yearning to be free" who were seeking liberty on the shores of the New World were mostly white Europeans. Italians, Irish, Germans, Dutch, and Poles were the primary immigrant groups passing through Ellis Island on their way to build a new life in America.

One hundred years later at least one thing has not changed: America remains a common destination for many immigrants worldwide. What has changed, however, is the national origin of these would-be American citizens. While immigration from Europe and Britain has declined dramatically since the late nineteenth and early twentieth centuries, the movement into the United States from Latin America, Mexico, and Asia has risen dramatically. After 1965, when Congress rescinded its immigration quota system, waves of immigrants from all over the world began to set course for America and its perceived limitless possibilities.

Among the reasons for the marked increase in Hispanics and Asians coming to America (though not the sole reason) has been a population explosion throughout the Third World, at times resulting in, among other difficulties, increased civil unrest in places like Africa, Asia, and Latin America. Unhappily, many nations which are growing the fastest in these final years of the twentieth century are among the poorest nations on earth. Whereas it is estimated that the population of the United States may increase twenty-nine percent in the next thirty years, Mexico during that same time will likely see a sixty-three percent rise.

The burden of population explosions is felt most acutely in many already-impoverished and overcrowded major cities worldwide. As increasing numbers of people flock to cities, many are being forced to live in shantytowns where the population density often reaches 130,000 people per square mile. It is estimated that by the year 2000 the population of many of the world's largest cities will burgeon to mind-numbing totals: Mexico City to 16.2 million, Bombay to 18.1 million, Calcutta to 12.7 million, São Paulo to a staggering 22.6 mil-

groups which are mixed and tossed together without losing their individual identities).

In Los Angeles, for instance, the Roman Catholic Church now celebrates mass in sixty different languages for at least ninety-nine distinct ethnic groups. Nationwide the percentage of foreign-born Americans has doubled since 1970. During the 1980s the United States welcomed ten million immigrants — the highest number for any decade of the twentieth century. What is perhaps most striking is the shift in national origin of these immigrants. During the 1950s, when there were only 2.5 million immigrants, only twenty percent of them came from Asia or Latin America. During the 1980s that percentage more than tripled: fully seventy-one percent of that decade's ten million immigrants came from Asia or Latin America.[1]

In the midst of these major changes on the American scene, denominations like the Christian Reformed Church have faced at once a great opportunity and a great challenge. The opportunity is to reach out to, tap into, minister to, and enfold the exploding ethnic populations, both indigenous and immigrant. The challenge comes from the fact that a successful reaching out to and enfolding of such groups inevitably changes the face of the denomination as it must make room for diverse languages, customs, worship styles, and even theological viewpoints.

The CRC, of course, was not unfamiliar with immigrant ethnicity within the church — but for most of its nearly 140-year history the immigrants of the Christian Reformed Church all came from one place: the Netherlands. This homogeneous Dutch ethos — with its own particular customs, style, and theology — was the anvil on which a distinctive Christian Reformed identity was hammered out in the New World. This monocultural immigrant ethos served the CRC well in its early history, creating in the midst of a large and strange new land a haven of security in which newcomers could form friendships and share worship without language barriers and cultural dislocation. Such separate enclaves are often incubators for assimilation, easing an ethnic population's adjustment to a new land and culture. Were assimilation not a gradual process, it would be highly threatening and overwhelming to the first generation in the new country.

Still, the late-twentieth-century challenge for the Christian Reformed Church, and for other one-time ethnically unified denominations like it, is to recognize and accept the increasing diversity which results when a denomination

FIGURE 1–2 The Statue of Libery welcoming the "huddled masses yearning to be free."

lion people. It is not surprising that this global population explosion, combined with the civil and national wars which now rage around the world, is leading many people to seek out what they hope will be the wide-open spaces and new opportunities of America.

Of course, America has long been home to several indigenous ethnic groups — including American Indians, Mexicans, and Spaniards — all of whom have long called portions of the United States home. Still, their numbers nationwide were rather modest until about the mid twentieth century. But recent surges in immigration have resulted in a greater ethnic diversity than America has ever known before — greater even than during the nineteenth-century heyday of European immigration. Equally important, America is waking up to the fact that the melting pot never actually melted and that individual ethnic groups are maintaining their distinct identities (leading some sociologists to speak not of a melting pot but of a salad bowl of various ceases to be a church with a heritage going back to a single mother nation. Beginning in the 1970s and 1980s, the challenge foreseen by many Home Missions leaders was to make room for the diversity which inevitably results when a formerly homogeneous Dutch immigrant church becomes a denomination of many *individual* immigrant churches, including congregations made up of Korean, Chinese, Vietnamese, and Hispanic peoples.

This challenge was tackled by the Christian Reformed Church and its Board of Home Missions primarily through church planting in areas with heavy concentrations of ethnic minorities. In 1995 Home Missions reported to synod that of the nearly fifty new churches it had planted since 1993, nearly half were ethnic congregations comprised of Hispanic, Korean, Indonesian, Vietnamese, and Navajo Christians.

But though the number of ethnically diverse congregations is now rising rapidly, Christian Reformed ministries to ethnic minorities actually go back to the middle of the twentieth century, when a few visionary leaders and congregations stepped out of their predominantly Dutch churches to welcome some very non-Dutch people for whom America had become home.

Beginnings

During the 1930s, as she grew up within the Christian Reformed Dutch subculture of Prospect Park, New Jersey, Bessie Vander Valk could not have guessed that in some small way her life would become mixed up with global politics. But

in the years ahead precisely that would happen as Bessie's life and career would intersect with the revolutionary actions of Fidel Castro on the Caribbean island of Cuba, ninety miles south of the United States.[2]

In 1940 Vander Valk attended a mission rally at her home church, Bethel CRC in Paterson, New Jersey. The evangelist speaking that day told the congregation about the great mission opportunities and the ripe harvest fields awaiting new mission workers in nearby Cuba. In the course of the evangelist's speech, Bessie Vander Valk heard the call of God's Spirit to the work of missions in Cuba.

Vander Valk knew that to engage in such work would require overcoming many obstacles. The first such barrier was the objection of her family, who feared what would happen to a young, single woman going off to a foreign land on her own. Another obstacle was finances. Unable to convince the World Missions branch of the CRC to support her with a sizable amount of money — the agency wanted her to go to Africa instead — Vander Valk knew she would have to raise her own support, which she did through the Bethel church, a local Baptist congregation, her family, and her friends.

By 1941 Vander Valk was ready to depart for Cuba. Passport in hand, Vander Valk — who at this point knew virtually no Spanish — departed from the United States and headed for the city of Matanzas, where she worked as a cook in an orphanage run by an American couple. In the course of her work in Matanzas, Vander Valk began to learn the Spanish language and the ways of the Cuban people. Once

FIGURE 3 From left to right, Clarence Nyenhuis, Ramón Borrego, Sara Menchaca, Betsy Vander Valk Izquierdo, and Fred Diemer.

her language skills increased, she began — completely on her own — to visit patients at a local women and children's hospital, comforting them in their times of need and presenting the hope of the gospel.

One of the patients whom Vander Valk visited was Virginia Gomez. Their relationship would soon open new doors of opportunity to the young would-be missionary. The relationship did not begin very auspiciously, however. One day Vander Valk brought Gomez what she assumed would be a cheering bouquet of flowers. After Gomez burst into tears, Vander Valk learned a quick lesson in her cross-cultural education: flowers in the Cuban culture are reserved for the terminally ill or the dead. Thus, when Vander Valk brought the flowers into the room, Virginia Gomez assumed her medical condition was considered terminal. Once this confusion was cleared up, a strong friendship developed between the two women, and Vander Valk succeeded in leading Gomez to a Christian conversion.

FIGURE 4 Jerry Pott.

By the time Gomez was ready to return to her home village of Jaguey Grande, she begged Vander Valk to return with her because many of her fellow villagers could benefit from the message of hope in Jesus which Vander Valk was bringing. Thus began what would prove to be nearly twenty years of vital ministry in Jaguey Grande — a place which, in the early 1940s, still had no electricity or indoor plumbing and which was accessible only by horse or on foot. Vander Valk focused her ministry especially on the children of Jaguey Grande, whom she taught the stories of Jesus in a Sunday school-like setting. Of all the people whom she encountered in this village, perhaps the most significant for Miss Vander Valk was Pastor Vicente Izquierdo, whom she later married.

The efforts of Vicente and Bessie Izquierdo resulted in the formation of the Interior Gospel Mission in 1955. By 1958 Christian Reformed World Missions took note of the work, sending Reverend Clarence Nyenhuis and Reverend Jerry Pott as the denomination's first official Cuban missionaries. But just one year later the revolution of Fidel Castro toppled the government of Fulgencio Batista, forever changing the Cuban situation.

One of the first results was a quick emigration of Cubans to the United States. Among those who returned to America at that time were the Izquierdos. Nyenhuis had intended to continue his mission work in Cuba despite the changed political conditions, but, having returned to the United States for a brief vacation in 1960, he discovered that the newly formed revolutionary government of Castro refused to allow him to reenter the country. Subsequently, Nyenhuis, along with the Izquierdos, began a new Spanish ministry in the United States.[3]

Suddenly, what had been a foreign mission field was transmuted into a home mission field located in southern Florida, where most Cuban refugees took up residence. Working with the Izquierdos and others, Nyenhuis used the facilities of the Shenandoah Presbyterian Church in downtown Miami to set up a medical clinic, food center, clothing ministry, and economic-support agency for the forming Cuban community. On December 18, 1960, the first official worship service of the new congregation was held. But despite aggressive canvassing in the neighborhood and many invitations to the community, this first service was attended only by the Nyenhuis family. A week later the Christmas Day service fared little better, attracting only two additional persons.

Still, Nyenhuis pressed on, concentrating much of his work on desperately needed refugee assistance. Unprepared to handle such a speedy influx of refugees from another country, the United States government relied on private and

FIGURE 5 Arlene and Clarence Nyenhuis.

FIGURE 6 El Buen Samaritano CRC, Miami, Florida.

FIGURE 7 El Redentor CRC in Hialeah, Florida.

church agencies to help meet the crisis. By February of 1961 there were already thirty thousand Cuban refugees in southern Florida, most of whom had fled their homeland with absolutely nothing in hand. Among the agencies formed in Miami to help the refugees was the Protestant Latin America Emergency Committee (PLAEC), to which Nyenhuis was quickly appointed a full member and to which Home Missions began to contribute much-needed funds. Through the help of denominational diaconal agencies as well as the Christian Reformed Latin Relief Committee, a Good Samaritan Center was set up to dispense food, clothing, and medical assistance through the help of volunteer doctors.

It was likely due in large part to Nyenhuis's willingness to engage in such a holistic ministry — to do the work of a good Samaritan — that in the course of just one year his church grew from two people on Christmas Day 1960 to a congregation of 210 by Christmas 1961. Soon thereafter a former Catholic chapel was purchased, and the El Buen Samaritano or "Good Samaritan" church was formally established on July 10, 1964, the first fully multinational Hispanic congregation in the denomination. Nyenhuis would pastor the church until 1969, when he moved to Anaheim, California, to begin a similar new ministry among the Cuban and Hispanic populations there. He was succeeded in Miami by Reverend Fred Diemer, who remained until 1979.

Over the years the Good Samaritan congregation con-

FIGURE 8 David Bosscher loading the Spanish Christian Reformed church of Miami bus.

FIGURE 9 Migrant workers entering South Olive church.

tinued to grow, graduating from Home Missions as a fully independent church in 1985, a congregation of over 250 persons attending worship services each Sunday. Despite various changes in leadership during the 1980s, Good Samaritan became the mother congregation for no fewer than three daughter churches in the south Florida area: the El Redentor church in Hialeah in 1982, the Buenas Nuevas church in Miami in 1989, and the Primera Iglesia Cristiana Reformada in West Palm Beach in 1992.

By 1995 the Hispanic Christian Reformed congregations in south Florida were ministering to well over seven hundred people and were planning even more new churches. In a real way this vital ethnic ministry can be traced back to the courageous, and for a very long time the solo, efforts of Bessie Vander Valk Izquierdo. Mrs. Izquierdo, who passed away in 1995 from complications of Alzheimer's disease, was a true pioneer in helping the CRC break out of its Dutch ethnicity and reach out to other peoples of the world, including that part of the world which arrives on the shores of this country.

The Backyard World

Bessie Vander Valk had to leave Prospect Park in order to meet up with the Spanish-speaking Cubans to whom she felt called in ministry. But as early as the 1940s, Christian Reformed church members in Holland, Michigan, realized that the Spanish-speaking world had already come to them. Each year Mexican *braceros,* or migrant workers, came to Holland to pick the beans and pickles grown in the area for the local Heinz food factory. Some local church members saw in these people the opportunity for at least a seasonal ministry if not, one day, an even larger year-round ministry.

Among the early leaders of this new work in the Holland area were Gerrit Bos and Chester Schemper. Schemper, a student at Calvin Theological Seminary, was asked to organize *bracero* worship services. Held in the Olive Center Town Hall

FIGURE 10 John P. Roberts reading the catechism to Mexican migrants in 1963.

and the Borculo school, the services attracted between thirty and one hundred migrant workers. Though the earliest work among the migrants was conducted in English, as the years passed, more and more Spanish-speaking evangelists and ministers were sought to make the work more inclusive and accessible to the *bracero* population.[4]

FIGURE 11 Chester Schemper.

By the early 1950s the work was being conducted by Everett Vanden Brink and Sylvia Stielstra, working under the auspices of Classis Zeeland. In 1953, under their leadership, a

A Cambodian Pastor's Painful, Prayerful Quest

One blustery winter day in early 1996, a distraught Cambodian refugee walked into Graafschap Christian Reformed Church near Holland, Michigan, and asked for help.

The man's wife had just left him. He had children at home. Here he was in this strange country, deep in the heart of west Michigan, and he didn't know where to turn. More than anything, he needed to talk to someone in his native language.

Providentially, the troubled man had come to the right place.

"We were able to give him assistance," said Socheth Na, evangelist for a fledgling Cambodian congregation based at the church on the outskirts of Holland, Michigan.

Na is a southeast-Asian refugee who is no stranger himself to adversity. He has experienced many of the massive emotional, spiritual, and psychological upheavals refugees undergo in changing countries, cultures, and even religions. As leader of one of eight CRC-supported Cambodian congregations in the United States and Canada, Na uses his own experiences as an immigrant in bringing the love of God to refugees who seek guidance, comfort, and love.

"There are a lot of casualties among the refugees," said Na, who escaped war-torn Cambodia in 1979 for a resettlement camp in Thailand. He came to this country in 1981.

"No one in my country had much freedom. When we come to the United States, it's like the dam breaks for some people. It is hard for them. There is a cultural breakdown. There is drinking, gambling."

About 650 Cambodians lived in the greater Holland area in 1996. Of these, about 50 regularly attended Sunday services conducted by Na at the church in Graafschap. Na, a graduate of Reformed Bible College, in Grand Rapids, Michigan, made sure he preached the gospel of Jesus in a manner that his fellow refugees could understand.

Colorful Cambodian traditions and southeast-Asian customs and music were woven, wherever possible, into the Christian services. A couple of times a year the group of Cambodians held a unity service with members of the much larger Graafschap congregation.

FIGURE 12 Socheth Na.

"They are finding their way," said Reverend Marv Hofman, pastor of the larger church. "It is not easy for either of us to mix our cultures and traditions. But we are doing it."

In the early 1980s several Holland-area churches sponsored Cambodians to come to this country from the refugee camps. Initially, many of the immigrants settled in larger cities. But a few made it to Holland.

Word of mouth encouraged them to come to west Michigan, said Dave Van Netten in a history he wrote about the influx of Cambodians to Holland. The majority of Cambodian immigrants in west Michigan are blue-collar workers. Some are homeowners; many are renters.

"Cambodians living in Holland have tended to adopt more Western values and life-styles," said Van Netten, a seminarian at Western Theological Seminary, in his article. "This includes such things as an orientation toward materialism, a hurried view of time and scheduling, and the rearing and marriage of their offspring."

There is a clash of cultures that is seen especially in the young, most of whom are forsaking the Cambodian language and some of whom have joined gangs of other southeast-Asian refugees as a way to develop self-identity.

The clash is especially evident in marriages. Back home, weddings are prearranged events. Not so in America.

"Parents struggle with letting their daughters date before they get married," he wrote.

Van Netten, who once worked with Cambodians at the Graafschap church and taught English in Cambodia, said many of the refugees are spiritually adrift.

"The adult Cambodians' perception of the Christian churches is currently one of attempting to 'proselytize' them to fit the 'American' religion," he said.

"Some take offense if they sense they are being encouraged to become a Christian or involved with the Christians in any way."

It is in the midst of this struggle for a place in a new world in which the ministry of Na and that of the larger CRC denomination plays such an important role.

In the winter of 1987, Na came to Graafschap to start a Bible study, which quickly grew from a few to a solid group of twenty regular attendees. He was still an RBC student at the time. In 1991, with the help of funding from Home Missions and the Synodical Council on Race Relations, he became a full-time missionary to the people with whom he shares similar hardships.

"I am saved by the grace of God and the atonement of Christ on the cross," said Na. "I really want to help other Cambodian people to get out of the darkness of the world of spirit worship, of ancestor worship, as well as the worship of untrue gods in nature."

Na was born in 1953 in a village on the delta of the Mekong River. He has three brothers and three sisters. The family was well off financially until a windstorm in 1958 destroyed his father's lumber business.

After the storm, his father took to the road to find work. Na stayed home, helped his mother sell rice cakes, and attended school. He heard of the Christian religion during his youth but considered it a confusing form of belief, "especially the part about accepting this man Jesus Christ as your Lord and Savior."

He continued to believe in many angels and gods until he came to this country and experienced a conversion while attending a CRC church in Denver, Colorado.

"I used to look down upon and laugh at students who became Christians and discussed the Good News in the shade of the coconut tree in front of my school," he recalled in a brief autobiography.

"Whenever I met a Cambodian Christian, I thought how stupid they were to waste their time studying this strange religion ... that belonged to the Western people."

Na was among the thousands of Cambodians who fled their country either during or after one of the bloodiest revolutions in history. The political party known as the Khmer Rouge, under the leadership of the infamous Pol Pot, killed millions of men, women, and children as part of a plan to return the country to its agrarian roots. This happened in the mid 1970s.

The educated, the Buddhist clergy, and any others considered enemies of the revolution were murdered by the Khmer Rouge. Millions of others were herded into countryside communes and forced to do hard labor with their hands.

Na was one of those sent to a camp. While there, he nearly died in a fall down a mountain, which he had climbed while at work. He survived and eventually was reunited with his family after the Vietnamese communists invaded Cambodia and defeated Pol Pot.

But Na was afraid of what the future might provide under any government in his homeland. So he escaped to Thailand. With other members of his family, he was able to come to the United States.

Once here, he started the long, painful process of changing his entire life and outlook. Conversion to the Christian faith helped, but nothing has been easy.

"My spiritual life has continued to be uneven at times," he said in his autobiography. "The weak point which has tempted me to fall into spiritual uncertainty was the conflict in my married life."

In Denver in the early 1980s, he met a woman, Lynn, with whom he had gone to school in Cambodia. They fell in love and married. But romance of that sort is unknown, or at least unsanctioned, in Cambodia. Members of his family did not approve of the marriage. Still, he and his wife endured.

They came to RBC on the suggestion of their pastor in Colorado. Life and school in west Michigan, he said, required adjustment. But then he found the job as an evangelist to his people.

The job in Graafschap is hard. Cambodians face many drawbacks in their attempt to blend in. Chief among those difficulties is the struggle for a spiritual life that feels comfortable and makes sense to them. With his education from RBC and ongoing assistance from denominational teachers, Na is making inroads.

"I'm so happy that the CRC has stepped away from how it used to be and has reached out to other groups of people," said Na. "The church has been part of God's plan, which has helped our group of Cambodians come this far."

"I'm so happy that the CRC has stepped away from what it used to be and has reached out to other groups of people."

— Evangelist Socheth Na

more permanent site for the ministry was established in the Calvary Mission Chapel on River Avenue in Holland. It was at this new site that the Iglesia Hispana CRC of Holland, Michigan, would be born. By 1958 the work was officially taken up by Holland Heights CRC, which moved the congregation to a new facility at the corner of Lincoln Avenue and Thirteenth Street. With a consistent congregation of thirty adults and sixty children, the work was clearly going very well.

In 1962 Reverend Juan Boonstra, later the first Spanish-language minister for *The Back to God Hour,* was brought into the work under the joint auspices of Holland Heights CRC and Classis Holland. During Boonstra's two years of work, a new facility was purchased at Maple Avenue and Twentieth Street. This permanent site became the official birthplace of the Iglesia Hispana CRC. The congregation became a formalized Home Missions ministry in 1964, when Reverend Carlos Tapia-Ruano became the church's first full-time pastor. In his five years of ministry, Tapia-Ruano was able to attract many new members, including a number of Cuban refugee families in the area. By 1969 the church was ministering to over 150 persons. Unhappily, however, Reverend Tapia-Ruano was accused of various moral and financial indiscretions, for which Classis Holland deposed him from the ministry of the Christian Reformed Church.

In the wake of this scandal, many of the Cuban members whom Tapia-Ruano had brought into the church left, but under the leadership of Reverend Frank Pott and his successors, Cornelius Persenaire and John Hutt, the church continued to grow until in 1991 it became an officially organized congregation. By 1995 the Iglesia Hispana CRC was ministering to over 165 persons, a congregation made up primarily of Mexicans but with representation also from Cuban, Puerto Rican, and Central

FIGURE 13 Everett Vanden Brink.

American Christians. By 1995 Reverend Hutt was being assisted by El Salvadoran evangelist Florencio Ramiro Lopez.

Located directly in the middle of one of the denomination's largest and oldest Dutch enclaves, this vital ministry is but a small reminder of the ways in which America is changing and the ways in which, as a result, denominations like the Christian Reformed Church are changing accordingly.

"Not All Latinos Eat Tacos"

To the uninitiated, all Hispanic or Latino groups may seem to belong to a monolithic ethnic group — people who look Mexican, speak Spanish, and share some kind of unified culture. In reality, Hispanic and Latino persons represent a broad spectrum of customs, cultures, and religious views because Hispanics and Latinos in the United States can trace their heritage to any one of twenty-six different nations in the Americas, a fact which gave rise to the proverb quoted above, "Not all Latinos eat tacos."

These cultural diversities are also represented in churches which minister to America's burgeoning Latino population. Whereas in 1970 America was host to a hundred thousand Latino evangelical Christians, by 1995 that number had jumped seventy-fold to seven million (out of an estimated total U.S. Latino population of thirty-five million). As the evangelical periodical *Christianity Today* has pointed out, evangelical leaders of the late twentieth century (including even Latino evangelical leaders) have had to become very creative in reaching out to a population of people which includes Mexican migrant workers, Salvadoran political refugees, post-Catholic fifth-generation Baptists, first-generation Pentecostals, dishwashing illegals, theological heavyweights, and rap-syncopating L.A. teenagers.[5]

FIGURE 14
Juan Boonstra.

As the Christian Reformed Church began seeking ways in the 1970s to plant more churches and do more vital ministry among American Latinos, it also had to wrestle with this diversity. It quickly became apparent, however, that if even Latino leaders sometimes found it difficult to innovate ministry programs to incorporate and take account of this rich tapestry of cultures and customs, then certainly successful outreach to Latinos could never be fully if done principally by Anglos.

In 1985, therefore, Reverend Al Mulder of Christian Reformed Home Missions and others, including Reverend Louis Wagenveld and Reverend Clarence Nyenhuis, challenged the denomination and its leaders to develop Spanish-language materials, manuals, and curricula to train new leaders in order to expand the denomination's ethnic ministries,

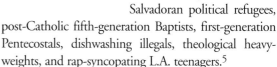

FIGURE 15 Alfred E. Mulder.   FIGURE 16 Ramón Borrego.   FIGURE 17 Duane E. VanderBrug.   FIGURE 18 Gary Teja.

particularly those among Latinos and particularly in California.

A 1986 report to the denomination states the need, challenge, and opportunity very clearly, pointing out that, according to a May 1986 directory of Protestant churches in California, the ratio of churches to Hispanic persons in California was 1:4294. It was urgently proposed, therefore, that the CRC begin planting new churches through the establishment of Bible-study core groups, neighborhood calling, and coordinated efforts with the Spanish *Back to God Hour* broadcasts and The Evangelical Literature League (TELL), which had been formed to provide Bibles and other materials in the Spanish language.

FIGURE 19 Spanish migrant service in New Era, Michigan, 1962.

Home Missions seized the opportunity, thus beginning a concerted and official effort to expand the vision and mission of the church in specifically ethnic directions. Mulder's efforts quickly led to several other initiatives in the late 1980s, including the convening of a Hispanic Planning Committee in 1986 and Home Missions' formal approval of a Hispanic Task Force in 1987.[6]

In just a few short years this work had borne enough fruit to warrant the appointment of the denomination's first Hispanic-ministry coordinator in the person of Ramón Borrego in 1989. Borrego's efforts helped to expand the ministry in the two years during which he worked for Home Missions, and the work grew even more after 1993, when Gary Teja took over. Under Teja's leadership, Christian Reformed Hispanic ministries expanded, even publishing its own quarterly newsletter called *Puentes,* or *Bridges.*

Though indigenous Hispanic and Latino leadership was the key to a successful Hispanic ministry, it was also the denomination's biggest deficit in that ministry. To meet this need, Home Missions, in cooperation with Calvin Theological Seminary and under the local auspices of the International Theological Seminary (ITS) in Los Angeles, opened a west-coast school for Latino evangelist training. Reverend Duane VanderBrug of Christian Reformed Home Missions made some initial proposals and sketches for the new program, but it was Reverend Gary Schipper who helped realize the dream of establishing a program to train new leaders for this growing area of the church. The new program dovetailed with the Hispanic Task Force in California to train leaders for new-church development, making use of some Spanish curriculum materials which were available through Christian Reformed World Missions.

In 1989 Schipper fully took over the Evangelism Training

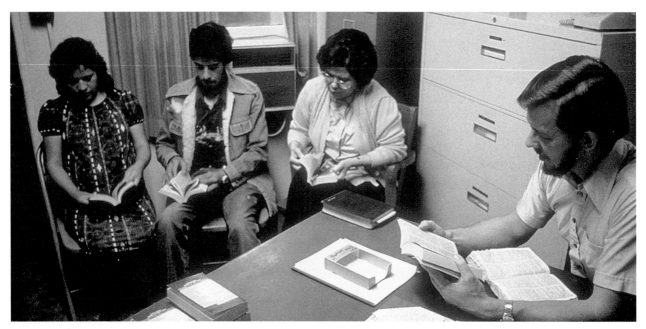

FIGURE 21 Louis Wagenveld.

FIGURE 20 Louis Wagenveld conducting a Bible study at a new church in Sun Valley, California.

evident as eight new churches were planted in California and still more in Florida, mostly through the work of graduates of the Evangelism Training Program. Other new churches were also begun in New Jersey, Texas, and Arizona. Indeed, by the mid 1990s Home Missions felt sufficiently encouraged to set a goal of having fifty Hispanic churches in place by the year 2003. This goal is being met through various strategies of leadership mentoring as part of ongoing efforts to train new Spanish-speaking leaders.

The challenges are great, however. Second- and third-generation Hispanics have a different set of needs, desires, and preferences than their parents and grandparents had. Additionally, leaders must frequently wrestle with the challenges inherent in bilingual communities as well as the challenge of developing unified strategies for ministry despite the fact that there is no typical Hispanic congregation — some congregations being well-off and middle-class, others being very poor.

To reach the new generation of Hispanics, Home Missions now works with regional task forces to develop comprehensive denominational strategies which take into account regional idiosyncrasies. Among the new strategies is the clustering of churches, whereby new church plants are placed as close as possible to an existing congregation which can serve as a parent church.

Additionally, new leaders are being recruited and educated through the resources available at Calvin Theological Seminary, Reformed Bible College, and the Evangelist Training Program. By making available internships in Hispanic ministry settings and by providing mentors or min-

Program in California, working half-time as a new-church developer in the El Monte area and half-time in teaching courses designed to help Latino leaders become equipped for evangelism and church planting. As the training program developed and spread — including expanding into Miami and New Jersey — leaders were trained for up to four years, with an eye toward their being ordained either as full pastors (this applying primarily to Latinos who had previously been ordained in other denominations) or as evangelists within the CRC.

The fruits of the new training program became quickly

FIGURE 22 Gary Schipper.

istry "coaches" to oversee and foster their training, Home Missions is making it possible for new candidates to learn new skills through on-the-job experience. A seminar entitled Church Planter's Bootcamp is also mandated early in the training process to fine-tune ministry skills. Through these and other new initiatives, Christian Reformed Home Missions is closing in on its goal of providing a loving Reformed ministry to Hispanics throughout North America.

The Koreans

On March 12, 1947, President Harry S. Truman announced a policy designed to contain the spread of Soviet influence worldwide. The Truman Doctrine, as it quickly became known, declared that "it must be the policy of the United States to support free peoples who are resisting attempted subjugation by armed minorities or by outside pressures."[7] When Truman spoke those words, few Americans knew much, if anything, about a small Asian country called Korea. However, on June 25, 1950, when communist North Korea invaded South Korea, the Truman Doctrine received its first test. Within months, thousands of U.S. troops joined a multinational force intent on keeping South Korea free. Thereafter, it would be a long, long time before Americans would forget Korea. Even after the war ended in 1953, U.S. troops would continue to be stationed along the Demilitarized Zone separating North and South Korea.

The story of the Christian Reformed Church and Korean Christians also dates back to the 1950s. Following the Korean War — which devastated so small a country, leaving in its wake thousands of orphans, wounded veterans, and impov-

erished peasants — Christian Reformed Home Missions and the Christian Reformed World Relief Committee cooperated in ministering to American soldiers in Servicemen's Homes as well as in other efforts aimed to bring relief to that ravaged country and its people.

By the late 1950s this contact resulted in a few Korean Presbyterian students' attending Calvin Theological Seminary. Even stronger ties between Korean Christians and the CRC were forged when Calvin Seminary president Dr. John H. Kromminga became a visiting professor to the Hapdong Seminary in Seoul during the spring of 1964. Kromminga's visit, and his subsequent positive report on the ripe conditions of Korea as a mission field, led to a 1965 synodical recommendation that the CRC raise $30,000 to donate toward the building of a new administration and classroom building for the Hapdong Seminary.

Writing in *The Banner* in 1965, Reverend Clarence Boomsma urged Christian Reformed congregations to take this goal seriously. At that time Boomsma, who was serving as secretary for the denominational Ecumenicity and Inter-Church Correspondence Committee, reminded readers that, although Korea was the most Christian of all Asian nations, Christians still represented only five percent of the general Korean population. Thus, support for Korean Christians and their pastors could go a long way toward reaching the ninety-five percent of Koreans who were not yet Christians while at the same time providing a real spiritual blessing to the CRC through ties forged with Reformed brothers and sisters in another part of the world.[8]

In 1965 few could have guessed how rich the Korean mission field was for harvesting or how great would be the eventual blessing for the CRC through its Korean ties. Indeed, few could have guessed how many of those Reformed Korean brothers and sisters would soon no longer be in another part of the world but right next door in the United States and Canada. For by 1996 Calvin Seminary was home to sixty Korean students, one-quarter of the seminary student body. Furthermore, by 1996 the CRC could boast fifty-six Korean congregations, ranging from California to Georgia. Located in forty North American cities, these congregations are home to over five thousand Christian Reformed members in fifteen states and provinces, including Hawaii, Alaska, and British Columbia.[9]

The growth of Christian Reformed Korean congregations correlates with a surge in Korean immigration in the late 1970s and early 1980s. In 1970 there were only modest numbers of Koreans residing in North America, accounting for only a small percentage of immigrants coming to the United States each year. But within a decade, that changed dramatically. Whereas in 1970 there were only 100 Korean congregations throughout the United States, by 1980 there were 1,000

Korean churches nationwide. That number would nearly triple in the following decade so that by 1991 there were 2,620 Korean churches in the United States.[10] Between 1981 and 1986, forty-seven percent of all immigrants to the United States came from Asia, with the Koreans representing the third-largest ethnic group among all immigrants.[11]

The largest geographic concentration of new Korean immigrants was in southern California, specifically, in the greater Los Angeles area. Indeed, by the time of the Los Angeles riots in 1992, over one-half of all businesses which were looted or destroyed in the riots belonged to Korean businesspersons. By that same year Los Angeles had become home to thirty Korean seminaries, which had, since their var-ious foundings, graduated a total of one thousand candidates for the ministry in various Korean denominations.

This surge in Korean seminaries and churches in the United States mirrored a religious revival in Korea itself, where, beginning in the early 1970s, Koreans began turning to Christianity in large numbers. By 1984 Korea had even become home to the largest Christian church in the world. Pastored by Reverend Paul Yonggi Cho, the Assembly of God congregation in Seoul had grown to 350,000 members by the mid 1980s and was gaining new members at a rate of 10,000 per month.[12]

The Work Begins

As noted earlier, the handful of Koreans who attended

A Visionary from the North

Early summer of 1984 was especially hectic for Reverend John T. Kim.

Kim, a native of North Korea, had just graduated from Calvin Theological Seminary and was assigned to start a new church among his fellow Koreans in southern California.

In the midst of figuring how he would move his family and all of his belongings west, he got an offer he could-n't refuse from Peter and Gladys Mulder, an elderly couple from Holland, Michigan.

The Mulders, members of Bethany CRC in Holland, asked if they could rent a truck, load it with his worldly goods, and drive it to the Los Angeles area. At first, the offer shocked him. Then he took them up on it.

"I was so overwhelmed," said Kim, a slender evangelist and seminary professor. "What they did is a symbol of how the CRC has cared for me and my ministry, which is for God and the Korean people."

A writer, teacher, preacher, and denominational leader, Kim in 1996 was among a handful of church-growth experts trying to form a vision of what the CRC must do as it moves into the next century. Having grown up a Methodist in North Korea and then having traveled the world as a Reformed evangelist, he believes he has a good idea of what has to happen for his church to survive and thrive in years to come.

"Our denomination has to become more multicultur-al," he said. "We will need to have more colors in the CRC. We need to be open to more races and to work harder to address the social and spiritual issues in our communities."

Kim attended a Presbyterian seminary in South Korea and eventually joined the CRC when he took a job as an outreach minister of a church in Orange County, California.

Early on, he wondered how he and his family would fit into the denomination founded in west Michigan by Dutch settlers. But experiences, such as when the Holland couple moved his family west, convinced him this was the church for him.

"The CRC opened up and let us into its family," said Kim. "I'm so grateful for the love and support that we have been given."

Unfortunately, not everyone feels such acceptance, he added.

Kim recalls a story related to him by one of his four children. This daughter slept over at a friend's house one night. While there, she asked her friend what church she attended. The friend said their family didn't go to church.

"My daughter then mentioned that there was a Christian Reformed church right across the street from their house. She asked why didn't they go there," said Kim.

The friend suggested to her parents that they try a ser-vice at the neighborhood house of worship. After some discussion, they decided to give it a try, said Kim. As it turned out, people in the church across the street weren't very friendly. The little girl and her family felt like strangers. No one talked to them. So they left and never went back.

"CRC churches need to expose their good gifts to lots of other people," he said. "Our congregational lives need

Calvin Seminary during the fifties paved the way for many more to attend in the years ahead. Among some of the first Korean seminarians who had done at least part of their educational work at Calvin were two men who would become pioneers in Christian Reformed Korean ministries: Dr. John E. Kim and Dr. Jin Tae Lee. Their work of church planting among Korean immigrants in California would begin what became a burgeoning of Korean congregations throughout the denomination.

In 1976 John E. Kim emigrated from Korea to southern California, where he received a call from Third Bellflower Christian Reformed Church to be a missionary to that area's large and growing Korean population. Kim began his work by

targeting one of the first major California Korean settlements in the greater Los Angeles area. After laying the groundwork to begin a new congregation, Kim held his first worship services in a movie theater on Brea Avenue in Los Angeles.

Through the guidance of Reverend Donald Negen of the Bellflower church as well as through the sponsorship and encouragement of the Classical Home Missions Committee of Classis California South and a grant-in-aid from Christian Reformed Home Missions, Kim steadily gathered a congregation. The congregation organized almost immediately and grew rapidly. Indeed, by 1990 it was able to purchase a seven-acre site on which to construct a large sanctuary to meet the worship and ministry needs of the now twelve-hundred-member congregation.

In 1977, one year after Kim had begun his church-planting work in Los Angeles, Jin Tae Lee began a similar ministry in Orange County. Beginning with just thirty-seven members meeting at the Fountain Valley Korean CRC, this congregation likewise grew rapidly. Within only one year Lee had gathered enough new members to formally organize the Orange Korean CRC in Fullerton. Like churches back in the Korean homeland, so also Korean congregations in the United States and Canada saw an explosion of church growth during the 1980s.

The church which Dr. Lee began in 1977 likewise exploded so that already by 1980 the congregation voted to spend a stunning $1 million to purchase the facility previously occupied by Pastor Charles Swindoll's First Evangelical Free Church. By 1996 the Orange Korean CRC, now under the leadership of Reverend Paul Yang, was home to nearly a thousand members, the largest Korean congregation in the CRC and one of the largest Christian Reformed congregations anywhere.

This congregation shows no signs of slowing down. Through its multiple programs — including a Korean gospel radio program — and its four full-time pastors (an additional six staff persons work part-time) the church is flourishing numerically and spiritually. During 1995 alone sixty new members were brought into the congregation through evangelism and outreach, and an additional ninety members transferred in from other denominations. On Sundays these new members, along with the rest of the congregation, worship

FIGURE 23 Paul Yang.

---

to explode and be alive. Generally, CRC congregations are too closed."

Koreans such as himself, he said, may be able to help the denomination open its doors. Having grown up in a society whose Christian faith has ignited in recent years, Koreans bring to the American Protestant church great vitality and powerfully expressive forms of religious expression.

"The Korean church has much to share with the CRC," he said. "We can bring spiritual fire and very strong evangelism to the denomination."

In his book *Protestant Church Growth in Korea*, Kim reports that Christianity is fairly new to his homeland. But Korea, once known as "the hermit nation," has seen numbers of Roman Catholics and Protestants increase tremendously in the last forty years. Much of this growth has been primarily in South Korea.

"Every day twenty new churches are planted, and 1,400 more Christians are added in Korea," he said. "The capital city, Seoul, is almost forty percent Christian, with over seven thousand churches, and it is also the home to ten of the twenty largest congregations in the world."

Exactly why there has been such growth is hard to say. Most likely it stems from the harsh political realities Koreans have faced as they have battled communism on one hand and tried to emerge into the larger capitalistic world on the other, said Kim.

"The Korean War, the poverty, and the oppression that we have faced have made us stronger in our religion," he said. "We also have a wider view of the world. We see the need to reach out for the gospel to the whole world."

at one or more of the many services throughout the day, the first one beginning already at six in the morning.[13] The church is now so large that it has given birth to a daughter congregation, which held its inaugural service on Easter Sunday 1996.

The steady influx of new immigrants to southern California created there the single richest area for church planting. As literally hundreds of new immigrants arrived each week during the 1970s and early 1980s, it was at times difficult to keep up with the needs of the Korean community. But in an effort to meet the spiritual needs of these people, the Christian Reformed Church focused its church-planting efforts in California, with the result that by 1996, thirty of the CRC's fifty-six Korean congregations are located in southern California.

Praying Communities

A hallmark of the Korean congregations, and a key spiritual ingredient in their growth, is the high-quality leadership which is routinely raised up within these congregations. But the central ingredient in Korean ministries is a fervent commitment to prayer by all church leaders. The worship, pastoral care, and evangelism programs of Korean congregations are all built upon and centered on never-ceasing prayer.

Another key element in the ability of Korean congregations to attract and disciple new members has been the Coffee Break program, an informal Bible-study and fellowship hour aimed at women and their children, for whom a Story Time program is provided (for a fuller explanation of Coffee Break ministries, see Chapter 8). Indeed, Coffee Break ministries have been so successful in Korean congregations that Christian Reformed Home Missions hired Myung Suk Lee to serve as Korean Coffee Break director. With Lee's help the Coffee Break materials which have been helpful denomination-wide since the early 1970s were translated into the Korean language. The Orange Korean CRC trained as many as 150 people to be Coffee Break leaders. Under their tutelage forty Coffee Break groups meet in the area of the Orange CRC.[14]

Beyond southern California, an additional twenty-six Korean CRCs have sprung up in Canada and the United States. Although most of these congregations are considerably smaller than their southern California counterparts (most numbering on average around one hundred members), they share the same commitment to prayer ministries, Coffee Break evangelism, and outreach to their communities.

To foster these ministries, Christian Reformed Home Missions hired Reverend John Choi as its first full-time Korean-ministry director. Choi lends

Chinese-Ministry Director — Peter Yang

Peter Yang serves Home Missions as the Chinese-ministry director. In this role he gives ministry guidance to eight Chinese ministries. These are located in eastern Canada, western Canada, California, and the Midwest. He is also the pastor of Golden Gate CRC in San Francisco, California, a church he founded in 1965.

FIGURE 24.

FIGURE 25 Korean Coffee Break director Myung Suk Lee.

FIGURE 26 An evening Bible study ends with a prayer circle at Orange Korean CRC.

FIGURE 27 John Choi.

support to congregations already in the denomination and also serves as a liaison between the CRC and Korean congregations which express interest in joining the denomination. Choi has been instrumental in bringing in a number of new leaders and congregations as well as in providing support for Christian Reformed Korean pastors, missionaries, and seminarians. At Calvin Theological Seminary Dr. John T. Kim, one of Orange Korean CRC's former pastors, now teaches some seminary courses and serves as mentor to the sixty Korean seminarians enrolled at the school.

Though the story of the Christian Reformed Church and Korean Christians is mostly one of blessing and success, issues which have divided the wider denomination have had an impact on Korean churches as well. The denomination's movement toward opening all church offices to women was a particular source of discomfort and distress to some Korean congregations and leaders. As a result of a 1993 synodical decision to remove the denomination's restrictions on women, some Korean congregations left the denomination, including Dr. John E. Kim's Los Angeles Korean CRC. In 1993 Kim's congregation was the denomination's largest Korean congregation, having grown to fifteen hundred members. Indeed, when it left the CRC, the congregation was large enough to form a Korean Presbyterian denom-

ination all its own. Five other Korean congregations soon followed Kim's lead and joined his newly formed federation of churches.

As noted above, however, the majority of Korean Christian Reformed congregations, leaders, pastors, and members have thus far remained with the denomination. However, some remain concerned about the CRC and its new policy on women serving as elders, evangelists, and ministers.

But far more Korean Christians face other challenges within their own communities. As immigration has begun to slow down, Korean pastors must wrestle with ministering to and holding on to their members, including the new generation of North American-born children and young people. While the older generation of immigrants seeks to hold on to traditional customs and ways and language, the younger generation grapples with fitting into North American culture. Hence, Korean CRC leaders are making earnest efforts to hold in creative and fruitful tension their dual identity as Koreans and North Americans.

Similarly, on a church-polity level, there are still some growing pains both for Korean congregations and for the denomination generally as both groups try to accommodate the other's styles, patterns, and traditional practices. Even as Korean church leaders seek to understand and practice

FIGURE 28 John T. Kim.

Christian Reformed patterns of church government and church life, so also non-Korean church leaders within the denomination are trying to appreciate and make allowances for Korean cultural and ecclesiastical patterns. Together the two groups are working to enhance each other's ministry to the mission field which North America has become.

As with any ministry which bears much spiritual fruit, the blessings also bring some challenges. As the traditionally Dutch, white, European Christian Reformed Church has opened its doors to ethnic-minority groups like the Hispanics and the Koreans (as well as to the Vietnamese, Cambodians, Chinese, and increasing numbers of others who now call North America home), it experiences various growing pains. Happily, however, they do appear to be pains which portend *growth* and not death as all seek to learn from one another so that the ministry of the whole may better reflect God's transcultural kingdom — a kingdom in which all are one through the waters of baptism into Christ Jesus, the Lord.

Chapter Eight

Gathering God's Growing Family

Evangelizing Toward the Twenty-First Century

"… you will be my witnesses in Jerusalem …."

Acts 1:8

Few bumper stickers have ever more succinctly summed up an entire generation than the commonly sighted 1960s sticker which advised, "Question Authority." Until the 1960s, despite subterranean cracks in the structure of American life, few people questioned the authority of the moral and religious traditions which many people believed undergirded life in America. Thus, it was comparatively easy for the average American to assume that most of his or her fellow citizens shared the same basic values and religious beliefs.

Certainly that was the case during the decade of the 1950s. Led by President Dwight D. Eisenhower's grandfatherly "faith in faith" ideals and bolstered by a sharp increase in attendance at churches and synagogues, most people found it easy to believe that America was still very much a religious, if not a thoroughly Christian, nation. Indeed, that decade's Cold War ideology was frequently stated as much in religious terms as in political ones, as the Christian West tried to stem the tide of godless communism in the East.

But then the 1960s arrived to shatter any remaining illusions about America's shared values and religious beliefs. As

the decade began, many fretted over the wisdom of electing a Roman Catholic to the White House for fear of papal intrusions into American politics. By the end of the decade, however, there had been so much religious upheaval and diversification that such an intramural concern would seem petty if not quaint by comparison.

For the sixties truly was a decade in which authority of any kind was questioned — political, biblical, religious, educational, and familial. As young people sought for meaning in the midst of a society they perceived to be adrift, there was a pronounced increase in religious experimentation, particularly experimentation in Eastern religions. When those four mop-headed and fairly clean-cut lads from Liverpool known as The Beatles arrived in this country in 1964, they looked like Anglican choirboys. But by the late sixties The Beatles had transmogrified into bearded, long-haired hippies who advocated Eastern mysticism and Hindu-like paths to serenity. Not a few American young people followed the path blazed by The Beatles and their favorite guru, the Maharishi Mahesh Yogi.

A CRC Crystal Ball

Trying to envision what Christian Reformed churches will look like in the coming century is not terribly hard for John Rozeboom.

The silver-haired executive director of Christian Reformed Home Missions only has to point to a half-dozen or more congregations in the United States and Canada. Several futuristic churches, big and small, are already hard at work gathering God's people into the kingdom.

FIGURE 1 John Rozeboom.

"The future is here," Rozeboom said. "It is happening in a full range of churches, from urban to suburban. We are seeing churches grappling with change and turning themselves into dynamic, outreaching congregations."

From one end of North America to another, the Holy Spirit is actively moving Christian Reformed people to face the demands of the coming century. They are catching a vision that says the church must minister to a range of human needs and ethnic groups, he said.

These are churches that are remaining steadfast to their Reformed roots at the same time they are making worship, prayer life, and various outreach ministries relevant to the lives of people today and are planning for tomorrow.

"The last word is not said, but there are churches that are metaphors of what we want to project into the future," commented Al Mulder, Home Missions' director of New-Church Development.

Exactly how CRC congregations will shape themselves in the future is unclear. God's will and the movement of his Spirit are always hard to predict. But there is a sense of what is needed and what might work in the twenty-first century.

"There is a shift from a church-shaped mission to a mission-shaped church," said Duane VanderBrug, Home Missions' director of Established-Church Development.

"Some of the sacred cows are diminishing. The kingdom is the whole breadth of God, and there are churches out there that have already seen that."

In this chapter, six churches are profiled that denominational leaders believe show God's grace flourishing in the land.

But even in more traditional theological circles academic theologians captured the spirit of the decade by a new stripe of theological inquiry — the "death of God" school of thought. Most of these scholars did not assert that a transcendent deity had actually passed away but rather that the *idea* of God had become untenable in the modern world. God, they claimed, had always been a particular kind of experience for individual persons, but, they further asserted, that kind of experience had now become rare for people who had "come of age." People were now too scientific, too empirically minded, too aware of the realities of evil in the world to maintain a naive belief in any traditional concept of God.

It was, they said, this old picture or conception of God which had died, leaving traditional forms of worship and piety bankrupt. Many of these theologians (or perhaps they are more aptly called a-theologians) recommended, therefore, that people seek God not through outdated forms of worship and religious experience but through personal introspection, through personal experience, and through engagement in the social causes of the larger society. In short, they advocated a thoroughly secular faith whereby God — if he existed at all — would be discovered to be a part of the wider world. God, in other words, was a sixties-style social activist.[1]

Combined with the decade's large-scale distrust in traditional authority structures, these new theological ideas led to a massive exodus out of mainline American churches and into many new mystical and individualistic religious patterns. The Baby Boomer generation (those born between 1945 and 1964) no longer accepted on authority the "truths" of the faith and therefore wanted to put some daylight between themselves and the purveyors of traditional religion. For the first time in American history, the number of citizens who were unabashedly willing to declare themselves officially "unchurched" was on the rise. (Indeed, the percentage of those who declared themselves nonreligious jumped three hundred percent between 1952 and 1985.)

Wade Clark Roof and William Mc Kinney, two sociologists who have tracked many of these changes, put it this way: "The 1960s marks a turning point in American religious life. It was as if the old synthesis of religion and culture fell apart." [2] In the words of Sidney Ahlstrom, "Presuppositions that had held firm for centuries — even millennia — were being widely questioned." [3]

As these changes sank their roots into America's

religious soil throughout the sixties and on into the seventies, many Christians began to realize that America had itself become a mission field. Whereas churches like the Christian Reformed Church had previously targeted mini mission fields within North America (Indian reservations, Jewish enclaves, the inner city), it slowly dawned on church leaders around the country that the need to do mission work in North America was no longer restricted to isolated segments of the population but now extended to the population as a whole, and especially to America's largest-ever generation: the postwar Baby Boomers.

Suddenly the evangelical and mainline denominations in America began to see themselves as an "exile church," as "resident aliens," as "strangers in a strange land." No longer could anyone assume that the morality or religious seriousness of one's next-door neighbor would be similar to one's own. No longer could one assume a common frame of reference when presenting the gospel even to people in one's own backyard.

Contextualization is the missiological term for tailoring the presentation of the gospel so that it can be clearly understood in new cultural settings. Contextualizing had long been seen as a vital and natural step to preaching the gospel in places like Nigeria or China, but now the American context had itself so radically changed that many saw a need for contextualizing the gospel presentation even for North American neighbors and friends. For America was now a mission field, and if the gospel was to make any headway in this new field, it was going to have to find a way into the hearts of millions of people who had been taught by their culture to "Question Authority."

Dropping In

By the 1980s the Baby Boomers who had been cultural dropouts during the turbulent sixties began to settle down, get married, and have children. In short, they began to drop back in on society. A few of these formerly antiestablishment folks even dropped so far back in as to embrace the materialism of American culture, thus creating the 1980s phenomenon of "yuppies" — young, urban, upwardly mobile professionals who distinguished themselves for

Name: Elmhurst Christian Reformed Church, Elmhurst, Illinois
Pastor: Reverend Bert De Jong
Founded: 1948
Membership: 1,000
Profile: Located twenty miles west of the Chicago Loop, this church began with the vision of one woman who held Sunday-school classes in her home. Church members are predominantly white middle-class adults and their families. The average age of church members is 30. The church

FIGURE 2–3

runs Discovery, an eight-hour program which helps adults learn what types of ministry best suit them. More than sixty percent of adult members are now involved in some type of ministry.

Ministries: Little Lambs, a youth ministry that meets in four weekly sessions, has enrolled 425 children. The church's Coffee Break ministry is active. There also is a MOPS (Mothers of Pre-Schoolers) group, which serves many mothers and their children. A daily vacation Bible school attracts more than three hundred children every summer. In early 1996 a prayer-team ministry began that contacted 3,500 homes in neighborhoods surrounding the church. Team members prayed through hundreds of requests with dozens of people. An active men's ministry is also available. In 1995, one hundred men attended Promise Keepers gatherings at locations throughout the United States. This activity alone began various study groups and a monthly men's breakfast. After two years of prayer and planning, a Saturday-night outreach service was slated to start in 1996.

FIGURE 4 Willow Creek Community Church.

FIGURE 5 Bill Hybels.

their massive acquisitiveness and greed. *Newsweek* magazine even declared 1984 "The Year of the Yuppie," highlighting those who collected cupboardsful of gourmet spices, who bought $1,200 worth of pots and pans (and who then ate out ninety percent of the time as part of "competitive eating"), who spent thousands each year on fitness gadgets and health clubs, and who generally would do almost anything in their climb to the top of the economic and corporate heap in order to buy shares in America's "good life."

But even as many sought solace and fulfillment in the accumulation of things, many others began to seek higher fulfillments. As these hippies-turned-yuppies began to have children of their own, they began to feel what psychologist James W. Jones recently described about children coming of age:

Growing up, children may learn to speak of God, envisioning God within the limits of their cognitive frame perhaps as a giant man (or woman) who lives above the clouds in a great white palace. But the time comes when children trudge off to school and leave behind the enchanted Eden of their private world. There they learn that beyond the clouds are only limitless curves of space bending back upon themselves; no great white palace, no friendly giant God …. [G]radually the child, now become a young man or woman, may cease to speak of God.

But perhaps one day, when staring into the face of his or her own newborn child, or when engulfed by the fierce beauty of the raging ocean or the soaring stillness of the mountains, or when confronted by the grave into which parents or friends have tumbled, the young man or woman, now become an adult, discovers that he or she has (in William James' words) "prematurely closed his accounts with reality" and that there is more to reality than can be dreamt of in any one philosophy. And the grown child may again speak of God. [4]

By the 1980s the "grown children" of the sixties were indeed speaking of God again, but they were doing so in their own language and speaking with their own peculiar religious accent. The remnants of their dropout ideology drove them to seek out a Christianity which was at once user friendly and useful. Many of them also maintained their "death of God"-induced distaste for traditional piety and worship, opting instead for more individualistic forms of religious expression in more experiential and nonthreatening churches which focused on the practical issues of their day-to-day lives. In fact, many Baby Boomers viewed mainline, traditional churches as irrelevant, quietly demanding a new kind of church.

In order to tap into this vast population of people, many established denominations began to open seeker-sensitive churches or "ministry centers" which were tailor-made for people suspicious of the old ways of piety, faith, and worship. The premier such church was the Willow Creek Community Church just outside Chicago, Illinois. Founded by Bill Hybels, a son of the Christian Reformed Church, Willow Creek was designed as a church which would look as little like a church as possible. Hymn books, pipe organs, offering plates, confessions of sin, and traditional sermons were dispensed with in favor of simpler, more upbeat songs projected onto a screen, rock bands, skits, and dramas through which the gospel was presented in new ways. The church also instituted a veritable shopping mall of programs and seminars dealing with everything from substance abuse and alcoholism to successful parenting and money management.

Willow Creek found a niche, growing from 150 members in 1976 to over 3,000 in 1979 and exploding still more to over 15,000 members by 1994 (most of these members coming from the Baby Boomer generation), making Willow Creek the second-largest Protestant church in the United States.

With the efforts of Willow Creek, the seeker-sensitive approach was born. Soon many other churches were trying to emulate the Willow Creek model by taking neighborhood surveys to determine what people liked and disliked about "church" and then tailoring seeker-sensitive alternative services which eliminated what was deemed offensive or irrelevant in order to maximize and add on what the surveys indicated as desirable. Such alternative services, like their Willow Creek prototype, tended to be upbeat, friendly, and decidedly modern, and the gospel — presented by them through skits and dramas as often as through sermons — was more focused on modern sensibilities, themes, and issues than on traditional theology, doctrines, and instruction.

400,000 by 2000

By the mid 1970s, in the middle of this vastly changed social and religious landscape, leaders in Christian Reformed Home Missions began to grapple with a fundamental question: How could the Christian Reformed Church fulfill Christ's Great Commission for this new generation of people? What would be required to evangelize and disciple people who had been raised in and who were living in this new situation? For it was very clear that North America was now a unique mission field in its own right. So what would a faithful, contextualized gospel presentation look like within the Christian Reformed setting?

Of course, the CRC was not the only denomination struggling with such vital questions. Many churches were waking up to the fact that they could no longer rely on immigration or biological growth to sustain themselves. Many were also realizing that if unsaved people were now all around in America, failing to seek ways of witnessing to these neighbors represented nothing less than disobedience to Christ's loving command to reach out to, to baptize, and to disciple all people. One result of this heightened awareness was the church-growth movement, unofficially headquartered at Fuller Theological Seminary in Pasadena, California. The leaders of this movement advocated that all Christians take personal responsibility for reaching their North American neighbors with the gospel.

Motivated by this kind of passionate care for the lost as well as a deep desire to be lovingly obedient to Christ's command, Home Missions asked the 1975 Synod of the Christian Reformed Church to adopt a document entitled "Statements on the Growing Church." This document declared,

Church growth is the work of the triune God which he accomplishes through moving God's people to faithful and urgent prayer and through blessing their total witness in the world. Growth refers both to numerical and spiritual

FIGURE 6 Promotional literature for *Gathering God's Growing Family*, 400,000 by 2000.

growth as necessary to the fulfillment of the mission which God gives the church. God, in building his kingdom, wills and enables his church, by his Word and Spirit, to grow. [5]

The statement then went on to list nine strategies for implementing such growth, including comprehensive training of all members in discipleship and personal evangelism; opening up the front door of the church genuinely to welcome, love, and enfold new members; diversifying accepted forms of worship and expressions of faith in order to reach a broader spectrum of people and cultures; and setting aside the needed funds and personnel to turn the whole church into a mission outpost.[6]

FIGURE 7.

By the mid 1970s, such a new mission thrust seemed more urgent when it was clear that the Christian Reformed Church was not growing, in part because of earlier failures to find new and creative ways to disciple people in the changed North American context. During the 1970s the denomination increased by only 7,642 members, or 2.8 percent. And the vast majority of that increase came via Canada, in part as a result of new churches planted among Dutch immigrants and their descendants. The result was that from 1970 to 1980 the Christian Reformed Church in the United States had a net gain of a scant 362 people. Indeed, the denomination declined in net membership in every year but one during the 1970s.[7]

By the mid 1980s it was believed that something more overt needed to be done to inspire the CRC to become energized around the Great Commission and, by so doing, perhaps turn around these distressing indicators of growth (or lack thereof). Since the only appreciable growth in the CRC had been coming from new-church planting, it was believed that this needed to be the direction in which future Home Missions' programs would go. Additionally, Home Missions foresaw that already-established congregations would also need to begin seeing themselves as mission outposts for the sake of gathering in the lost from within their local communities and not only as enclaves of the already saved.

Thus, in the early 1980s Home Missions began to partner with local congregations through a grant-in-aid program which provided the funds and resources necessary to develop local evangelism leadership. Home Missions, in short, began to shift from being an agency which oversaw denomination-wide programs like follow-up to *The Back to God Hour* and Native American missions to being a partner agency for developing and fostering local mission ministries which would more and more be owned by local churches and classes. Though Home Missions had always been active on the local level, it took new initiatives to make this aspect of the work primary. Indeed, by 1994 Home Missions put essentially all its projects on a declining-grant basis, helping to start local programs but then gradually backing off from them in favor of indigenous leadership and ownership.

Home Missions also encouraged local church programs such as Coffee Break ministries. Begun by Neva Evenhouse

FIGURE 8 Coffee Break prayer time.

FIGURE 9 Story Time at Zion Christian Reformed Church, Oshawa, Ontario.

and Alvin Vander Griend at Peace CRC in South Holland, Illinois, in 1970, Coffee Break evangelism targeted women and their children with the message of the gospel. In 1981 Home Missions formally adopted Coffee Break ministries, providing materials, resources, and leadership training for the program. By providing a friendly and relaxed environment for women and also by underwriting an entertaining and informative Story Time for children, Coffee Break presented the basics of the gospel to women who had never before heard the story of Christ or who had wandered away from church. By Coffee Break's twenty-fifth anniversary, in 1995, the ministry was a part of over five hundred Christian Reformed congregations.

Another Home Missions program was Congregational Evangelism Training (CET), based on the Evangelism Explosion methodology of Dr. James Kennedy. Through the efforts of Reverend Wesley Smedes and Reverend Milton Doornbos, by the mid 1980s, CET, along with the Witnessing Where You Are program, had been implemented to one degree or another in over half of the denomination's nearly nine hundred congregations. The CET method aimed to train lay people to speak freely about their faith and to give their personal testimonies to friends and neighbors

as a first step toward inviting them to church and, ultimately it was hoped, introducing them to Christ.

In the area of new-church development Home Missions set a goal in 1984 to establish thirty new churches by 1989. By concentrating on areas without churches and by targeting various ethnic populations previously not ministered to by the CRC in any formal way, Home Missions reached its goal of thirty new churches in just three years instead of the six originally envisioned. Mission leaders felt that this success was a clear indicator that the one-time isolated Christian Reformed Church was now coming alive to the gospel's call to "seek the lost and disciple the found."

Largely as a result of this new push in church planting

FIGURE 10 Milton Doornbos.

FIGURE 11 Wesley Smedes.

FIGURE 12 Linda and John Rozeboom with granddaughter Katie Elgersma.

(particularly in the area of ethnic ministry), the denomination slowly began to show marked increases in new members. Whereas growth through evangelism during the sixties and seventies had been between 1,000 and 1,500 people per year, by the end of the 1980s that number rose to around 2,000 per year, increasing to 2,600 by the mid 1990s. During the eighties the denomination also saw a burgeoning number of new congregations, increasing the total number of churches in the denomination by 113 between 1980 and 1990.

In 1986 Home Missions welcomed a new executive director in the person of Reverend John Rozeboom. Rozeboom had long been invested in the mission outreach of the church, having served as the regional home missionary for the entire West Coast of the United States from 1976 to 1986 and prior to that as a new-church developer in southern California. Under Rozeboom's leadership the Home Missions board implemented a new program in 1987 to capitalize on and encourage recently renewed zeal for evangelism and also its byproduct of new gains in membership. The program was called *Gathering God's Growing Family*, and its energizing slogan and goal was a numerical one: 400,000 by 2000.

In 1987 the denomination stood at approximately 310,000 members. Through new-church planting as well as through evangelism programs like Coffee Break and CET in already-established congregations, it was hoped that 90,000 new members could be added to the denomination in the years between 1988 and 2000, bringing the total to 400,000 Christian Reformed Church members. The goal was more modest than it appeared, reflecting a mere two percent growth per year during that twelve-year period.

To meet that goal — but more importantly to inspire the denomination toward greater faithfulness in fulfilling Christ's call to evangelism and discipleship — Home Missions adopted a number of core values which it desired to communicate through all of its programs. The key values for the *Gathering* program included passionate care for those living apart from God in Christ, a fervent desire to move people to pray for those who were lost, and a multivalent strategy to mobilize the local churches toward mission and outreach resulting not only in numerical growth but also in an ethnic diversification which would better reflect the culture in which the Christian Reformed Church was situated.

Unhappily, however, the time was not ripe for increasing the net number of Christian Reformed members. Despite a zeal for evangelism on the part of many and despite genuine gains in the number of new churches planted by Home Missions — as well as a commensurate number of new converts to the faith — other issues in the denomination brought about an overall decline in membership.

In the late 1980s the writings of Calvin College astronomy professor Howard Van Til, particularly his book *The Fourth Day*, created a storm of controversy over issues relating to the biblical book of Genesis and its relationship to science, especially to theories of evolutionary cosmic development. Although Van Til was investigated by the college and seminary board of trustees and cleared of any heretical teachings, many conservative members of the denomination felt betrayed by what they perceived to be new and unbiblical teachings at their beloved denominational college.

At the same time, the debate over the role and place of women in the offices of the church — a debate which had begun already in the early 1970s — continued to passionately engage synod after synod. As the church lurched toward a more gender-inclusive ministry in which women could be ordained as deacons, elders, and ministers, many more conservatives became convinced that the Christian Reformed Church was heading in an unholy and liberal direction. The confluence of the women-in-office debate and the creation controversy swirling around Van Til and some other Calvin College scientists led to large-scale defections from the denomination both of individual members and, at times, even of whole congregations. So, despite the efforts of Home

Missions to achieve numerical increases, the denomination actually declined between the years 1988 and 1995 until by 1995 the total number of Christian Reformed members in the United States and Canada had dropped almost 16,000, to approximately 294,000 people. By the early nineties, in the wake of these setbacks, the numerical goal of 400,000 by 2000 was quietly dropped from the *Gathering God's Growing Family* agenda.

Understanding Postmodernism

But there was far more to the *Gathering* program than just numerical growth. The real goal was inspiring faithfulness and generating zeal to tell others the Good News of the gospel. To do that well in a denomination which had a long history of isolation and ethnic homogeneity, Home Missions sensed that it would need to educate its pastors and lay leaders both on the nature of life in North America after the six-

ties and on what kinds of gospel contextualizing was working for other religious groups.

Toward that end Home Missions sought the assistance of various scholars, speakers, pastors, and lay leaders who were in key positions to help in this educational component of *Gathering*. Among those asked by Home Missions to educate the CRC as to the contours of what some were calling "the first post-Christian generation" was Craig Van Gelder. A professor of missiology at Calvin Theological Seminary, Van Gelder had the advantage of a broad cultural perspective, having recently come into the CRC from the outside; he had formerly worked as a staff consultant and professor in the Presbyterian Church (U.S.A.). But his new-found love for the CRC and its excellent theology motivated him to do all he could to help the denomination effectively communicate the gospel to its North American neighbors. Van Gelder became a valuable consultant to Home Missions, helping to bring

Name: Zion CRC, Oshawa, Ontario

Pastor: Reverend Henry Wildeboer

Founded: 1963

Membership: 1,000

Profile: Located in the greater Toronto area, the town of Oshawa is dominated by the overwhelming presence of General Motors, which has huge manufacturing and assembly plants in the area. The church offers weekly worship services that make rich use of music, poetry, drama, and other arts. Church membership was stable until about 1985. From 1985 until 1990, membership doubled and then slowed. Because the church is now overcrowded, the congregation has purchased land on which to build a bigger facility. The church was once mostly blue collar. Much of its recent growth has come as younger professionals have joined.

Ministries: Coffee Break ministry has brought many women, and then their children and their husbands, into the church. There are also a vacation Bible school, Men's Life groups, a food bank, and a ministry that works with the needy who live in the inner city.

FIGURE 13–15.

CRC ministers and its members up to speed on the shape of new American religious patterns.

Van Gelder, and Home Missions generally, repeatedly reminded the denomination that in the midst of seismic changes on the American religious landscape, there was no question that to stay relevant the CRC would have to change. "The issue [was] not 'whether' the CRC [would] change, but 'what' the CRC [would] choose to become."[8] In a world characterized by pluralism, relativism, and constant change, in the midst of a generation of Baby Boomers — and Baby Busters, the children of Boomers — for whom the meeting of felt needs was the paramount mark of a successful church, no church could hope to minister without keeping pace with the times and contextualizing the gospel message accordingly.

Borrowing from church-growth experts like Kennon Callahan, Home Missions began to include among its strategies alternative models to the traditional church and to the traditional worship service. Though no one model was advanced, one thing became increasingly clear: the old model of single-cell, ethnically homogeneous churches with only one style of fairly traditional worship services led by a pro-

fessional minister was not the wave of the future. Van Gelder himself suggested eight principles which he believed could determine the relative success or failure of the CRC in the years ahead:

1. *From ethnic unity to shared vision;*
2. *From top-down decision-making to process planning;*
3. *From the professional minister to the missionary pastor;*
4. *From single cell churches to multiform congregations;*
5. *From the primacy of preaching to the centrality of worship;*
6. *From a closed system to seeker-sensitive;*
7. *From central ecclesiastical authority to local initiative;*
8. *From cultural uniformity to unified diversity.*[9]

Home Missions and Van Gelder also suggested that, although the church should remain deeply committed to the traditional "forms of unity" as represented by the creeds and confessions of the denomination, these documents and the truths contained within them needed to be made relevant and comprehensible to the new generation of seekers. Further, Home Missions and Van Gelder suggested, since Baby Boomers were wary of traditional ecclesiastical structures and establishments, it might be missiologically wise to put a bit of distance between the denomination and various local ministries. As another Home Missions leader, Reverend Dirk Hart, put it,

FIGURE 16 Dirk Hart.

It is important today that we learn to wear our denominational affiliation lightly. In an unchurched culture a denominational name can be a hindrance to our outreach. Some of our newer churches ... underplay the name "Christian Reformed." Well they should because their primary purpose is to reach people with the gospel, not build a denomination.[10]

Together We Gather

Robert Schuller has long been an enigma in Reformed circles. Though coming from a theological tradition which highlights the depravity of human nature, Schuller repeatedly emphasizes positive self-esteem through pondering the wonders of possibility thinking. Though his Sunday worship services are recognizably Reformed in character, they take place in the massive Crystal Cathedral, complete with indoor water fountains, palm trees, and a Jumbotron large-screen television. Though the congregation sings primarily traditional hymns, accompanied by a magnificent pipe

Name: First Christian Reformed Church, Sioux Falls, South Dakota

Pastor: Reverend Stanley Scripps

Founded: 1923

Membership: 830 members, including children

Profile: Located in a growing city on the high plains at the crossroads of northbound and westbound interstates, this congregation is racially homogeneous. Most members are between the ages of 25 and 40, work in medical, financial or food-processing jobs, or own their own businesses. Nearly twenty percent of adults are not married, a slowly growing trend. Most husbands and wives work outside the home. People who join most likely come from other churches.

Ministries: The church has a strong desire for solid programs to nurture the youth, and it has an aggressive evangelistic thrust. In 1978 it "cloned" a sister church, Shalom, which presently has 406 members. Recently an effort has been launched to start another church. First CRC has also established a ministry called THEOS, geared to help persons who are grieving a death or a loss. Another ministry, SPIN, which was started in 1994 by a church member, reaches out to single parents with the message of God's love through Christ.

FIGURE 17
Robert Schuller.

organ, and though Schuller himself continues to don a traditional preaching robe, he is frequently joined on his podium by Hollywood stars, sports heroes, and political figures who come to share winning stories of how they have "made it" in life through the power of possibility thinking.

Still, despite such enigmas, many believe that Schuller is a master at tailoring the gospel message to the southern-California population in Orange County and nearby Los Angeles. Therefore, when Schuller began hosting an annual conference called the Institute for Successful Church Leadership, some in the Christian Reformed Church saw the opportunity to further the goals of *Gathering* by dovetailing with and participating in this Reformed cousin's Institute (a few Christian Reformed leaders had begun attending Schuller Institutes already in the mid 1970s).

One such Christian Reformed person was Amway co-founder Richard De Vos. Indeed, De Vos believed so firmly in the goals of *Gathering* and was so convinced that Schuller's conference could further those goals that he and Home Missions entered an agreement which stated that if Home Missions could get seventy-five percent of a given classis' ministers and leaders to sign up for the Schuller conference, he would subsidize the cost so it would be financially possible for every one of the denomination's forty-six classes to have the opportunity to attend the annual conference. Between 1990 and 1993 Home Missions was able to do precisely that, and over 1,100 Christian Reformed ministers and lay leaders attended the week-long event held each January at the Crystal Cathedral in Garden Grove, California.

In a 1990 speech at Calvin Theological Seminary, De Vos articulated the views which led him to believe that his denomination's leaders could benefit from the perspectives and ideas of the Schuller conference. Applying the same methods of business by which he had transformed Amway into the world's largest and most profitable privately owned corporation, De Vos gave

"a view from the pew," telling the seminary community that for the church to grow and survive, it must watch its "bottom line" — it must ask this question: How many new people were brought in last year? The unhappy fact, De Vos claimed, was that the CRC was flat — filled with potential but generally lacking in excitement and in the ability to communicate its message to the wider world. If the church is similar to a business, then it must do more than just manage what it has — it must build and expand, or it dies.

The key way for such building and expansion to happen, according to De Vos, was by bringing in new people and doing so constantly. Such an atmosphere of expectation needed to be created that church members would bring peo-

FIGURE 18 Exterior view of the Crystal Cathedral.

FIGURE 19 Inside the Crystal Cathedral.

ple in, that they would invite people to church, and that once people got there, the church itself would be an inviting place to which they would want to return.[11]

Toward accomplishing these goals, De Vos lent his financial support to make possible the week-long January *Gathering* Conferences. At these conferences Christian Reformed Home Missions held its own separate seminars prior to and following the larger Schuller conference. In these seminars Home Missions attempted to educate conference attenders about why and how the modern situation was different from earlier times and how that fact should reshape the ways by which the Christian Reformed Church would present the gospel.

Name: New Life CRC, Abbotsford, British Columbia

Pastor: Reverend John Poortenga

Founded: 1986

Membership: 750

Profile: New Life is a young church, with almost no members older than 60. The church began with a core of second-generation Dutch families. Early on, members were largely blue collar. More recently, more white-collar workers have joined as the town has become a bedroom community to Vancouver. The church is now comprised of people from many religious backgrounds. New Life tends to attract "broken-winged" people with many emotional, spiritual, psychological, and physical hurts. This is a "cell-based" church in which more than ninety percent of church members are members of small groups. These groups break down into groups for men, women, and young adults. There also are prayer groups and groups for support/recovery from addictions. Worship here is contemporary.

Ministries: New Life has commissioned and sent out nearly twenty people into full-time ministry in the last ten years. They are working for various missions around the world and in North America with a group called Youth with a Mission. In addition, two persons are missionaries for the Union Gospel Mission, one works with Youth for Christ in the public high schools, and one ministers to prostitutes with Crossfire Ministries in Seattle. Four missionaries are establishing new churches, and one missionary is a teacher among the Inuit Indians. There also is Sonshine Ministry, which works with young children in the church. This includes a puppet team, story-tellers, and care groups.

Conference attenders were helped to see that regional classes needed to become mission stimulators by assisting their local congregations to become mission outposts on the frontier of this now largely unchurched land. Pastors in attendance were alerted to the dangers of seeing themselves as professional maintenance ministers and to start viewing themselves as missionaries-in-residence whose goal should be teaching people how to reach out. Through lectures and worship, through reflection and prayer, Home Missions attempted to achieve its overarching goal of making Christ's Great Commission the central impetus for all that the church does.

In the larger Schuller conference — typically attended by over two thousand people from all over the United States — conferees listened to speeches by Robert Schuller and many other megachurch leaders from around the country, who told their stories of church growth and who, thereby, tried to inspire others to go and do likewise. Through speeches, workshops, and networking with church leaders from other denominations, leaders of the Christian Reformed Church heard in many varied ways the same basic *Gathering* message articulated by Home Missions in its slogan message: *God wants his lost children to be found. The Christian Reformed Church intends to be a church where these people can be enfolded, challenged to live for him, and equipped to be his witnesses. In short, God wants the Christian Reformed Church to seek the lost, disciple the found, all for God's glory.*[12]

Evaluations

As is perhaps inevitable in the midst of huge changes on the American scene and in the light of new approaches to meet the challenge of such changes, Home Missions received some criticism. In the early days of *Gathering,* when the numerical goal of "400,000 by 2000" was still being promoted, many questioned whether it was biblically sound to make numbers the main indicator of one's faithfulness (or lack thereof). Church growth, critics alleged, cannot be measured solely by how many people come in the door each year; it must also — and perhaps more importantly — be measured by how well those people are discipled, by how much they grow in the knowledge of the faith. Others feared that a

FIGURE 20 Richard De Vos.

primarily numerical goal might lead churches and Home Missions generally to do anything in their power to meet that number, whether or not such methods accorded well with the true nature of the Christian faith.

In response, Home Missions reminded critics that true church growth is indeed a both-and prospect — both numerical growth and spiritual growth, both a seeking of the lost and a discipling of the found. But it also pointed out that for too long the Christian Reformed Church had focused only on spiritual growth within congregations with the result of a flat, almost zero numerical growth. Having a goal to shoot for was to be an incentive to remind the church that God expects those in the church to seek out and bring in new people who can then become part of the spiritual discipleship process. The CRC has much to offer by way of a rich spiritual and theological heritage — all the more reason to reach as many people as possible in genuine Christ-like love and concern.

On other fronts, by the early 1990s a number of theologians and church leaders in the wider evangelical world also began to raise critical questions regarding the direction in which the overall church-growth and seeker-sensitive movements were moving American churches. Authors David Wells and Os Guinness both upbraided the larger megachurch movement in America, particularly in those places where there had been a nearly wholesale abandonment of theology and traditional forms of worship in favor of pop psychology and anything-goes entertainment spectacles designed more to titillate than to foster true worship.[13]

Similarly, but much closer to home, Calvin Theological Seminary professor Dr. Cornelius Plantinga, Jr., in a 1993 speech at Calvin College's The January Series, wondered what message gets presented about the nature of Christianity when worship services are so thoroughly altered from their past forms. Plantinga lamented the "nightclub format" of many contemporary worship services in the wider church world — services advertised on the entertainment pages of newspapers as proffering would-be worshipers "fun." Though recognizing the intelligent creativity of some of

Name: Oasis Community Church, Moreno, California
Pastor: Reverend Alan Breems
Founded: 1991
Membership: 161
Profile: Seventy percent of Oasis Community members come from an unchurched background. Sixty-five percent of families are white, twenty-five percent are Latino, five percent are Asian, and five percent are African American. The main thrust of the church has been to reach young families in southern California who have little or no church background.

FIGURE 21–23

Ministries: There is a strong Coffee Break ministry in the morning and later in the day. Small-group Bible studies are offered to various groups five nights per week. A group of prayer warriors got together in 1995 and began to pray regularly for thirty families that had once attended the church. Within weeks, several of the families returned to Oasis. Twelve of the families began to attend services on a regular basis.

those involved in planning such alternative services — particularly the ones at Willow Creek — Plantinga asserted that hard questions needed to be faced regarding this approach to the Baby Boomer generation — hard *theological* questions. For when being sensitive to the nonreligious leads one to plan a worship service which is accordingly as nonreligious as possible, more than just the service may get changed.

In short, Plantinga wondered,

How much do such services reflect the Christian faith? [For]

FIGURE 24.

Name: Oasis Community Church, Orlando, Florida
Pastor: Reverend Stanley Workman
Founded: 1959
Membership: 150
Profile: Oasis began with six people in a home. All age groups are represented in the church, but the main age range encompasses young families with parents between 20 and 40 years old. Many church members have never gone to church before. Diverse cultures and ethnic groups are represented in church services and ministries. The church's mission is "to grow in our walk with the Lord and to share that walk with the community." Services are contemporary and geared to bringing in new members. A vibrant Hispanic congregation shares space in the church.
Ministries: Many church members are part of small groups for Bible study, prayer, and discussions. Small as this church is, it works to establish other congregations in the Orlando area. Two churches are already up and running, one is soon to start, and more are planned. The church works with many "lost souls" who are part of the congregation for a time and then move on.

if the popular changes in worship do represent a contextualized version of the historic Christian faith, then we are going to have to face the fact that the Christian religion is very different from the one most of us learned. How likely is it that a popular God is really God, that a user-friendly God will rebuke sin?[14]

Of course, the Christian Reformed Church had never systematically adopted megachurch methodology, and Home Missions in particular made clear that in all its work — including the planting of new churches — it desired to "maintain integrity with the confessions and mission vision of the CRC denomination." Still, Plantinga's critique — as well as the criticism of others in and outside the denomination — pointed to a longstanding difficulty which missionaries have always faced: how to contextualize the gospel's pre-

FIGURE 25
Cornelius Plantinga, Jr.

sentation without thereby also changing or obscuring the gospel. In a denomination which had at mid century still been characterized by a fairly uniform order of worship and a very standard and traditional style of doctrinal preaching, making changes in these critical areas was as difficult as it was — in the opinion of many — utterly necessary.

But in an effort to do its work carefully, and following its participation in the Schuller conferences, Home Missions continued to try to educate church leaders, particularly through participating in conferences at the Willow Creek church. For Willow Creek is in many ways a shining example of a church wholly committed to the Great Commission without compromising theological integrity and biblically educational preaching. While recognizing that Willow Creek cannot be duplicated elsewhere — particularly in already-established congregations — many leaders who attend the invigorating Willow Creek seminars come away with renewed enthusiasm for the task of gathering God's people into churches faithful to the Lordship of Christ, relevant to the social, physical, and spiritual needs of people living in the late twentieth century, and committed to telling as many people as possible the Good News that is the gospel.

Gathering Toward the Twenty-First Century

As the world approaches the end of the twentieth century and also the end of the second millennium A.D., pundits

Home Missions Regional Directors

John Van Til serves as the Home Missions regional director for Central and Eastern Canada. In this role he guides the development of twenty-two newly emerging churches and supervises grants to twelve growing, established churches. All of the regional directors are front line *Gathering* leaders. They facilitate new-church development, guide the revitalization of established churches, and support mission pastors.

Name	Region	New Churches	Growing, Established Churches
John Van Til	Central and Eastern Canada	22	12
Dirk Hart [†]	Eastern USA	8	4
Gary Teja [†]	Florida	13	3
Allen Likkel [†]	Lake Erie	4	3
James Osterhouse	North-Central	13	3
Martin Contant	Northern Pacific	14	10
Ernest Benally	Red Mesa	19	1
Peter Holwerda	Southern Pacific	61	9
Alvin Vander Griend [†]	Siouxland	4	1
Jerry Holleman	West Central USA	25	16
Milton Doornbos	West Michigan	10	20

[†] Part-time Home Missions regional director

FIGURE 26
John Van Til

FIGURE 27
Dirk Hart

FIGURE 28
Gary Teja

FIGURE 29
Allen Likkel

FIGURE 30 James
Osterhouse

FIGURE 31
Martin Contant

FIGURE 32
Ernest Benally

FIGURE 33
Peter Holwerda

FIGURE 34 Alvin
Vander Griend

FIGURE 35
Jerry Holleman

FIGURE 36
Milton Doornbos

and prognosticators of all stripes are busy making predictions. What will be the shape of the church in the twenty-first century? What changes will there be theologically, pastorally, ecclesiastically? Of course, even the most educated of guesses regarding the future are still just guesses — guesses which may prove to be as wide of the mark in the actual twenty-first century as were all of those late-nineteenth-century optimistic predictions made about the glory of the coming twentieth century. For contrary to the most educated opinions one hundred years ago, the foreseen forward march of technology and science did not lead to a peaceful twentieth century of amity and goodwill. Technology did indeed exceed even the wildest of nineteenth-century predictions, but as it did so, it led to a century in which that very same technology was frequently harnessed to make more effective various purges, holocausts, and ethnic cleansings.

What can be said with certainty in the late 1990s is that America will remain a unique mission field as ethnic diversity increases and the children and grandchildren of the Baby Boomers continue to struggle to make their religious way in the world. It is with an eye to these people that Christian Reformed Home Missions will begin its second century of work.

As local initiative and local ownership of mission projects have become a reality, Home Missions finds itself in a position to plant and water the seeds — seeds of plants that will be tended and harvested by others. By 1995 Home Missions was involved in helping to fund approximately 250 various projects, including established-church development, new-church plantings, campus ministry, the ongoing Native American mission in the Southwest, and helping inner-city churches to find the staff and the resources for ministry to that increasingly needy field. But Home Missions is doing this with an eye toward helping others to catch and then own for themselves the vision of *Gathering God's Growing Family*, which is the vision of the Great Commission itself.

In addition to its directly funded ministries, Home Missions has also partnered with a total of 750 congregations which make some kind of use of Home Missions' materials and programs. Headed by Reverend Duane VanderBrug, the Established-Church Development wing of Home Missions includes programs to help established congregations plant daughter churches and to do Congregational Master-Planning, wherein consultants move congregations through a series of self-evaluation steps designed to help them take account of their resources and then mobilize themselves into more mission-oriented churches. Pastors are aided by Home Missions through the formation of *Gathering* networks which link pastors together in their mutual focus on evangelism and outreach. Home Missions also

FIGURE 37 Men's Life.

FIGURE 38 Men's Life.

continues to promote local out-reach through Coffee Break ministries and its Story Time program, Men's Life ministries, small-group Bible studies, and annual conferences and conventions for the leaders of these various programs.

Home Missions also continues to promote prayer as the vital starting point for all church and mission work. Home Missions' minister of evangelism resources, Reverend Alvin Vander Griend, has been effective in developing prayer resources for congregations and in organizing prayer summits to mobilize local leaders for mission in North America.

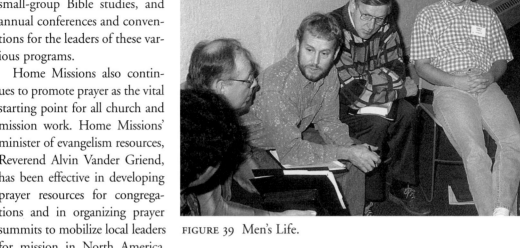

FIGURE 39 Men's Life.

The agency is also involved in energizing whole classes to become not just administrative conclaves but enthusiastic local mission agencies through and by which the congregations under their care will also more and more engage their neighbors in the cause of Christ.

Home Missions reported to the 1995 Synod that through all such efforts since the beginning of the *Gathering* program in 1987, 19,484 persons had been brought into the Christian Reformed Church. (Despite these gains, however, the denomination continued to show a net decline of nearly two percent annually due to transfers to other denominations, defections, and other such losses of members.) Many of the denomination's newest members have come in through new churches, which Home Missions helps to plant at a rate of about twenty per year.

Now under the leadership of Reverend Alfred Mulder, the New-Church Development Department of Home Missions was able to report in 1995 that the agency had planted 130 churches since the start of *Gathering*, 122 of them still being

alive and well. Overall, the agency continues to work with 163 emerging churches and their staffs, dedicating fifty-eight percent of its annual $9 million budget to such new-church starts. Fully one-half of these new congregations consist of various ethnic-minority groups.

Though the Christian Reformed Church may be suffering membership setbacks because of other issues, Christian Reformed Home Missions is doing its level best to keep the denomination alive and moving spiritually in zestful and heartfelt fulfillment of Christ's Great Commission. Christ called the church to bring the gospel to all nations but to begin in "Jerusalem," that place which one calls home. For the Christian Reformed Church that home is North America — the place from which and in which God's family needs to be gathered together in love.

Conclusion

This book chronicles a journey of sorts — the Christian Reformed Church's century-long journey in home missions. Of course, a temporal journey differs from a geographic one. Whereas the goal of a geographic journey is to arrive in a new and perhaps foreign place, a temporal trip can be taken without ever leaving home. It is possible to travel temporally while staying put geographically.

This book has been about a temporal journey which has never left home — this was a time trek through North American *home* missions. In 1996, though the work of Christian Reformed Home Missions is still occurring here at home in North America, even as it was in 1896, the landscape has so changed that it almost feels as though we have journeyed to a new place after all. We live in a radically changed situation.

Many, but by no means all, of those changes are chronicled in this book. One thing which has not changed is the gospel and the call of the Great Commission to go forth and make disciples. The question which each generation must face is how to witness to that unchanging gospel in ways relevant to the current time and place without compromising the truth of the living Christ, who is the gospel's core. In the twentieth century that question could not be asked and answered just once or twice. Rather, it kept coming up again and again as this topsy-turvy time repeatedly presented the church with new circumstances, innovations, challenges, and problems.

Since the time of Christ few, if any, centuries can boast as many changes as the twentieth century can. When this book's story began, we saw Andrew Vander Wagen setting out on horseback to roam the mesas of New Mexico in search of Navajo to whom he could preach the gospel. As the book closes, Baby Boomer missionaries are networking through the Internet, e-mailing one another from laptop computers in an attempt to reach the first post-Christian generation.

Perhaps this unsettling constancy of change explains why, as the previous chapters show, almost every mission effort — including those which eventually became wildly fruitful —

was met with initial wariness and often with penetrating criticism. For it has not been easy to make sense of innovations like radio and television. It has not been easy to be faithful to Christ through world wars abroad and urban squalor at home. It has not been easy to keep on speaking the old, old gospel truths to a generation loathe to accept anything on authority. It has not been easy to shuck a staunchly Dutch identity and to open the front door of the church to many different ethnic groups and traditions.

None of this has been easy, but through the faithful, prayerful efforts of the missionary pioneers and workers chronicled in this book, the Word of God has gone forth. As the Christian Reformed Church awaits the advent of a new century, few dare to guess what that new century will hold, though continued rapid change seems inevitable. As the denomination continues to gather God's growing family, doing mission work will continue to be a challenge, a delicate balance between preserving the Reformed heritage and making it speak faithfully to new mission situations.

In 1903 Christian Reformed missionaries stood on the edge of that vast tract of land known as Smith's Ranch and declared, "Now the Lord has given us room and we will flourish in the land." As the century closes, today's mission workers stand on both shores of this continent, surveying not an isolated tract of land here or there but seeing the whole continent from Vancouver to New York, from Halifax to Houston as a mission field — a field ripe for harvesting, full of people yearning for meaning and Good News.

As Christian Reformed Home Missions enters its second century of work, it can truly be said that now the Lord has given room aplenty for others to join the Frylings and the Vander Wagens, the Eldersvelds and the Rozendals, the Vander Meulens and the Verduins, the Van Schouwens and the Callenders in seeking the lost and discipling the found so that, by God's Spirit and grace, God's great gospel mission may continue to flourish in the land.

Chapter and Vignette Notes

Introduction

1. For general background on late nineteenth- and early twentieth-century America, see Mark Noll, *A History of Christianity in the United States and Canada* (Grand Rapids: Eerdmans, 1992) 163–310. See also Winthrop Hudson, *Religion in America,* 4th ed. (New York: Macmillan, 1987) 195–302.
2. See preceding references and James A. Scherer, *Gospel, Church, and Kingdom: Comparative Studies in World Mission Theology* (Minneapolis: Augsburg, 1987) 9–50.
3. Noll 293.
4. Henry Beets, *The Christian Reformed Church* (Grand Rapids: Baker, 1946) 134.
5. See Harvey A. Smit, "Mission Zeal in the Christian Reformed Church: 1857–1917," *Perspectives on the Christian Reformed Church,* ed. Peter De Klerk and Richard R. De Ridder (Grand Rapids: Baker, 1983) 225–40. See also Dick L. Van Halsema, *The Rise of Home Missions in the Christian Reformed Church: 1857-Present* (diss., Union Theological Seminary, New York, 1953).
6. Smit 236.
7. Smit 237.
8. Smit 239.

Chapter One: Going West

1. Herman Fryling, personal memoir prepared for John C. De Korne, ed., *Navajo and Zuni for Christ: Fifty Years of Indian Missions* (Grand Rapids: Christian Reformed Board of Missions, 1947). The portion here cited was not published in the final book.
2. Robert J. Groelsema, "Christian Assimilation," *Origins* 5:1 (1987): 43.
3. Fryling, personal memoir.
4. Much of the background information on Fryling comes from his archive folder in Heritage Hall, Hekman Library, Calvin College, Grand Rapids, Michigan.
5. Vander Wagens, personal papers.
6. Much of the historical and background information on

the Navajo tribe comes from Peter Iverson, *The Navajo,* ed. Frank W. Porter III, Indians of North America Series (New York: Chelsea, 1990).

7. See archive folder on Leonard P. Brink in Heritage Hall, Hekman Library, Calvin College, Grand Rapids, Michigan.
8. John C. De Korne, ed., *Navajo and Zuni for Christ: Fifty Years of Indian Missions* (Grand Rapids: Christian Reformed Board of Missions, 1947) 19.
9. Leonard P. Brink, "Our Indian Mission: A Retrospect of 1901," *Banner of Truth* Dec. 1901: 90–92.
10. Leonard P. Brink, "Mission Notes," *The Banner* 6 June 1909: 274.
11. Leonard P. Brink, "Mission Notes," *The Banner* 26 May 1905: 222.
12. Background information on Indian boarding school largely drawn from *In the White Man's Image,* The American Experience Series, Public Broadcasting System, videotape, 1990.
13. Edward T. Begay and Keith Kuipers, personal interviews, Mar. 1995.
14. Groelsema 44.
15. Cocia Hartog, *Indian Mission Sketches* (n.p.: self-published, 1910) 12.
16. Hartog 13.
17. Hartog 14.
18. De Korne 184.
19. Drawn from Donald L. Parman, "J.C. Morgan: Navajo Apostle of Assimilation" (unpublished paper) and J.C. Morgan, "Voice from an Indian" (unpublished paper).
20. Groelsema 45.
21. "Letter from Rehoboth," *The Banner* 16 Jan. 1913: 40-41.
22. Jacob H. Bosscher, unpublished memoir n.d., n.p.
23. This historical background information was drawn principally from Alfonso Ortiz, *The Pueblo,* ed. Frank W. Porter III, Indians of North America Series (New York: Chelsea, 1994). See also C. Gregory Crampton, *The Zunis of Cibola* (n.p.: U of Utah P, 1977).

24. Crampton 118.
25. General background on mission work in Zuni drawn from Cornelius Kuipers, *Zuni Also Prays* (Grand Rapids: Christian Reformed Board of Missions, 1946).
26. Roger Posthuma, "A Stone Fell in Zuni," *The Banner* 25 Apr. 1975: 15–17.
27. Andrew Vander Wagen, "History of Zuni Missions," *The Banner* 1 June 1906: 142–44.
28. Crampton 154.
29. *The Banner* 17 Mar. 1910: 171.
30. Agnes Natewa, personal interview, Mar. 1995.
31. Reverend Mike Meekhof, personal interview, Mar. 1995.
32. Harry Boer, *Our Mission Budget and the Indian Field* (unpublished pamphlet, n.d.) 11.
33. Boer 17.
34. Boer 22.
35. *Our Indian Missions: Pietistic or Reformed?* (n.p.: General Conference of Christian Reformed Missionaries on the Indian Field, n.d.) 20–21.
36. Rodger Buining, "First Americans and First-Rate Churches," *The Banner* 29 Sept. 1986: 8–9.
37. Edward T. Begay, personal interview, Mar. 1995.
38. Some of these perspectives come from interviews conducted by Reverend Al Mulder in October 1994 and are based on his notes.

Churches in Classis Red Mesa

Compiled by Alfred E. Mulder, director of New-Church Development for Christian Reformed Home Missions, from various sources, including *Go and Tell*, a seventy-fifth anniversary booklet by Cornelius Kuipers.

Sage, Sand, and Silence

"The End of an Era." *The Banner* 16 Sept. 1977: 19–20.

Navajo Nurse

"Navajo Nurse Remembers Nursing During the 1900s," *Health Care News* Aug. 1988: 4–5
L.J. Lamberts, *The Life Story of Dr. Lee S. Huizenga* (Grand Rapids: Eerdmans, 1950).

A Witch Finally Finds His True Fate

Cornelius Kuipers, *Zuni Also Prays* (Grand Rapids: Christian Reformed Board of Missions, 1947) 141–43.

A Week at Crownpoint

Reverend Jacob Bolt, *A Week's Work: Christian Reformed Mission, Crownpoint, New Mexico* (privately published pamphlet, n.d.).

Keith Kuipers: Locker-Room Missionary

Keith Kuipers, scrapbook.

Personal Interviews

Loren Tuscon, interview, June 1995.
Marla Jasperse, interview, June 1995.
Stanley Jim, interview, June 1995.
Keith Kuipers, interview, June 1995.
Michael Meekof, interview, June 1995.
James Nakhai, interview, June 1995.
Agnes Natewa, interview, June 1995.
Marian Roskamp, interview, June 1995.
Ray Slim, interview, June 1995.
Dennis Van Andel, interview, June 1995.
Elmer Yazzie, interview, June 1995.

Chapter Two: A Chosen People

1. Quoted in John Rozeboom, "The Christian Reformed Church in Mission to the Jews," diss., Calvin Theological Seminary, 1973, 111.
2. Statistics from Winthrop S. Hudson, Religion in America, 4th ed. (New York: Macmillan, 1987) 305–06.
3. From Fles family correspondence in Home Missions archives, n.d.
4. Rozeboom 10. Quotations from *De Wachter* articles are translated by John Rozeboom.
5. Rozeboom 13.
6. Rozeboom 18.
7. Herman Schultz, "The Paterson Hebrew Mission," *The Banner* 27 Nov. 1931: 1062.
8. Rozeboom 44.
9. Frederick S. Voss, *The Presidents* (Washington, DC: Smithsonian Institute Press, 1991) 67.
10. See Rozeboom 52ff.
11. Albert Huisjen, correspondence with Christian Reformed Board of Home Missions.
12. Nathanael Institute, *25th Anniversary Booklet* (n.p.: n.p., 1944) 40.
13. Nathanael Institute 41.
14. William Yonker, "Nathanael Institute," *The Banner* 16 Mar. 1928: 212.
15. Rozeboom 60.
16. Nathanael Institute 30.
17. Many of these details were drawn from monthly missionary reports submitted to the office of the Board of Home Missions.
18. Rozeboom 69.
19. Edith Vander Meulen, monthly report, June 1958.
20. Vander Meulen, personal correspondence with Board of Home Missions, 21 Jan. 1967.

21. Vander Meulen, personal correspondence, 21 Jan. 1967.
22. Grace Hoekstra, letter to Board of Home Missions, 21 Mar. 1967.
23. Hoekstra.
24. Vander Meulen, personal correspondence, 1971.

Johannes Rottenberg: A Love for His People

S.P. Tabaksblatt, *Ds. Johannes Rottenberg* (self-published).

Gerrit Koedoot, *A History of the Christian Reformed Church and Jewish Missions* (self-published, 1963).

Isaac A. Rottenberg, interview, 16 Apr. 1995.

New Teeth, Tracts, and Prayer

Minutes of Workers' Meeting, 25 Oct. 1945 – 7 Sept. 1957.

Home Missions in Canada

Albert Vander Mey, *To All My Children* (Jordan Station, ON: Paideia, 1983).

Tymen E. Hofman, *The Strength of Their Years* (Saint Catharines, ON: Calvinist Contact, 1983).

Tymen E. Hofman, interview, 19 Feb. 1996.

Chapter Three: The Electronic CRC

1. Albert E. Brumley, "Turn Your Radio On," *Country Western Hymnal* (Grand Rapids: Zondervan/Singspiration, 1972) no. 43.
2. Much of this historical information is from Quentin Schultze, "The Wireless Gospel," *Christianity Today* 15 Jan. 1988: 19–23.
3. Christian Reformed Church in North America, *Acts of Synod 1928* (Grand Rapids: Office of the Stated Clerk, 1928) 16.
4. Christian Reformed Church in North America, *Acts of Synod 1930* (Grand Rapids: Office of the Stated Clerk, 1930) 245.
5. Christian Reformed Church in North America, *Acts of Synod 1938* (Grand Rapids: Office of the Stated Clerk, 1938) 202.
6. Christian Reformed Church in North America, *Acts of Synod 1939* (Grand Rapids: Office of the Stated Clerk, 1939) 31.
7. David De Groot, *Worlds Beyond: The Story of* The Back to God Hour *1939–1979* (Palos Heights: The Back to God Hour, 1979) 8. Throughout this chapter much of the general information comes from this fortieth-anniversary book.
8. Much of the biographical information on Peter Eldersveld is drawn from his archive folder in Heritage Hall, Hekman Library, Calvin College, Grand Rapids, Michigan.
9. Peter Eldersveld, "Radio Religion," *The Banner* 4 Nov. 1949: 1287.
10. James De Jonge, "Reflections of a Friend," *Torch and Trumpet* Jan. 1966: 7–8.
11. Quoted in *The Banner* 29 July 1960: 27.
12. See Paul E. Freed, *Towers to Eternity* (Chatham, NJ: Trans World Radio, 1967).
13. Joel Nederhood, "Peter Eldersveld, 1911–1965: In Memoriam," *The Banner* 19 Nov. 1965: 22–23.
14. Joel Nederhood, "CRC-TV Progress Report," *The Banner* 1 Oct. 1976: 16–17.
15. Ben Armstrong, *The Electronic Church* (Nashville: Nelson, 1979) 141ff.
16. See Quentin Schultze, *Televangelism and American Culture* (Grand Rapids: Baker, 1991).
17. Joel Nederhood, "Evaluating the Electronic Church," *The Banner* 2 Feb. 1981: 8–9.
18. *The Banner* 19 Sept. 1989: 8–15.

Opening-Morning Jitters

Radio Bulletin of The Back to God Hour, III.4, 1954.

"Looking Back: December 7 Marked the Fifth Anniversary of Network Broadcast," *The Banner,* 30 Jan. 1953.

Choir members John Hofman, Lucile De Stigter Poel, Elaine Ryskamp Hofman, and Helen Brondsema Opperwall, interviews, 22 Feb. 1995.

Preaching the Word over the Air Without Flair

David Feddes, interview, 21 Mar. 1995.

Joel Nederhood, interview, 21 Mar. 1995.

"Back to God Hour Is Looking at Bright Side of Televangelism," *Grand Rapids Press,* 5 Mar. 1988,

Chapter 4: Going to School

1. George M. Marsden, *The Soul of the American University: From Protestant Establishment to Established Nonbelief* (New York: Oxford UP, 1994).
2. Marsden 15.
3. Statistics drawn from Henry Beets, *The Christian Reformed Church* (Grand Rapids: Baker, 1946) 117–22.
4. James Bratt, *Dutch Calvinism in Modern America* (Grand Rapids: Eerdmans, 1984) 55ff.
5. Bratt 89.
6. Leonard Verduin, personal correspondence with the author, 1994.
7. Leonard Verduin, report to the Ann Arbor Committee.
8. "A Chapel of Our Own at Ann Arbor," *The Banner* 10 Apr. 1942: 348.
9. "A Chapel of Our Own at Ann Arbor" 349.
10. Verduin, personal correspondence.

11. This article was reprinted in the January 1953 edition of *The Calvin Forum.*

12. Christian Reformed Church in North America, *Acts of Synod 1967* (Grand Rapids: Board of Publications, 1967) 279–80.

13. See various articles on campus chaplaincy in *The Reformed Journal* Jan. 1971.

14. Alvin Hoksbergen, "Where the Church Meets the Campus," *The Reformed Journal* Jan. 1971: 7.

15. Marvin P. Hoogland, "The Campus Ministry and the Crisis of Authority," *The Reformed Journal* Oct. 1971: 11–14.

16. Much of the information on the ministry at Queen's University was provided by Bill Van Groningen.

17. Edson "Bill" Lewis and the Campus Ministry Task Force provided copies of its minutes and other information relevant to current discussions on this subject.

A Ministry to the Heart and Soul

Donald Postema and members of Campus Chapel, University of Michigan, Ann Arbor, Michigan, interview, 12 Jan. 1995.

Kent State "Massacre"

"The Campus Ministry and the Crisis in Authority," *Reformed Journal* Oct. 1971.

"The Campus in Crisis," *The Banner* 28 Aug. 1970.

Henry Post, interview, 18 Feb. 1995.

Roger Van Harn, interview, 16 Feb. 1995.

John Schuring, interview, 6 Mar. 1995.

Chapter 5: The Great Cities

1. Winthrop S. Hudson, *Religion in America,* 4th ed. (New York: Macmillan, 1987) 272.

2. Sean Dennis Cashman, *America in the Gilded Age: From the Death of Lincoln to the Rise of Theodore Roosevelt* (New York: New York UP, 1984) 1.

3. Cashman 10.

4. Hudson 274.

5. Mark Noll, *A History of Christianity in the United States and Canada* (Grand Rapids: Eerdmans, 1992) 306–07.

6. Hudson 278.

7. James D. Bratt, *Dutch Calvinism in Modern America* (Grand Rapids: Eerdmans, 1984) 72.

8. See James D. Bratt and Christopher H. Meehan, *Gathered at the River: Grand Rapids, Michigan, and Its People of Faith* (Grand Rapids: Eerdmans, 1993).

9. This section on Grand Rapids, Michigan, draws heavily from John Knight's book *Echoes of Mercy, Whispers of Love,* published in 1989 by the Grand Rapids Area Ministries in honor of one century of mission work in the Grand Rapids area.

10. Knight 43ff.

11. Knight 11–22.

12. Bratt and Meehan 128–29.

13. Knight 29–31.

14. Knight 47–49.

15. Knight 63.

16. Nicholas Monsma, "Mr. Eugene S. Callender Introduced to Our Readers," *The Banner* 11 Jan. 1952: 45.

17. Quotations from Callender's monthly reports are drawn from Christian Reformed Home Missions file archives.

18. Callender, report, 28 Feb. 1952.

19. Letter, 4 Aug. 1952.

20. Report to the board, Feb. 1952: 4.

21. Report, Sept. 1955.

22. Report, 19 Nov. 1956: 12.

23. Annual report, 1957: 2, 4.

24. Henry Blystra, letter, 27 Nov. 1957, filed in Christian Reformed Home Missions archives.

25. Callender, report, May 1958.

26. Callender, report, May 1958.

27. Committee report, 27 June 1955.

28. Earl Marlink, report, 19 Sept. 1962.

29. Timothy Christian School Board, minutes, *The Reformed Journal* Mar. 1970: 5.

30. *Chicago Tribune,* Nov. 11, 1969.

31. Henry Stob, "Let Us Repent," *Reformed Journal* Mar. 1970: 3.

32. Christian Reformed Church in North America, *Acts of Synod 1968* (Grand Rapids: Board of Publications, 1968) 562.

33. William Ipema, monthly report to Christian Reformed Home Missions, Aug. 1969.

34. Karl J. Westerhof, monthly report to Christian Reformed Home Missions, Aug. 1969.

35. Lawndale report to Christian Reformed Home Missions, Feb. 1970.

36. "God Was Not Wasting His Time," *The Banner* 14 Jan. 1972: 8.

37. Richard Grevengoed, MAP ("Ministry Assessment Profile") study history (n.p., 1976).

38. Robert Price, "Understanding the Dutch-American Christian Reformed Church Subculture and Tradition," diss., Northern Baptist Theological Seminary, 1 Aug. 1994, 20.

God's Glory in the Inner City

Reginald Smith, interview, 7 Oct. 1995.

Life and Love in the City

Stanley Vander Klay, interview, 22 May 1996.
Ministry Profile (privately published pamphlet, n.d.).

An Iowa Farm Boy Comes to the City

Anthony Van Zanten, *When Things Don't Fit* (unpublished autobiography).
Anthony Van Zanten and members of Roseland CRC, interview, 22 Sept. 1995.

Doing the Job in L.A.

Thomas Doorn, Stanley Ver Heul, and members of Los Angeles Community CRC, interview, 22 Sept. 1995.

Chapter 6: The Reverend Chaplain

1. Christian Reformed Church in North America, *Acts of Synod 1918* (Grand Rapids: Office of the Stated Clerk, 1918) 42.
2. David C. McCullough, *Truman* (New York: Simon and Schuster, 1992) 104.
3. William Manchester, *Visions of Glory: 1874–1932, The Last Lion*, 2 vols. (New York: Dell, 1983) 1:650.
4. Doris Kearns Goodwin, *No Ordinary Time* (New York: Simon and Schuster, 1994) 186–87.
5. Diedrich Kromminga, *The Banner* 24 Nov. 1944: 1109.
6. J.M. Vande Kieft, "The Chaplain Situation," *The Banner* 23 Oct. 1942: 964.
7. Goodwin 133.
8. "Ordination Services of Chaplain Harry R. Boer," *The Banner* 27 Nov. 1942: 1080.
9. Wezeman papers, Chaplaincy Ministries archives.
10. Harry R. Boer, "Tarawa: A Chaplain Reminisces," *The Banner* 19 May 1944: 464–65.
11. Jacob Heerema, *The Banner* 14 Sept. 1995: 12–14.
12. All quotations in this section are from Cornelius Van Schouwen, *The Life and Work of a Chaplain: Second World War* (1943–1946), a privately published diary.
13. Henry R. Van Til, "Address to Synod of Chaplain Henry R. Van Til," *The Banner* 30 June 1944: 608–09.
14. Elton Holtrop, "The Opportunities of a Chaplain in a VA Hospital," *The Banner* 26 Mar. 1948: 391.
15. Robert A. Caro, *The Years of Lyndon Johnson: Means of Ascent* (New York: Knopf, 1990) xxiii.
16. Caro xxiv.
17. Jan Friend, "What Do You Do?" *The Banner* 1 Apr. 1966: 4–5.

Ministering to the Bottom Line

Jack Vander Laan, interview, 17 Oct. 1995.

Offering Hope in the Valley of Death

Robert Korneef, interview, 5 Dec. 1995.

Not Just a Jail-House Religion

Raymond Swierenga, interview, 23 Nov. 1995.

Chapter 7: The Backyard World

1. Statistics here are drawn from "Here Comes the World," *Christianity Today* 15 May 1995: 18–25, and "Must It Be the West against the Rest?" *Atlantic Monthly* Dec. 1994: 61–79.
2. For information on Bessie Vander Valk Izquierdo I am indebted to Mrs. Arlene Nyenhuis, who wrote a series of memoirs about Vander Valk and provided them for this project.
3. Information on the history of work in the Miami area, as well as a good deal of the other historical information in this chapter, was drawn from John Wagenveld, "Brief History of the Hispanic Christian Reformed Church," a resource complied in connection with Wagenveld's thesis work and given to Home Missions in connection with the writing of this book.
4. Information on the work in Holland, Michigan, was drawn from Wagenveld and from a paper provided by the Iglesia Hispana itself.
5. *Christianity Today* 6 Feb. 1995: 38–42.
6. Much of the information on recent work in Hispanic ministries was provided by Gary Teja and Gary Schipper, who also read and commented on the manuscript in progress in ways which were extremely helpful.
7. David C. McCullough, *Truman* (New York: Simon and Schuster, 1992) 548.
8. Clarence Boomsma, "Urgent—Gifts Needed for Seminary in Korea," *The Banner* 5 Nov. 1965: 16–17.
9. Statistics and general background information on Koreans in the CRC was provided by Christian Reformed Home Missions.
10. Euntae Jo, "Sociological Implications for Growing Churches Among Korean Immigrants in the U.S.A," diss., Southwest Baptist Seminary, 1993, 27.
11. William J. Serow, et. al., eds., *Handbook on International Migration* (Westport, CT: Greenwood, 1990) 348.
12. See *Christianity Today* 18 May 1984: 50.
13. Much of this information was provided by Ruth Donker, *Gathering Magazine* 3.2 (Fall 1995): 2–3.
14. Donker 3.

A Cambodian Pastor's Painful, Prayerful Quest

Marvin Hofman and Socheth Na, interview, 6 Mar. 1996.
Socheth Na, *My Life Story* (unpublished autobiography).

Van Netten, David, unpublished term paper on Cambodian immigration to Holland, Michigan.

A Visionary From the North

John T. Kim, interview, 23 Feb. 1996.

John T. Kim, *Protestant Church Growth in Korea,* introduction.

Chapter 8: Gathering God's Growing Family

1. Information drawn from Millard J. Erickson, *Christian Theology* (Grand Rapids: Baker, 1983) 114–16.
2. Wade Clark Roof and William Mc Kinney, *American Mainline Religion: Its Changing Shape and Future* (New Brunswick: Rutgers, 1987) 9.
3. Roof and Mc Kinney 11.
4. James W. Jones, *In the Middle of This Road We Call Our Life: The Courage to Search for Something More* (San Francisco: Harper, 1995) 22.
5. Christian Reformed Church in North America, *Acts of Synod 1975* (Grand Rapids: Board of Publications, 1975) 232–33.
6. Christian Reformed Church in North America, *Acts of Synod 1975* (Grand Rapids: Board of Publications, 1975) 232
7. The statistics and related information for this chapter were provided by John Rozeboom, executive director of Christian Reformed Home Missions.
8. *Together We Gather: Understanding the Mission of the Church* (Grand Rapids: Christian Reformed Home Missions, 1994) 57.
9. *Together We Gather* 58–61.
10. *Together We Gather* 44.
11. Richard De Vos, "Developing the Church and Motivating Members," 1990 Special Lectures, audiotape provided by Calvin Theological Seminary.
12. *Together We Gather*, v.
13. See David Wells, *No Place for Truth, or Whatever Happened to Evangelical Theology* (Grand Rapids: Eerdmans, 1993) and Os Guinness, *Dining with the Devil: The Megachurch Movement Flirts with Modernity* (Grand Rapids: Baker, 1993).
14. Cornelius Plantinga, Jr., "Fashions in Folly: Sin and Character in the Nineties," The January Series, Calvin College, 15 Jan. 1993.

A CRC Crystal Ball

Information supplied by Elmhurst CRC, Elmhurst, Illinois; New Life CRC, Abbotsford, British Columbia; Oasis Community Church, Moreno Valley, California; Zion CRC, Oshawa, Ontario; and Oasis Community Church, Orlando, Florida.

Picture Credits

Introduction

1, 3. *100 Years of Home Missions,* pamphlet, Christian Reformed Home Missions.

2, 4. Christian Reformed Home Missions.

Chapter One: Going West

1-2, 6-7, 9, 15-17, 20-27, 29, 34, 36-39, 41-42, 44-46, 48-53, 55-56, 58-59, 61-64, 66, 68-74, 85, 89. Christian Reformed Home Missions.

3-5, 8, 10-14, 19, 30-33, 35, 40, 43, 57, 65, 67, 75-76, 81. Heritage Hall, Hekman Library, Calvin College.

18. *Jesus Dayoodláanii Biyiin,* Navajo hymn book.

28, 77. Sandra DeGroot.

47. Rehoboth archives.

54. Mike Meekhof.

60. Indian booklet, Christian Reformed Home Missions.

78-80, 82-84, 86, 90. Mary Meehan.

87-88. Keith Kuipers.

65. *The Banner* 17 Mar. 1910: 171.

35. *The Banner* 27 Nov. 1913: 755.

Chapter Two: A Chosen People

1, 5-6, 18, 22-25, 31-32. Christian Reformed Home Missions.

8. Heritage Hall, Hekman Library, Calvin College.

2, 7, 15-16, 19, 21. *Twenty-Fifth Anniversary of the Chicago Jewish Mission,* souvenir booklet published under the auspices of the Board of the Nathanael Institute.

3-4, 14, 17, 20. *The Banner* 14 Aug. 1925: 1487.

9-13. Nathanael Institute pamphlet.

26. Donald Levy.

27-30. Nathanael Institute pamphlet.

Home Missions in Canada

1. Tymen E. Hofman, *The Strength of Their Years,* (St. Catharines, ON; Calvinist Contact, 1983) 33.

4, 6, 8-9. Tymen E. Hofman.

2, 3, 5, 7. *Nobleford Christian Reformed Church 1905-1980* (Lethbridge, Alberta: Ronalds Western, 1981) 182, 2, 16, 182.

Chapter Three: The Electronic CRC

7. Christian Reformed Home Missions.

1, 15. David De Groot, *Worlds Beyond: The Story of* The Back to God Hour *1939-1979,* (Palos Heights: The Back to God Hour, 1979).

2-4, 8-14, 16-29. Courtesy of Advertising Marketing Group, Inc.

5-6. Heritage Hall, Hekman Library, Calvin College.

Chapter 4: Going to School

1. B.K. Kuiper, *The Church in History,* 13th ed. (Grand Rapids, Christian Schools International, 1964) 315.

2. Booklet, *Home Missions, Christian Reformed Church, 1935* 2.

4. Jacob D. Eppinga, *A Century of Grace* (Grand Rapids, LaGrave Avenue CRC, 1987) 116.

3, 6, 8. *The Banner* 10, Apr. 1942: 348-49.

5, 11, 17-21. Donald Postema.

7, 10, 13. Christian Reformed Home Missions.

9. Gwen Pott.

12. Duane E. VanderBrug.

14-16. Bill Van Groningen.

Chapter 5: The Great Cities

1, 11, 21, 23-24, 27, 30-33. Duane E. VanderBrug.

2, 10. Heritage Hall, Hekman Library, Calvin College.

3-7. Roger Van Harn, Grace CRC.

8-9. Grand Rapids Public Library.

12. *The Banner* 14 Nov. 1952: 1389.

28. *The Banner* 5 Dec. 1958: 13.

13-20, 22, 25, 26, 29, 34, 43-44. Christian Reformed Home Missions.

35. John Hamilton.

36-38. Tymen E. Hofman.

39-42. *Chimes,* 3 Oct. 1969.

45–51. Los Angeles Community Christian Reformed Church.

Chapter 6: The Reverend Chaplain

1, 5. Heritage Hall, Hekman Library, Calvin College.

2. Grand Rapids Public Library.

6–9, 19–21, 24–27. Christian Reformed Home Missions.

18. *The Banner* 13 July 1992: 10.

3, 10, 17. CRC Chaplain Committee pamphlet.

4. Clarice Ribbens.

11–16. Cornelius Van Schouwen, *The Life and Work of a Chaplain: Second World War* (1943–1946), a privately published diary.

22–23. Herbert L. Bergsma, *Chaplains with Marines in Vietnam 1962–1971* (Washington, DC: U.S. Navy, 1985).

Chapter 7: The Backyard World

1, 2. Duane E. VanderBrug.

3–10, 12–22, 27–28. Christian Reformed Home Missions.

11. Heritage Hall, Hekman Library, Calvin College.

23–26. Orange Korean CRC.

Chapter 8: Gathering God's Growing Family

1, 6–10, 12, 16, 26–39. Christian Reformed Home Missions.

2–3. Elmhurst CRC.

4–5. Brochure, Willow Creek Community Church.

11. Heritage Hall, Hekman Library, Calvin College.

13–15. Zion CRC.

17–19. Dr. Robert Schuller, Crystal Cathedral.

20. Richard De Vos

21–23. Oasis CRC, Moreno Valley, California.

24. Oasis CRC, Orlando, Florida.

25. William B. Eerdmans Publishing Company.

William B. Eerdmans Sr., left, and G.J. Vande Riet visited the Bowery Mission in New York City in 1910 as theology students in New Jersey (to study the residents lives, they dressed accordingly).

Index of Names

Rozeboom, John, 53, 186, 192, (x, 186, 192)
Rozeboom, Linda, (192)
Rozendal, Martha, 52, (52)
Rozendal, John, 52–53, 55, 59, 63–64, 135, (53, 59)
Rutgers, William, 79
Sandoval, Jerome, 10, 42
Sandoval, Lolee, 42
Schemper, Chester, 173, (173)
Schipper, Earl, 103
Schipper, Gary, 177–78, (179)
Schooland, Casey, 165–66, (71, 153)
Schoon, Winnie, (33)
Schuller, Robert, 194–95, (195)
Schultz, Herman H., 52–53, 64, (52)
Schultze, Quentin, 74, 93
Schultze, Henry, 79, 81, 94, (79)
Schuring, Gladys, (103)
Schuring, John, 102, (103)
Schuurman, John, (71)
Sheldon, Charles, 114
Slim, Ray, 10, 38, 45, (38)
Slotemaker, H., (71)
Smedes, Wesley, 66, 191, (191)
Smit, Harvey, xiii, 163
Smith, Reggie, 119
Spann, Sam, (143)
Speer, Robert E., xi
Spoelstra, P., (71)
Sprik, Bert, 32, (33)
Spyker, John, Sr., 13, (30)
Spyker, Mrs. John, Sr., (30)
Stap, John, (71)
Steen, Mr. and Mrs. Barney, (33)
Steigenga, J., (71)
Stek, Henrietta, 57, (57)
Stielstra, Sylvia, 173
Stob, George, (153)
Stob, Renzina, 17, (17, 33)
Sweetman, Leonard, (71)
Swets, John, (33)
Swets, Seymour, 80
Swierenga, Raymond, 162
Sytsma, Richard, III
Tabachnick, Ben, (59)

Taft, William, I
Tanis, E.J., 99
Tanis, Evert, (71)
Tapia–Ruano, Carlos, 176
Taplin, Aleem, (145)
Teja, Gary, 177, (177, 199)
Tiemersma, Klaas, (71)
Toeset, Carl, (71)
Toonstra, Martin, (116)
Trap, Leonard, 75, 148, (75, 148)
Trotter, Mel, 117–18, (118)
Truman, Harry S., 156, 160, 179
Tso, Zah, 21, 40
Tuit, Wilhelmina, 54, 57, 59, (58)
Tumaka, Nick, 27–28, (29)
Tuscon, Loren, 39, (39)
Tuyl, Carl, 166
Van Baalen, J.K., (71)
Van Dyk, Peter, (71)
Van Dyke, J.R., (71)
Van Dyken, Harry, (71)
Van Gelder, Craig, 193–94
Van Groningen, Bill, 106–07, (107)
Van Harn, Roger, 103, 116–17, (117)
Van Houten, Siebert, 167
Van Katwijk, Peter, 167
Van Laar, Gerard, (71)
Van Mersbergen, Julie, (59)
Van Reken, Everett, (59, 60)
Van Schouwen, Cornelius, 157–160, (153, 157, 158)
Van Schouwen, Sue, (157)
Van Til, Henry R., 160
Van Til, John, 167, (199)
Van Til, Howard, 192
Van Wyck, Mr. And Mrs., (33)
Van Zanten, Donna, (132)
Van Zanten, Tony, 132–34, (132)
Vande Kieft, Henry, (153)
Vande Kieft, J.M. , 70, 99, 135, 151–52, (71, 151)
Vande Lune, James, 10
Vande Water, John, 118
Vanden Akker, Wm., (71)

Vanden Bosch, Tamme, xii, xiii, 2–3, (xiii)
Vanden Brink, Everett, 173, (176)
Vander Ark, C., (71)
Vander Ark, Jay, 163
Vander Beek, Meindert, 32, (16)
Vander Griend, Alvin, 191, 201, (199)
Vander Griend, M., (71)
Vander Griend, W., (71)
Vander Kieft, John M., 70
Vander Klay, Stanley, 122–23, (122)
Vander Kooi, George, (153)
Vander Laan, Jack, 150, (150)
Vander Meer, John, (153)
Vander Meulen, Edith, 54–55, 57, 63–66, (58, 59, 64, 66)
Vander Mey, Albert, 70
Vander Veer, Andrew and Cornelia, 118
Vander Vliet, John, 70
Vander Wagen, Andrew, 1–5, 7–8, 15, 24, 26–31, 37, 202, (2, 15, 27, 33)
Vander Wagen, Dena, (33)
Vander Wagen, Edward, (33)
Vander Wagen, Effa, (33)
Vander Wagen, Effa, 4, 27–28, 31, (2, 8, 27, 33)
Vander Wall, Fannie, (33)
Vander Weide, Marie, (21, 33)
Vander Werp, Henry, 49
Vander Werp, Jennette, (33)
Vander Woude, (71)
VanderBrug, Duane, 131, 135, 139, 177, 200, (199)
Veenstra, Johanna, 117, (49)
Vellinga, John, 72
Ver Heul, Stanley, 142–46, (143, 44)
Verbrugge, John, (71,155)
Verduin, Henry, 75, (75)
Verduin, Leonard, 97, 99–101, 104, (97)
Visser, Marjorie, 126
Vos, Clarence, (71)
Vreeman, Jerry, 93, (93)

Wagenveld, Louis, 178, (178)
Walters, Dick, 78
Ward, Luther, (116)
Washington, Henry, (116)
Waslander, H., (71)
Weidenaar, J., (71)
Wesseling, Betty, (59)
Westerhof, Karl J., 138
Westra, Isaac, 75
Wezeman, Richard, 155–56, 165
Whipple, Catherine Hood, 22, (22)
Wierenga, Herman, 72, (71)
Wildeboer, Henry, 193
Will, Hubert L., 139
Wilson, Woodrow, 17, 97, 147–48
Withage, C.T., (71)
Wolff, James E., 140, (141)
Workman, Stanley J., 198
Yang, Paul, 181, (181)
Yang, Peter, 182, (182)
Yazzie, Elmer, 46, (46)
Yazzie, Sampson, 45
Yff, George, 32, 34
Yonggi Cho, Paul, 180
Yonker, William, 57–58, 65, (57)
Young, La Verne, 140
Zandstra, Jack, 54–55, 58–59, 64, (54)

Colophon

❧ Cover and interior page design is by Aaron Phipps. Garamond type was set in 10.5 pt on 2.5 pt leading. ❧ This book was produced on a Power Macintosh 7100/66 and paginated with Quark XPress 3.31. The photos were digitally imaged in Adobe Photoshop 3.0. ❧ Film of the electronic pages was accomplished by Electronic Publishing Center.

✝